DISCARD

■ United States Holocaust Memorial Museum
Jack, Joseph and Morton Mandel
Center for Advanced Holocaust Studies

Documenting Life and Destruction
Holocaust Sources in Context

SERIES EDITOR

Jürgen Matthäus

DOCUMENTING LIFE AND DESTRUCTION

HOLOCAUST SOURCES IN CONTEXT

This groundbreaking series provides a new perspective on history using first-hand accounts of the lives of those who suffered through the Holocaust, those who perpetrated it, and those who witnessed it as bystanders. The United States Holocaust Memorial Museum's Jack, Joseph and Morton Mandel Center for Advanced Holocaust Studies presents a wide range of documents from different archival holdings, expanding knowledge about the lives and fates of Holocaust victims and making these resources broadly available to the general public and scholarly communities for the first time.

BOOKS IN THE SERIES

1. *Jewish Responses to Persecution, Volume I, 1933–1938*, Jürgen Matthäus and Mark Roseman (2010)
2. *Children during the Holocaust*, Patricia Heberer (2011)
3. *Jewish Responses to Persecution, Volume II, 1938–1940*, Alexandra Garbarini with Emil Kerenji, Jan Lambertz, and Avinoam Patt (2011)
4. *The Diary of Samuel Golfard and the Holocaust in Galicia*, Wendy Lower (2011)
5. *Jewish Responses to Persecution, Volume III, 1941–1942*, Jürgen Matthäus with Emil Kerenji, Jan Lambertz, and Leah Wolfson (2013)
6. *The Holocaust in Hungary: Evolution of a Genocide*, Zoltán Vági, László Csősz, and Gábor Kádár (2013)
7. *War, Pacification, and Mass Murder, 1939: The Einsatzgruppen in Poland*, Jürgen Matthäus, Jochen Böhler, and Klaus-Michael Mallmann (2014)
8. *Jewish Responses to Persecution, Volume IV, 1942–1943*, Emil Kerenji (2014)
9. *Jewish Responses to Persecution, Volume V, 1944–1946*, Leah Wolfson (2015)
10. *The Political Diary of Alfred Rosenberg and the Onset of the Holocaust*, Jürgen Matthäus and Frank Bajohr (2015)
11. *Nazi Persecution and Postwar Repercussions: The International Tracing Service Archive and Holocaust Research*, Suzanne Brown-Fleming (2016)

A project of the

United States Holocaust Memorial Museum

SARA J. BLOOMFIELD
Director

Jack, Joseph and Morton Mandel Center for Advanced Holocaust Studies

PAUL A. SHAPIRO
Director

JÜRGEN MATTHÄUS
Director, Applied Research

under the auspices of the

Academic Committee
of the
United States Holocaust Memorial Council

PETER HAYES, *Chair*

This publication has been made possible by
support from

Claims Conference ועידת התביעות
The Conference on Jewish Material Claims Against Germany

The William S. and Ina Levine Foundation

and

The Blum Family Foundation

Documenting Life and Destruction
Holocaust Sources in Context

NAZI PERSECUTION AND POSTWAR REPERCUSSIONS

The International Tracing Service Archive
and Holocaust Research

Suzanne Brown-Fleming

Foreword by Paul A. Shapiro

Advisory Committee:

Christopher R. Browning
David Engel
Sara Horowitz
Steven T. Katz
Alvin H. Rosenfeld

Rowman & Littlefield
in association with the United States Holocaust Memorial Museum
2016

For USHMM:
Project Manager: Mel Hecker
Translator: Kathleen Luft
Researchers: Holly Robertson Huffnagle, Amanda Pridmore

Published by Rowman & Littlefield
4501 Forbes Boulevard, Suite 200, Lanham, Maryland 20706
www.rowman.com

Eastover Road, Plymouth PL6 7PY, United Kingdom

Front cover: USHMMPA WS# 43574

British Library Cataloguing in Publication Information Available

Library of Congress Cataloging-in-Publication Data Available

Brown-Fleming, Suzanne, author.
Nazi persecution and postwar repercussions : the International Tracing
    Service archive and Holocaust research / Suzanne Brown-Fleming.
Lanham : Rowman & Littlefield, [2016] | Series: Documenting life
    and destruction: Holocaust sources in context | Includes bibliographical
    references and index.
LCCN 2015026631| ISBN 9781442251731 (cloth : alkaline paper) |
    ISBN 9781442251755 (e-book)
LCSH: International Tracing Service. | Concentration camp inmates—
    Archival resources—Germany—Arolsen. | War victims—Archival
    resources—Conservation and restoration—Germany—Arolsen. | World War,
    1939–1945—Archival resources—Conservation and restoration—Germany—Arolsen.
LCC HV6762.G3 .B76 2015 | DDC 026/.9405318--dc23 LC record available at
    http://lccn.loc.gov/2015026631

∞™ The paper used in this publication meets the minimum requirements of American
National Standard for Information Sciences—Permanence of Paper for Printed Library
Materials, ANSI/NISO Z39.48-1992.

Printed in the United States of America

CONTENTS

FOREWORD
by Paul A. Shapiro

DURING THE years that I worked to open the archive of the International Tracing Service (ITS)—nearly a decade that culminated in the ratification by eleven countries of formal amendments to the international agreements governing the ITS—it was difficult to fully comprehend the multiple levels of significance that would emerge once the tens of millions of documents locked up at ITS headquarters in Bad Arolsen, Germany, became fully accessible. Kept out of the reach of survivors, researchers, educators, and others with potential interest, the documents had been utilized for over 60 years almost exclusively for tracing and name search purposes and were being used as the twenty-first century began to validate slave and forced labor compensation claims that flowed in from an already disappearing generation of survivors, who had suffered persecution at the hands of Nazi Germany and her allies. The most common notion regarding ITS was that the archive contained millions of name cards and name lists of various sorts and provenances, and little else. The International Committee of the Red Cross (ICRC), which administered ITS on behalf of an eleven-country International Commission, made only minimal information available regarding the archive's contents and fostered this limited understanding of the archive precisely in order to stifle curiosity and reduce the likelihood that pressure would be brought to bear to open its doors. The ICRC also restricted the information that was available to member states of the International Commission, information that might have motivated Commission members to act sooner than they did, and even recruited well-known specialists, some of whom had enjoyed privileged personal access to the archive, to reinforce the notion that the ITS archive's potential for purposes other than tracing and name search would be minimal.[1]

At the time, this mischaracterization of the ITS archive seemed highly credible. It was, after all, difficult to believe that six decades after the end of World War II there remained a place where one could find, hidden from public view, between 50 and 100 million documents relating to the fates of millions of people, Jews and members of virtually every other nationality as well, who were victimized by the Nazis: millions of concentration camp documents; transport and deportation lists; Gestapo arrest warrants; prison records; forced and slave labor documentation that revealed thousands of government, military, corporate, and other users of cheap labor, and the consequences of treating human beings as disposable assets to be used up and discarded; displaced persons (DP) files; and millions of inquiries from around the world from survivors and their families, all hoping at first to find someone still alive, and later simply needing to better understand what had happened to loved ones who had been murdered. And it was difficult for most people to believe that six decades after the end of World War II, the democratic governments on the International Commission, nine from Europe plus the United States and Israel, were responsible for keeping this documentation out of the reach of survivors (and everyone else), and appeared ready, as the twenty-first century began, to see the last remnant of the survivor generation disappear without giving survivors access to records that contained precious information about themselves and their families, and without providing them with the comfort of knowing that the documentary record of what happened to them would not be conveniently kept under wraps, "swept under the rug," as one pained Holocaust survivor expressed it to me one day in my office at the United States Holocaust Memorial Museum (USHMM), once the survivors were gone.

I was told on more than one occasion by representatives of most countries on the Commission that there had to be some misunderstanding. Still, when the issue of access was raised, it was more convenient for most of the governments involved to believe that the documents held in the ITS archive were of little significance, rather than to entertain what might be a different reality and, after decades, confront their own responsibility for the closed-door policy that prevailed at ITS. By the end of the twentieth century, the Holocaust was broadly considered the century's defining event, and it was just as broadly understood

---

1. See, for example, Wolfgang Benz, "Kein grösstes Holocaust-Archiv der Welt—Der Internationale Suchdienst Arolsen und die historische Forschung," in *Tribune. Zeitschrift zum Verständnis des Judentums*, Vol. 179, 3rd Quarter 2006, pp. 107–13; also available at www.tribuene-verlag.de/TRI_Benz_1.pdf (accessed on August 24, 2015).

that knowingly concealing documentation of the Holocaust could be considered a form of Holocaust denial.[2]

And yet, with each year of disappointment, disappointment that I measured against the actuarial table of the survivor generation, the multiple levels of significance of the archival collections at ITS became clearer. In the face of legal arguments, technical impediments, and bureaucratic procedure, I saw **moral imperative**—a moral obligation to Holocaust survivors and their families, and to others who were targeted during the Nazi era, to provide not only the closure that information held in the archive might provide, but reassurance that the names and fates of lost loved ones, as well as their own experiences, would not remain hidden away forever. Fulfilling this moral obligation became for me the highest and most urgent ethical priority.

The archive was also of immense **memorial significance**, clarifying the fates of millions and adding precious information to the growing databases of survivors and victims that were being maintained at the United States Holocaust Memorial Museum and Yad Vashem.

From my perspective, the moral argument and the memorial significance of the ITS records, grounded in the raw history of the Holocaust, provided more than sufficient rationale for action. But there was more. Layers of contemporary relevance and powerful warnings for the future became clearer as my effort to open the archive proceeded. In the face of **rising Holocaust denial** in all its forms, whether emerging as a trend in some European countries or emanating from Iran during the presidency of Mahmoud Ahmadinejad, the tens of millions of pages of irrefutably authentic evidence in the ITS archive could serve for all time as a potent weapon against the deniers, trivializers, relativizers, and minimizers. It also became clearer as the actions necessary to open ITS became more extreme that the campaign itself held a **warning about ourselves, our organizations, and our governments**: The struggle that was required to open the ITS archive was a powerful reminder of the ability of even good governments, good organizations, and good people to fail to give adequate attention to the voices and concerns of people perceived as having little power or influence. Who, after

---

2. Media coverage played a significant role in driving the International Commission toward a final decision to open the archive. Concern regarding the issue of Holocaust denial increased after the issue was aired in the media. See, for example, Roger Cohen, "U.S.-German Flare-Up Over Vast Nazi Camp Archives," *New York Times*, February 20, 2006; the German *Das Erste* network television documentary segment *"Kein Zutritt für Holocaust-Forscher. In Deutschlands wichtigstem NS-Archiv lässt man sich nicht in die Karteikarten schauen,"* by Peter Gerhardt and Christine Rütten, aired on the program *Titel, Thesen, Temperamente*, March 12, 2006; and the *Washington Post* editorial board's lead editorial entitled "A Holocaust Denial," March 25, 2006.

all, could appear more powerless than the survivors of a genocide, bereft of their families, bereft of their possessions, displaced and resettled far from their original homes, and struggling to rebuild some semblance of normality in their lives?

There was a **warning about genocide** as well. Tragic events in the Darfur region of Sudan provided a vivid reminder that we live in a world characterized by repeated genocides—Rwanda, Cambodia, Bosnia, Darfur. Clearly, no world region is immune. The ITS archive reveals in excruciating detail the price of failing to act to prevent genocide and the decades-long consequences that such a failure to act can generate. And finally, the archive provided a graphic **warning about the danger of resurgent antisemitism**. The Nazi regime set out to target Jews. But once the ethnic and religious hatred bound up in antisemitism was unleashed, with the gross disregard for the dignity of **every** human being that such prejudice inevitably produces, the targeting, the persecution, the suffering, the killing did not stop with the Jews. A majority of the documents in the ITS archive deal with the fates of non-Jewish victims of Nazi-era persecution. A visit to ITS makes it extraordinarily clear that while antisemitism is bad for Jews, it is extremely dangerous for everyone else as well. I knew that making people aware of the records at ITS could provide a reminder regarding the consequences of unchecked antisemitism, for which there appeared to be increasing need as the new century began.

All of this became clear, even without detailed knowledge of the full contents of the several buildings in which the ITS archive was stored. What was less clear was the degree to which what was locked away in those buildings would offer new insights and opportunities for advanced research and teaching. Logic dictated that tens of millions of documents, much of it unique in character and little of it ever examined by specialists, would enable research and teaching that had not been possible before. But for as long as the archive remained sealed, it was impossible to know in what ways and to what degree.

Thus, in 2008, shortly after the treaty amendments opening the archive took effect, one of the first things the USHMM and ITS agreed to do was sponsor a two-week research workshop at the archive in Bad Arolsen. The fifteen scholars who participated were to be given free rein to explore the institution's archival holdings in order to begin to evaluate and debate the significance of the collections for scholarship.

It was obvious that the ITS archive, through its size alone, would add significantly to the enormous archival puzzle regarding the Holocaust that was being assembled, piece by piece, through the international archival acquisition programs of both the Washington and the Jerusalem memorial institutions, the Mémorial de la Shoah in Paris, and other institutions that were determined to gather and preserve for posterity the evidence of Holocaust-era crimes and the consequences of those crimes.

Factors beyond mere scale also appeared to offer promise. The ITS collections cover the entire period from Hitler's rise to power in 1933 to the spring of 1945, that is, the entire period of Nazi rule. They also extend through the whole of the Displaced Person and survivor repatriation and resettlement era, and through postwar inquiries and responses, reflect varying interests in and uses of the records right up until today as well. Few, if any, other archival repositories offered similar "longitudinal" coverage of the infrastructure of persecution during the Nazi era and its long-term legacy, measured in its consequences for individuals, individual countries, and the international community writ large—a chronology extending from 1933 literally to the present day.

Moreover, due to the specific purposes of tracing and name search for which the collections at Bad Arolsen had been used throughout the postwar era, and because of the organizational structure of the archive created to pursue those purposes, ITS had the potential to add to the typically perpetrator-focused approach to Holocaust study the ability to see the event through the eyes and experiences of the victims, of survivors, of forced laborers, of Displaced Persons, etc.—the very people the United States Holocaust Memorial Museum and related institutions elsewhere had been created to remember. The suffering and perspective of those specifically targeted for persecution on racial or religious grounds—Jews, Roma and Sinti, Jehovah's Witnesses and other minority Christian sects, homosexuals, people with disabilities, Poles, Ukrainians, Russians and other Slavs, Soviet prisoners of war—might emerge with sharper contour from documentation that had been systematically reorganized to focus on the victim.

The fifteen researchers who participated in that first research workshop came together in Bad Arolsen from the United States, France, Germany, the United Kingdom, Israel, Poland, and Australia. They formed four teams according to the specific interests each participant had expressed when applying to the workshop. In addition to archival fonds that had been regularly consulted by ITS staff and that the staff expected the participants to utilize, some of the participants explored the basements and the attics of the buildings where collections were housed and found long-untouched collections of UNRRA (United Nations Relief and Rehabilitation Administration) and IRO (International Refugee Organization) documents from the 1940s and 1950s; labor records not of prisoners of the Nazis, but of Displaced Persons; and fifty-year old hand-written registers of the flow of documentation to the predecessor organizations of ITS, as well as massive collections of institutional correspondence, all of which revealed in one fashion or another how the ITS itself had evolved over time. It quickly became evident that the ITS repository held more, and more diverse, collections than anticipated, which actually was not surprising. ITS had never had a trained archivist on staff, and no comprehensive physical inventory of what the ITS buildings contained had been undertaken since the Allied High Commission for Germany turned over administration of the repository to the ICRC in 1955.

While these "discoveries" were important and signaled the need for a thorough inventory to protect the integrity of the collections, it was the content analysis—the assessment of potential—by the four teams that was most critical. Given the challenges that might be encountered working in collections that had few finding aids, had been systematically reorganized for purposes of name search, and where the disappointments might be as great as any exciting prospects, expectations regarding the results of the research workshop had been intentionally kept in check.

The team that examined the "Incarceration" or *Inhaftierung* collections emphasized, first, that the collections indeed spanned the entire period of Nazi rule. The records were "astonishing" in their detail, regarding individual prisoners, relations among different groups of prisoners, prisoner functionaries, and what has come to be known among Holocaust scholars as the "gray zone."[3] The participants felt the material would permit the creation of scrupulously documented social histories of some of the camps and open new understanding of prisoner categorization practices and the systematic use of categorization to exert control. One member of the team focused on the unique insights provided by the records—in particular, the massive medical and sexual-issues-related files of various kinds—into the still-resonant issue of the power of the state over people's bodies. Another stressed the opportunity to study patterns of violence in the camps over time. A third wanted to explore the ways in which the documentation could corroborate, or might contradict, sensitive issues regarding the camp experience that were addressed in postwar survivor testimonies.

The team that explored the massive forced labor records—designated at ITS as *Kriegszeit* (wartime) records, though many were created after the war on order of Allied occupation authorities—reported on the diversity of the documents in this section of the ITS archive: directives of all sorts, labor detail assignments, social insurance records, marriage and birth records of forced laborers, infirmary records, death records, and more. The participants focused on the

---

3. The concept of the "gray zone" was introduced by Primo Levi as he reflected on the camp reality that he had experienced, in which moral ambiguity and compromise were pervasive. For a scholarly exploration of the "gray zone," see Jonathan Petropoulos and John Roth, eds., *Ambiguity and Compromise in the Holocaust and its Aftermath* (New York: Berghahn Books, 2005).

records of industrial companies that exploited slave and forced laborers—
thousands of companies according to their quick sweep through the material,
not just well known major industrial firms like I.G. Farben or Daimler-Benz—
and on the extensive use of such labor everywhere and by everyone: in industry,
by the military, by government offices, on farms, in churches, etc.[4] In the few
days during which they had access to the records, the team produced a list of
over twenty-five categories of forced laborer and was able to document "fluidity"
in the system, as laborers moved or were moved from one category to another,
with fewer or greater privileges or risks, according to a variety of factors, most
under the control of the perpetrators and users of forced and slave labor, but
some under the control of the laborers themselves. The team discovered remarkable cases in which forced laborer complaints about their "employers" resulted
in detailed investigations and penalization of the "employers" by the SS. These
cases appeared more likely to occur in the latter part of the war. The team
stressed that there would be much to be learned from studies of aspects of the
forced labor experience over time. Because of the omnipresence of forced labor
in towns and villages throughout the Third Reich, in other Axis states, and the
territories occupied by Axis forces—there were, for example 352 separate users
of forced labor in the town of Saarbrücken, 16 in one small village in France—
the group saw the potential for revelatory new micro-studies of individual towns
or regions. A sociologist on this team, perhaps cognizant of the horrific use of
similar techniques by Soviet authorities after the war, focused on the Nazis' use
of "schizophrenia" diagnoses, in regions with euthanasia facilities, to simply
make troublesome forced laborers "disappear."

The team that worked with the Displaced Persons material—designated at
ITS as *Nachkriegszeit* (postwar) records—reported being "overwhelmed" by the
research possibilities. They found records on 2,500 camps for survivors, including camps that operated for a time in what became the Soviet zone of Germany,
and massive information about the stages through which DPs passed on the path
from prisoner to a future, "from inhumanity to rehabilitation." The relevance of
the records, team members asserted, extended far beyond the Holocaust and
related Nazi-era crimes to the broadest European and global impact of the waves
of people who moved through DP camps and on to somewhere else. The team
suggested that the materials at ITS could stimulate study of the impact of the

---

4. The pervasiveness of forced labor detention sites is reflected in the over 30,000 such
sites identified in the course of research for the United States Holocaust Memorial Museum's
Encyclopedia of Camps and Ghettos, 1933–1945, being prepared under the general editorship
of Geoffrey P. Megargee. See, for reference, the Museum's web site (www.ushmm.org) and
Eric Lichtblau, "The Holocaust Just Got More Shocking," *New York Times*, March 3, 2013.

end of Jewish life in Europe and its reconstruction elsewhere, and perhaps even lead to the creation of a "center for aftermath studies" to inform the policies of contemporary state and international actors that wrestle with modern refugee issues and the long-term consequences of genocide and related population displacements. While contemplating the scale of the postwar crisis that involved millions of displaced persons, the team, citing the impact on individual DPs and their families of snap value judgments by Allied "intake officers" at DP camps, stressed the need for studies that might lead to better training today to address the individual physical and psychological needs of survivors of future crises. Making reference to the records relating to Nazi medical crimes and the physical consequences of starvation, deprivation, and exhausting physical labor that can be found in both the Incarceration and the Displaced Persons sections of the ITS archive, the team drew attention to the importance of the archive for scholars of the history of medicine.[5] The participants also reflected on the abuse of the DP system by war criminals to leave Europe and, in most cases, escape without ever being held accountable for their crimes. As the last trials of alleged Holocaust-era perpetrators were being debated and, in a few instances, carried through to judgment, the fact that the ITS archive contained substantive files on alleged war criminals like John (Ivan) Demjanjuk, Laszlo Csatary, Johann "Hans" Breyer, and others led this team to suggest the need for serious new analysis of how such individuals navigated to safety through the cloudy aftermath of the genocide of European Jewry. They also proposed renewed study of the individuals and institutions that failed to investigate such people, or found nothing objectionable in what they had done, and therefore helped them.

The final team worked in the section of the archive labeled "Topical Documents" (*Sachdokumente*) and in the well over three million "Tracing and Documentation" (T/D) or postwar inquiry files. Not surprisingly, each inquiry sent to ITS provided important information known to the inquirer at the same time as it sought information from the ITS archive. Team members summarized the research possibilities as "broad" and "expansive." They emphasized the potential for refugee compensation studies; for study of the institutional history of ITS as a case study of the management of the needs of survivors of genocide and mass displacement; and for study of the *Lebensborn* program and the planning, under

---

5. See Paul Weindling, *Victims and Survivors of Nazi Human Experiments: Science and Suffering in the Holocaust* (London: Bloomsbury Academic Publishing, 2015). Weindling, Wellcome Trust Research Professor in the History of Medicine at Oxford Brookes University, is currently leading a multi-year Arts and Humanities Research Council research project on "Victims of Human Experiments under National Socialism." Project researchers have made extensive use of the ITS archive.

Heinrich Himmler's direct supervision, of techniques to create the "perfect Aryan child." One researcher described the potential for an important project on mass graves and the graves of victims who died at forced labor. Another advocated for serious study, based on these materials, of the manner in which information on Nazi crimes was first gathered by Allied authorities during the last phase and immediately following the end of World War II. The discussion that followed the team's presentation also identified the unique significance of the T/D files for studies of post-Holocaust emigration and resettlement patterns, a kind of post-Holocaust geography of the survivors of persecution, of perpetrators, and of hundreds of thousands of others who had been displaced for some reason, including in particular the return of Soviet authority to prewar Soviet territories that had been occupied and the Soviet military occupation of much of East Central Europe. The intertwined fates of perpetrators and collaborators, their victims, bystanders, and beneficiaries, so evident in so much of the ITS documentation, did not end when the war ended.

During the research workshop's summary discussions, possibilities for future research initiatives emerged that spanned the document sections covered by each team and integrated many of the themes they had raised. Participants advocated for comparative study of every kind—for example, study of the diversity of prisoner, labor, DP, resettlement, and memory-seeking experiences made possible by the incarceration, labor, DP and resettlement, and T/D sections; for exploration of the geography of the Holocaust, including refugee and migration studies and the "geography of memory," tracing the nature of inquiries received by ITS, where they came from, and when; for longitudinal studies, and in particular for study of behaviors in the post-Holocaust "chronological gray zone" or "fluid temporal space" from late 1943 to 1948, when perpetrators, victims, users of forced labor, bystanders, and then DPs, allied authorities, and potentially implicated perpetrators all lived in a situation of great uncertainty, changing prospects, and the unpredictable possibilities presented by growing awareness that the Allies would win the war and that Germany would be defeated, followed ever so quickly by the onset of the Cold War. The ITS archive, workshop participants concluded, would be "a goldmine for scholars."

* * *

Seven years after that initial research workshop, some misconceptions regarding the ITS archive persist. Many people, understanding correctly that there are millions of name cards and lists of names in the archive, still consider that to be the full measure of it. But the collections are much more diverse, and the name cards and lists, knowledgeably consulted, analyzed, and aggregated, speak with the powerful voice of individual human beings and provide a foundation for the multiple research possibilities outlined by the workshop participants, and undoubtedly many more. The perception that the archive is relevant principally for research into events in Western Europe, especially in Germany itself, and dramatically less relevant to events further east, while valid to a degree, requires significant qualification and needs to be tested case-by-case, lest researchers fail to consult the important documentation relating to events in Eastern Europe and the former Soviet Union that can be found in ITS records.[6] And while it is true, as was often asserted as an argument against opening the records, that the ITS archive does not house records of grand strategy making or of the perpetrators' planning and implementation of the "Final Solution," on the basis of which so much history has been written, ITS powerfully documents the human factor—the grinding routine of man's inhumanity to man, of prisoners' efforts to survive one more day, of perpetrator calculations of how to reap the most benefit from disposable human assets consigned to their control, of occasional acts of courage and rescue, and of the herculean efforts of survivors to live after so much death.

The seven years have also witnessed dramatic change. The ICRC withdrew from its administrative role at ITS, and the International Commission hired an internationally respected research scholar and professor of Holocaust studies to serve as the first post-ICRC director of the institution. As a result of the treaty amendments signed in 2006 and ratified by the final International Commission member state in 2008, the United States Holocaust Memorial Museum and national repositories in several other Commission member countries have received over 150 million document scans from the ITS archive, and the scanning continues. At the USHMM, we have responded to over 15,000 requests from survivors and their families for information about lost loved ones. And for the first time, responses to such requests, whether provided from Washington, from ITS in Bad Arolsen, or elsewhere, are being accompanied by copies of the actual documents that relate to the inquirer's question, rather than via the bureaucratic form letter that previously characterized ITS responses, if they materialized at all. The difference for survivors and their families who are still seeking answers seventy years after the end of World War II has been immense.[7]

---

6. See Paul A. Shapiro, "Vapniarka: The Archive of the International Tracing Service and the Holocaust in the East," *Holocaust and Genocide Studies*, 27, No. 1 (Spring 2013), pp. 114–137.

7. In some cases revelations in the ITS collections have led to and had a dramatic impact on important new survivor and survivor family publications. See, for example, Sarah Wildman, *Paper Love—Searching for the Girl My Grandfather Left Behind* (New York: Penguin/Riverhead Books, 2014), and Thomas Buergenthal, *A Lucky Child—A Memoir of Surviving*

A comprehensive list of the document collections at ITS, based on a physical search of the institution, now exists. Work is being done on catalogues and finding aids to facilitate research—something that prior to opening the archive had been considered unnecessary for documentation to which no one was supposed to gain access. Institutionally, ITS has become a more welcoming venue for research and has begun to publish a yearbook of ITS-related scholarship.[8]

The concern raised by the ICRC and shared by some national representatives on the International Commission that opening the archive might lead to an immediate spate of lawsuits relating to data privacy (*Datenschutz*) proved to be unwarranted. Irrespective of whether the records have been consulted at Bad Arolsen under the access rules established by the Commission for the ITS headquarters, or in digital form at one of the national copy repositories in the member states of the Commission, where the national privacy and archival laws and practices of the respective member state apply, no such lawsuits have materialized. Given the positive impact for both survivors and their families and for researchers since the archive has been open, even the sensitivity that once existed regarding the potential for scholars to explore the uses that various national governments made of the collections at ITS, or to study the ways in which states and international organizations met or failed to adequately address survivor-related issues and needs after World War II, has diminished. There is no question that the ITS archive offers these possibilities to serious researchers, just as it offers the possibility to examine the manner in which the administrators of ITS—whether UNRRA or the IRO, the Allied High Commission for Germany or the ICRC—responded to requests by governments for information regarding alleged war criminals and collaborators whose names, wartime behavior, and generally self-expiating approaches to DP and Allied occupation authorities after the war can be found in the archive.[9]

Auschwitz as a Young Child, expanded edition (New York: Little Brown and Company/Back Bay Books, 2015).

8. To date, four annual volumes of *Freilegungen: Jahrbuch des International Tracing Service* have appeared, published by Wallstein Verlag (Göttingen).

9. There was considerable discussion of this issue as the Commission debated access rules. ITS responses to government inquiries relating to alleged war criminals were often edited multiple times before being finalized. The drafts were generally retained in the respective work file, making it possible to see whether edits clarified or obfuscated the information shown in ITS archival material relating to the person who was the subject of the inquiry. In some instances it is also clear from the file that the absence of a trained historian on the ITS staff for many decades left the institution ill-equipped to evaluate the significance of documents in the collections. ICRC sensitivity regarding this issue led to a suggestion by the ICRC, as it prepared to relinquish its administrative control at ITS and as the scanning of inquiry (T/D) files began, to scan and make available for research only the incoming inquiry

In the seven years since the archive has been open, the International Commission has become increasingly aware of the breadth of subject matter for which the ITS holdings constitute a unique resource for scholarly research or add new perspectives on topics that may have already been studied in some depth using other archival collections. There is growing awareness, as well, that the archive can serve as a vital resource for future education and training regarding the Holocaust, other related Nazi-era crimes, and the enormous task of dealing effectively with the aftermath of genocide. Recognizing all of this, the Commission has recently decided to work toward making all of the documentation in the ITS archive accessible on line. This transformation of approach in just a few years, from near-total denial of access to plans to make the documentation accessible everywhere, will surely encourage greater use of the archive for research of the sorts identified by participants in that first jointly sponsored USHMM-ITS workshop, which took place in Bad Arolsen just a few months after research access to the archive became possible.

It took years to open the ITS archive, and more years have passed since. During this period, the actuarial table of the survivor generation has caught up with tens of thousands of survivors of Nazi-era persecution and displacement, some of them my friends, some my inspirations, and all people who deserved better than what they endured even after the Holocaust ended. Since the opening of the ITS archive, many survivors have received information and documentation that had been denied to them for decades regarding lost loved ones and regarding their own experiences. But many more did not live long enough to be granted that opportunity for closure. One may ask what debt is owed to them. Is there any meaningful way to acknowledge the ethical wrong that they suffered as a result? The ITS archive contains tens of millions of documents with the potential to ensure that neither the victims nor the survivors, nor what happened to them, will ever be forgotten. In my view, it must be the responsibility of today's scholars and educators and those of future generations to make use of the archive and capitalize on that potential.

*   *   *

The United States Holocaust Memorial Museum dedicated considerable energy to opening the ITS archive. The Museum continues to work with ITS in Bad Arolsen and with the other national repositories of digital copies of the

---

and the final response that was sent by ITS to the inquiring government, destroying all intermediate drafts. The International Commission unanimously rejected the proposal, leaving open for future research the manner in which inquiries regarding alleged war criminals had been handled at ITS.

archive on projects designed to facilitate its use. Suzanne Brown-Fleming is the senior coordinator of the programs of the Jack, Joseph and Morton Mandel Center for Advanced Holocaust Studies that are dedicated to advancing scholarly use of the ITS archive. In *Nazi Persecution and Postwar Repercussions: The International Tracing Service Archive and Holocaust Research*, she has undertaken the first serious effort to guide scholars, researchers, and educators through some of the challenges and complexities of working with the ITS archive, and simultaneously to illustrate the rewards of engaging this important new resource for Holocaust research and teaching. The powerful case studies that Dr. Brown-Fleming provides illustrate some of the possibilities for innovative and cutting-edge research approaches that the ITS collections offer. She has made a significant contribution through this unique publication. Thanks to her work, others will be able to proceed with greater confidence in identifying and utilizing ITS archival riches that relate to their own academic and educational pursuits.

Paul A. Shapiro, Director
Jack, Joseph and Morton Mandel Center for Advanced Holocaust Studies
United States Holocaust Memorial Museum
October 2015

Acknowledgments

THIS BOOK was made possible first and foremost by Paul Shapiro, who led the United States Holocaust Memorial Museum's herculean efforts to open the International Tracing Service (ITS) to survivors and scholars the world over, often without considering the potential and actual personal costs to himself. I only hope he will one day write that full story. I also thank ITS former director Rebecca Boehling (January 1, 2013 to December 31, 2015), whom I met as a graduate student when she sat on my dissertation committee. She has been a crucial and supportive force since that time. This is my sixteenth year in the Museum's Jack, Joseph and Morton Mandel Center for Advanced Holocaust Studies, where I first arrived as a fellow in 2000. I have amazing colleagues across the institution whose expertise, hard work, and generosity with their time, when this project consumed mine, have made this book possible. I must mention them each personally. Diane Afoumado, Betsy Anthony, William Connelly, Jo-Ellyn Decker, Robert Ehrenreich, Mel Hecker, Fritz Kainz, Alexandra Lohse, Jürgen Matthäus, Amanda Pridmore, Jude Richter, and Robert Williams: thank you.

Colleagues around the world have also proved invaluable to me along the way, and I owe special thanks to Ruth Balint, Ben Barkow, Lauren Bartsche, Daniel Cohen, László Csősz, Edward Holland, Laure Humbert, Susan Miller, Christine Schmidt, Gerald Steinacher, Johannes-Dieter Steinert, Dan Stone, and Susanne Urban for pointing me in the right direction or reviewing sections of this manuscript to offer improvements and corrections. All errors are my own responsibility.

I must thank my husband, Mark Fleming, for his constant love and support, and also our daughters, Madison, Eleanor, and Giselle Fleming, for doing without their mother on many occasions so that this book could become a reality. I hope the product is a source of pride for them, as I could not have completed it without their patience.

This volume is the culmination of the early and continued support shown by several key individuals and foundations: Betty-Jean and David Bavar, Edie and David Blitzstein, and K. Peter and Yvonne R. Wagner; and the Braman Family Foundation, the Harris Family Foundation, the Manya Friedman Memorial Fund, the Pulier Foundation, and the the Curt C. and Else Silberman Foundation. Finally, I would like to dedicate this book to Randolph L. Braham and to Theodore "Zev" Weiss and his wife, Alice, to whom I owe a tremendous personal debt for reasons they understand.

Abbreviations

AG	*Aktiengesellschaft* (corporation)
AJDC	American Jewish Joint Distribution Committee (also referred to as JDC)
BEG	Bundesentschädigungsgesetz (Federal Indemnification Law)
BLEA	Bayerisches Landesentschädigungsamt (Bavarian State Compensation Office)
CDPX	Combined Displaced Persons Executive
CM/1	International Refugee Organization care and maintenance—welfare and support forms
CNI	Central Name Index
CTB	Central Tracing Bureau
DP	Displaced person
DP-2	Displaced person registration record
EVZ	Stiftung "Erinnerung, Verantwortung und Zukunft" (Foundation "Remembrance, Responsibility, and Future")
Fa.	*Firma* (company)
FRG	Federal Republic of Germany
GBI	Generalbauinspektor für die Reichshauptstadt (Inspector General of Construction for the National Capital City)
IC	International Commission
ICEM	Intergovernmental Committee for European Migration
ICRC	International Committee of the Red Cross
IIO	International Information Office

IMT	International Military Tribunal
IRO	International Refugee Organization
ITS	International Tracing Service
NSDAP	Nationalsozialistische Deutsche Arbeiterpartei (National Socialist German Worker's Party)
NSV	Nationalsozialistische Volkswohlfahrt (National Socialist People's Welfare)
OT	Organisation Todt
PCIRO	Preparatory Commission for the International Refugee Organization
POW	Prisoner of war
RuSHA	SS-Rasse- und Siedlungshauptamt (SS Race and Resettlement Main Office)
SA	Sturmabteilung (Nazi storm troopers)
SDG	*Sanitätsdienstgrad* (SS medical orderly)
SHAEF	Supreme Headquarters/Allied Expeditionary Forces
SS	Schutzstaffel (Nazi Security Squad)
T/D	tracing and documentation
UNESCO	United Nations Educational, Scientific, and Cultural Organization
UNHCR	United Nations High Commissioner for Refugees
UNRRA	United Nations Relief and Rehabilitation Administration
USFET	United States Forces, European Theater
USHMM	United States Holocaust Memorial Museum
UUSC	Unitarian Universalist Service Committee
YMCA	Young Men's Christian Association
YWCA	Young Women's Christian Association

CHAPTER 1

THE INTERNATIONAL TRACING SERVICE HOLDINGS

O N JUNE 25, 2007, the CBS television news network program *60 Minutes* aired the segment "Hitler's Secret Archive." Program host Scott Pelley warned viewers, "You are about to see secrets of the Holocaust that have been hidden away for sixty years. What we found ranged from the bizarre to the horrifying." Pelley was reporting on the International Tracing Service (ITS) in Bad Arolsen, Germany, which was, until November 2007, the largest closed Holocaust-related archival collection in the world. The documents, said Pelley, had been "taken to a town in the middle of Germany called Bad Arolsen, where they were sorted, filed and locked away, never to be seen by the public until now."[1] This is but one rendering—and among the most public—of the tale of the ITS holdings, which, then and now, continue to fascinate.

Recently inscribed into the United Nations Educational, Scientific, and Cultural Organization (UNESCO) Memory of the World Register,[2] the size and scope of the collection, staggers the imagination. In tens of millions of documents, the ITS holdings capture the Nazi and Axis attempt to remake all

---

1. "Hitler's Secret Archive," *60 Minutes*, CBS News Archive, www.cbsnews.com/videos/hitlers-secret-archive (accessed January 2, 2015).
2. "Archive of the International Tracing Service Listed in UNESCO Register 'Memory of the World,'" Press Release, ITS, Bad Arolsen, June 19, 2013.

of Europe under the fascist juggernaut and the terrible, decades-long aftermath for families, institutions, and nations. The ITS holdings relate to millions of people subject to incarceration, forced labor, displacement, or death as a result of World War II; to their persecutors; to witnesses and accomplices;[3] and to the countries and agencies that addressed their needs at war's end. The documents' organization focuses on the perspective of victims and survivors of the Holocaust, both Jews and non-Jews.[4] Consider this description by Paul A. Shapiro, the principal driver in opening the ITS holdings:

> [The ITS holdings] represent a rare case of archives gathered in a single location that span chronologically from the moment Adolf Hitler's National Socialist Party rose to power in Germany [in 1933], through the years of Nazi domination and mass persecution of Jews and other targeted groups on the European continent, through the years when both Jewish and non-Jewish survivors of persecution (as well as many perpetrators) passing through hundreds of displaced persons facilities sought emigration, resettlement and the opportunity to construct new lives in the postwar, post-Holocaust era; and continuing right up to our own day through the millions of inquiries that both sought and provided important information, submitted to the ITS by survivors, governments, and other institutions and individuals.[5]

Decades before the inaccurately titled "Hitler's Secret Archive" aired and scholars gained access to the ITS holdings, many myths and misconceptions about the archive circulated. These are well summarized and articulated by Shapiro and will not be repeated here.[6] Rather, this brief volume offers a point of

---

3. I use the term "witnesses" with caution. In the case of his forthcoming study on Buczacz, for example, Omer Bartov writes poignantly that "the distinction between rescue and denunciation was often blurred and at times nonexistent, as was the distinction between perpetrators and victims; and that the category of bystander in these areas was largely meaningless, since everyone took part in the events, whether he or she suffered or profited by them." Omer Bartov, "Wartime Lies and Other Testimonies: Jewish-Christian Relations in Buczacz, 1939–1944," *East European Politics and Societies* 25 (2011): 491.

4. Paul A. Shapiro, "History Held Hostage," *Reform Judaism* (winter 2009), available at www.reformjudaism.org/history-held-hostage (accessed 23 September 2015). See also his foreword in this volume.

5. Paul A. Shapiro, "Vapniarka: ITS and the Holocaust in the East," in *Freilegungen: Auf den Spuren der Todesmärsche*, ed. Jean-Luc Blondel, Susanne Urban, and Sebastian Schönemann. Jahrbuch des International Tracing Service I (Göttingen: Wallstein Verlag, 2012), 26. See also Paul A. Shapiro, "Vapniarka: The Archive of the International Tracing Service and the Holocaust in the East," *Holocaust and Genocide Studies* 27, no. 1 (spring 2013): 114–37.

6. See Shapiro, "History Held Hostage"; Shapiro, "Vapniarka," 114–16.

entry into a complex collection with great potential to advance twenty-first-century scholarship and education on the Holocaust and its aftermath. Far from providing the final word, this volume intends to demystify the ITS holdings and make the contents of the archive more accessible. The curious reader seeking new sources and perspectives on the Holocaust and its postwar repercussions will find many questions and some answers in these pages. If this volume stimulates more comprehensive and in-depth work utilizing the ITS holdings going forward, it will have fulfilled its purpose.

Reports describing the creation and early years of ITS can be found in the collection itself.[7] In 1943, the British Red Cross Bureau for International Affairs (London) was converted into a tracing service. In February 1944, the Supreme Headquarters/Allied Expeditionary Forces (SHAEF) assumed leadership of it. SHAEF transferred the administration of the tracing service to the United Nations Relief and Rehabilitation Administration (UNRRA)[8] in late 1945, at which point its primary mission became the tracing of civilians, although ultimate authority over the tracing service and its policies remained with the military governments.[9] In January 1946, the Central Tracing Bureau (CTB) moved to Bad Arolsen. Not bombed during the war, the town was home to large, intact buildings and undisturbed telegraph and telephone lines. It was also centrally located relative to the four zones of occupied Germany.[10]

---

7. "Historical Survey of Central Tracing Activity in Germany, 1945–1951," 6.1.1/82492856–3231/ITS Digital Archive, USHMM. All citations in this manuscript follow the format stipulated by the ITS, which, for ITS digital collections, is as follows: [title or description of document], [archival subcollection number]/[digital document number]/ITS Digital Archive, [location]. See "Format for Citing Documents from the ITS Archives," ITS, www.its-arolsen.org/fileadmin/user_upload/Dateien/Benutzerregelung/Citation_Engl_2014.pdf (accessed February 9, 2015). For the history of ITS from its creation through the decades of the Cold War, see Bernd Joachim Zimmer, *International Tracing Service Arolsen: Von der Vermisstensuche zur Haftbescheinigung; die Organisationsgeschichte eines "ungewollten Kindes" während der Besatzungszeit* (Bad Arolsen: Waldeckischer Geschichtsverein, 2011); Jennifer Rodgers, "From the 'Archive of Horrors' to the 'Shop Window of Democracy': The International Tracing Service and the Transatlantic Politics of the Past" (PhD diss., University of Pennsylvania, 2014).

8. Founded in November 1943, the UNRRA was an international relief agency representing forty-four nations. For a thorough history of the UNRRA, see George Woodbridge, *UNRRA: The History of the United Nations Relief and Rehabilitation Administration*, 3 vols. (New York: Columbia University Press, 1950).

9. Martin Weinmann, *Das Nationalsozialistische Lagersystem* (Frankfurt am Main: Zweitausendeins, 1990), 138–39.

10. For the history of Bad Arolsen during the National Socialist era, see Bernd Joachim Zimmer, "Arolsen," in *The United States Holocaust Memorial Museum Encyclopedia of Camps*

As early as October 1945, the UNRRA Central Tracing Bureau recommended that "indexes of names of former concentration camp inmates, or any other record of concentration camps that would aid in identifying such persons, be located, safeguarded and their location made known."[11] By the following month, the mandate had expanded to include lists of labor detachments sent out from main concentration camps, lists of graves and burial places of displaced persons (DPs), food and labor office lists, cemetery records, church records, records of vital statistics bureaus, personnel records, hospital records, and reports from DPs on names of concentration camps.[12]

In July 1947, the International Refugee Organization (IRO) took over administration of the CTB, and on January 1, 1948, it was renamed the International Tracing Service.[13] In April 1951, the High Commission for Occupied Germany assumed authority over ITS, a measure intended as provisional until the service could be transferred to the administration of the West German government. Instead, in 1955, the International Committee of the Red Cross (ICRC) in Geneva assumed administration of the ITS, subject to the authority of an International Commission (IC) consisting at that time of eight countries (Belgium, the Federal Republic of Germany, France, Israel, Italy, the Netherlands, the United Kingdom, and the United States).[14]

---

and Ghettos, 1933–1945, Vol. 1: *Early Camps, Youth Camps, and Concentration Camps and Subcamps under the SS-Business Administration Main Office (WVHA)*, ed. Geoffrey P. Megargee (Bloomington: Indiana University Press in association with USHMM, 2009), 307–8; Bernd Joachim Zimmer, *Deckname Arthur. Das KZ-Aussenkommando in der SS-Führerschule Arolsen* (Kassel: Verlag Gesamthochschule-Bibliothek Kassel, 1994); Anke Schmeling, *Josias Erbprinz zu Waldeck und Pyrmont. Der politische Werdegang eines hohen SS-Führers* (Kassel: Verlag Gesamthochschule-Bibliothek Kassel, 1993); Jonathan Petropoulos, "Prince zu Waldeck und Pyrmont: A Career in the SS and Its Murderous Consequences," in *Lessons and Legacies, Volume IX: Memory, History, and Responsibility: Reassessments of the Holocaust, Implications for the Future*, ed. Jonathan Petropoulos, Lynn Rapaport, and John K. Roth (Evanston, IL: Northwestern University Press, 2010), 169–84.

11. "UNRRA Central Tracing Bureau and Records Office, Requirements of the Central Tracing Bureau and Records Office, UNRRA, Regarding Concentration Camp Records, October 23, 1945," 6.1.1/82510743/ITS Digital Archive, USHMM.

12. "Documents to Look For, November 27, 1945," 6.1.1/82510791–2/ITS Digital Archive, USHMM.

13. Weinmann, *Das Nationalsozialistische Lagersystem*, 139.

14. For the broader political context of Nazi crimes and the documentary record in West German politics in the 1950s, see, among others, Norbert Frei, *Adenauer's Germany and the Nazi Past: The Politics of Amnesty and Integration*, trans. Joel Golb (New York: Columbia University Press, 2002); Astrid Eckert, *The Struggle for the Files: The Western Allies and the Return of German Archives after the Second World War*, trans. Dona Geyer (New York: Columbia University Press, 2012).

According to a June 1946 report by Maurice Thudicum, the first director of the CTB, the "first set of concentration camp records [the tracing bureau] was to gather and exploit" came from the Dachau concentration camp. (See document 1.1.[15]) Dachau Registration Office records saved by prisoners employed there and first kept by the International Information Office (Dachau) were transferred in their entirety to the US Zone Tracing Bureau in August 1946. Original documentation from the Buchenwald concentration camp arrived next, obtained from the US Document Center in Wiesbaden, followed by Flossenbürg documentation from the 3rd Army Berlin Document Center and the War Crimes Tribunal in Dachau. Additional original material from these camps amounting to "126 crates" arrived from the US Document Center in Oberursel at the end of 1947. Materials relating to the Mauthausen concentration camp were discovered in Munich in December 1948 and sent on to the tracing bureau. By the end of 1948, "these documents constituted the largest and most complete collection of original concentration camp records in Europe."[16]

Thousands of other collections continued to be deposited there after 1955 and as late as 2008, "sometimes," writes Shapiro, "sent by individuals and organizations seeking to assist ITS in the fulfillment of its mandates and sometimes deposited at Bad Arolsen by governments that did not care to preserve the records or believed that if they were at ITS, no one would ever see them."[17] (See document 1.2.[18]) The history of the opening of this archive in 2007, the man-

---

15. Dachau Registration Office card for Szulim Goldberg, 1.1.6.7/96338956/ITS Digital Archive, USHMM. Card is original. For document 1.1, see also the discussion in chapter 4 of the Dachau Registration Office. This and other documents profiled in this volume are meant to be illustrative and have been selected for their visual power, unusual content, or representativeness as a "typical" document in the ITS holdings. The documents selected for this volume are not meant to be comprehensive but rather to stimulate further research and interest in the ITS holdings.

16. "History of the International Tracing Service, 1945-1951," undated report, pp.140-41, 6.1.1/82493071–2/ITS Digital Archive, USHMM. 6.1.1/82493071–2/ITS Digital Archive, USHMM.

17. Shapiro, "Vapniarka," 27. For hundreds of pages of documentation on how files came to rest in Bad Arolsen, see files in ITS collections, 6.1.1/82510715–1769/ITS Digital Archive, USHMM.

18. In March 1990, the Bavarian Red Cross in Bamberg turned over to ITS eleven original letters addressed to Vladislaus Razyn while he was incarcerated in the small fortress of Theresienstadt and subsequently, according to further ITS-held documentation, in Dresden and Bautzen. He must have kept these letters with him during his incarceration in Ebrach prison in Bamberg—his last place of imprisonment before he was liberated there on May 20, 1945. Document 1.2 presents one of the letters, found in the attic of a dwelling on Judenstr. 15, Bamberg, an important clue signifying that Razym was probably Jewish and remained in

date that all IC member states have the option to received a scanned (i.e., digital) copy upon request, and the withdrawal of the ICRC from the administration of ITS in 2012 is most compelling and deserves its own full-length study.[19]

Managed directly by the IC and under the directorship of Floriane Hohenberg (effective January 1, 2016), the ITS is undergoing a "reorientation [and] shift of focus" in its work in recognition of the reality that "clarifying individual fates, tracing family members [and] restitution issues will gradually fade into the background."[20] The Berlin Agreements signed by IC members on December 9, 2011, at the Foreign Office in Berlin and effective from January 1, 2013, define ITS guidelines.[21] Currently, the IC consists of eleven member states (Belgium, France, Germany, Greece, Israel, Italy, Luxembourg, the Netherlands, Poland, the United Kingdom, and the United States). Both the ICRC and the German Federal Archive (Bundesarchiv) have permanent observer status in the IC. The Bundesarchiv has been designated as an institutional partner to "advise the ITS in archival questions such as digitization, conservation and archival description."[22]

THE INTERNATIONAL TRACING SERVICE HOLDINGS

Broadly speaking, the ITS holdings consist of (1) original material located only in the ITS holdings, (2) copies of documentation for which the originals might

Bamberg at least temporarily after liberation. See the letter from "Zdena" to prisoner V. Razyn (circa 1944) sent to ITS by Bamberg Red Cross in 1990, 1.2.2.1/11817287/ITS Digital Archive, USHMM. This is an example of a tiny and fascinating collection among thousands of others that arrived in Bad Arolsen in the decades following World War II.

19. Shapiro, "History Held Hostage"; Kenneth Waltzer, "Opening the Red Cross International Tracing Service Archives," *John Marshall Journal of Computer and Information Law* 26, no. 1 (fall 2008): 166; Paul Belkin, "Opening of the International Tracing Service's Holocaust-Era Archives in Bad Arolsen, Germany," CRS Report for Congress, Order Code RS22638, April 5, 2007.

20. *Perspectives for the ITS Annual Report* (Bad Arolsen: ITS, 2012), 15. ITS today defines itself as "a centre for documentation, information and research on Nazi persecution, forced labor and the Holocaust" (3). See also the ITS website (www.its-arolsen.org, accessed July 9, 2013).

21. *Perspectives for the ITS Annual Report* (2012): 12–13. For the full text of the law, see "Agreement on the International Tracing Service," ITS, www.its-arolsen.org/fileadmin/user_upload/Dateien/gesetzestexte/Bundesgesetzblatt_ITSagreement.pdf (accessed July 9, 2013). ITS is financed by the budget of the Federal Republic of Germany's Commission for Culture and the Media (Bundesministerium für Kultur und Medien).

22. *Perspectives for the ITS Annual Report* (2012): 9. Also see "Partnership Agreement between the German Federal Archives and the ITS," ITS, www.its-arolsen.org/file

no longer exist, (3) original material within the ITS holdings and also held in copy in other archives around the world, and (4) copies of material initially gathered from other archives for tracing purposes and today extremely useful for researchers.[23] It would be difficult at this point to estimate the percentage of materials unique to the ITS holdings. However, using currently available tools (to which we will return at a later point), we can make a beginning in identifying that material that exists only and uniquely in the ITS holdings. That said, there is great utility for researchers in having colocated copies of relevant collections. Further, these ITS-held copies guide scholars to the original sources.

A large portion of the ITS holdings have been scanned. As of 2015, the scanned portions of the ITS holdings are organized into the following units:

- Special Inventories and Finding Aids
- Subunit Zero: Global Finding Aids
- Subunit One: Incarceration and Persecution
- Subunit Two: Registration of Foreigners and German Persecutees by Public Institutions, Insurance Companies, and Firms (1939–1947)
- Subunit Three: Registrations and Files of Displaced Persons, Children, and Missing Persons
- Subunit Four: Special NSDAP[24] Organizations and Actions
- Subunit Five: Miscellaneous
- Subunit Six: Records of the ITS and its Predecessors

Under the terms of the 2011 Berlin Agreements, the ITS has provided copies of the scanned documents to designated institutions within seven of the IC member states. These scanned copies constitute the ITS digital archive.[25] To date, the United States Holocaust Memorial Museum (USHMM), Israel's Yad Vashem, the Institute of National Remembrance (Warsaw) in Poland, the Luxembourg Documentation and Research Centre on Resistance, the Belgian and

---

admin/user_upload/Dateien/gesetzestexte/Vertragstext_PV_Original.pdf (accessed July 9, 2013).

23. For discussions regarding the centralized "collection of documents and records" for the purpose of tracing individuals, see "Historical Survey of Central Tracing Activity in Germany, 1945–1951," 6.1.1/82492875–6/ITS Digital Archive, USHMM, 16–17.

24. Nationalsozialistische Deutsche Arbeiterpartei (National Socialist German Worker's Party).

25. Per the citation guidelines issued by the ITS in Bad Arolsen, the scanned portions of the ITS holdings should be cited as the "ITS Digital Archive."

French national archives, and the Wiener Library for the Study of the Holocaust & Genocide (London) in the United Kingdom have received a copy of the ITS digital archive. In each respective IC member state, national archival law and practice, as well as institutional preparedness, govern access to and use of the ITS digital archive.

SUBUNITS ONE AND TWO[26]

Subunits One (Incarceration and Persecution) and Two (Registration of Foreigners and German Persecutees by Public Institutions, Insurance Companies, and Firms, 1939–1947) are best discussed in tandem, as the camp universe[27] and the phenomenon of forced labor (*Zwangsarbeit*)[28] frequently went hand in hand. In addition to the centralized and SS-run[29] camps that have made their

---

26. Special inventories and finding aids and Subunit Zero will be covered later in the text.

27. In 1933 the Nazi regime opened the first concentration camps in a network that ultimately became "perhaps the most pervasive collection of detention sites that any society has ever created." See Geoffrey P. Megargee, "Editor's Introduction to the Series and Volume I," in Megargee, *The United States Holocaust Memorial Museum Encyclopedia of Camps and Ghettos*, 1:xxiii–xxxvi.

28. The foundational work on the use of forced labor during the Third Reich is still Ulrich Herbert, *Hitler's Foreign Workers: Enforced Foreign Labor in Germany under the Third Reich*, trans. William Templer (New York: Cambridge University Press, 1997). See also Dieter Pohl and Tanja Sebta, *Zwangsarbeit in Hitlers Europa: Besatzung, Arbeit, Folgen* (Berlin: Metropol, 2013); Wolf Gruner, *Jewish Forced Labor under the Nazis: Economic Needs and Racial Aims*, trans. Kathleen M. Dell'Orto (New York: Cambridge University Press in association with USHMM, 2006); Laura J. Hilton and John J. Delaney, "Forced Foreign Laborers, POWs and Jewish Slave Workers in the Third Reich: Regional Studies and New Directions," *German History* 23, no. 1 (2005): 83–95; Mark Spörer, *Zwangsarbeit unter dem Hakenkreuz: Ausländischer Zivilarbeiter, Kriegsgefangene und Häftlinge im Deutschen Reich und im besetzten Europa, 1939–1945* (Stuttgart: Deutsche Verlags-Anstalt, 2001).

29. The sprawling Schutzstaffel (SS, Nazi Security Squad) was established in 1925 as a protective service for prominent Nazi Party functionaries and ultimately became the key exeutive organization, together with the police, of the Nazi state, commanded by Heinrich Himmler. After 1940, the SS also played a significant economic and military role, comprising by war's end roughly one million men and several thousand women and was deeply involved in camp slave labor networks. See Peter Longerich, *Heinrich Himmler*, trans. Jeremy Noakes and Lesley Sharpe (Oxford: Oxford University Press, 2012); Jan Erik Schulte, *Zwangsarbeit und Vernichtung: Das Wirtschaftsimperium der SS: Oswald Pohl und das SS-Wirtschafts-Verwaltungshauptamt 1933–1945* (Paderborn: Ferdinand Schöningh, 2001); Hans Safrian, *Eichmann's Men*, trans. Ute Stargardt (New York: Cambridge University Press in association with USHMM, 2010); Michael Wildt, *An Uncompromising Generation: The Nazi Leadership of the Reich Security Main Office*, trans. Tom Lampert (Madison: University of Wisconsin Press, 2009).

way into the world's consciousness—Auschwitz, Bergen-Belsen, Buchenwald, Dachau—Geoffrey P. Megargee cites a "bewildering array" of other persecution sites. These included "killing centers, ghettos, forced labor camps, prisoner-of-war (POW) camps, so-called resettlement camps, brothels, prisons," and more, run by the SS, the German military, the police, and other governmental agencies, as well as private industry. Axis powers too began their own camp systems stretching from "France to Romania and Norway to Italy." As records in the ITS holdings so ably demonstrate, prisoners came from every country over which the Nazi and Axis regimes held power.[30] Work "was a central element of the Nazis' camp regimen," and most prisoners had to perform some sort of labor.[31]

Historians differentiate between groups of forced laborers and their sites of incarceration. Common factors included laborers' inability to leave or change their work deployments/work sites or to exercise control over their work and living conditions. Ulrich Herbert proposes four main groups of forced laborers: (1) foreign civilians transferred into German territory over the course of the war specifically for the purpose of labor deployment, becoming the largest group of foreign laborers in Germany and including millions of *Ostarbeiter* (eastern workers) from Poland and the former Soviet Union; (2) foreign POWs and military detainees deployed in the German economy; (3) inmates of concentration camps exploited under the auspices of the SS, enduring particularly brutal conditions and often complete disregard for life and health, leading some historians to classify them as "slave laborers"; (4) German and foreign Jews forced to work in their towns and later ghettos in occupied Europe.[32] An estimated 8 million foreign forced laborers had been deployed in the German economy by 1944.[33]

Many victims subjected to forced labor found themselves in the camp system at some point and subject to slave labor within it. In the ITS holdings, they thus appear in both Subunits One and Two. Subunit One includes collections relating to camps, ghettos, and prisons of various types, the Nazi or Axis agencies that ran them, and slave labor within the concentration camp universe. Many aspects of the incarceration and persecution process, including surveillance,

---

30. Megargee, "Editor's Introduction to the Series and Volume I," 1:xxiii.

31. Ibid., 1:xxiv.

32. Ulrich Herbert, "Forced Laborers in the Third Reich: An Overview," *International Labor and Working-Class History* 58, no. 1 (2000): 192–93; Idit Gil, "Jewish Slave Laborers from Radom in the Last Year of the War: Social Aspects of Exploitation," in *Freilegungen: Spiegelungen der NS-Verfolgung und ihrer Konsequenzen*, ed. Rebecca Boehling, Susanne Urban, Elizabeth Anthony and Suzanne Brown-Fleming. Jahrbuch des International Tracing Service IV (Göttingen: Wallstein Verlag, 2015); Alexandre Doulot, "'No Number Tattooed': The Cosel Convoys from France in the ITS Holdings," in Boehling, Urban, Anthony and Brown-Fleming, *Freilegungen*.

33. Herbert, "Forced Laborers in the Third Reich," 192–39.

arrest, detention, deportation, and slave labor (especially Jewish slave labor) in main camps and sprawling subcamps, can be studied in Subunit One. Larger collections within Subunit One include over two million scans of documents on individual Buchenwald prisoners and other original camp records. Moving digital images of concentration camp prisoners' belongings, from watches to wedding rings to photographs to personal papers, to be found in subunit 1.2.9 bring home the insatiable nature and real human cost of Nazism. (See document 1.3.[34])

Aside from the aforementioned Buchenwald-, Dachau-, Flossenbürg-, and Mauthausen-related wartime documents that arrived in Bad Arolsen in the immediate years after the war, Subunit One contains thousands of scans of original documents located only in the ITS holdings concerning prisoners in Gross-Rosen[35] (1.1.11.1) and its subcamps, including the Wolfsberg labor camp,[36] as well as tens of thousands of scans of original questionnaires, postal control cards, infirmary cards, and illness and death certificates for prisoners in Mittelbau-Dora[37] (1.1.27). Subunit One also holds substantial material from Natzweiler-Struthof[38] (1.1.29), Ravensbrück[39] (1.1.35), Niederhagen-Wewelsburg[40] (1.1.31), and a host of other camps too numerous to list here.[41] Scholars have begun to work with materials in Subunit One to study individual camps

---

34. Ring belonging to Dachau prisoner Arthur Becker, prisoner number 45341, 1.2.9.1/ 108019938/ITS Digital Archive, USHMM.

35. Gross-Rosen concentration camp was located in Lower Silesia (today Rogoźnica, Poland). For an overview of Gross-Rosen and its subcamps, see Leslaw Braiter et al., "Gross Rosen," in Megargee, *The United States Holocaust Memorial Museum Encyclopedia of Camps and Ghettos*, 1:693–812.

36. For more information on the Wolfsberg labor camp, established to "provide manpower" for the construction of the underground headquarters for Hitler in Lower Silesia, see Piotr Kruszyński, "Riese/Wolfsberg," in Megargee, *The United States Holocaust Memorial Museum Encyclopedia of Camps and Ghettos*, 1:796–97.

37. See Michael J. Neufeld, "Mittelbau Main Camp (Dora)," in Megargee, *The United States Holocaust Memorial Museum Encyclopedia of Camps and Ghettos*, 1:965–1002.

38. For an overview of Natzweiler-Struthof and its subcamps, see Jean-Marc Dreyfus, "Natzweiler-Struthof," in Megargee, *The United States Holocaust Memorial Museum Encyclopedia of Camps and Ghettos*, 1:1003–71.

39. See Bernhard Strebel, "Ravensbrück," in Megargee, *The United States Holocaust Memorial Museum Encyclopedia of Camps and Ghettos*, 1:1187–1228.

40. See Kirsten John-Stucke, "Wewelsburg Main Camp (Niederhagen)," in Megargee, *The United States Holocaust Memorial Museum Encyclopedia of Camps and Ghettos*, 1:1517–21.

41. For a full list of those camps and ghettos identified as stand-alone subcollections, organized in the ITS holdings by geographic location (e.g., "Buchenwald") or by country (e.g., "Camps in France" or "Camps in Norway"), see "General Inventory," ITS, www.its -arolsen.org/en/archives/collections/general-inventory/index.html (accessed June 19, 2013). The geographically based headings of these subcollections should not be considered compre-

at a deeper level.[42] ITS holdings are not limited to camps in Germany. Shapiro has written about the many myths surrounding the ITS holdings. One is that they "have greatest relevance to what happened in Western Europe [. . .] and are dramatically weaker [. . .] the further east in Europe one looks."[43] Shapiro argues that this generalization requires qualification, as ITS holdings concerning the camp Vapniarka (1.1.47.1), today in Ukraine, show.[44]

Also in Subunit One are nearly 1 million records of the Secret State Police (Geheime Staatspolizei, Gestapo).[45] These include 467 original individual case files of Gestapo headquarters in Düsseldorf and its branches in Essen, Duisburg, and Krefeld; of Gestapo headquarters in Linz, Austria;[46] and of the Gestapo units in the concentration camps Neuengamme and Sachsenhausen as well as Rudersberg (subordinate to the Stuttgart Gestapo).[47] Original and not yet utilized by researchers are court-martial proceedings against foreign-born members

hensive. Information on a particular camp or ghetto may be found elsewhere and outside that particular subcollection in the ITS holdings.

42. One example is Hinzert (1.1.13), for which the ITS holdings contain original photographs of the first camp commandant, Hermann Pister (October 1939–December 1941), and material on *E-Polen* (*Eindeutschungs-Polen*, Poles to be Germanized) and other special groups of inmates. See Beate Welter, "Die Zusammenarbeit der Gedenkstätte SS-Sonderlager/KZ Hinzert mit dem ITS Bad Arolsen," in Blondel, Urban, and Schönemann, *Freilegungen: Auf den Spuren der Todesmärsche*, 50, 52–53. The Hinzert camp was 30.6 kilometers (19 miles) southeast of Trier and 1.6 kilometers (1 mile) west of the village of Hinzert (Moselgau). See Evelyn Zegenhagen, "Hinzert," in Megargee, *The United States Holocaust Memorial Museum Encyclopedia of Camps and Ghettos*, 1:823–45. Stefan Wilbricht has used documents from the ITS holdings to study the female and youth prisoner populations in Moringen (1.1.28), near Göttingen. See Stefan Wilbricht, "'Dem KZL. Moringen zugeführt worden': Ergebnisse der Personenrecherche zu den Moringer KZ," in Blondel, Urban, and Schönemann, *Freilegungen: Auf den Spuren der Todesmärsche*, 57. Moringen was a men's camp in 1933 and an early women's camp from 1933 to 1938. In 1940 it became a youth protection camp. See Jürgen Harder and Joseph Robert White, "Youth Protection Camp Moringen," in Megargee, *The United States Holocaust Memorial Museum Encyclopedia of Camps and Ghettos*, 1:1530–32.

43. Shapiro, "Vapniarka," 26.

44. Vapniarka was located in Romanian-administrated Transnistria from 1941 to 1944 and today is in southwestern Ukraine.

45. The Gestapo, subsumed under the SS and Office (*Amt*) IV within the Reich Security Main Office (Reichssicherheitshauptamt, RSHA), were political police engaged in counterespionage, ferreting out so-called enemies of the Third Reich, and, during the war, in the deportation and murder of Jews. See Wildt, *An Uncompromising Generation*.

46. 1.2.2.1/folders 512–20, 1.1.6.1/folder 138, and 1.2.7.13/ITS Digital Archive, USHMM.

47. The finding aid "R 2—Files of the Geheime Staatspolizei (Gestapo)" organizes these 467 files by geographic location, allowing a researcher to see all cases for a particular office (*Gestapostelle*). See "Findbuch zum Bestand R 2—Geheime Staatspolizei (Gestapo)," ITS, www.its-arolsen.org/en/archives/finding-aids/index.html (accessed September 24, 2015).

of German military units from all over Europe and the Middle East, some
of them volunteers, conducted between 1940 and 1945 (1.2.8.1). British and
American authorities discovered these documents in Düsseldorf and Würzburg
in 1950. After passing through several other stations, the records made their
way to Bad Arolsen. Because the cases fell outside the ITS mandate to trace
victims, most documents were released to the defendants' countries of origin.
Of these, 679 cases remained in Bad Arolsen.[48] They can include long and
fascinating narratives about the events and actions that triggered arrest. The
court-martial proceedings offer fresh material for researchers studying a particular unit, examining specific ethnic groups willingly or unwillingly recruited into
the German military, or seeking to construct patterns in what grounds were
cited for disciplinary measures. Those studying the Security Service (Sicherheits-
dienst des Reichsführers-SS, SD)[49] will find original Frankfurt am Main SD
(Aschaffenburg branch) records relating to *Ostarbeiter*; Polish, Belgian, and
French prisoners of war; and those who employed them (1.2.3.0, folder 2).
Subunit One also includes documentation relating to Red Army POWs whom
the SS conscripted from Wehrmacht POW camps as forced laborers.[50]

Subunit Two is a primary source base for the study of labor camps functioning outside the aegis of the SS camp complex, usually operated by private companies or municipalities, utilizing Jewish slave laborers, *Ostarbeiter*, prisoners of
war, and civilian contractors. It contains records of relevant administrative bodies, for example, local or regional labor departments (*Arbeitsämter*) or the German Labor Front (Deutsche Arbeitsfront, DAF),[51] and the records of hospitals,

48. See the finding aid "Findbuch zum Bestand M 1: Kriegsgerichte der Deutschen
Wehrmacht [Courts Martial of the German Army]" ITS, www.its-arolsen.org/en/archives/
finding-aids/index.html (accessed September 24, 2015). Most cases are army (Wehrmacht)
cases, but some are air force (Luftwaffe) cases. The finding guide is organized by military unit
(e.g., Gericht der 1. Luftwaffen-Felddivision or Gericht der 16. Infanterie) and then by first
name.

49. The SD was formed in 1931 as the intelligence service of the NSDAP and later acquired
broader state functions before its main office was merged into the RSHA as Office III. See
George C. Browder, *Hitler's Enforcers: The Gestapo and the SS Security Service in the Nazi
Revolution* (New York: Oxford University Press, 1996); George C. Browder, *Foundations of the
Nazi State: The Formation of Sipo and SD* (Lexington: University of Kentucky Press, 1990).

50. Eric Steinhart, "Toiling for the Reich: New Findings on Soviet Laborers in Nazi
Germany from the International Tracing Service Digital Archive" (unpublished paper deliv-
ered at the American Association for the Advancement of Slavic Studies annual conference,
Los Angeles, California, November 18–21, 2010).

51. The most comprehensive study on the German Labor Front is Rüdiger Hachtmann,
Das Wirtschaftsimperium der Deutschen Arbeitsfront 1933–1945 (Göttingen: Wallstein Verlag,
2012).

health insurance companies, police, and other institutions that regulated different aspects of foreign labor in Germany, including millions of registration cards,
employees' record books, and individual correspondence relating to forced
labor. (See document 1.4.[52]) Subunit Two contains documents that Nazi authorities and large-scale German employers, including the German military, the
Inspector General of Construction for the National Capital City (Generalbauinspektor für die Reichshauptstadt, GBI),[53] the Organisation Todt (OT),[54] and
the Warsaw Labor Office (Arbeitsamt Warschau), produced to manage both
their voluntary foreign workers and those they engaged in forced labor.[55] One
can also find postwar documentation created by foreign governments and tracing services as they searched for missing POWs. This includes documentation
generated by the German Armed Forces Information Office for War Losses and
Prisoners of War (Wehrmachtsauskunftstelle für Kriegverluste und Kriegsgefangene) and the French High Commission for Germany.[56]

Many documents in this subunit, including grave registration forms, were
produced in response to a November 1945 Allied Control Council order issued
to local German authorities tasked with obtaining "nominal rolls by nationalities of Prisoners of War, forcibly evicted persons, workmen and refugees who
have resided temporarily or permanently in occupied territory or who were in
transit through these territories, as well as lists of institutions in which these
persons worked."[57] (See document 1.5.[58]) The resulting records yield a detailed
picture of the nature and implementation of forced labor in Nazi-and Axis-
dominated Europe and allow for locating and describing previously unknown

---

52. Identity card (*Ausweis*) for eastern worker (*Ostarbeiterin*) Lena Iwansowa, 2.2.2.1/
72830650/ITS Digital Archive, USHMM. Document is original.

53. For a description of GBI-related material in ITS and other archives, see "Findbuch
R 1 Generalbauinspektor für die Reichshauptstadt (GBI)," ITS, www.its-arolsen.org/en/
archives/finding-aids/index.html (accessed September 24, 2015).

54. The OT was a construction and public works agency established in 1938 by Fritz
Todt, for the purpose of building highways and military installations. The OT used approximately 1.4 million men—forced laborers, POWs, and slave laborers from concentration
camps—for labor in deadly and inhumane conditions.

55. Lists of the employment office in Warsaw of Polish forced laborers in Germany (agriculture), 2.2.4.1/ITS Digital Archive, USHMM.

56. Steinhart, "Toiling for the Reich."

57. Legal Division, Office of Military Government for Germany, *Enactments and
Approved Papers of the Control Council and Coordinating Committee, Allied Control Authority
Germany* (Berlin: Legal Division, Legal Advice Branch, Drafting Section, Office of Military
Government for Germany, 1945), 1:209a.

58. Grave registration form of French POW Georges Devaux, Oberbernbach/Landkreis
Aichach, Upper Bavaria, attached to grave registration form, 2.1.1.1/69786340/ITS Digital
Archive, USHMM. Drawing is original.

camp sites and inmate populations. Entire inmate groups can be traced through-out the war. Researchers can reconstruct patterns and trends in evolving Nazi wartime labor policy and its implementation on the ground.

Subunit Two illuminates the unprecedented mass movement of European populations by German and Axis military and civilian authorities during the war. It demonstrates both the complex administrative infrastructure directing logistics from the top and the tremendous energy generated—and often wasted—on the bottom as foreigners were transferred in and out of towns and villages, companies, and camps. Most of all, documentation in the ITS holdings brings into sharp relief the high visibility and ubiquity of racism and the per-ceived benefit of exploitation in day-to-day life in wartime Europe. A single barrack or even a barn could be fenced off and serve as a site of persecution and exploitation for its inmates. Current understandings of what constituted a "camp" will change as a result of documents in the ITS holdings, as will our understanding of what Alexandra Lohse calls the "texture" of forced labor. Researchers for the USHMM's Camps and Ghettos Encyclopedia project esti-mate that at least forty thousand sites utilizing forced labor (foreign civilians, prisoners of war, concentration camp inmates, and Jews) existed.[59]

SUBUNIT THREE

Subunit Three (Registration and Files of Displaced Persons, Children, and Missing Individuals) includes the massive body of administrative paperwork to cope with millions of DPs when World War II ended. These included former concentration camp inmates, forced laborers, prisoners of war, those in hiding, and those who had returned from Communist eastern Europe.[60] According to

---

59. This estimated number includes camps for foreign forced laborers, main POW camps, forced labor camps for Jews, ghettos, and concentration camps and subcamps, but it does not include tens of thousands of POW subcamps and various kinds of work sites. See Alexandra Lohse, "Forced Labor in ITS" (unpublished paper delivered at the "Introduction to Holocaust Studies" ITS seminar for undergraduate, master's, and early doctoral students, USHMM, July 2013). For a case study detailing the ubiquity of forced labor in the life and function of a single town and the utility of the ITS holdings for drawing out a detailed picture, see chapter 2.

60. There has been an explosion of recent scholarly work regarding the experiences of displaced persons in postwar Europe, including Gerard Daniel Cohen, *In War's Wake: Europe's Displaced Persons in the Postwar Order* (New York: Oxford University Press, 2012); Margaret Myers Feinstein, *Holocaust Survivors in Postwar Germany, 1945–1957* (Cambridge: Cambridge University Press, 2010); Atina Grossmann, *Jews, Germans and Allies: Close Encounters in Occupied Germany* (Princeton, NJ: Princeton University Press, 2007); Anna Holian, *Between National Socialism and Soviet Communism: Displaced Persons in Postwar Ger-many* (Ann Arbor: University of Michigan Press, 2011); Laura Jockusch, *Collect and Record!*

Gerard Daniel Cohen, "Approximately eight million civilians in Germany qualified as DPs under UNRRA and Allied military directives" by war's end. Military
and UNRRA officials "succeeded in returning six to seven million" to their
"countries of origin" by the fall of 1945. Approximately 1.2 million refugees
remained. Who were the so-called last million, as they were called in media
descriptions of that era? Nearly 50 percent were Polish (an estimated 400,000 in
March 1946), and a large percentage were Estonians, Latvians, and Lithuanians
(150,000 to 200,000) or ethnic Ukrainians (100,000 to 150,000), rounded out
by Jews, Yugoslavs, Slovaks, Hungarians, and other eastern Europeans.

What Cohen calls a "second and longer phase of the DP episode" began in
early 1946, when the "last million" became rapidly augmented by so-called
posthostilities refugees and dislocated people. This new wave included 9 to 12
million ethnic Germans expelled from east-central Europe—records of whom
are also to be found in ITS holdings—and 250,000 ethnic Italians who left
Yugoslav-controlled Istria and Dalmatia. It included also 520,000 ethnic Ukrainians, Belarusians, and Lithuanians transferred out of Poland by the end of
1946 and 1.5 million ethnic Poles repatriated from Soviet Ukraine, Belarus, and
Lithuania between 1944 and 1948. These refugees coming from the Soviet
Union were often fleeing the brutality of Soviet occupation; in other cases,
they were collaborators fearing retribution after Nazi and Axis defeat. Political
upheaval and nascent nationalism in other parts of the world meant that millions of refugees from India, Pakistan, Israel, Hong Kong, Taiwan, Korea, and
Arab nations also fled to Europe after 1947. Records of these non-European
refugees who found themselves in European DP camps can also be found in the
ITS holdings.[61]

Jewish Holocaust Documentation in Early Postwar Europe (New York: Oxford University Press,
2012); Angelika Königseder and Juliane Wetzel, *Waiting for Hope: Jewish Displaced Persons in
Post–World War II Germany* (Evanston, IL: Northwestern University Press, 2001); Hagit
Lavsky, *New Beginnings: Holocaust Survivors in Bergen-Belsen and the British Zone in Germany,
1945–1950* (Detroit, MI: Wayne State University Press, 2002); Tamar Lewinsky, *Displaced
Poets: Jiddische Schriftsteller im Nachkriegsdeutschland, 1945–1951* (Göttingen: Vandenhoeck & Ruprecht, 2008); Zeev W. Mankowitz, *Life between Memory and Hope: The Survivors of the Holocaust in Occupied Germany* (Cambridge: Cambridge University Press, 2002);
Avinoam Patt, *Finding Home and Homeland: Jewish DP Youth and Zionism in the Aftermath
of the Holocaust* (Detroit, MI: Wayne State University Press, 2008); Avinoam J. Patt and
Michael Berkowitz, eds., *"We Are Here": New Approaches to Jewish Displaced Persons in Postwar Germany* (Detroit, MI: Wayne State University Press, 2010); Jessica Reinisch, *The Disentanglement of Populations: Migration, Expulsion and Displacement in Postwar Europe,
1944–1949* (New York: Palgrave Macmillan, 2011); Tara Zahra, *Lost Children: Reconstructing
Europe's Families after World War II* (Cambridge, MA: Harvard University Press, 2011).
   61. Cohen, *In War's Wake*, 5–7. See also chapter 5.

With regard to Jews, UNRRA statistics for September 1945 showed that among remaining DPs in Germany, Austria, and Italy, roughly fifty thousand (3.6 percent) were Jewish. The *she'erit hapletah* (the surviving remnant) came from all parts of Europe.[62] When the refugee population began to increase significantly in 1946, the Jewish DP population increased from 50,000 to 145,000 in 1946 alone. By the summer of 1947, about 182,000 Jewish DPs lived in Germany, 80 percent of them from Poland. The remainder came predominantly (but not exclusively) from Hungary, Czechoslovakia, Russia, and Romania. Among the Jewish refugees were eastern European nationals who had sought refuge from the Nazis in the Soviet Union in 1939 and returned to their homes only to encounter rampant antisemitism. Thus they sought refuge once again, primarily in the western zones of occupied Germany. Even at its peak in 1947, the Jewish displaced persons population never exceeded more than 10 to 20 percent of all DPs.[63]

ITS holdings consist of materials generated by the international organizations tasked with caring for DPs, including UNRRA, IRO, the International Red Cross, the Intergovernmental Committee for European Migration (ICEM),[64] and the United Nations High Commissioner for Refugees, and religious or national bodies like the American Jewish Joint Distribution Committee (AJDC), the Jewish Organization for Rehabilitation through Training (ORT), the Hebrew Immigrant Aid Society (HIAS), the Jewish Agency for Israel, the National Catholic Welfare Conference, and many, many others. Allied Expeditionary Forces authorities prepared a standardized two-sided registration form called a DP registration record (DP-2) for each person upon arrival at an assembly center.[65] (See document 1.6.[66]) Millions of DP-2 cards are part of the ITS holdings, and scans of the cards are available at the national repositories as part of the ITS digital archive. DP-2 cards contain basic personal details about refugees that typically include name, place of birth, date of birth, occupation, country of origin, and religion.

Subunit Three also holds 350,000 envelopes containing so-called IRO care and maintenance—welfare and support (CM/1) forms from assembly centers in

---

62. Michael Brenner, *After the Holocaust: Rebuilding Jewish Lives in Postwar Germany*, trans. Barbara Harshav (Princeton, NJ: Princeton University Press, 1997), 139.

63. Yehuda Bauer, *Out of the Ashes: The Impact of American Jews on Post-Holocaust European Jewry* (Oxford, UK: Pergamon Press, 1989), 45.

64. Later renamed the International Organization for Migration.

65. William Charles Connelly, ed., "DP/2 Karte," in *Glossary of Terms and Abbreviations Found in the Archive of the International Tracing Service (ITS)* (Washington, DC: USHMM, Holocaust Survivors and Victims Resource Center, 2011).

66. DP-2 card for Greinom Golub, 3.1.1.1/67203489/ITS Digital Archive, USHMM. Document is original.

Austria, Germany, Italy, Switzerland, and the United Kingdom. (See document
1.7.[67]) These were compulsory screening questionnaires, standardized across the
Allied zones, that required applicants to answer biographical questions about
their prewar and wartime activities in order to obtain support and DP status
from the IRO. CM/1 envelopes also contain processing documentation, and so
forth, as Allied authorities prepared applicants for resettlement. Despite the
great potential inherent in these records, scholars must apply appropriate scru-
tiny to the information contained therein. Ruth Balint writes, "The answers
DPs gave to the authorities and the testimonies and petitions they wrote were
crafted for a certain purpose and a specific audience. To secure DP status meant
both access to welfare and a ticket to the West, and getting the story 'right' often
meant the difference between securing a future in a new country, remaining
stuck in Germany as an unwanted fringe dweller, or being repatriated back to
the Communist East. What people wrote was not necessarily what they thought,
nor was it necessarily the truth."[68] Put another way, applicants needed to demonstrate their eligibility.[69] Thus, CM/1 forms can include lengthy testimonies
about the applicant's wartime experience; notes by IRO interviewers, who were
often DPs themselves, with their own CM/1 forms and fluency in the applicant's language; photographs; internal IRO correspondence on the merit of the
application; health records; marriage certificates; employment affidavits and
applications; emigration information; and other often unexpected documentation, all subsequently aggregated by ITS staff and placed in the applicant's
CM/1 form and organized by name.

If applicants obtained DP status, IRO officers tried to determine their resettlement in the most viable or appropriate country. IRO "screeners" were "tasked

---

67. IRO CM/1 form for Wolfgang Goldstein, 3.2.1.1/79130519/ITS Digital Archive,
USHMM. Document is original.

68. Ruth Balint, "The Use and Abuse of History: Displaced Persons in the ITS Archive"
(paper presented at the "International Tracing Service Collections and Holocaust Scholarship" conference, USHMM, Washington, DC, May 12–13, 2014). For further information
see "The International Tracing Service Collections and Holocaust Scholarship," USHMM,
www.ushmm.org/m/pdfs/20140506-ITS-Conference-Program.pdf (accessed May 5, 2014).

69. According to the IRO's 1948 constitution, "The term 'displaced person' applies to a
person who, as a result of the actions of [. . .] the Nazi or fascist regimes or of regimes which
took part on their side in the Second World War [. . .] has been obliged to leave his country
of nationality or of former habitual residence." The constitution made explicit reference to
"persons who were compelled to undertake forced labor or who were deported for racial,
religious or political reasons." See "Constitution of the International Refugee Organization,
August 20, 1948," in Department of State, *Germany, 1947–1949: The Story in Documents*
(Washington, DC: Department of State, Division of Public Affairs, 1950), 129.

with identifying and purging war criminals, collaborators and ethnic Germans (*Volksdeutsche*), all of whom, if identified, were excluded from the DP community."[70] To prove they fell into the correct category, the IRO required applicants to record their activities and places of employment in their former home countries, and so we see scrawled across the pages of tens of thousands of CM/1 forms, in aggregate, the entire range of behaviors and roles that victims, perpetrators, collaborators, and beneficiaries played across Europe between 1933 and 1945, from the fascist Hungarian Arrow Cross officer to the Polish peasant put to forced labor on a German farm to the Jewish survivor of several concentration camps. Used responsibly and in conjunction with other postwar records available within and outside the ITS holdings, these documents help elucidate the fate of individuals and entire groups stranded in Europe.

CM/1 forms and those generated by other relief organizations are also a source for scholars who wish to track in great detail the administrative practices of the agencies involved, as well as the social and cultural attitudes of DP interviewers, whose impressions often determined the outcome of each case. "Poor, old, sick woman," wrote an ICEM caseworker about seventy-five-year old ethnic German Lina Geisler, originally from Grottau, Czechoslovakia.[71] In other instances, caseworkers and intake officers could be far less kind, making recommendations on the basis of an applicant's bad haircut or child born out of wedlock. Scholars studying gender-based assumptions and attitudes have much rich material here. "She is the type of person who is unable to make decisions independently," wrote IRO interviewer J. Ziverts about then twenty-three-year-old Ewhenia Kowalska, a Ukrainian Greek Catholic from Buczacz deported to Germany in April 1942.[72]

SUBUNIT FOUR

Subunit Four (Special NSDAP Organizations and Actions) consists of files concerning two Nazi organizations: the National Socialist People's Welfare (Nationalsozialistische Volkswohlfahrt, NSV)[73] and the SS-Lebensborn (Fount of Life)

---

70. Balint, "The Use and Abuse of History," 4. For greater detail, see chapter 5.

71. Lina Geisler, 3.2.2.1/81392301/ITS Digital Archive, USHMM.

72. Ewhenia Kowalska, 3.2.1.4/81053579/ITS Digital Archive, USHMM. For a longer discussion about the role played by intake officers, see chapter 5.

73. The NSV was a "charitable" organization that operated according to Nazi racial doctrine—that is, it discriminated against "so-called asocials, inferior races, genetic defectives, and Jews." NSV causes included fighting diseases and promoting health in schools. Implicated in the Holocaust, the NSV sent to "deserving" Germans the valuables of those murdered by the Nazi regime, an understudied aspect of the NSV for which the ITS holdings offer promise. See also David F. Crew, *Germans on Welfare: From Weimar to Hitler* (New

program, founded by Heinrich Himmler. (See document 1.8.[74]) Comparatively speaking, Subunit Four is a small archive. Lebensborn was established in 1935 within the SS Race and Resettlement Main Office (SS-Rasse- und Siedlungs-hauptamt, RuSHA)[75] in the context of orders by Himmler charging every SS man to produce at least four children, whether in or out of wedlock. Lebensborn provided birth documents and basic support and recruited adoptive parents. By 1944, the SS maintained a total of thirteen homes in which approximately eleven thousand children were born. After the beginning of the Russian campaign, non-German European children deemed "of good blood" were taken from their parents, evaluated by Lebensborn, and passed on to adoptive parents.[76] Few Lebensborn records other than those in the ITS holdings are known to have survived.

Documents in the ITS holdings reflect the multiple roles of Gregor Ebner, who, among other posts, served as medical director of the Lebensborn facility Hochland in Steinhöring, near Munich.[77] Because of his broad responsibilities, in addition to documentation of the Hochland facility, this subcollection includes material concerning other facilities. These include the "homes" (*Heime*) Harz (in Wernigerode/Harz), Kurmark (in Klosterheide/Mark), Pommern (in

York: Oxford University Press, 1998); Peter Hammerschmidt, *Die Wohlfahrtsverbände im NS-Staat: Die NSV und die konfessionellen Verbände Caritas und Innere Mission im Gefüge der Wohlfahrtspflege des Nationalsozialismus* (Opladen: Leske & Budrich, 1999); Hans Otte and Thomas Scharf-Wrede, eds., *Caritas und Diakonie in der NS-Zeit: Beispiele aus Niedersachsen* (Hildesheim: Georg Olms Verlag, 2001).

74. Letter bearing facsimile signature of Heinrich Himmler, 4.1.0/82448314/ITS Digital Archive, USHMM. Document is original.

75. An important study of the RuSHA is Isabel Heinemann, *Rasse, Siedlung, deutsches Blut: Das Rasse- und Siedlungshauptamt der SS und die rassenpolitische Neuordnung Europas* (Göttingen: Wallstein Verlag, 2003).

76. See Angelika Baumann and Andreas Heusler, eds., *Kinder für den "Führer": Der Lebensborn in München* (Munich: Franz Schiermeier Verlag, 2013); Thomas Bryant, *Himmlers Kinder: Zur Geschichte der SS-Organisation "Lebensborn" e.V. 1935–1945* (Wiesbaden: Marix Verlag, 2011); Volker Koop, *"Dem Führer ein Kind schenken": Die SS-Organisation Lebensborn e.V.* (Cologne: Böhlau, 2007); Georg Lilienthal, *Der Lebensborn e.V.: Ein Instrument nationalsozialistischer Rassenpolitik* (Frankfurt am Main: Fischer Verlag, 1993).

77. From February 1938 to March 1942, Ebner was executive director (*geschäftsführendes Vorstandsmitglied*) of the Lebensborn e.V. (*eingetragener Verein*) and director (*Leiter*) and senior physician (*leitender Arzt*) at the Hochland facility (1937–1945). He was also responsible for medical supervision (*ärztliche Überwachung*) of all Lebensborn homes and in March 1940 became curator for medical and ideological questions (*Kurator für ärztliche und weltanschauliche Fragen*) for the Lebensborn board of trustees. In 1943 he took over the Central Department G (Health Care). See "NS 1—Lebensborn e.V.," ITS, www.its-arolsen.org/en/archives/finding-aids/index.html (accessed September 24, 2015).

Bad Polzin), Friesland (in Hohehorst near Bremen), Taunus (in Wiesbaden), Schwarzwald (in Nordrach/Baden), and Sonnenweise (in Kohren-Salis/Saxony); in Austria, Ostmark (subsequently named Wienerwald, in Pernitz/Muggendorf near Vienna); and in Luxemburg, Moselland (in Bofferding). American forces captured the Hochland facility and the documentation therein. After use in Nuremberg successor trial eight, the collection was sent to Bad Arolsen in August 1948. The RuSHA trial documents are an example of a subcollection for which the originals and copies can be found in other archives or are published. However, the colocation of the copies with the Lebensborn and NSV files is convenient for the researcher.[78]

SUBUNIT FIVE

Subunit Five (Miscellaneous) consists of trial-related documentation (5.1) and records concerning Allied investigations of so-called death marches and identification of so-called unknown dead, meaning all graves of non-German nationals, be they death march victims, camp or labor brigade prisoners, local forced laborers, soldiers killed in battle, or prisoners of war (5.3). On October 1, 1945, the Allied and German Military Graves Service issued an order to all mayors (*Bürgermeister*) across Germany to "register the graves of all Allied nationals in Germany" on a specified grave registration form.[79] This directive resulted in the receipt by the Allies of not only the returned forms but also cartographical and other materials. (See document 1.9.[80]) The so-called graveyard surveys held in subunit 5.3.5 (Grave Investigation/Cemetery Maps) are among the most moving and visually compelling documents in the ITS holdings.

These maps, organized in the ITS holdings by *Land* (state) and then by *Kreis* (district), were created locally and submitted to Allied authorities in the

---

78. The finding aid "Allied Military Tribunals, Nuremberg Follow-Up Trial against War Criminals No. 8: SS Main Office for Racial and Settlement Issues" (*Nürnberger Nachfolge-Kriegsverbrecherprozess Nr. 8: Rasse- und Siedlungshauptamt*/RuSHA) describes the October 1947 to February 1948 trial and ITS's acquisition of copies of the proceedings from the Berlin Document Center in 1948 alongside the NSV organizational records, with each set distinct.

79. "Alliierter und Deutscher Kriegergräberdienst/Allied and German Military Graves Service/Etat Civil Militaire Allie et Allemand, Richtlinien an alle Bürgermeister zum Suchen, Erfassen, Betreuen und Melden der Kriegergräber des zweiten Weltkriegs," 6.1.1/82506627–30/ITS Digital Archive, USHMM.

80. Hand-drawn map of Hoppstädten-Weiersbach Jewish Cemetery depicting graves of Paul Aleschin (a Russian), five unknown Russians, and five Poles, 5.3.5/101105355/ITS Digital Archive, USHMM.

first months and years after war's end. They are yet another testament to the familiarity of the local population with the presence, death, and burial of concentration camp prisoners, forced laborers, and POWs in their midst. One potential use of the hand-drawn maps in subunit 5.3.5 might be to look specifically at those German towns where hundreds of subcamps opened only in 1944 and where hundreds and sometimes thousands of prisoners died of starvation and disease.[81] The maps in subunit 5.3.5 can provide details and reveal patterns concerning where these victims were (or were not) buried. If, for example, one looks at the maps for the town of Vaihingen an der Enz (hereafter Vaihingen),[82] where a so-called *Krankenlager* (hospital camp) opened in the fall of 1944,[83] one can identify several dozen graves of Vaihingen inmates who must have been among the eighty-four former prisoners who died after liberation and were buried in the town's cemetery.[84]

With regard to death march victims specifically, in April 1946 the CTB inaugurated a project to "identify the burial places of the victims of the death marches during the last months of the war," publishing their first findings in the paper "Death Marches (*Marches de la Mort*): Routes and Distances, Volumes I–III."[85] Carried out over approximately four years, the project terminated in

---

81. Recent scholarship identifies a major shift in the development of the concentration camp universe during the last twelve months of the war. In 1944, 588 new concentration camps were established, 310 of them opening between July and October 1944. See Nikolaus Wachsmann, "The Dynamics of Destruction: The Development of the Concentration Camps, 1933–1945," in *Concentration Camps in Nazi Germany: The New Histories*, ed. Jane Caplan and Nikolaus Wachsmann (New York: Routledge, 2010), 32–33.

82. Vaihingen is a small town located between Stuttgart and Karlsruhe in southern Germany. During World War II, it was the site of an unused quarry owned by Baresel AG, which captured the attention of Albert Speer and became a test site for V-1 rocket engines. Work on construction of this subcamp began in the summer of 1944. Jean-Marc Dreyfus, "Vaihingen/Enz," in Megargee, *The United States Holocaust Memorial Museum Encyclopedia of Camps and Ghettos*, 1:1064–65.

83. For cutting-edge analysis of Vaihingen and its subcamps using ITS holdings, see Gil, "Jewish Slave Laborers from Radom in the Last Year of the War."

84. See 5.3.5/101099850–51 and, for the maps themselves, 5.3.5/101099894–907/ITS Digital Archive, USHMM. The map showing the graves of former prisoners (identifiable by their names, as with the prisoner population from Belgium, France, Germany, the Netherlands, Norway, Poland, and Russia) can be seen in 5.3.5/101099902–03/ITS Digital Archive, USHMM. For a history of the liberation of the camp and the eventual construction of the concentration camp cemetery in 1958 for the majority of the victims who died in Vaihingen, see "History of the Camp," KZ-Gedenkstätte, www.gedenkstaette-vaihingen.de/3019-Geschichte-des-Lagers.html (accessed September 24, 2015).

85. "Records of the ITS on Death Marches: Introduction," Subject-Oriented Special Inventories on the Archival Holdings of the ITS (Bad Arolsen, 2010), ITS, www.its-arolsen .org/en/archives/finding-aids/index.html (accessed September 24, 2015).

June 1951. These three volumes, as well as thousands of pages of investigative records about death marches from Buchenwald, Dachau, Mittelbau-Dora, Flossenbürg, Neuengamme, Sachsenhausen, and some of their satellite camps and documentation about "hundreds of cemeteries and mass graves," are now part of the ITS holdings and have already started to receive scholarly attention.[86]

Investigative materials in the ITS holdings include both early testimonies of survivors and also "thousands of questionnaires" completed by "mayors, policemen, and other civilians."[87] (See document 1.10.[88]) In complying with Allied regulations, a German resident of Heilbronn-Böckingen, one Herr Gessinger, described a death march through his town in early April 1945. "When we asked," he testified, "we were told that the prisoners were from Neckarelz.[89] Neckarelz was a subcamp of the Natzweiler concentration camp, which was used for armaments production in those days. The prisoners were in a state of utter exhaustion."[90] He described efforts by German onlookers to provide food, cigarettes, and clothing and the open murder by their guards of sixteen prisoners who collapsed.[91] Scholars have begun the work of analyzing the Allied tracing bureaus' origins and aims in order to "identify unknown dead,"[92] examining UNRRA questionnaires and correspondence with local German authorities[93]

---

86. Daniel Blatman, "On the Traces of the Death Marches: The Historiographical Challenge," in Blondel, Urban, and Schönemann, *Freilegungen: Auf den Spuren der Todesmärsche*, 85–107; Daniel Blatman, *The Death Marches: The Final Phase of Nazi Genocide* (Cambridge, MA: Belknap Press, 2011). The finding aid "Special Inventory Records of the ITS on Death Marches," ITS, www.its-arolsen.org/en/archives/finding-aids/index.html (accessed September 24, 2015), gives a brief history of the CTB/ITS "Attempted Identification of Unknown Dead" program and organizes most (but not all) materials in this subcollection alphabetically by community (i.e., maps and documentary material compiled by tracing staff in the community of Abenberg on evacuation marches, transports, eyewitness reports, death certificates, places of burial, and related evidence in or through that community specifically). The alphabetical structure is extremely useful for researchers seeking evidence on a particular community or route.

87. Blatman, "On the Traces of the Death Marches," 105–6.

88. Testimony of "Gessinger" about the death march through Heilbronn-Böckingen, 5.3.1/84597251/ITS Digital Archive, USHMM.

89. See Jean-Marc Dreyfus, "Neckarelz I and II," in Megargee, *The United States Holocaust Memorial Museum Encyclopedia of Camps and Ghettos*, 1:1045–47.

90. 5.3.1/84597251/ITS Digital Archive, USHMM.

91. Ibid.

92. Sebastian Schönemann, "'Accounting for the dead': Humanitäre und rechtliche Motive der alliierten Ermittlungsarbeit zu den Todesmärschen," in Blondel, Urban, and Schönemann, *Freilegungen: Auf den Spuren der Todesmärsche*, 122–51.

93. Martin Clemens Winter, "Frühe Ermittlung zu den Todesmärschen: Quellen im Ver-

and the registration and renumbering of some death march victims upon arrival at their destination.[94] Studies of specific death marches have also been published recently.[95] Documenting regional patterns is also possible, as Katrin Greiser's work on death marches across Bavaria demonstrates.[96] Not yet tapped is the promise these documents have for the study of the geography of the Holocaust, a new and growing research area.[97]

SUBUNIT SIX

Subunit Six (Records of the ITS and Its Predecessors) contains three main components: first, administrative records of predecessor organizations, discussed earlier in this chapter; second, records of the Child Search Branch; and third, tracing and documentation (T/D) correspondence files. The Child Search Branch was established as a separate department within the UNRRA in 1945 and continued as a separate unit within the IRO. In September 1950, the Child Search Branch became integrated into the ITS and remains in place today.[98] The records of the Child Search Branch include correspondence sent and received in the context of the search for missing Jewish and non-Jewish children and the identification of and care for so-called unaccompanied children. It includes field, monthly, and annual reports written by UNRRA or IRO staff dealing with the steadily changing buildup and organization of the Child Search Branch.[99]

---

gleich," in Blondel, Urban, and Schönemann, *Freilegungen: Auf den Spuren der Todesmärsche*, 136.

94. Susanne Urban, "'Vernehmungsunfähig': Registraturen nach der Ankunft von Räumungstransporten in KZ," in Blondel, Urban, and Schönemann, *Freilegungen: Auf den Spuren der Todesmärsche*, 262–81.

95. Arno Huth, "Die Auflösung des KZ Natzweiler und seines Aussenlagerkomplexes," in Blondel, Urban, and Schönemann, *Freilegungen: Auf den Spuren der Todesmärsche*, 184–97; Josephine Ulbricht, "Die Untersuchungen der UNRRA zu den Todesmärschen des KZ Flossenbürg," in Blondel, Urban, and Schönemann, *Freilegungen: Auf den Spuren der Todesmärsche*, 152–68. For an overview of Natzweiler-Struthof and its subcamps, see Dreyfus, "Natzweiler-Struthof," 1003–71.

96. Katrin Greiser, "Grabstätten und Sterbeorte in Bayern: Eine Suche nach den Opfern der Todesmärsche," in Blondel, Urban, and Schönemann, *Freilegungen: Auf den Spuren der Todesmärsche*, 300–313.

97. See Anne Kelly Knowles, Tim Cole, and Alberto Giordano, eds., *Geographies of the Holocaust* (Bloomington: Indiana University Press, 2014).

98. "Child Search Branch," in "Glossary," ITS, www.its-arolsen.org/en/help-and-faq/glossary/index.html (accessed September 24, 2015).

99. See "Bestand ITS 1: Child Search Branch," ITS, www.its-arolsen.org/en/archives/finding-aids/index.html (accessed September 24, 2015).

The label "T/D" was introduced in 1948 as shorthand to describe correspondence files that now number over 3 million individual cases.[100] The T/D files in subunit 6.3.3.2 (Repository of T/D Cases) date from 1947 onward[101] and contain incoming and outgoing correspondence between the tracing service, public and government authorities, and victims of Nazi persecution and their family members (i.e., "Inquirers"). T/D files include letters, bureaucratic forms and documentation, and even early testimonies written by those who turned to the tracing service to obtain documentation or to search for family members. Inquirers who were victims or claimed to be victims of the Nazis needed documentary evidence to qualify for compensation or to verify their pension applications. T/D files more than twenty-five years old are accessible for historical research.[102]

When an inquirer wrote to Bad Arolsen, tracing staff created a so-called inquiry card, recording both the inquirer and the information the inquirer provided, and assigned the case a processing number (discussed below).[103] Original inquiry cards[104] were filed in the Central Name Index (CNI), with a copy also deposited in the T/D file.[105] If no documents could be found, ITS staff identified the set of correspondence with a letter (*Briefnummer*), and these materials constitute subcollection 6.3.3.3 (Repository of Inquiries with a Negative Check Result Filed under *Briefnummern*).[106] (See document 1.11.[107]) Tracing staff recorded all future inquiries on a single person on the outside cover of an ITS-

---

100. "Tracing/Documentation," in "Glossary," ITS, www.its-arolsen.org/en/help-and-faq/glossary/index.html (accessed September 24, 2015).

101. Tracing inquiries received in 1945 and 1946 (6.3.1.1) are not yet part of the ITS digital archive.

102. "Deposit of T/D Correspondence Files," in "Glossary," ITS, www.its-arolsen.org/en/help-and-faq/glossary/index.html (accessed September 24, 2015).

103. For the specifics of this process, see "PCIRO Central Tracing Bureau Revised Procedure for Registration and Processing of Records," October 15, 1947, 6.1.1/82504655–64/ITS Digital Archive, USHMM.

104. The "Attributes" tab provides the researcher with the following key information gathered from the inquiry card created upon receipt at ITS of the first piece of correspondence requesting information on a given individual: last name, given name, date of birth, place of birth, religion, nationality, kind of data record (i.e., "inquiry"), T/D number, name of claimant, date of inquiry, and notes on "further indications provided by the claimant."

105. "Inquiry Card," in "Glossary," ITS, www.its-arolsen.org/en/help-and-faq/glossary/index.html (accessed September 24, 2015).

106. The "Briefnummer" filing process was used by ITS staff from 1958 to 1980. See "Letter Numbers," in "Glossary," ITS, www.its-arolsen.org/en/help-and-faq/glossary/index.html (accessed September 24, 2015).

107. Outside cover of ITS-generated T/D file for Theresia Müller, 6.3.3.2/85371006/ITS Digital Archive, USHMM.

generated file folder. The outside cover of an individual's T/D file can range from a record of a single inquirer to a long series of inquirers over decades.

The T/D files offer the researcher the opportunity to ask broad and wide-ranging questions. Scholars studying Holocaust awareness and memory might examine T/D files to determine patterns in who was asking, when, and why. Scholars studying the ITS itself might use T/D files to examine changes over time in how ITS staff responded to inquiries, which has broader implications for the tangled Cold War and post–Cold War policies of the ITS.[108] One might write a history of treatment of so-called humanitarian requests by ITS staff over time.[109] Many other areas of research are possible. Which governments made inquiries, when, and why? How might we weave these inquiries into the histories of restitution and legal action against wartime collaborators and what we think of today as "Holocaust trials"?

Let us turn to how researchers might begin to aggregate T/D files for such studies. Researchers interested in inquires about a particular national group could run a keyword search by nationality (e.g., "Ukrainian" or "Polish"). Further, not all T/D files pertain to victims. Some pertain also to collaborators and perpetrators who abused the DP system.[110] In the ITS holdings, the T/D files are organized by their aforementioned processing number (hereafter referenced as the T/D number). As of this printing (and readers should note that new documents are regularly added to the ITS digital archive), T/D numbers 1 through 1,250,000 (i.e., over 1 million individual correspondence files) are already part of the ITS digital archive and are open for research. Scanning of the nearly 2 million additional correspondence files is ongoing in Bad Arolsen. T/D numbers are recorded on the upper-right-hand corner of CNI cards or are sometimes handwritten by ITS staff on CM/1 forms or other documents pertaining to a particular individual. To locate a specific single T/D file, the standard avenue for researchers is to find the T/D number and then to locate the T/D number sequentially in subunit 6.3.3.2.

Researchers could also use a keyword search to aggregate T/D files. T/D

---

108. The only study to date of this aspect of the history of ITS itself is the aforementioned dissertation by Jennifer Rodgers titled "From the 'Archive of Horrors' to the 'Shop Window of Democracy': The International Tracing Service and the Transatlantic Politics of the Past."

109. ITS defines so-called humanitarian requests as "an ITS expression for inquiries by survivors or family members of victims in order to receive information from the documents, to clarify the fate of persecutees or to reunite families." See "Humanitarian Requests," in "Glossary," ITS, www.its-arolsen.org/en/help-and-faq/glossary/index.html (accessed September 24, 2015).

110. For an example of this, see the Caballero case in chapter 5.

files are also indexed by the name of the person being inquired about, the date of birth of the person being inquired about, and the first and last year inquiries were made. For example, for a study of the work carried out by the Bavarian State Compensation Office (Bayerisches Landesentschädigungsamt, BLEA) over time, the researcher would run a keyword search using "BLEA." As of this printing, such a search results in 52,144 "hits" for inquiry card data held in subunit 0.1 (CNI). Researchers could then use each hit to locate the T/D number and thus gain access to over fifty thousand BLEA-related correspondence files. For a smaller study on the role of a particular private legal office, a researcher could replicate this method. For example, a keyword search under the term "Kossoy" will aggregate all inquiries made by A. M. Apelbom & Kossoy Law & Notarial Offices (Munich and Tel Aviv). Apelbom & Kossoy made over 4,256 inquires to ITS. Researchers can locate the T/D number for each case and study who used this law office, as well as its successes and failures over time.[111]

A researcher interested in the impact of the American television miniseries *Holocaust* (aired by NBC in 1978) on inquiries to ITS could run a keyword search for "1978," resulting as of this printing in 13,208 T/D file (6.3.3.2) hits. Now, armed with the information that ITS received over thirteen thousand inquiries in 1978, the diligent researcher might look at each T/D file to study who was inquiring and why to discern what impact the miniseries might have had. A different and perhaps more efficient way to conduct the same search would be to run an "attributes" search and under "date of inquiry" to search by each single day, beginning with April 16, 1978, and going forward.

Regarding postwar compensation issues, subcollection 6.2.1 contains the records of the Finance Ministry of the Federal Republic of Germany (FRG) tracking the amounts and breakdown of compensation payments made following the Federal Indemnification Law (Bundesgesetz zur Entschädigung für Opfer der nationalsozialistischen Verfolgung, or Bundesentschädigungsgesetz) between November 1, 1953, and January 1, 1978. Subcollection 6.3.3.4 holds over 1 million scans of documents dating from 2000 to 2006 and relating to inquires in the context of the efforts of the Foundation "Remembrance, Responsibility, Future" (Stiftung "Erinnerung, Verantwortung und Zukunft," EVZ), the German federal organization responsible for compensation to (primarily) former forced and slave laborers.[112]

---

111. An inquiry made by Apelbom & Kossoy will be discussed in chapter 3.

112. For information on the EVZ, see "Origins of the Foundation EVZ," EVZ, www .stiftung-evz.de/eng/the-foundation/history.html (accessed June 20, 2013). As of this printing, the scans of documents contained in subcollection 6.3.3.4 have not been provided to the designated institutions outside Bad Arolsen.

NONSCANNED MATERIALS

A significant percentage of materials amassed at ITS in Bad Arolsen are not yet available in scanned form (i.e., not yet part of the ITS digital archive). These materials exist in their original paper form, microfilm, microfiche, CD-ROM, and other media. ITS staff have assigned these materials subunit numbers ten through thirteen:

- Subunit Ten: Documentary Fonds of the Archival Management Section
- Subunit Eleven: Institutional File Deposit for All Departments
- Subunit Twelve: Institutional File Deposit of the Directorate
- Subunit Thirteen: Library

Many documents in Subunit Ten are duplicate copies already accessible in the ITS digital archive in Subunits Zero through Six. The IC is in the process of identifying those materials on microfilm, microfiche, and CD-ROM not yet incorporated into the ITS digital archive. While the total scope of nonscanned materials is difficult to estimate with precision, their prominence in the 5,803-page "General Inventory" of all ITS holdings (to be discussed at a later point)[113] gives some indication of the overall size of these collections.[114] An ITS-generated inventory, "NInv—Non-inventoried Acquisitions" offers guidance to these subcollections.[115]

The CD-ROM collections relate to *Ostarbeiter* attempting to return to their homes after the war and also include wartime camp-related material copied from archives in Kiev, Odessa, Ternopol, and Vinnitsa in Ukraine; Ljubljana in Slovenia; Prague in the Czech Republic; and Szczecin in Poland. While much of the nonscanned material is copied from other archives, it also includes work cards (*Arbeitskarten*) and work books (*Arbeitsbücher*) in their original form, sent by claimants or the labor user (*Arbeitgeber*) to the ITS in Bad Arolsen in the context of the efforts of the EVZ. "Three work books produced by the Rheine

113. *Gesamtinventar des Internationalen Suchdienstes (ISD)*, January 13 2013, PDF document subsequently available to repositories of the ITS digital archive. Hereafter cited as the "General Inventory."

114. The 5,803-page "General Inventory" details all Subunits, beginning with Subunit Zero through Subunit Thirteen. Subunits Zero through 10.1 are either already scanned, in the process of being scanned for inclusion in the ITS digital archive, or consist of security copies (10.1), and constitute pages 1 through 4,184. Pages 4,185 through 5,803 describe Subunit 10.2 through Subunit 13.

115. See "General Inventory," ITS, www.its-arolsen.org/en/archives/collections/general-inventory/index.html (accessed June 20, 2013).

[Westphalia] labor office, employer: Deutsche Reichsbahn Rheine—books found in an attic" is a typical entry for original materials sent by the EVZ to Bad Arolsen in recent years.[116]

One never knows what to expect when inquiring about nonscanned materials. They include, for example, "Sixty large wooden cases" of claims files "assembled by the Communist government of Romania in the early 1970s" for the purpose of seeking a "lump sum hard currency settlement" from the FRG "for damages suffered by Romanians during World War II as a result of German persecution." In 2008, the German Foreign Ministry "shipped all the cases, still intact, to ITS."[117] Or one finds a wartime "Most Wanted" list produced by the Criminal Police (Kriminalpolizei, or Kripo) in Berlin, unearthed by a police officer's granddaughter upon going through old family papers.[118] To cite another case, the nonscanned materials include 3,238 card catalogue cards (*Karteikarten*) found in a basement in Hamburg in a steel cabinet (*Stahlschrank*). A better description awaits the curious historian who requests access to "Ninv (non-inventoried)—174."[119]

USING THE INTERNATIONAL TRACING SERVICE HOLDINGS

The history and original mandate of the ITS in Bad Arolsen—a tracing service, not an archive—meant that documents were organized according to their utility in clarifying individual fates rather than by their origin or provenance.[120] Broken up on receipt by ITS staff for reorganization according to their utility for *tracing*, archival collections in the ITS holdings are filed by subject and "chronologically

---

116. "General Inventory," 4,886: Akte 10.9.2.1.94: Arbeitsbücher ausgestellt vom Arbeitsamt Rheine, Arbeitgeber: Deutsche Reichsbahn.

117. Shapiro, "Vapniarka," 32–33.

118. "General Inventory," 4,889: Akte 10.9.2.1.111.

119. "General Inventory," 4,902: Akte 10.9.2.1.177.

120. An apt description appears in the "Historical Survey of Central Tracing Activity in Germany, 1945–1951," 6.1.1/82492860/ITS Digital Archive, USHMM, published in 1946. At that time, a "consolidated tracing service" was imagined as a "single consolidated agency which brings together all available records and information, and in turn receives all enquiries. It implies the maintenance of a gigantic index of information concerning each person known to have been displaced or to have perished as a result of persecution. It also implies a wide network of investigators to carry out field work, or an interlocking system of agencies which will provide the service under centralized direction." "Historical Survey, 6.1.1/82492886." This design played a strong role in shaping ITS operations and records management until 2007.

by date of receipt."[121] Let me return here to the assumption, referred to earlier by Shapiro, that "no one would ever see" documents deposited at Bad Arolsen. Today, existing search tools and finding guides do not yet contain consistent and adequate descriptions of collection-level contents or file-level contents therein. In early 2013, as required in connection with the withdrawal of the ICRC, ITS staff created a 5,803-page "General Inventory" of all ITS holdings, including not only those documents already scanned with copies provided to the aforementioned designated institutions (the ITS digital archive) but also those materials in microfilm, microfiche, CD-ROM, and their original paper form and as of this printing only available on-site in Bad Arolsen. Meant "to offer a first overview of the archives kept at ITS," the descriptions for each subcollection are still rudimentary.[122] Even so, scholars may glean from the inventory larger subcollections potentially relevant to their topics.[123]

Several years ago, as a predecessor to the "General Inventory," the USHMM created a searchable "Inventory of the Archive of the International Tracing Service" (*Inventar*). In English and German, it provides a limited over-view of more than twenty-one thousand separate historical collections. For the reasons suggested at the beginning of this section, the *Inventar* is organized chronologically by date of registration/accession of each "deposit," starting with the massive deposits already accumulated by 1955. After 1955, governments, private organizations, other archives, and private individuals sent additional col-lections of documentary material to ITS, sometimes in the original and some-times in copy form. Those deposits were also recorded chronologically by date of registration. ITS staff copied some collections from other archives and recorded the addition of these collections. Each discrete deposit of documentary material at ITS is thus defined as a "collection" in the *Inventar*.

Some "collections" have just a few pages, whereas others may contain tens of thousands of pages.[124] For collections acquired after 1955, ITS staff made so-called *Inventar Blätter* (inventory pages or archival accession cover sheets). If created, an *Inventar Blatt*, a green piece of paper titled "registration of new material" (*Anmeldung von Neu-Eingängen*) or "inventory of new material" (*Inventarisierung von Neumaterial*), is still colocated with each separate collection

---

121. See "Information on Use," ITS, www.its-arolsen.org/en/archives/collections/general -inventory/information-on-use/index.html (accessed November 6, 2015).

122. See "Information on Use."

123. The "General Inventory" PDF document is a useful starting point for all researchers as it can be searched by keyword.

124. "International Tracing Service Inventory Search," USHMM, www.ushmm.org/on line/its-inventory/simple.php (accessed July 28, 2015).

and is the first scanned page of each collection, and it is sometimes the only description of the documents therein available. One can find on the green *Inventar Blätter* staff notes concerning where the material would be filed, a description of the contents, the origin of the documents, their status as either originals or copies, the number of pages in the collection, the date it was received, and other notes, especially regarding the number of names that the documents contain for tracing purposes.[125] Users should note that the *Inventar* is not comprehensive of all of the ITS holdings. For example, it does not include the over 3 million T/D files, the millions of individual name files, or the non-scanned materials that are crucial, and extremely large collections.

The massive Central Name Index is the main card catalogue for name searches. Also inscribed into the UNESCO Memory of the World Register, the approximately 50 million CNI name cards referencing approximately 17.5 million individuals may include date and place of birth, other names used or name variants, maiden name, parents' names, nationalities, religion, known location(s) during World War II, prisoner number(s), and other information, such as profession. As already discussed, tracing service staff recorded the names of individuals in newly arrived collections on small cards, similar in size to a modern-day 3 × 5 index card. In the early days of mass tracing efforts, these cards were organized phonetically by last name, then by first name, name equivalents (i.e., "Elizabeth" with "Elisabeth"), and date of birth, thus aggregating all references to one person, allowing staff to find references to one individual more easily among massive amounts of paper.

Such CNI cards, then, are a starting point to locate further information on "carded" individuals. As a next step, users must identify, locate, and examine the document from which the card was created. In other cases, tracing service staff created entirely separate card files attached to a particular collection and thus not in the CNI.[126] The CNI is inconsistent in that it is not comprehensive of every single individual who appears in the ITS holdings. It includes many (but not all) people deemed victims and often does not include the names of perpetrators, users of forced labor, or Allied or DP aid organization authorities.[127] Even with regard to victims, for many collections, victims' names were not "carded" at all.

---

125. For two examples, see 1.1.47.1/5160333 and 2.1.1.2/70504569/ITS Digital Archive, USHMM.

126. Examples include subcollections 2.2.2.1 (War-Time Card File of registration cards, employees' record books, individual correspondence), 3.1.1.1 (DP-2 Card File), 4.1.1 (Lebensborn Card File), and 6.3.2.1 (Files of Children Identified by Name).

127. For example, individuals appearing in the so-called Service Watson (1.2.4.3) and Service CCC lists are not always carded in the CNI. Electronic archival subunits 2.1.5.3

Various guides and search tools have been created by the staff of the USHMM's Holocaust Survivors and Victims Resource Center, including a highly useful glossary of terms and abbreviations.[128] Also, in the decade after World War II, ITS staff created several catalogues of their concentration camp– and prison-related holdings.[129] From 2010 to 2012, the USHMM, Yad Vashem, and the ITS in Bad Arolsen together carried out a pilot cataloguing and indexing project on select concentration camp records and the CM/1 case files from assembly centers in Germany (3.2.1.1) and Italy (3.2.1.2). These records are now indexed by—in addition to name, place, and date of birth—the categories of religion, nationality, ethnicity, sex, and the DP camp name at which the applicant completed his or her CM/1 form. A check box exists to alert researchers to photographs in the CM/1 case file. As a result, users of the ITS digital archive can aggregate or parse files by using particular variables—for example, "Polish + Jewish + Female + DP Camp Feldafing." As the CM/1 files originating in Germany (3.2.1.1) and Italy (3.2.1.2) are the only subcollections for which this deeper indexing has been completed, much more such work is needed to increase the scholarly utility of other name-related collections in the ITS holdings.

SCHOLARLY OPPORTUNITIES

The ITS holdings are invaluable in reconstructing the experiences of individuals and families at the micro level.[130] Documents in the ITS holdings clarify the

(Hospital Files, Berlin), 2.1.4.4 (Hospital Files, Soviet Zone), 2.3.3.1 (Index of Persecutees in the French Occupation Zone Including French Nationals in Other Zones), and 1.1.14.6 (Italian Index) are not always carded.

128. Connelly, *Glossary of Terms and Abbreviations*.

129. These include (1) *Catalogue of Camps and Prisons in Germany and German-Occupied Territories, September 1st, 1939—May 8, 1945*, 1st ed. (Bad Arolsen: International Tracing Service Records Branch, Documents Intelligence Section, July 1949), in Weinmann, *Das Nationalsozialistische Lagersystem*, for the purpose of offering a guide to incarceration locations using maps available at ITS; and (2) the *Katalog der Konzentrationslager-Dokumente die sich bei dem International Tracing Service Allied High Commission for Germany befinden/Catalogue of Concentration Camp Records Held by the International Tracing Service Allied High Commission for Germany*, 2 vols. (1951), with a second edition published in 1954. Three subsequent editions were published between 1955 and 1957.

130. See Zvi Bernhardt and Kinga Frojimovics, "The Synergy of Documents: Making Shards into a Whole," in Blondel, Urban, and Schönemann, *Freilegungen: Auf den Spuren der Todesmärsche*, 19–25; Suzanne Brown-Fleming, "'Wiedervereinigung Ersehnend:' Gender and the Holocaust Fates of the Müller and Gittler Families," In *Different Horrors/Same Hell: Gender and the Holocaust*, Myrna Goldenberg and Amy Shapiro, eds. (Seattle: University of Washington Press, 2013), 177-197.

fates of individual families and are especially powerful when combined with other sources, such as photographs, family letters, and oral testimonies.[131] These documents can be used to gather detail not only on victims but also on perpetrators who abused the DP system to flee justice postwar.[132] (See document 1.12.[133]) The case of SS auxiliary Ivan Demjanjuk is among the best known. Convicted in May 2011 for assisting the SS in the murder of 28,060 Jews at the Sobibor death camp in eastern Poland, Demjanjuk had applied for and received DP status from the IRO after World War II, enabling him to emigrate to the United States. In his 1948 CM/1 form, Demjanjuk claimed to have fled the Soviet Union for Poland in 1937 and, from there, to have been deported to Germany as a forced laborer in 1943. On his application, Demjanjuk did not acknowledge his role as a Ukrainian auxiliary for the SS,[134] leaving only the clue that he was a truck driver in Sobibor during the war. At the time he completed his CM/1 form in 1948, Sobibor's key role as one of the Operation Reinhard killing centers[135] was not well known, and Demjanjuk received DP status.[136]

131. Examples include Suzanne Brown-Fleming, "'*Wiedereiningung Ersehnend*,'" 177–97; Umberto Gentiloni and Stefano Palermo, *16.10.43 Li hanno portati* (Rome: Fandango Libri, 2012), which traces the fate of 230 Jewish children deported from Rome to Auschwitz on October 16, 1943. It extends beyond the wartime fates of the children to utilize T/D files containing correspondence between victims' families, Italian authorities, and tracing service officials.

132. See Eric C. Steinhart, "The Chameleon of Trawniki: Jack Reimer, Soviet *Volksdeutsche*, and the Holocaust," *Holocaust and Genocide Studies* 23, no. 2 (fall 2009): 239–62.

133. DP identity card for Ivan Demjanjuk, 3.1.1.1/66866153/ITS Digital Archive, USHMM.

134. For the role played by SS auxiliaries in the Nazi military machine, see Peter Black, "Foot Soldiers of the Final Solution: The Trawniki Training Camp and Operation Reinhard," *Holocaust and Genocide Studies* 25, no. 1 (2011): 1–99; Valdis O. Lumans, *Himmler's Auxiliaries: The Volksdeutsche Mittelstelle and the German National Minorities of Europe, 1933–1945* (Chapel Hill: University of North Carolina Press, 1993).

135. See Yitzak Arad, *Belzec, Sobibor, Treblinka: The Operation Reinhard Death Camps* (Bloomington: Indiana University Press, 1987); Bogdan Musial, ed., *Aktion Reinhardt: Der Völkermord an den Juden im Generalgouvernement 1941–1944* (Osnabrück: Fibre, 2004); Jules Schelvis, *Sobibor: A History of a Nazi Death Camp* (New York: Berg in association with USHMM, 2007).

136. See Eric C. Steinhart, "Displaced by War and Conquest: New Findings on DPs from Eastern Europe and the Soviet Union" (paper delivered at the 2012 "Beyond Camps and Forced Labour" conference, Imperial War Museum, London, January 2012). Secondary sources on this storied case include Angelika Benz, *Der Henkersknecht: Der Prozess gegen John (Iwan) Demjanjuk in München* (Berlin: Metropol, 2011), and Lawrence Douglas, *The Right Wrong Man: John Demjanjuk and the Last Great Nazi War Crimes Trial* (Princeton, NJ: Princeton University Press, 2016).

Information on many collaborators and perpetrators can be found in the ITS holdings.

Although crucial, researching individuals and families and ferreting out war criminals together represent only one dimension of the promise of the ITS holdings. Scholars are beginning to utilize these documents for many other avenues of scholarly inquiry. For example, Johannes-Dieter Steinert's recent book on Polish and Soviet children in Nazi Germany and occupied eastern Europe utilizes the subcollections on the Łódź (1.1.22.0)[137] and Lebrechtsdorf (Potulice, Poland; 1.1.61.0)[138] youth detention and education camps. In 2012, the release of *Freilegungen: Auf den Spuren der Todesmärsche* marked the first publication in the ITS Yearbook series. The second book in the series, *Freilegungen: Überlebende—Erinnerungen—Transformationen*, was published in early 2013,[139] and the third, on DPs, appeared in 2014.[140] The fourth volume takes advantage of the rich material on sites of persecution and deeper studies of Jewish victims in particular.[141]

As discussed in the foreword, key academic gatherings have played a role in instigating and thereafter furthering scholarly exposure to the ITS holdings, with the goal of assessing and testing their research and educational potential. The 2008 international research workshop "Exploring the Newly Opened International Tracing Service Archive," co-organized by the USHMM and ITS, permitted an international group of fifteen scholars from around the world to survey the ITS holdings for ten days. Asked to give an impression of significant topical areas for which the ITS holdings might redefine our understanding of the Holocaust, this first international scholarly group to explore the just opened holdings produced the following list: social histories of camps and sites of forced labor spanning the entire 1933–1945 period; changing patterns of behavior, violence, and obedience to orders over time from the perspectives of perpetrators, prisoners, laborers, witnesses, and labor users; prisoner categorization prac-

---

137. Johannes-Dieter Steinert, *Deportation und Zwangsarbeit: Polnische und Sowjetische Kinder im Nationalsozialistischen Deutschland und im besetzten Osteuropa, 1939–1945* (Essen: Klartext, 2013), 178.

138. Steinert, *Deportation und Zwangsarbeit*, 235. The subcollection he references consists of photocopies from microfilm obtained from the State Museum of Auschwitz in 1972.

139. Rebecca Boehling, Susanne Urban, and René Bienert, eds., *Freilegungen: Überlebende—Erinnerungen—Transformationen.* Jahrbuch des International Tracing Service II (Göttingen: Wallstein Verlag, 2013).

140. Rebecca Boehling, Susanne Urban, and René Bienert, eds., *Freilegungen: Displaced Persons—Leben im Transit: Überlebende zwischen Repatriierung, Rehabilitation und Neuanfang.* Jahrbuch des International Tracing Service III (Göttingen: Wallstein Verlag, 2014).

141. Rebecca Boehling, Susanne Urban, Elizabeth Anthony and Susan Brown-Fleming, eds., *Freilegungen: Spiegelungen der NS-Verfolgung und ihrer Konsequenzen.*

tices; medical practices and abuses; labor utilization in particular towns, regions, camps, or institutions; the impact of gender on one's fate and status; and other potential avenues of exploration.[142]

In 2014, scholars from the United States, the United Kingdom, Germany, Austria, France, Israel, Spain, and Australia pursued these and other themes in the first scholarly conference to highlight significant new and original research using the ITS holdings since their opening. Topics included an analysis of early testimonies, sexual violence, postwar death march investigations, Jewish and non-Jewish slave and forced labor, medical experiments, the Reich Association of Jews in Germany (Reichsvereinigung der Juden in Deutschland, RVJD)[143] card file, the Lebensborn program, the Nazi prison system, biographies of prisoners of Mauthausen and its subcamps, DPs, and the history of ITS itself.[144] A selection of these first research results have been published in the 2015 ITS Yearbook.

It is no accident that this volume is part of the Jack, Joseph and Morton Mandel Center for Advanced Holocaust Studies's *Documenting Life and Destruction: Holocaust Sources in Context* series, which features firsthand accounts from those who perpetrated, witnessed, and/or suffered through the Holocaust. ITS-held documentation is an excellent resource for such studies. It is worthwhile testing the possibilities of working with documentation in the ITS holdings via a series of four case studies, each utilizing materials across the main Subunits One through Six. These case studies are designed to stimulate fresh thinking about the ITS holdings and the questions we might ask of them. They are not meant to be comprehensive; nor do they represent the only possibilities for scholarly use of the ITS holdings: far from it! Rather, they illustrate the utility of the ITS holdings for addressing broader topics across scholarly disciplines and over decades, from history to gender to geography to Jewish studies, and for examining the questions that still plague us about how human behavior and agency could play the central role in so many aspects of the Holocaust.

Chapter 2, "'Our Mothers, Our Fathers': Lahnstein," focuses on one small

---

142. Paul A. Shapiro, "Exploring the Newly Opened ITS Archives" (keynote address delivered at the Seventh Stephen S. Weinstein Holocaust Symposium at Wroxton College, Oxfordshire, England, July 2008).

143. The RVJD was established in 1939 and had three purposes: first, to further emigration; second, to maintain Jewish schools, and third, to maintain the Jewish welfare system. See Beate Meyer, *A Fatal Balancing Act: The Dilemma of the Reich Association of Jews in Germany, 1939–1945*, trans. Bill Templer (New York: Berghahn Books, 2013).

144. For a full conference agenda, see "International Conference," USHMM, www.ushmm.org/research/scholarly-presentations/conferences/its-conference (accessed December 24, 2014).

German town in the heart of the Rhineland to examine the devastating universe of collaboration, greed, and persecution and its aftermath across victim groups and types of sites of detention. Chapter 3, "Jewish Voices," samples the many kinds of documents in the archive in which Jews describe their experiences, such as questionnaires, letters to ITS in search of missing family members (often contained in T/D files), applications for DP status, compensation applications, transcripts of interviews with German prosecutors, and correspondence and interviews with relief agencies, to name only a few.

Chapter 4, "Hour Zero: The Year 1945," uses documentation across the ITS holdings to describe this key year of upheaval and transition from the viewpoints of many actors, from Nazi perpetrators and accessories who did not see the futility and bankruptcy of the Nazi worldview, to the prisoners finally freed, to shocked Allied troops and aid workers who struggled to cope with what they found as they liberated Europe. Chapter 5, "Imagining the Displaced," highlights the global nature of the Holocaust by focusing on documentation concerning refugees from across not only Europe but also North Africa, Asia, Latin America, and the Middle East. Taken together, these four case studies show that the ITS holdings have a unique ability to capture World War II and the Holocaust in a way that reaches far beyond Germany and even Europe to touch nearly every nation, religion, and ethnic group.

DOCUMENT LIST

DOCUMENT 1.1. Dachau Registration Office card for Szulim Goldberg, 1.1.6.7/96338956/ITS Digital Archive, USHMM.

DOCUMENT 1.2. Letter from "Zdena" to prisoner Vladislaus Razyn (circa 1944) sent to ITS by Bamberg Red Cross in 1990, 1.2.2.1/11817287/ITS Digital Archive, USHMM. (followed by translation).

DOCUMENT 1.3. Ring of Dachau prisoner Arthur Becker, prisoner number 45341, 1.2.9.1/108019938/ITS Digital Archive, USHMM.

DOCUMENT 1.4. Identity card for eastern worker Lena Iwansowa, 2.2.2.1/72830650/ITS Digital Archive, USHMM.

DOCUMENT 1.5. Drawing of grave of French POW Georges Devaux, Oberbernbach/Landkreis Aichach, Upper Bavaria, 2.1.1.1/69786340/ITS Digital Archive, USHMM.

DOCUMENT 1.6. DP-2 card for Greinom Golub, 3.1.1.1/67203489/ITS Digital Archive, USHMM.

DOCUMENT 1.7. IRO care and maintenance form for Wolfgang Goldstein, 3.2.1.1/79130519/ITS Digital Archive, USHMM.

DOCUMENT 1.8. Memorandum from Heinrich Himmler to Lebensborn e.V. personnel, October 27, 1939, 4.1.0/82448314/ITS Digital Archive, USHMM. Document is original; signature is a facsimile (followed by translation).

DOCUMENT 1.9. Hand-drawn map of Hoppstädten-Weiersbach Jewish Cemetery depicting graves of Paul Aleschin (a Russian), five unknown Russians, and five Poles, 5.3.5/101105355/ITS Digital Archive, USHMM.

DOCUMENT 1.10. Statement of E. Gessinger about the death march through Heilbronn-Böckingen, 5.3.1/84597251/ITS Digital Archive, USHMM (followed by translation).

DOCUMENT 1.11. Cover of ITS-generated T/D file for Theresia Müller, 6.3.3.2/85371006/ITS Digital Archive, USHMM.

DOCUMENT 1.12. DP identity card for Ivan Demjanjuk, 3.1.1.1/66866153/ITS Digital Archive, USHMM.

DOCUMENTS

DOCUMENT 1.1*

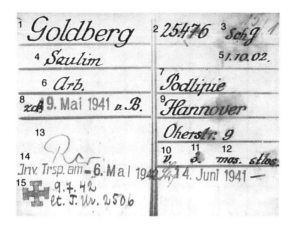

1. **Surname**: Goldberg
2. **Dachau Prisoner Number**: 25,476
3. **Prisoner Category**: SchJ [in full: *Schutzhäftling-Jude*, English: protective custody prisoner-Jew]
4. **Forename**: Szulim
5. **Date of Birth**: 1 October 1902
6. **Occupation**: Arb. [*Arbeiter*, English: laborer]
7. **Place of Birth**: Podlipie
8. **(Latest) Arrival in Dachau**: zck. 19. Mai 1941 v. B. [*zurück 19. Mai 1941 von Buchenwald*, English: returned 19 May 1941 from Buchenwald]
9. **Residence before Incarceration**: Hannover, Oherstr. 9
10. **Marital Status** v. [*verheiratet*, English: married]
11. **Number of Children** [3]
12. **Race and Nationality Codes**: mos. stlos. [*mosaisch, staatenlos*, English: Jewish, stateless]
13. The handwritten "Rtk" in pencil indicates that a card in the "Revier-Toten-Kartei" [English: clinic card catalog of deaths] had been prepared.
14. The red hand-stampings and notations read "Inv. Trsp.—6. Mai 1941, n. Strf. 14. Juni 1941" [in full: *Invaliden-Transport—6 Mai 1941, nach Strafkommando 14 Juni 1941*, English: Invalid Transport—6 May 1941, to Punishment Detail 14 June 1941.]
15. "[Cross] 9.7.42 lt. T. Ur. 2506" [in full: *9 Juli 1942 laut Todes-Urkunde. 2506*, English: died 9 July 1942 according to Death Certificate 2506].

---

*Numbers 1 to 15 added for translation purposes.

DOCUMENT 1.2

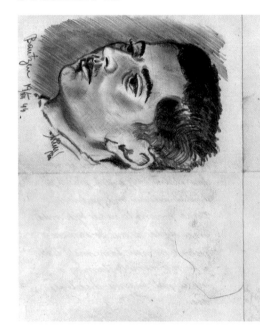

Dear Vladicku,

First, please accept my fond greetings and a remembrance of you.

I was at your house on Monday. Your mother is amazingly good, she said that you had written to her. She gave me your address, and that is why I am writing to you. First I should give you the news from here. We are all going to exercise, it is all the same just like when you were here. As to what concerns me [illegible] You know the whole week I have to work 12 hours a day like everywhere, Sundays are verily awful. It is difficult to live that way. Occasionally we go to the movies with the girls at work. If you were here it would be different. Vlada, please, I really would like to have your photo. Our Jitka gave me yours. But what good is it to me if you want it back. And I, poor thing, won't have any. Vlada, I really would like my own. I miss you. I don't go to the dance hall, there are young boys and that doesn't mean anything. I wait until you return, then we will go together.

I am ending the letter because I don't know what else to write. Next time I will try to write you more. All the boys and girls send you their regards. Also Jirka Linda, Jarka Kastic. Vlada, once more I am asking you for a photo.

I leave you thinking of the memories and the days that we spent together. Once more, I say good-bye and send you thousands of kisses.

Your always loving

Zdena

[Right corner]
I wouldn't give you the pleasure to go with somebody else, I am only waiting for you, you know.

[Left corner]
Vlada, I still am very fond of you and hope you are proud (?) of me.

DOCUMENT 1.3

DOCUMENT 1.4*

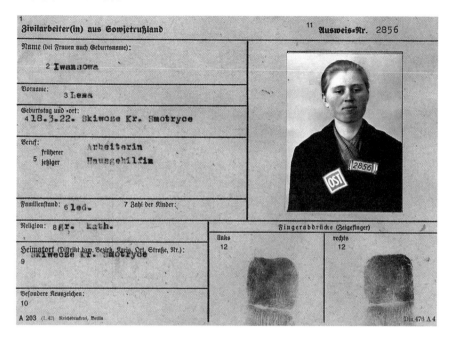

1. **Prisoner category**: civilian worker from Soviet Russia
2. **Last name** (for women, maiden name also): Iwansowe
3. **First name**: Lena
4. **Date and place of birth**: March 18, 1922, in Skiwoze Kr. Smotryce
5. **Occupation: previous**: Arbeiterin [English: worker]; **current**: Hausgehilfin [English: maid]
6. **Marital status**: led. [*ledig*, English: single]
7. **Number of children**: blank
8. **Religion**: gr. Kath. [English: Greek Catholic]
9. **Home town** (district, county, place, street, number): Skiwecze Kr. Smotryce
10. **Distinguishing marks**: blank
11. **ID number**: 2856
12. **Fingerprints** (index fingers): left, right

---

*Numbers 1 through 12 added for translation purposes.

DOCUMENT 1.5

DOCUMENT 1.6

A.E.F. D.P. REGISTRATION RECORD form filled in by hand:

- **(1) Registration No.:** INFILTREE / 6988216942
- **Original □ Duplicate ☒**
- **(2) Family Name:** GORLUB GREINOM
- **Other Given Names:** (blank)
- **(3) Sex:** M. ☒ F. □
- **(4) Marital Status:** Single ☒ Married ☒ Widowed □ Divorced □
- **(5) Claimed Nationality:** JEWISH
- **For coding purposes:** A. B. C. D. E. F. G. H. I. J.
- **(6) Birthdate:** 25.X.1917   **Birthplace:** LUBLIN   **Province:**   **Country:** POLAND
- **(7) Religion (Optional):** MOS.
- **(8) Number of Accompanying Family Members:** —
- **(9) Number of Dependents:**
- **(10) Full Name of Father:** HONIA
- **(11) Full Maiden Name of Mother:** ESTER RACHLIN
- **(12) Desired Destination:** PALESTINE — City or Village / Province / Country
- **(13) Last Permanent Residence or Residence January 1, 1938:** LUBLIN — City or Village: LUBLIN   Province: Country: POLAND
- **(14) Usual Trade, Occupation or Profession:** CARPENTER Woodworkment
- **(15) Performed in What Kind of Establishment:**
- **(16) Other Trades or Occupations:**
- **(17) Languages Spoken in Order of Fluency:** a. POLISH, b. YIDDISH, c. HEBREW
- **(18) Do You Claim to be a Prisoner of War:**
- **(19) Amount and Kind of Currency in your Possession:** Yes / No
- **(20) Signature of Registrant:** Golub G.
- **(21) Signature of Registrar:**
- **Date:** 23.1.46
- **Assembly Center No.:**
- **(22) Destination or Reception Center:** — Name or Number / City or Village / Province / Country
- **(23) Code for Issue:** 1 2 3 4 5 6 7 8 9 10 11 12 13 14 15 16 17 18 19 20 21 22 23 24 25 26 27 28
- **(24) Remarks:** R4/7

UNRRA
Team 100

DOCUMENT 1.7

DOCUMENT 1.8

3/2,

`·22`

Der Reichsführer-ᛋᛋ   Berlin, den 27. Oktober 1939

Betr.: Bestellung des "Lebensborn" e.V. als Beistand für die
ehelichen Kinder und Übernahme der Vormundschaft für
die unehelichen Kinder gefallener ᛋᛋ-Kameraden.

Um den Frauen und den Kindern unserer gefallenen ᛋᛋ-Kameraden in jeder Hinsicht wirksam Hilfe zu gewähren,
gleichgültig ob es sich um die Wahrnehmung der Rechte
der Hinterbliebenen gegenüber Dritten oder ob es sich
z.B. um die Erziehung, Ausbildung der Kinder handelt
usw., beauftrage ich den "Lebensborn" e.V.

a.) sich in denjenigen Fällen als Beistand für die ehelichen Kinder gefallener ᛋᛋ-Kameraden vormundschafts-
gerichtlich bestellen zu lassen, wenn dies dem Wun-
sche der Mutter entspricht oder im Interesse der
Kinder liegt;

b.) die Vormundschaften für die unehelichen Kinder zu
übernehmen.

Das ᛋᛋ-Personalhauptamt und das Hauptfürsorge und Versor-
gungsamt-ᛋᛋ haben laufend die eingereichten Meldungen
über die gefallenen ᛋᛋ-Kameraden dem "Lebensborn" e.V.
zu übersenden.

Der "Lebensborn" e.V. hat sich mit den Hinterbliebenen
in Verbindung zu setzen und festzustellen, ob die Bestellung als Beistand oder die Übernahme der Vormundschaft in Betracht kommt.

Sämtliche ᛋᛋ-Dienststellen und ᛋᛋ-Führer haben die vom "Lebensborn" e.V. zu leistende Arbeit im weitestgehendem
Masse zu unterstützen.
Der "Lebensborn" e.V. hat mir laufend über die Bestellun-
gen als Beistand oder Vormund zu berichten.

Der Reichsführer-ᛋᛋ

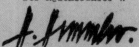

The Reichsführer-SS   .   Berlin, October 27, 1939

<u>Re</u>: Appointment of Lebensborn e.V. as advocate for the legitimate children and assumption of guardianship for the illegitimate children of SS comrades who were killed in action.

In order to furnish assistance effectively and in every way to the wives and children of our fallen SS comrades, whether it is a matter of exercising the rights of the surviving dependents with regard to third parties or, for example, of raising and educating the children, etc., I instruct Lebensborn e.V.

    a.   to have itself appointed by the guardianship court as advocate for the legitimate children of fallen SS comrades in instances when this is in keeping with the desire of the mother or is in the interest of the child;

    b.   to assume guardianship of the illegitimate children.

The SS Personnel Main Office and the SS Welfare and Pensions Main Office must routinely forward to Lebensborn e.V. the notifications submitted with regard to fallen SS comrades.

Lebensborn e.V. must get in touch with the surviving dependents and determine whether appointment as advocate or assumption of guardianship comes into consideration.

All SS offices and SS leaders must support to the greatest possible extent the work to be performed by Lebensborn e.V.

Lebensborn e.V. must routinely report to me concerning the appointments to act as advocate or as guardian.

The Reichsführer-SS
[signed] H. Himmler

DOCUMENT 1.9*

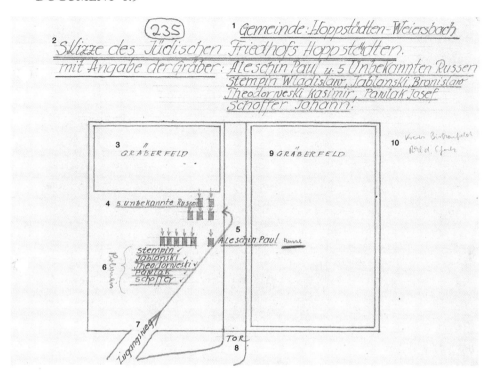

1. Community: Hoppstädten-Weiersbach
2. Sketch of the Hoppstädten Jewish Cemetery with Indication of Graves:
   Paul Aleschin and 5 unknown Russians
   Wladislaw Stempin, Bronislaw Jablanski, Kasimir Theodorweski, Josef Pawlak, Johann Schoffer
3. Burial ground
4. 5 unknown Russians
5. Paul Aleschin (Russian)
6. Poles: Stempin, Jablanski, Theodorweski, Pawlak, Schoffer
7. Access path
8. Gate
9. Burial ground
10. [at right, handwritten] Kreis Birkenfeld

---

*Numbers 1 through 10 added for translation purposes.

DOCUMENT 1.10

Aussage von Herrn G e s s i n g e r, Heilbronn-Böckingen,
zu den ermordeten A u s l ä n d e rn.

31.August 1946.

Ich habe am 3. oder 4.April 1945 einen Zug von Konzentrations-
lagerhäftlingen durch Böckingen führen sehen. Auf Befragen er-
fuhren wir, dass die Häftlinge von Neckarelz kamen. Neckarelz
war ein Aussenkommando des Konzentrationslagers Natzweiler, das
damals für Rüstungszwecke eingesetzt war. Die Häftlinge waren im
vollkommen erschöpften Zustand. Es dürften sich in der Hauptsa-
che um Ausländer gehandelt haben. Ein Teil der Böckinger Ein-
wohnerschaft versuchte, sich den Häftlingen zu nähern und ihnen
Lebensmittel, Rauchwaren und Kleidungsstücke zuzuwerfen. Sie
wurden jedoch dafür von den begleitenden Wachmannschaften mit
Erschiessen bedroht.
Ein Teil der Häftlinge, die in vollkommen erschöpftem Zustande
waren, brachen von den Strapatzen der Wanderung zusammen. Wer
nicht mehr weiter konnte, wurde von den Wachmannschaften durch
Fusstritte, Kolbenstösse oder Genickschuss vollends ermordet.
Nachdem der Zug Böckingen passiert hatte, wurden die 16 Tote
weggeräumt und zunächst in Bombentrichtern verscharrt.
Nach der Befreiung Böckingens durch Truppen der Vereinten Nationen hat der antifaschistische Teil der Bevölkerung von Bö-
kingen diese Toten wieder ausgegraben und auf dem Böckinger
Friedhof beigesetzt. Irgendwelche dokumentarische Unterlagen,
wer die Toten waren, sind nicht vorhanden. Sie wurden auch
nicht durch ein Militärgericht verurteilt und es wurde deshalb
auch keinerlei Todesbenachrichtigung an irgend ein Standesamt
gegeben. Es waren einfach auf dem Weg zurückgebliebene Häftlinge, namenlos und unbekannt, die nicht mehr weiter kamen und
deshalb sterben mussten.

                         /t.E.Gessinger./

Statement of Mr. G e s s i n g e r, Resident of Heilbronn-Böckingen,
regarding the Murdered F o r e i g n e r s
August 31, 1946

On April 3 or 4, 1945, I saw a procession of concentration camp prisoners being led through Böckingen. When we asked, we were told that the prisoners were from Neckarelz. Neckarelz was a subcamp of the Natzweiler concentration camp, which was used for armaments production in those days. The prisoners were in a state of utter exhaustion. These men probably were mainly foreigners. A part of the Böckingen population tried to approach the prisoners and throw food, tobacco products, and articles of clothing to them. As a result, however, the accompanying guards threatened to shoot them. Some of the prisoners, who were totally exhausted, collapsed from the exertions of the march. Anyone who could not go on was killed by the guards: kicked to death, beaten with rifle butts until dead, or shot in the back of the neck. After the procession had passed through Böckingen, the 16 dead bodies were cleared away and first buried in bomb craters. After the liberation of Böckingen by troops of the Allied nations, the antifascist segment of the population of Böckingen exhumed these bodies and interred them in the Böckingen Cemetery. No documentary records telling who the dead men were are available. They were also not convicted by a court-martial, and thus no notification of death whatsoever was sent to any bureau of vital statistics. They were simply prisoners who fell behind along the way, name-less and unknown, who could walk no farther and for this reason had to die.

E. Gessinger

DOCUMENT 1.11

SCANNED					No. T- *100 615*
05. Aug. 2010					X - Ref: *T: 86 793*
Name: w *ILd*					
And. GERMANY	✓		*19*/*8.* ✓ *50*		*Jhw.*
Origin of Case	Int.–Reb.	Loc.	Not Loc.	Re–R.	Nationality

KL

n. Srissmann

NAME: MÜLLER *Theresa (nee: zrossmann).*

	CASE REVIEW
re-opened Case Received:	*18 FEB 1950*
Statistics IN: *mr*	*Case Rev. 9-2-50*
Statistics OUT: 5 MAR 1950 16. AUG. 1950	*Report 20 MAR 1950*
Case Closed: 17 AUG 1950 R	*Consp. 5.90*
	Files 20-E 50

ACTION OF CORRESPONDENCE SECTION

		Dat	Res			Dat	Res	
T, Feb. R X Harm			*3 68*	*Tz to enquire*		29 MAR 1950		*Reports 14850 28*
briefam: 24. Okt. 1958				*83 to enq.*		47 *1950* R		*Files 20/4 50*
24. Okt. 1958								*16. 9. 50*
Fotokopie d. Schr								
von E.P. Berlin 8. Mar								*3 - Jan. 1963*
21. Mai 1973								*4. März 1963*
0.B. 24 Jun 1990								MAP LOCATION
								11. Mai 1973
								Country:
								28 Jun 1990
								Kreis:
								Area:

ACTION OF RECORDS BRANCH	FIELD TRACING Destination		MASS TRACING
22 FEB 1950 Rekords Checking Section			*Action Famm 9-3-50*
Library			*S.L. Nr. 10 20.6.50*

OBSERVATIONS:

Closed; not closed
1 Kh Karte ohne Gewicht
Zurück am 21. Okt. 1958 Rm.

Deadline Dates: *15*				

100 615

Brichgez Sauerland, Valkxorzan

DOCUMENT 1.12

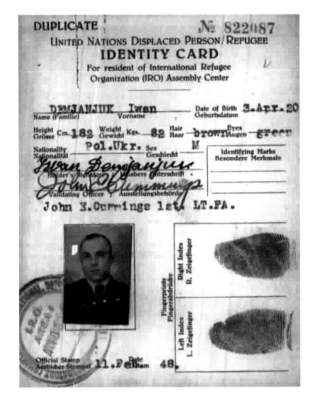

"OUR MOTHERS, OUR FATHERS":[1] LAHNSTEIN

"**O**N EITHER side of the Lahn [river] are two charming towns, Nieder-lahnstein and Oberlahnstein, connected with each other by an avenue of trees, which seem to exchange smiles and salutations," wrote Victor Hugo in 1845.[2] In 1933, the two towns admired by Hugo constituted what is today Lahnstein: Niederlahnstein on the north side of the Lahn and Oberlahnstein on the south side—sleepy towns situated at the juncture of the Lahn and Rhine rivers, approximately 6 kilometers (3.7 miles) south of Koblenz.[3] In the heart of the middle Rhine valley, Lahnstein, like the International Tracing Service (ITS),

---

1. This phrase is the title of the German television 4.5-hour miniseries *Unsere Mütter, Unsere Väter* (2013). The miniseries has been produced as a film with English subtitles, renamed *Generation War* (2013). When asked why he used this particular title, German producer Nico Hofmann, born in 1959 in Heidelberg, told a group of young German journalists that the film is a dialogue with his own mother and father, and parts of the film represent his parents' experiences as expressed in their diaries and memories. Hofmann acknowledged that "the title is a confession" (*der Titel ist Bekenntnis*). See Werner D'Inka et al., "Es Ist Nie Vorbei [It is never over]," *Frankfurter Allgemeine Zeitung*, March 18, 2013.

2. Victor Hugo, *The Rhine* (Boston: Dana Estes, 1902), 279.

3. Until 1969, the municipalities (*Gemeinden*) of Nieder- and Oberlahnstein were part of the Prussian province (*Provinz*) Hessen-Nassau in the district (*Landkreis*) of Sankt Goars-hausen. During the Nazi era, the two towns belonged to the Nazi province (*Gau*) of Hessen-Nassau in the district (*Kreis*) Sankt Goarshausen (after 1939, Rheingau-Sankt Goarshausen).

is inscribed in the United Nations Educational, Scientific, and Cultural Organization (UNESCO) Memory of the World Register. It is a beautiful place. In 1933, Niederlahnstein had a population of 5,421 and Oberlahnstein a population of 9,609.[4] Although the National Socialist German Worker's Party (Nationalsozialistische Deutsche Arbeiterpartei, NSDAP) won the largest percentage (53.8 percent) of votes in the district of St. Goarshausen in the March 1933 elections, support was lower but still significant in Ober- and Niederlahnstein, where the Nazi Party captured roughly three to four votes out of every ten.[5] During the Nazi period, these two towns and surrounding villages were sites of labor camps for Jews and prisoners of war (POWs), mobile construction brigades made up of slave laborers from concentration camps, civilian work camps owned by local businesses and filled with forced laborers from all over Europe, and a special court prison (*Gerichtsgefängnis*) run by the nazified Reich Ministry of Justice (Reichsjustizministerium, RJM)—this in addition to the regular police prison. American[6] and then French troops occupied the town in 1945 and established a displaced persons (DP) transit camp in Niederlahnstein. The ITS holdings tell us the story of Nazi persecution and its aftermath in this single small town. This same story played itself out with local variations in every village, town, and city in Germany. Researchers will find they need only ask the question, and through the ITS holdings, they will be able to reconstruct the histories of so many places where charm and grace became transformed into ugliness, terror, and greed.

---

4. Michael Rademacher, "Deutsche Verwaltungsgeschichte von der Reichseinigung 1871 bis zur Wiedervereinigung 1990," www.verwaltungsgeschichte.de (accessed September 24, 2015).

5. In the March 1933 elections, the Nazi Party received 41 percent of the vote in Oberlahnstein and 29.5 percent in Niederlahnstein. Other major parties also received significant support. The Center (*Zentrum*) captured 33.1 percent of the vote in Oberlahnstein and 35.6 percent in Niederlahnstein, a surprisingly low number given that Niederlahnsteiners were 85.1 percent Catholic. The Communist Party received 21 percent of the vote in Niederlahnstein. Violent repression of political enemies and "forced coordination" (*Gleichschaltung*) were quick, so that the Nazi Party received over 90 percent of the vote in both towns by the November 1933 elections. See Hubertus Seibert with Judith Sommer, eds., *Vom kurfürstlichen Ort zur grossen kreisangehörigen Stadt: Die Geschichte Lahnsteins im 19. und 20. Jahrhundert* (Lahnstein: Görres-Druckerei, 1999), 146, 150–54. See also *Wie war das damals in Lahnstein? Herausfordernde Geschichten aus den Jahren 1933–1945* (Lahnstein: Imprimatur Verlag, 2010). For biographical information on local Nazis, see Franz Maier, *Biographisches Organisationshandbuch der NSDAP und ihrer Gliederungen im Gebiet des heutigen Landes Rheinland-Pfalz* (Mainz: Hase & Koehler, 2007).

6. The first American troops entered Ober- and Niederlahnstein from the direction of Horchheim on March 27, 1945. Seibert with Sommer, *Vom kurfürstlichen Ort zur grossen kreisangehörigen Stadt*, 202.

Small Jewish communities had lived in Ober- and Niederlahnstein since 1266 and constituted approximately 0.4 percent of the otherwise Christian population.[7] A postwar compilation of deported, deceased, and emigrated Jews living in Oberlahnstein between 1933 and 1945 records forty-nine families comprising 133 individuals; for Niederlahnstein, the compilation indicates another four families of 13 individuals.[8] The synagogue, located on Oberlahnstein's main street, Hochstrasse, near the city hall (*Rathaus*), was gutted and the prayer books taken and thrown into the Rhine on November 10, 1938. Eleven-year-old Ingeborg Eichberg recollected this well, as on that day her father was arrested on the street outside her family's apartment and sent to Buchenwald.[9] (See document 2.1.[10]) Minutes later, the apartment was looted and destroyed while she, her mother, and her sister looked on in shock. It was Ingeborg's first experience with antisemitic violence that she could recall, but not her last.[11] Her parents, butcher Josef Eichberg and his wife, Emmy, could not say the same. (See document 2.2.[12]) Ingeborg and her family left Oberlahn-

---

7. Paul Arnsberg, *Die jüdischen Gemeinden in Hessen: Anfang, Untergang, Neubeginn* (Frankfurt: Landesverband der Jüdischen Gemeinden in Hessen/Societäts-Verlag, 1971), 151–53; "Duldung-Integration-Vernichtung-Erinnerung: Juden in Lahnstein," in Seibert with Sommer, *Vom kurfürstlichen Ort zur grossen kreisangehörigen Stadt*, 719.

8. "Namensliste der in Oberlahnstein und Niederlahnstein ansässig gewesenen Personen der israelischen Gemeinde," 1.2.5.1/12851819–29/ITS Digital Archive, USHMM. The compilation submitted for Ober- and Niederlahnstein alphabetically lists 146 individuals in total. For each person, the compilation lists first and last name, date and place of birth, profession, former address by city and street, arrest date or date and destination of emigration, and date of death. ITS accession notes indicate the compilation consists of "extracts" (*Auszüge*), presumably from local archives, and was received by ITS in December 1965.

9. File Josef Eichberg, 1.1.5.3/5812933–5/ITS Digital Archive, USHMM. There is no folder number, as the documents in 1.1.5.3 are organized by name. Eichberg was incarcerated at Buchenwald by December 2 and appears to have been released on December 12, 1938. His file consists of a postal money order indicating that Emmy Eichberg sent 30 Reichsmark (RM) to one Paul Wertheim on December 2, 1938, and an additional 30 RM for her husband, as the money order is for a total of 60 RM. The documents are copies from the Berlin Document Center received by ITS in 1993.

10. Prisoner account record (*Geldüberweisungsformular*) with record of money order from Emmy Eichberg to Paul Wertheim and Josef Eichberg, 1.1.5.3/5812934/ITS Digital Archive, USHMM. Copy from Berlin Document Center received by ITS in 1993.

11. USC Shoah Foundation testimony for Irene Osbourne (born Ingeborg Eichberg).

12. "Transport to the Auschwitz Concentration Camp on August 14, 1942/Train from Drancy Departing on August 14, 1942," p. Dukes, Friedrich, through Eisemann, Samuel, 1.1.9.9/11188105/ITS Digital Archive, USHMM. Postwar compilation.

stein in 1939 and thus began their Holocaust odyssey. She and her older sister survived; her parents did not.[13]

Emil Baer, chair (*Vorsteher*) of the Jewish Community (*jüdisches Kultusgemeinde*) of Oberlahnstein and prominent owner of an iron and scrap-metal business (*Eisen- und Schrotthandel*) at Martinstrasse 2, lived with his family in the stately Villa Baer at Ostallee 11, a few blocks' walk from the city hall and synagogue. Storm troopers (Sturmabteilung, SA) destroyed the family villa on November 10, 1938. Eighth-grade students from a nearby school destroyed the windows and garden at the behest of Nazi Party members. In February 1939, Baer was forced to move to his place of business, declared a *Judenhaus* (Jew house), a building managed or administered by the Jewish Religious Federation.[14] In the summer and fall of 1941, those Jewish families still remaining in the districts (*Landkreise*) of Lower Lahn–Limburg, Westerwald, and Rheingau–St. Goarshausen were deported to an abandoned mining facility turned labor and residential camp for Jews in Friedrichssegen, a bare few kilometers east of Lahnstein and today a suburb of the town.[15] Baer was among them.[16] Living in dilapidated buildings without running water or electricity, the women were conscripted for brick making and the men for iron and scrap-metal work.[17] Emil Baer died in Sachsenhausen on October 15, 1941, purportedly of a heart

---

13. Numerous CNI cards as well as further ITS-held documentation corroborating the fates of Josef and Emmy Eichberg are not included here for the sake of brevity.

14. "Familie Baer (z.T. auch: Bär)," Lahnsteiner Altertumsverein, www.lahnsteiner-alter tumsverein.de/baer.html (accessed July 20, 2013). Quoted from "Erschütternde Schicksale von Lahnsteiner Juden," *Rhein-Lahn Zeitung* No. 156 (July 7, 2012).

15. In May–June 1941, Gestapo offices, in collaboration with Nazi city and district administrators, created a new "labor and residential camp" network for Jewish families (*Arbeits- und Wohnlager für deutsche Juden*), alongside and separate from the already existing labor and Reich Association (Reichsvereinigung) camps. Forty, all in the so-called Old Reich (*Altreich*), were created in total. The purpose of these camps was the "concentration" of Jewish families "in preparation for the coming deportations, monitoring of those families, and using them for forced labor." Wolf Gruner, *Jewish Forced Labor under the Nazis: Economic Needs and Racial Aims*, trans. Kathleen M. Dell'Orto (New York: Cambridge University Press in association with USHMM, 2006), 61–63, 64, 67.

16. "Namensliste der in Oberlahnstein und Niederlahnstein ansässig gewesenen Personen der israelischen Gemeinde," 1.2.5.1/12851819–29/ITS Digital Archive, USHMM. The residency complex consisted of a single street and several buildings in very poor condition. The compilation lists all Jewish individuals incarcerated there.

17. Walter Rummel, "Ein Ghetto für die Juden im Tal der Verbannten. Die Umwandlung der ehemaligen Bergarbeitersiedlung in Friedrichssegen (Lahn) zum Wohnlager für jüdische Zwangsarbeiter und -arbeiterinnen, 1938–1942," *Jahrbuch für westdeutsche Landesgeschichte* 30 (2004): 419–507.

attack.[18] (See document 2.3.[19]) His spouse, Johanna Baer, and his sister, Minna Baer, perished later. They were among those on two 1942 transports from Friedrichssegen to the east: on June 10 to Sobibor via Frankfurt am Main and on August 28 to Theresienstadt and then Auschwitz, where they were murdered.[20] Of this small yet vibrant community, only Hilde (Levi) Emmel returned to Niederlahnstein after the war, spared deportation to the east by a prison stay in Frankfurt am Main, followed by two years in the Ravensbrück concentration camp.[21]

"To the left, on the Lahn, at the verge of the horizon, the sun and the clouds intermingle with the gloomy ruins of [Castle/Burg] Lahneck, fraught with mystery for the historian," wrote Victor Hugo. More than 150 years later, it is still an unforgettable sight, one that subscriptions salesman (*Abonnentenwerber*) Otto Wilhelm Böhm would have seen each day from the comfortable postwar home he shared with his wife at Gymnasialstrasse 18 in Oberlahnstein. He was arrested

---

18. Civil registry, Oranienburg I, secondary death book Vol. IIa—1.10.1941—31.12.1941/entry for Emil Baer, 1.1.38.1/4081939/ITS Digital Archive, USHMM. Photocopy received by ITS in 1957.

19. CNI card for Emil Baer, 0.1/14598352/ITS Digital Archive, USHMM. Note that the date of presumed death on the CNI card is incorrect. See chapter 1 regarding the manner in which ITS generated CNI cards based on information received from a third party, which had to be corroborated by ITS-held documentation.

20. "Namensliste der in Oberlahnstein und Niederlahnstein ansässig gewesenen Personen der israelischen Gemeinde," 1.2.5.1/12851819–29/ITS Digital Archive, USHMM.

21. Born in Niederlahnstein in 1906 and living on Goethestrasse 4, Emmel was deported to Tagschacht/Friedrichssegen on August 12, 1941. See "Namensliste der in Oberlahnstein und Niederlahnstein ansässig gewesenen Personen der israelischen Gemeinde," 1.2.5.1/12851823/ITS Digital Archive, USHMM. From there, she was transferred from the Gestapo-run police prison (*Polizeigefängnis*) on Gutleutstrasse 13 (part of Klapperfeld prison, Frankfurt am Main) to the Ravensbrück concentration camp on August 26, 1943. See 0.1/20097665–73 and "Transporte am Donnerstag den 26.8.43," 1.2.2.1/11363916/ITS Digital Archive, USHMM. She arrived in Ravensbrück on September 3, 1943, where she was classified as a political prisoner, assigned prisoner number 22717, and put to work as a seamstress in the tailoring shop. See list dated March 9, 1943, ITS Digital Collection, 1.1.35.1/3765109/ITS Digital Archive, USHMM. After the war, Emmel returned to Niederlahnstein and lived on Schillerstrasse 44 in January 1949. See "Inventarverzeichnis allen persönlichen Eigentums von Emmel (geb. Levi), Hilda (Sara), August 10, 1950," 2.1.1.1/70347457; "American Committee of O.S.E. (Organization to Save the Children/L'Oeuvre de Secours aux Enfants) List of Jewish Persons at Present in Germany in the French Zone of Occupation, August 1, 1946," 3.1.1.3/78810773; Hilde (Levi) Emmel, 3.2.1.1/79066434–7/ITS Digital Archive, USHMM. There is no folder number, as documents in 3.2.1.1 are organized by name. See also Rummel, "Ein Ghetto für die Juden im Tal der Verbannten," 419.

on April 10, 1957[22] and tried in 1960 by West German authorities in the regional court (*Landgericht*) of Düsseldorf, as part of what we today refer to as the Sachsenhausen trials.[23] (See document 2.4.[24]) He, Horst Hempel, and August Höhn stood charged with a long list of crimes at Sachsenhausen, where Emil Baer, Böhm's social superior in Oberlahnstein before the Nazi rise to power, perished. Specifically, charges against the three men included taking part in summary executions of approximately 10,800 Soviet prisoners of war;[25] shooting twenty-seven prisoners from isolation block 58 and then burning their bodies in the crematorium on an October day in 1944, after having told them that they were being taken to the camp's *Industriehof* to load a truck;[26] murdering between 250 and 700 ill patients from the camp infirmary (*Revier*) at the

---

22. Böhm was born on July 11, 1890, in Heilbronn, the son of a station chief in the Württemberg Gendarmerie. Trained in technical school to be a bookbinder, he fought in World War I and joined the NSDAP and the SS in October 1932. He was first stationed in Sachsenhausen as an SS guard in 1938. The camp itself came to comprise the so-called SS camp, which included the SS barracks; the "protective custody camp," triangular in shape; a separate camp for Allied officers and high-profile prisoners; the so-called industry yard; and the brickworks (*Klinkerwerk*), which ultimately became a subcamp in its own right. Böhm's duties were in the *Schutzhaftlager*. After further training, Böhm returned in October 1941 as platoon leader in the guard force. In 1943, he was transferred to the camp commandant's office (*Kommandantur*), where he was roll call leader (*Rapportführer*). By the time of the camp's evacuation, he had been promoted to SS master sergeant (*Hauptscharführer*). See "Documents in Criminal Matters for the Sachsenhausen Concentration Camp Trials, Indictment, Copy: The Senior Public Prosecutor for the Regional Court to the Regional Court in Düsseldorf, June 12, 1959," 5.1/82298495 and 82298844–91/ITS Digital Archive, USHMM. No accession date for ITS acquisition of the copies is available. Biographical information on Böhm is on pp. 1, 18–19 of the indictment (82298844 and 82298861–2). Information on the organization of the camp is on pp. 20–23 (82298863–6).

23. Ibid., 82298495 and 82298844. C. F. Rüter and D. W. de Mildt, *Die westdeutschen Strafverfahren wegen nationalsozialistischer Tötungsverbrechen 1945–1997: Eine systematische Verfahrensbeschreibung mit Karten und Registern* (Munich: K. G. Saur Verlag, 1998), 114–15.

24. "Documents in Criminal Matters for the Sachsenhausen Concentration Camp Trials, Indictment, Copy: The Senior Public Prosecutor for the Regional Court to the Regional Court in Düsseldorf, June 12, 1959," 5.1/82298844/ITS Digital Archive, USHMM.

25. Ibid., 82298868.

26. Ibid., 82298873–5.

time of the camp's evacuation;[27] and shooting at least 400 Jewish prisoners transferred to Sachsenhausen from Lieberose.[28] This list includes just a fraction of all the charges against the three men. Böhm received a life sentence.

Beginning in October 1939,[29] the wartime economy of Landkreis Sankt Goarshausen relied on prisoners (*Gefangene*) and POWs, *Zivilarbeiter* (non-Jewish foreigners working in Nazi Germany voluntarily or as forced labor), and *Ostarbeiter*, so-called eastern workers, from across western, southern, and eastern Europe.[30] (See document 2.5.[31]) Documents in the ITS holdings pertaining to Ober- and Niederlahnstein relate to citizens of Belgium, Croatia, Czechoslovakia, England, France, Holland, Italy, Latvia, Lithuania, Poland, Romania, Russia, and Yugoslavia, somehow caught up in the Nazi web of exploitation and toiling through the war in Ober- and Niederlahnstein, the largest towns in Landkreis Sankt Goarshausen. Each had hundreds of such laborers. The French National Tracing Bureau lists 275 and 375 occupants of civilian work camps in Oberlahnstein and Niederlahnstein, respectively.[32]

A striking document lists *Zivilarbeiter, Ostarbeiter*, and *Gefangene* who died in Oberlahnstein from January 1, 1940, to December 31, 1945. *Ostarbeiter* Marian Babiaczyk, listed as a Russian chimney sweep, hanged himself (*Selbst-*

---

27. Ibid., 82298884–8.

28. Ibid., 82298888–9.

29. On October 1, 1939, the leader of the labor office in Niederlahnstein wrote to the president of the regional (*Land*) labor office for Hesse (located in Frankfurt) to request eight hundred POWs for labor. See Seibert with Sommer, *Vom kurfürstlichen Ort zur grossen kreisangehörigen Stadt*, 174.

30. For a fuller picture of the economy of Landkreis Sankt Goarshausen and the use of forced labor therein, see Alexandra Lohse, "Landkreis Sankt Goarshausen," in *The United States Holocaust Memorial Museum Encyclopedia of Camps and Ghettos*, ed. Martin Dean, vol. 6 (Bloomington: Indiana University Press in association with USHMM, forthcoming). Other sources for Niederlahnstein include Walter Rummel, "Zwangsarbeitereinsatz im Gebiet des heutigen Rheinland-Pfalz: Die bürokratische Dokumentation und ihr Verbleib," in *Zwangsarbeit in der Rheinland-Pfalz während des Zweiten Weltkriegs*, ed. Hedwig Brüchert and Michael Matheus (Stuttgart: Franz Steiner Verlag, 2004), 8–9.

31. The Niederlahnstein cemetery map including graves of French, Dutch, Polish, Russian, and Italian citizens who perished and were buried there during World War II. 5.3.5/ 101105363/ITS Digital Archive, USHMM.

32. Martin Weinmann, *Das Nationalsozialistische Lagersystem* (Frankfurt am Main: Zweitausendeins, 1990), 529.

mord durch Erhängen) on August 22, 1941, two months after the German invasion of the Soviet Union. French *Zivilarbeiter* and assistant lathe operator (*Hilfsdreher*) Henri Yacinthe drowned while bathing (*ertrinken beim Baden*) in Oberlahnstein on August 8, 1944. So did French *Zivilarbeiter* and blacksmith (*Schmied*) Jacques Perraudin two weeks later, on August 26, the day Charles de Gaulle entered a free Paris. Russian *Ostarbeiterin* Irina Zararow died of a nutritional disorder (*Ernährungsstörung*) on December 17, 1944. Meningitis, tuberculosis, cancer, asthma, bronchitis, and other maladies are all cited as causes of death for foreign-born workers in Oberlahnstein. The list bears witness to several stillborn babies whose Russian and Polish mothers sometimes died with them, either in the rigors of childbirth or due to maltreatment or even murder.[33]

We know, too, thanks to a visually interesting report in the ITS holdings, that between December 27, 1944, and January 8, 1945, a train with prisoners belonging to a railroad construction brigade from Oranienburg was based in the town of Kamp (today Kamp–Bornhofen am Rhein).[34] (See document 2.6.[35]) The prisoners were put to work on the railroad line between Oberlahnstein and neighboring Braubach with no protection from British and American bombing raids. During one such raid, six were killed and subsequently buried in a common grave in Kamp. According to the local cemetery attendant, the prisoners themselves had to dig the grave for their fallen, and it was

---

33. "Standesamt Oberlahnstein, Liste der in der Zeit vom 1. Januar 1940 bis heute hier verstorbenen ausländischen Staatsangehörigen, December 31, 1945," 2.1.3.1/70828150/ITS Digital Archive, USHMM. The document is original; it was compiled by Oberlahnstein's registrar, Mr. Pott (*Standesbeamter*) and dutifully stamped with the town registrar's seal on December 31, 1945.

34. The *SS-Baubrigaden* (construction brigades) were "mobile subcamps assigned to repair bomb damage." Todd Huebner, "Sachsenhausen Main Camp," in Megargee, *The United States Holocaust Memorial Museum Encyclopedia of Camps and Ghettos*, 1:1256. Created in December 1944, the railroad construction brigade (*Eisenbahnbaubrigade*) formally called SS-Eisenbahn-Baubrigade XII (SS EBB XII), a detachment from Sachsenhausen-Oranienburg, worked at Kamp. SS-Eisenbahn-Baubrigade XIII, a detachment from Dachau created in January 1945, worked in Bad Kreuznach, then Reichertshofen, then Neuhof bei Fulda, and finally in the Oberlahnkreis. The prisoners buried in Kamp were presumably from SS EBB XII. Karola Fings, "SS-Baubrigaden and SS-Eisenbahnbaubrigaden," in Megargee, *The United States Holocaust Memorial Museum Encyclopedia of Camps and Ghettos*, 1:1353–59.

35. "Certified Copy from the Death Register of the Bureau of Vital Statistics in Kamp (Rhine)," 2.2.0.1/82447342/ITS Digital Archive, USHMM. This document is original; it forms part of a subcollection of originals and copies from Deutsche Dienststelle in Berlin, received by ITS in 1991.

they who testified as to the number to be buried. No names were recorded in the death register maintained by the Kamp municipal authorities. The dead were thought to be Russian nationals.[36] Documents in the ITS holdings attest to many more such cases in Oberlahnstein and Niederlahnstein, recording death by bombs in the latter half of 1944 and early 1945. The status of prisoners and foreign forced laborers as disposable individuals comes through in a popular saying making its way around Oberlahnstein by the winter of 1944: "The English and Americans rule the sky; foreigners the streets; and the German people the bomb shelters."[37]

ITS holdings are a treasure trove for understanding the use of forced labor by ordinary companies and municipal bodies, large and small, in this region. (See document 2.7.[38]) Niederlahnstein was the location of a labor office responsible for monitoring working conditions, wages, and discipline.[39] When one assembles documents in the ITS holdings on this topic, a very specific picture of the regular human labor trafficking across the towns becomes clear. The city of Oberlahnstein used thirty-seven Italian POWs for labor between November 1943 and March 1945. Three Italian POWs worked for Geschw. Helbach O.L. (Helbach Siblings Oberlahnstein).[40] Alexandra Lohse uses documents in the ITS holdings to name larger companies that used foreign forced labor in Ober- and Niederlahnstein. Fa. (*Firma*, firm) Feldmühle AG (*Aktiengesellschaft*, corpora-

---

36. Ibid.
37. "Die Engländer und Amerikaner beherrschen die Luft, die Fremdvölkischen die Strasse und das deutsche Volk die Luftschutzkeller." Seibert with Sommer, *Vom kurfürstlichen Ort zur grossen kreisangehörigen Stadt*, 180, 183.
38. "Inquiry into the Whereabouts of Civilian and Military Members of the United [Allied] Nations (Italy), the Mayor, Dept. IV, Oberlahnstein, April 18, 1946," 2.1.3.1/ 70828180/ITS Digital Archive, USHMM.
39. "Labor Offices in French Zone, 1941," 6.1.1/82514613/ITS Digital Archive, USHMM. The document is a postwar compilation based on *Die Dienststellen der Arbeitseinsatz-, der Reichstreuhänder -und der Gewerbeaufsichtsverwaltung* (Berlin: Montanus-Druckerei, 1941), issued by the Reich Labor Ministry (Reichsarbeitsministerium). Thirteen officials constituted the Reich trustees of labor (*Reichstreuhänder der Arbeit*), one for each economic region of the Reich and responsible to the minister of labor, Franz Seldte. Their offices set wages and moderated conflicts between employers and workers. See Adam Tooze, *The Wages of Destruction: The Making and Breaking of the Nazi Economy* (London: Allen Lane, 2006), 40.
40. "Labor Offices in French Zone, 1941," 6.1.1/82514613/ITS Digital Archive, USHMM. Helbach was one of several local businesses that agreed only to hire members of the German Labor Front (Deutsche Arbeitsfront) in September 1935, which excluded "non-Aryans." Seibert with Sommer, *Vom kurfürstlichen Ort zur grossen kreisangehörigen Stadt*, 156.

tion),[41] one of the largest German paper manufacturers, registered thirty-seven Estonians working in its Oberlahnstein plant between 1944 and 1945,[42] in addition to thirty-seven Russians.[43] In 1944, seven Italian POWs,[44] six Latvians,[45] eleven Lithuanians,[46] and two Poles[47] joined them. Fa. Otto Kaiser Kommanditgesellschaft (limited partnership) in Oberlahnstein, involved in armaments manufacture,[48] registered seven Italian POWs as early as March 1943,[49] sixty-three Russians,[50] and one Pole, Michael Francol, from October 1943 to June 1944.[51] Jakob Bollinger & Co., a chemical factory in Oberlahnstein,[52] registered two Poles, Marian and Helene Pinta,

---

41. Feldmühle was one of several local businesses that agreed only to hire members of the German Labor Front in September 1935, which excluded "non-Aryans." Seibert with Sommer, *Vom kurfürstlichen Ort zur grossen kreisangehörigen Stadt*, 156.

42. "Der Bürgermeister als Ortspolizei Behörde, Stadt Oberlahnstein, zu Ib, Namentliche Liste der in Liste Ia aufgeführten Personen, Estland. Oberlahnstein, 27.4.1946," 2.1.3.1/70828177/ITS Digital Archive, USHMM.

43. "Der Bürgermeister als Ortspolizei Behörde, Stadt Oberlahnstein, zu Ib, Namentliche Liste der in Liste Ia aufgeführten Personen, Russland. Oberlahnstein, 27.4.1946," 2.1.3.1/70828214/ITS Digital Archive, USHMM.

44. "Der Bürgermeister als Ortspolizei Behörde, Stadt Oberlahnstein, zu Ib, Namentliche Liste der in Liste Ia aufgeführten Personen, Italien. Oberlahnstein, 27.4.1946," 2.1.3.1/70828181/ITS Digital Archive, USHMM.

45. "Der Bürgermeister als Ortspolizei Behörde, Stadt Oberlahnstein, zu Ib, Namentliche Liste der in Liste Ia aufgeführten Personen, Lettland. Oberlahnstein, 27.4.1946," 2.1.3.1/70828184/ITS Digital Archive, USHMM.

46. "Der Bürgermeister als Ortspolizei Behörde, Stadt Oberlahnstein, zu Ib, Namentliche Liste der in Liste Ia aufgeführten Personen, Litauen. Oberlahnstein, 27.4.1946," 2.1.3.1/70828189/ITS Digital Archive, USHMM.

47. "Der Bürgermeister als Ortspolizei Behörde, Stadt Oberlahnstein, zu Ib, Namentliche Liste der in Liste Ia aufgeführten Personen, Polen. Oberlahnstein, 27.4.1946," 2.1.3.1/70828203/ITS Digital Archive, USHMM.

48. Seibert with Sommer, *Vom kurfürstlichen Ort zur grossen kreisangehörigen Stadt*, 168.

49. "Der Bürgermeister als Ortspolizei Behörde, Stadt Oberlahnstein, zu Ib, Namentliche Liste der in Liste Ia aufgeführten Personen, Italien. Oberlahnstein, 27.4.1946," 2.1.3.1/70828181/ITS Digital Archive, USHMM.

50. "Der Bürgermeister als Ortspolizei Behörde, Stadt Oberlahnstein, zu Ib, Namentliche Liste der in Liste Ia aufgeführten Personen, Russland. Oberlahnstein, 27.4.1946," 2.1.3.1/70828214–5/ITS Digital Archive, USHMM.

51. "Der Bürgermeister als Ortspolizei Behörde, Stadt Oberlahnstein, zu Ib, Namentliche Liste der in Liste Ia aufgeführten Personen, Polen. Oberlahnstein, 27.4.1946," 2.1.3.1/70828203/ITS Digital Archive, USHMM.

52. Bollinger was one of several local businesses that agreed only to hire members of the German Labor Front in September 1935. In September 1937, Jakob Bollinger was also responsible for reporting a Catholic youth group celebrating mass in the Josefskapelle to the local SS and SA for gathering illegally, resulting in their arrest. Seibert with Sommer, *Vom kurfürstlichen Ort zur grossen kreisangehörigen Stadt*, 156, 161–62.

from 1944 to March 1945.[53] Zschimmer & Schwarz registered one Russian[54] and ten Polish men from 1944 to March 1945.[55] In 1942, over 150 POWs, half of them French, were kept in a camp (*Lager*) in the Johanneskloster (St. John's Abbey) on the Rhine. Seventeen of them, recollected Father Peter Egenolf, were from Belgium and the Netherlands, impressed into the Transportflotte Speer to build ships able to carry stone to the Reich capital.[56] Fa. Farbwerk Schroeder & Stadelmann AG in Oberlahnstein[57] operated its own camp for eastern workers. Sixty-seven Russians, male and female, were registered there.[58] As shown later in this chapter, for many of the individuals appearing in subunit 2.1.3.1 (Lists of All Persons of United [Allied] Nations and Other Foreigners, German Jews, and Stateless Persons; French Zone), further documentation is available in other subunits, especially regarding their postwar experiences in DP camps.

The ITS holdings illuminate these laborers' daily challenges, lived wartime experiences, and exchanges with the local population. Fa. Didier-Werke AG in Niederlahnstein,[59] a factory involved in armaments manufacture,[60] employed

---

53. "Der Bürgermeister als Ortspolizei Behörde, Stadt Oberlahnstein, zu Ib, Namentliche Liste der in Liste Ia aufgeführten Personen, Polen. Oberlahnstein, 27.4.1946," 2.1.3.1/ 70828203/ITS Digital Archive, USHMM.

54. "Der Bürgermeister als Ortspolizei Behörde, Stadt Oberlahnstein, zu Ib, Namentliche Liste der in Liste Ia aufgeführten Personen, Russland. Oberlahnstein, 27.4.1946," 2.1.3.1/70828214/ITS Digital Archive, USHMM.

55. "Der Bürgermeister als Ortspolizei Behörde, Stadt Oberlahnstein, zu Ib, Namentliche Liste der in Liste Ia aufgeführten Personen, Polen. Oberlahnstein, 27.4.1946," 2.1.3.1/ 70828203/ITS Digital Archive, USHMM.

56. Karl-Joseph Hummel and Christoph Kösters, *Zwangsarbeit und katholische Kirche 1939–1945: Geschichte und Erinnerung, Entschädigung und Versöhnung. Eine Dokumentation* (Paderborn: Verlag Ferdinand Schöningh, 2008), 338–39. The Transportflotte Speer was a private shipping business founded in 1941 as part of the effort of the Generalbauinspektor für die Reichshauptstadt Berlin (Inspector General of Building for the Reich Capital Berlin) to "organize its own transportation network for shipping on the extensive canal system through Germany." Paul B. Jaskot, *The Architecture of Oppression: The SS, Forced Labor and the Nazi Monumental Building Economy* (London: Routledge, 2000), 98.

57. Schroeder & Stadelmann was one of several local businesses that agreed only to hire members of the German Labor Front in September 1935. Seibert with Sommer, *Vom kurfürstlichen Ort zur grossen kreisangehörigen Stadt*, 156.

58. "Namentliche Liste der in Liste Ia aufgeführten Personen, Russland. Oberlahnstein, 27.4.1946," 2.1.3.1/70828216/ITS Digital Archive, USHMM.

59. The Niederlahnstein branch of Didier-Werke AG had closed in 1932 and reopened at the end of October 1936. In 1937, the workforce consisted of 175 persons. Seibert with Sommer, *Vom kurfürstlichen Ort zur grossen kreisangehörigen Stadt*, 155.

60. An unspecified number of Didier-Werke laborers were killed in an air raid on September 21, 1944. The company was targeted because of its role in arms manufacture. A significant portion of the factory was destroyed during one bomb attack on December 28,

and housed in a camp (*Lager*)[61] at least twenty Lithuanian *Zivilarbeiter*.[62] (See document 2.8.[63]) In one incident, on July 1942 at 8:45 p.m., "Weinheimer," the *Ortsbauernführer* (local farmers' leader)[64] for neighboring Horchheim, called "Moll," the field watchman (*Feldhüter*), to report a group of Lithuanian workers making their way toward the Lag neighborhood, bordering the Lahnstein forest. Weinheimer suspected they intended to steal food from the fields (*Felddieb-stähle*). Moll and a reserve police senior constable (*Polizei-Oberwachtmeister, Meister der Reserve/Pol.Oberw. Mstr.D.Res.*),[65] one "Pabel," bicycled as fast as their legs could take them toward the area to discover four men near a garden owned by a "Hoffeller." According to Moll's report, the men had been at the Didier-Werke for only a few weeks. Two potato plants had been plucked, and one of the workers had an empty leather satchel around his waist. The *Feldhüter* and Pabel returned the men to their foreman (*Meister*) at Didier-Werke, "Klein."[66] Weinheimer also asked a "Frau Bouillon" to call a police senior con-

---

1944, and another on January 29, 1945. Seibert with Sommer, *Vom kurfürstlichen Ort zur grossen kreisangehörigen Stadt*, 168, 172.

61. The camp was located on Markstrasse, one of the main thoroughfares in Niederlahnstein. Seibert with Sommer, *Vom kurfürstlichen Ort zur grossen kreisangehörigen Stadt*, 175.

62. "Liste der in unserem Betrieb beschäftigt gewesenen litauischen Staatsangehörigen, Didierwerke, Niederlahnstein," 2.1.3.1/70828195/ITS Digital Archive, USHMM. See also Lohse, "Landkreis Sankt Goarshausen."

63. "Meldung, Niederlahnstein, 20. Juli 1942," 2.1.3.1/70828194/ITS Digital Archive, USHMM.

64. Part of the structure of the Reich Agricultural Organization (Reichsnährstand), a cartel dealing with agricultural affairs that set price and production controls. The *Ortsbauern-führer* was responsible for overseeing day-to-day activities. See Tooze, *The Wages of Destruction*, 186–87.

65. Pabel held ranks within the Order Police (Ordnungspolizei, or Orpo) or regular police. When appointed chief of police in 1936, Heinrich Himmler divided the German police into two branches, each with its own office in Berlin: the Security Police (Sicherheitspolizei) and the Order Police (Ordnungspolizei). The infamous Secret State Police (Geheime Staatspolizei, or Gestapo) and the Criminal Police (Kriminalpolizei, or Kripo) were subordinate to the Security Police Main Office. Subordinate to the Order Police Main Office were the city/municipal police (Schutzpolizei, or Schupo), the rural police (Gendarmerie), and the local community police (Gemeindepolizei or Ortspolizei). Reservists were those born between 1901 and 1909. Christopher Browning, *Ordinary Men: Reserve Police Battalion 101 and the Final Solution in Poland* (New York: HarperCollins, 1992), 4–5.

66. According to reports, the four men were Alfons Bauzys, Johann Kardalis, Bronislaus Paszun, and Johann Ruksenhs. "Meldung, Niederlahnstein, 20. Juli 1942," 2.1.3.1/70828194/ITS Digital Archive, USHMM. The Didier-Werke camp on Markstrasse had a camp leader (*Lagerführer*) and a guard (*Wachmann*). Foreman (*Werkmeister*) Johann K[lein] was tasked with the former duty. Seibert with Sommer, *Vom kurfürstlichen Ort zur grossen kreisangehörigen Stadt*, 175.

stable (*Oberwachtmeister der Schutzpolizei des Reichs/O.Wachtm.d.Sch.d.R.*)[67] because of two additional Lithuanian *Zivilarbeiter*, Josef Bacelis and Hubert Schelenikas. Both were caught in Horchheim with full sacks of potatoes on the same evening at the same time. Ultimately, all six men received a warning from "Gehrke," a senior police officer (*Polizeihauptwachtmeister*) in the municipal police unit attached to the mayor's office (*Bürgermeister als Ortspolizeibehörde, Schutzpolizeidienstabteilung*). Gehrke determined that severe punishment would follow any further episodes and recommended that all Lithuanians employed at Didier-Werke be in their quarters one hour before the onset of darkness.[68]

In a second incident, a few days later on July 27, 1942, Lithuanian *Zivilarbeiter* Ksoveri Jasiulis and Franz Siomänas failed to report to work. One "Vierkrantz" of Didier-Werke wrote to the Niederlahnstein local police (*Ortspolizeibehörde*). He suspected that Jasiulis had gone to visit his brother and that Siomänas had fled with the intention of returning to Lithuania. In this document, one finds the first reference to a camp on the premises of Didier-Werke AG, when Vierkrantz notes, "After searching the camp, [we found] they had left behind their clothing."[69] Jasiulis's employment record book (*Arbeitsbuch für Ausländer*) indicates that his first day of work at Didier-Werke was March 21, 1942, and a postwar card tells us he was still employed there until March 16, 1945. Whether he returned voluntarily or, more likely, given his status, was forced to do so, we do not know.[70]

A third incident also involved two Lithuanian *Zivilarbeiter* who did not return from visits to their families. Didier-Werke requested the aid of the local police in contacting their hometowns to aid in the process of their recapture.[71]

---

67. The Schutzpolizei was a detachment of Order Police used during World War II for security, police, and antipartisan activities.

68. "Urschrift nebst Anlage dem Herrn Bürgermeister als O.P.B. (Ortspolizeibehörde) in Niederlahnstein, Der Landrat, Pol[.] 301, St. Goarshausen, 25. Juli 1942," 2.1.3.1/ 70828193/ITS Digital Archive, USHMM.

69. "Eigenmächtiges Verlassen der Arbeitsstelle durch litauische Zivilarbeiter," copy (*Abschrift*) of letter from J. A. Vierkrantz, Didier-Werke AG, Niederlahnstein, to the local police (*Ortspolizeibehörde*), Niederlahnstein, 27.7.42, 2.1.3.1/70828192/ITS Digital Archive, USHMM.

70. See photocopy of Jasiulis's employment record book for foreigners (*Arbeitsbuch für Ausländer*), 2.2.2.1/72725879/ITS Digital Archive, USHMM. There is no folder number, as the documents in 2.2.2.1 are organized by name. A card created postwar indicates he never gained the status of free worker (*Freier Arbeiter*). See photocopy of card for Jasiulis, 2.3.3.1/ 77549796/ITS Digital Archive, USHMM. There is no folder number as the documents in 2.3.3.1 are organized by name.

71. Letter, "Becker, Didier-Werke A.G. to Kreispolizeibehörde St. Goarshausen/Rhein, weitergereicht durch die Ortspolizeibehörde Niederlahnstein, 2.8.43," 2.1.3.1/70828191/ ITS Digital Archive, USHMM.

Lohse writes about a fourth and final incident, described in a February 6, 1944, report by Fa. Farbwerk Schroeder & Stadelmann AG to the Niederlahnstein local police concerning "Lithuanian *Ostarbeiter*" visiting the women's work camp (*Ostarbeiterinnenlager*) who refused to leave when requested to do so by the camp's guard (*Wachmann*). When the guard called a supervisor (*Meister*) to the scene, the men ran away. Two, Hubert Walkutier and the aforementioned Siomänas, both employed at Didier-Werke, hid. Upon their discovery, their identity papers (*Ausweispapiere*) were confiscated, and they were ultimately fined three Reichsmark apiece.[72]

If caught begging in public, refusing to work (*Arbeitsverweigerung*), or failing to have proper identification on their person, among other offenses, the foreign forced laborers in Ober- and Niederlahnstein found themselves subject to arrest and incarceration. Niederlahnstein held the distinction of maintaining one of four court prisons in Higher Regional Court District Ten, *Oberlandesgericht* Frankfurt am Main,[73] which formed part of and came under the control of the nazified Reich Justice Ministry (RJM).[74] The RJM[75] also oversaw the deployment of prisoners for work, including those incarcerated in *Gerichtsgefängnis* Niederlahnstein. (See document 2.9.[76]) One 1944 report notes that the three male prisoners incarcerated there were impressed into

---

72. Letter, "Farbwerke Schroeder & Stadelmann Aktiengesellschaft an die Ortspolizei, Niederlahnstein, 7 Februar 1944," 2.1.3.1/70828190/ITS Digital Archive, USHMM. See also Lohse, "Landkreis Sankt Goarshausen."

73. "Verzeichnis über die offenen Gerichtsgefängnisse der Reichsjustizverwaltung mit einer Belegfähigkeit unter 50 Köpfen," 1.2.2.0/82159800/ITS Digital Archive, USHMM. The other three were located in Höhr-Grenzhausen, Limburg/Lahn, and Usingen (Taunus). This document is a photocopy from the German Federal Archive (Bundesarchiv) received by ITS in 1970.

74. Ibid., 82159796.

75. The German justice system became so compromised that it was subject to trial after World War II (*United States of America v. Josef Altstoetter et al.*, "The Justice Case"). All courts were subordinated to the Reich Justice Ministry in 1935. See, among others, Ingo Müller, *Hitler's Justice: The Courts of the Third Reich* (Cambridge, MA: Harvard University Press, 1991); Michael Stolleis, *Recht im Unrecht: Studien zur Rechtsgeschichte des Nationalsozialismus* (Frankfurt am Main: Suhrkamp, 1994); Michael Stolleis, *The Law under the Swastika: Studies on Legal History in Nazi Germany* (Chicago: University of Chicago Press, 1998).

76. "Generalstaatsanwalt, Frankfurt-Main, an den Herrn Reichsminister der Justiz, Dresden, 24 Juli 1944,"1.2.2.0/82158434/ITS Digital Archive, USHMM. This document is a photocopy from the German Federal Archive (Bundesarchiv) received by ITS in 1970.

reprocessing iron clasps for "the corporation C.[S.] Schmidt.[77] This task is quite important to the wartime economy."[78]

We know much about arrest and imprisonment in *Gerichtsgefängnis* Niederlahnstein thanks to a thirty-eight-page document in the ITS holdings listing 244 Croatian, Czech, Lithuanian, Polish, Romanian, Russian, Ukrainian, and Yugoslav laborers incarcerated there between 1941 and 1945.[79] (See document 2.10.[80]) The document lists first and last name, date and place of birth, nationality, status (e.g., *Landwirtschaftlicher Arbeiter, Ostarbeiter*), reason for arrest (in some but not all cases), dates of imprisonment, prisoner category, referring authority (e.g., Amtsgericht, Kriminalpolizei, Bahnpolizei, Gestapo, among many others), and subsequent fate (e.g., released, transferred, location of transfer, etc.). What might seem on its face a simple list could yield statistical analyses to determine patterns and changes over time, depending on the questions the researcher asks. How many men were arrested? How many women? Which nationalities were arrested most or least frequently? What grounds for arrest were most prominent? Were some nationalities more likely to be released versus

---

77. The corporation C. S. Schmidt, small family-run businesses, and larger firms engaged in the use of forced labor *not* to be found in ITS include Rheinisch-Nassauische Lagerei und Spedition; the army grain provisioning office (*Heeresverpflegungsamt*); the forestry office (*Forstamt*) Lahnstein on Emserlandstrasse 8; the city government (*Stadtverwaltung*) of Niederlahnstein; farmer (*Landwirt*) Josef Schimmel on Emserstrasse 34; Heinrich Dehe and Johann Schmitz on Holzgasse 2; merchant (*Händler*) Nikolaus Dommermuth on Emserlandstrasse 3; Johann Ems on Emserstrasse 21; Georg Herbel on Brückenstrasse 3; the baker Heinrich Dötsch on Emserstrasse; Heinrich Daniel on Emserstrasse 15; the bakery of Wilhelm Kretzer on Brückenstrasse 7; the book shop Hans Staudt on Bahnhofstrasse 5; the butcher Josef Moos on Brückenstrasse 4; Franz Schmidt on Emserstrasse 30; shoemaker Josef Meurer on Emserstrasse 14; Franz Hoffmann on Sauergasse 6; and the Jakob Schönberger engineering works (*Maschinenfabrik*), also with its own *Ostarbeiterlager* on Koblenzer Strasse, near that run by the wire works company (*Drahtwerke*) C. S. Schmidt. In Seibert with Sommer, *Vom kurfürstlichen Ort zur grossen kreisangehörigen Stadt*, 175, citing a lecture (*Vortragsmanuskript*) by Hans Steil, *Vor fünfzig Jahren. Lahnstein erlebte den totalen Luftkrieg* (Lahnstein, 1994), 9–19.

78. "Generalstaatsanwalt, Frankfurt-Main, an den Herrn Reichsminister der Justiz, Dresden, 24 Juli 1944," 1.2.2.0/82158434/ITS Digital Archive, USHMM.

79. "Gerichtsgefängnis Niederlahnstein," 1.2.2.1/11369841–78/ITS Digital Archive, USHMM. Niederlahnstein's *Amtsgerichtgefängnis* under discussion here is not to be confused with its police prison (*Polizeigefängnis*). For the role of prisons in the Nazi state, see Nikolaus Wachsmann, *Hitler's Prisons: Legal Terror in Nazi Germany* (New Haven, CT: Yale University Press, 2004).

80. Romanians incarcerated in the Niederlahnstein Court Prison, 1943. "Niederlahnstein Court Prison," 1.2.2.1/11369856/ITS Digital Archive, USHMM.

transferred to a new and often harsher location of punishment? Did specific months or years yield greater or lesser numbers of arrests, and if so, why? Were the Jews of Ober- and Niederlahnstein incarcerated and abused there?[81] These are just some of the questions a document like this one allows researchers to explore.

One of the least documented aspects of the hybrid population and range of persecution in wartime Ober- and Niederlahnstein is that of POW labor detachments (DTs, *Arbeitskommandos*) there. A document created by International Committee of the Red Cross (ICRC) authorities after the war, located in the ITS holdings,[82] includes lists of labor detachments, including DT 872 from Stalag[83] XII A (Limburg/Lahn) in Oberlahnstein[84] and DT 1040 from Stalag XII D (Trier) in Niederlahnstein.[85] (See document 2.11.[86]) Who were the men in these detachments? Where were they from? Where did they work, and what kind of work did they do? Very little secondary literature exists on these POW labor detachments. The only available secondary source reveals that the labor office in Niederlahnstein had already requested the first eight hundred POWs in October 1939 and that on December 18, 1940, the aforementioned Drahtwerke C. S. Schmidt[87] received its first contingent of French POWs from Stalag XII A. The men were required to live in camps, usually guarded by Wehrmacht soldiers. The aforementioned camp in the Johanneskloster was established in July 1940, and by 1942 at least seven camps for POW *Arbeitskommandos* existed in Oberlahnstein.[88] We do not know the total number of POWs used for forced labor

---

81. This was the case, though further research is required. See Melanie Wehr et al., "Zentrale Stelle der Landesjustizverwaltungen B 162 (Teilfindbuch)," Ludwigsburg 2012, 20, for a reference to file 14264, "Misshandlungen jüdischer Häftlinge im Gerichtsgefängnis Niederlahnstein."

82. "Liste III," 2.2.5.3/82363711/ITS Digital Archive, USHMM. This document is a cover sheet created by ITS staff. No date is given.

83. Stalags XII A and XII D were in Wehrmacht (army) district (*Wehrkreis*) 12 (Wiesbaden). "Stalag" is an abbreviation *Stammlager* (base camp). See "Former DW Installations in the U.S. Zone of Germany," 2.2.5.1/82362700/ITS Digital Archive, USHMM.

84. "Stalag XII A," 2.2.5.3/82363781/ITS Digital Archive, USHMM.

85. "Stalag XII D," 2.2.5.3/82363784/ITS Digital Archive, USHMM.

86. "Stalag XII A," 2.2.5.3/82363781/ITS Digital Archive, USHMM.

87. In July 1942, Soviet forced laborers joined their French counterparts. The firm kept its own camp on Koblenzer Strasse. Drahtwerke C. S. Schmidt engaged in armaments manufacture during the war and thus was a target of the 8th US Air Force attack on Niederlahnstein on January 29, 1945. Seibert with Sommer, *Vom kurfürstlichen Ort zur grossen kreisangehörigen Stadt*, 153, 168, 172, 175.

88. A remarkable number; these include Camp 871, run by the Reichsbahn (National Railway) with 120 French POWs; Camp 873, run by Feldmühle AG, with 90 French POWs;

in these camps. Documents in the ITS holdings can also tell us about Allied soldiers who did not survive to be captured. Between April 14 and 18, 1945, for example, several American pilots were shot down or crashed over Oberlahnstein. Only one, infantryman Henry W. Schriefer, could be identified.[89]

We encounter fewer difficulties tracing sources on the Niederlahnstein transit camp for DPs. Despite the recent increase in research on DP camps, those in the French Zone are still understudied. Thus little can be found in secondary sources about the Niederlahnstein camp,[90] located in the town's former army barracks, the Deines-Bruchmüller Kaserne at Hermsdorferstrasse 2,[91] just west of the Lag where Weinheimer, Pabel, and Moll had so successfully prevented the attempted potato theft. A June 1945 United Nations Relief and Rehabilitation Administration (UNRRA) report lists "4,200 Poles and 3,400 Italians" in the camp and states that the Italians were to be repatriated by the end of the summer. It notes that the camp consisted of "German barracks considerably damaged by bombardment," with a functioning sewage system and good water supply. "The camp is overcrowded but will accommodate the 4,200 Poles in winter when the Italians are evacuated." Milk and petrol were not available, and other supplies were "delivered irregularly since the French took over the area," with shortages in "soap, all welfare supplies, clothing, and shoes." Medical services are described as "well organized," and patients were treated in the French-

---

Camp 874, run by the Bollinger chemical factory, with 35 French POWs; and Camp 1103, run by Schroeder & Stadelmann, with 17 French POWs. The labor detachments/camps appear to be numbered in sequence (871, ITS referenced 872, 873, 874, presumably from Stalag XII A/Limburg). Seibert with Sommer, *Vom kurfürstlichen Ort zur grossen kreisangehörigen Stadt*, 174–76.

89. "Sterbeurkunde Nrs. 64–67," 2.2.2.9/77165238–41/ITS Digital Archive, USHMM. These documents are original to ITS.

90. The few exceptions include Julia Maspero, "French Policy on Postwar Migration of Eastern European Jews through France and the French Occupation Zones in Germany and Austria," *Jewish History Quarterly* no. 2 (June 2013); Petra Weiss, "Die Koblenzer Lager für Displaced Persons, 1945–1947," *Jahrbuch für westdeutsche Landesgeschichte* no. 29 (2003): 467–507. Other sources include the *Biuletyn Obozu Polskiego w Niederlahnstein* (Bulletin of the Polish camp in Niederlahnstein) and *Pobudka: Informacyjne pismo tygodniowe* (Niederlahnstein weekly news magazine, 1945).

91. Petra Weiss, "Eine Kaserne als Wartesaal: Displaced Persons in der Horchheimer Gneisenau-Kaserne," *Kirmes: Das Horchheimer Magazin* (2005). The barracks were constructed for Wehrmacht use in 1938 and still exist today, operated by the Bundeswehr. While used as a DP camp, it formed one of three former army-barracks-turned-DP camps in the Koblenz area, the other two being the Augusta-Kaserne in Koblenz-Pfaffendorf and the Gneisenau-Kaserne in der Horchheimer Höhe (Alte Heerstrasse 149).

run hospital in Oberlahnstein.[92] The camp had a school, a Boy Scouts club, and dances and concerts. "The Poles in the camp," notes the report, "are well organized and fairly contented."[93]

French authorities and the UNRRA reorganized the Niederlahnstein camp to "make space" for Jewish DPs in late 1946, sending most of the Polish occupants to another camp in mid-November. Julia Maspero writes, "French authorities transferred 500 Jewish DPs from Calw (Baden-Württemberg) to Niederlahnstein at the beginning of December," where they "had to live next to the remaining 300 Polish DPs." According to Maspero, no other Jews were ever sent to the Niederlahnstein DP camp, and the Jewish DPs sent from Calw "did not stay long in Niederlahnstein: on January 8, 1947, 495 Jews were in the camp; a few days later, only 80 remained." Maspero continues, "Others disappeared during the night and are believed to have fled to the US zone. By April 1947, all Jews had left the camp."[94]

ITS-held documents offer some additional clues. French administrative records referencing the Niederlahnstein camp are scattered throughout various subcollections.[95] Hundreds of pages list DPs (of various nationalities) in the Niederlahnstein transit camp between December 1947 and 1951.[96] Though

---

92. Note that ITS contains French Zone hospital files, searchable only by name, in 2.1.3.2 (Hospital Files, French Zone).

93. This report can be found in HA6B-2/1 and HA5–4/5 (S-0436–0059, S-0425–007, and PDR6_493), Wiener Library for the Study of the Holocaust and Genocide, London. See also document collection 1407 (Jewish Relief Unit: Personnel Files, 1940s–1950s), Item 1407/9, reports by Dixi Heim, Jewish Relief Unit, UNRRA Team 48, Becherhöll, Niederlahnstein, Wiener Library, www.wienerlibrary.co.uk/Search-document-collection?item = 14 (accessed September 25, 2015).

94. Maspero, "French Policy on Postwar Migration of Eastern European Jews." These five hundred DPs had "illegally entered from the American zone into the French zone in Austria, and were later moved by French authorities from Bregenz to Calw." See the entry for Niederlahnstein in Angelika Königseder and Juliane Wetzel, *Waiting for Hope: Jewish Displaced Persons in Post–World War II Germany* (Evanston, IL: Northwestern University Press, 2001), 255, which notes that it is in the northern district and had a kibbutz; the entry lists the number of Jewish camp residents as only thirty-five on February 28, 1947, eight on May 31, 1947, and zero as of July 30, 1947.

95. "L'attaché d'administration de Fontenailles, Officier des Recherches, Subdivision de Coblence, à Monsieur le Chef Régional des Recherches Rhénie-Hesse-Nassau. Niederlahnstein, 12 Novembre 1946," 1.1.29.0/82127438; "Certificat Réservé aux 'Cas de Détresse,' Transit Niederlahnstein, 4 août 1949," 3.1.1.0/82384626; Station Lists, UNRRA Assembly Centers, May–December 1946, 3.1.1.0/82383124, 82383195, 82383225, 82383249 and 82383254/ITS Digital Archive, USHMM.

96. "DP Listen Niederlahnstein," 3.1.1.2/82020169–520/ITS Digital Archive, USHMM.

predominantly from Poland, they also came from Belgium, Bulgaria, Czechoslovakia, Ecuador, France, Germany, Holland, Hungary, Iran, Italy, Latvia, Lithuania, Luxembourg, Norway, Romania, the Soviet Union, Spain, Turkey, and Yugoslavia; of course, many were "stateless." A portion of these individuals were presumably Jewish.[97] We should not, however, assume that these lists capture everyone and every nationality that passed through this camp. Individual DPs residing in the Niederlahnstein camp can be found in the so-called DP-2 card file.[98] One undated document lists 964 Polish DPs living in Niederlahnstein.[99] ITS holdings include a list of 123 Catholic, Protestant, and Orthodox DPs claiming experience in agricultural work, from Bulgaria, Czechoslovakia, Hungary, Lithuania, Poland, Romania, Ukraine, and Yugoslavia (as well as some "stateless"), who emigrated from the Niederlahnstein transit camp to Brazil in two waves, on December 20, 1948, and January 14, 1949.[100] A researcher might analyze these files to determine what kind of profile was required for success in emigrating to Brazil with regard to gender, age, marital status, occupation, and religion—all categories included in these detailed lists. Care and maintenance (CM/1) forms indicate that Jewish DPs continued, if briefly, to enter the camp in its transit capacity in 1948 and 1949.[101]

The ITS holdings contain nearly eight hundred "forms of application for [International Refugee Organization (IRO)] assistance" (the above-mentioned CM/1 forms) originating in Germany from applicants currently in the Niederlahnstein transit camp, including applicants identifying themselves as Jewish. IRO "screeners" were "tasked with identifying and purging war criminals, collaborators and ethnic Germans (*Volksdeutsche*), all of whom were excluded from the DP community."[102] Thus, a doctoral student examining all CM/1 applications forms is likely to find, in aggregate, the entire range of behaviors and roles

---

97. Ibid.

98. DP-2 card file, 3.1.1.1/ITS Digital Archive, USHMM. This subcollection is currently searchable by name only.

99. "Délégation supérieure de la Sarre, avis de mutation semaine des personnes déplacées," 2.1.3.1/70828114–31/ITS Digital Archive, USHMM.

100. "Niederlahnstein," 3.1.3.2/81769689–725/ITS Digital Archive, USHMM. DPs continued to emigrate to Brazil or be repatriated to their home countries via the Niederlahnstein transit camp. See 2.2.0.1/82423281 and 82423283/ITS Digital Archive, USHMM.

101. CM/1 forms for Ukrainian-Polish Jew Gerald Löw-Drutjanow and Romanian Jew Mendel Soifer (Sojfer), 3.2.1.1/79420033–7 and 79735220–2/ITS Digital Archive, USHMM.

102. Ruth Balint, "The Use and Abuse of History: Displaced Persons in the ITS Archive" (paper presented at the "International Tracing Service Collections and Holocaust Scholarship" conference, USHMM, Washington, DC, May 12–13, 2014).

that victims, aggressors, and beneficiaries played across Europe, concentrated
and living side by side, for a few short days, months, or years, in Deines-
Bruchmüller Kaserne at Hermsdorferstrasse 2.

Two examples will suffice here. The first concerns the Polish Catholic Halas
family: Zygmunt, age thirty-one, Antonia, age twenty-five, and Zygmunt Jr., age
two. (See document 2.12.[103]) The form recommending them for employment
includes a charming picture of a healthy-looking and well-dressed family. We
learn that Zygmunt Halas was deported to Germany for forced labor in 1940,
where he worked on various farms. He became an inmate in the Niederlahnstein
DP camp in 1945 and a camp guard in 1946. Beginning in 1947, he held a
series of jobs in Koblenz, in a sawmill, then in a quarry, and finally in construction. All of his postwar employers provided good references. French Zone IRO
officials filling out the form in 1950 noted the family "may be recommended
from all points of view. Very neat and tidy. The husband is conscientious and
fond of work and is bringing up his family in a correct and worthy manner.
Will give satisfaction to employers. Highly recommendable."[104]

Next there is the case of Kálmán Abay, born in 1899 in Pécs, Hungary.[105]
He was a colonel in the Hungarian gendarmerie, a "military-style" body that
served the 1919–1944 Miklós Horthy regime "unconditionally" and "maintain[ed] internal order." Contemporary research confirms that recruits were
carefully selected. Training emphasized a "militant, anticommunist worldview"
and "reinforced prejudices against Jews and others." Tellingly, after Germany
occupied Hungary in March 1944, the Nazi regime "saw no need to cleanse the
organization": no district commanders were purged. "Thousands of survivors'
eyewitness accounts mention the gendarmes' brutality"; gendarmes werè "notorious" for "beating Jews during the ghettoization and deportations" of Hungarian Jewry, alongside other cruelties.[106]

The ugly role of the Hungarian gendarmerie in what we today call the
Holocaust was no secret after war's end; otherwise Abay's interviewer and IRO
screener,[107] fellow Hungarian and former Hungarian army officer Alexander

103. CM/1 form for Zygmunt Halas, 3.2.1.4/80998233/ITS Digital Archive, USHMM.
104. Ibid., 80998231–41. The comments of the IRO officer appear to have been translated from the original German, though the name of the commentator is not included.
105. CM/1 form for Kálmán Abay, 3.2.1.1/78861851–63/ITS Digital Archive,
USHMM.
106. Zoltán Vági, László Csősz, and Gábor Kádár, *The Holocaust in Hungary: Evolution
of a Genocide* (Lanham, MD: Alta Mira Press in association with USHMM, 2013), lvii.
107. For a detailed explanation of the process of obtaining necessary IRO documentation
for migration, including the interview process at IRO resettlement centers that followed
completion of the CM/1 form and other required initial documentation, see Louise W.

(Sándor) Pásztor,[108] would not have felt the need to write the following in his September 8, 1951, report: "He [Abay] had nothing to do with Jewish cases." On the basis of this statement presumably, Abay's form bore the official stamp of US Zone eligibility officer Wilhelmis Reinders,[109] declaring the recipient as "within the mandate of IRO [and] eligible for resettlement services."[110] Interned by the US Army after Axis defeat and investigated for alleged war crimes for a year and half, Abay had been released from US Army custody without charge in May 1947.[111] And so he came to the French Zone and worked as a locksmith.[112] In December 1947, he was transferred from the Ehrenbreitstein facility in Koblenz to the Niederlahnstein facility, where he filed an application for assistance requesting emigration to Argentina, Canada, or Brazil, in order of preference.[113] He moved on to the American Zone and settled in Munich, acquiring a wife, Erzsébet, and a mother-in-law, also named Erzsébet.[114] The new family filed again for emigration in 1949, this time with Canada as the preferred desti-

---

Holborn, *The International Refugee Organization: A Specialized Agency of the United Nations. Its History and Work, 1946–1952* (Oxford: Oxford University Press, 1956).

108. Pásztor, born in 1902 in Košice, was a Protestant salesman working in Košice (Kassa) and Budapest until 1944. Fluent in Hungarian, German, English, and Slovak, with some skills in French, after the war he applied for a translation license. He worked for the IRO as an interviewer in Augsburg from March 1948 to January 1951. In an amendment dated August 1951, he acknowledged his role in the Hungarian army, writing, "I concealed my military service because I could not have got[ten] my job with [the] IRO if I had told [them] of my military service at that time (March 1948)." CM/1 form for Alexander-Sandor Pásztor, 3.2.1.1/79570204–7/ITS Digital Archive, USHMM. We learn more about Pásztor's wartime military service in the Hungarian army in Vrútky, Slovakia (December 1944 to January 1945), his promotion to lieutenant when stationed in Diószeg (January 1945 to March 1945), and his move to Munich in 1951 from his tracing and documentation file (6.3.3.2/99109083–91/ITS Digital Archive, USHMM). He emigrated to the United States from Munich in 1957, sponsored by the National Catholic Welfare Conference (3.1.1.1/68539953–4/ITS Digital Archive, USHMM). Many IRO interviewers were displaced persons themselves, with their own records in ITS. We see from this case the added dimension and richness of the backgrounds of the interviewers.

109. A photograph of Wilhelmis Reinders can be found in the Yad Vashem Photo Archive, Item #45421, Archival Signature #7908, Album #FA 378/3. We do not have further information about him.

110. CM/1 form for Kálmán Abay, 3.2.1.1/78861855/ITS Digital Archive, USHMM.

111. Ibid.

112. Ibid., 78861854.

113. Ibid., 78861852.

114. Ibid., 78861851 and 78861856–7.

nation[115] and, as a Roman Catholic family, with the backing of the National Catholic Welfare Conference.[116]

Sam Moskowitz, vice consul in the consular suboffice of the Funkkaserne DP facility in Munich, remained suspicious. Writing to Charles T. Snively, senior officer, US Displaced Persons Commission in August 1951, he noted,

> It appears from the consular interview that the applicant was a colonel in the Hungarian gendarmerie and was at one time wanted as a war criminal. His account of his activities as a gendarmerie officer is inconclusive, and his only documentation on the war crimes charge is a release from a prisoner of war camp. [I] request that [the] case be reinvestigated by the [US Counter-intelligence Corps] on [the] 'war crimes' matter [. . .] and that the case be returned to the IRO for [an] eligibility check. If eligibility is confirmed, [the] letter should state that [the] applicant's service and high rank in the Hungarian gendarmerie, an organization known to have persecuted minorities, have been considered.[117]

Moskowitz's concerns were considered and discarded by the aforementioned Pásztor in Abay's resulting follow-up interview on September 8, 1951. (See document 2.13.[118]) Pásztor's notes confirm what Abay had already acknowledged on his own when filling out his IRO care and maintenance form back in 1947: Abay was a gendarme officer and promoted to the rank of colonel on November 1, 1944, two weeks after the establishment of the Nazi-oriented Arrow Cross (Ferenc Szálasi) regime.[119] Abay denied the implications of this time line, claiming that his promotion "had [already] been prepared by the

---

115. Ibid., 78861854.

116. Memorandum from Sam Moskowitz, vice consul, consular suboffice, Funkkaserne, to Charles T. Snively, senior officer, US Displaced Persons Commission, dated August 27, 1951. Ibid., 78861858.

117. Ibid.

118. Ibid., 78861855.

119. Former army major Ferenc Szálasi established the Hungarian National Socialist Party, the Arrow Cross, in 1937. On October 15, 1944, after unsuccessfully attempting to pull out of Hungary's alliance with Germany, Hungarian regent Miklós Horthy was forced to resign and transfer power to Szálasi and the Arrow Cross Party. Vági, Csősz, and Kádár, *The Holocaust in Hungary*, 147–48.

Horthy regime[120] in July/August 1944 and it was a normal promotion, not an extra-ordinary one."[121] Abay claimed that "he was an expert in personnel and disciplinary cases," had "nothing to do with Jewish cases," and "was not a member of any [political] party." And so Pásztor—and, on the basis of Pásztor's notes, Reinders—deemed Abay eligible for emigration. "There are no proofs and no signs that he is a war criminal—his service during the war cannot be regarded as voluntary," wrote Pásztor.[122]

Materials from the Historical Archives of the Hungarian State Security Office confirm that Kálmán Abay was indeed an officer of personnel and disciplinary cases, as he claimed in his CM/1 form. In 1944, he served in Gendarmerie Department XX in the Ministry of Defense. He was not a party member, as any party membership was forbidden to officers, but he was a staunch Arrow Cross loyalist, as witnessed by party documents. He even took part in the preparations for the Arrow Cross takeover in October 1944. His promotion might have been a regular one, but he was a clear supporter of the rabidly antisemitic and murderous Arrow Cross regime. No evidence of his direct involvement in the persecution of Jews has been uncovered.[123]

What do such documents tell us about day-to-day life in Nazi Germany in a small town that one can easily traverse on foot in under two hours? In the Lahnstein case, documents in the ITS holdings demonstrate how Nazi ideology and economic practice permeated the entire social fabric and economy of this tiny town. Lahnstein's Jews, part of the town's history for centuries, were put to slave labor in a mining facility before they were deported east; one returned. The local abbey became a POW camp. Prisoners of war and forced laborers performed work for entities ranging from the town's ceramic factory to the Berlin-based Transportflotte Speer, sending stones to create monumental buildings for the thousand-year Reich. Small businesses—the bakery of Wilhelm Kretzer at Brückenstrasse 7, the bookshop of Hans Staudt at Bahnhofstrasse 5, the establishments of butcher Josef Moos at Brückenstrasse 4 and shoemaker

---

120. Miklós Horthy (1858–1957) was regent of Hungary from 1919 until his arrest by the Nazis in October 1944.

121. CM/1 form for Kálmán Abay, 3.2.1.1/78861855/ITS Digital Archive, USHMM.

122. Ibid.

123. Historical Archives of the Hungarian State Security, file no. V-130.792, case of Gendarme Colonel István Láday, a state secretary in the Arrow Cross Ministry of the Interior. Quoted by András Zoltán Kovács, "A Szálasi-kormány belügyminisztériuma [The Ministry of the Interior of the Szálasi government]" (PhD diss., University of Pécs, 2008), 202.

Josef Meurer at Emserstrasse 14—used one, two, or three forced laborers. A visible and ubiquitous part of the town's wartime daily life, these workers died of causes ranging from malnutrition to drowning to giving birth in inadequate facilities. The local population was quick to report a stolen potato despite knowing that doing so might land the thief in jail for punishment as the war dragged on. Local cemeteries hold mass graves for Russian and Polish *Ostarbeiter* killed in air attacks because they were forced to perform labor in dangerous areas. Accounts of the treatment of the centuries-old Jewish community in Ober- and Niederlahnstein, beginning in 1933 and culminating in its total destruction, are violent and heartbreaking.[124]

In the immediate postwar years, victims of the Nazi and Axis powers lived in agonizingly close proximity to supporters of these regimes, forced by circumstance to share space and scarce resources. St. John's Abbey shed its brief role as home to POWs to become a home for orphaned children by 1950,[125] before returning again to its function as a place of worship. Today, one can marry, baptize children, celebrate mass, or light candles in prayer for deceased loved ones there. Oberlahnstein's former synagogue never reopened. The history described here is hardly evident to the naked eye in Lahnstein today. A small local Catholic charitable body, Kolpingfamilie Lahnstein St. Barbara, initiated the first *Stolperstein*, or "stumbling stone," in memory of murdered Lahnstein Jews in the summer of 2012.[126] Not a single Jew lives in Lahnstein as of this printing. Not one. One must wonder, then, how Lahnstein once again became the idyllic and captivating place that so fired Victor Hugo's imagination, and my own.

DOCUMENT LIST

DOCUMENT 2.1. Prisoner account record with record of money order from Emmy Eichberg to Paul Wertheim and Josef Eichberg, 1.1.5.3/5812934/

---

124. Hubertus Seibert, "Duldung-Integration-Vernichtung-Erinnerung: Juden in Lahnstein," in Seibert with Sommer, *Vom kurfürstlichen Ort zur grossen kreisangehörigen Stadt*, 719–52.

125. 3.3.1.1/82287868/ITS Digital Archive, USHMM.

126. In 2013, the Lahnsteiner Altertumsverein carried out a yearlong program commemorating the seventy-fifth anniversary of Reichskristallnacht. The program, titled "Rheinisches Judentum," consisted of a lecture series on Jewish life and culture in the Rhineland and excursions to former Jewish sites of worship and persecution. See "Jahresprogramm 2013," Lahnsteiner Altertumsverein, www.lahnsteiner-altertumsverein.de/jahresprogramm-2013 .html (accessed May 4, 2014). On the Lahnstein *Stolpersteine* program, see www.lahnsteiner -altertumsverein.de/lahnstein.html and www.kolping-lahnstein.de/pdf/stolpersteineflyer.pdf (accessed May 4, 2014).

ITS Digital Archive, USHMM. Copy from Berlin Document Center received by ITS in 1993.

DOCUMENT 2.2. "Transport to the Auschwitz Concentration Camp on August 14, 1942/Train from Drancy Departing on August 14, 1942," p. Dukes, Friedrich, through Eisemann, Samuel, 1.1.9.9/11188105/ITS Digital Archive, USHMM. Postwar compilation.

DOCUMENT 2.3. CNI card for Emil Baer, 0.1/14598352/ITS Digital Archive, USHMM.

DOCUMENT 2.4. "Documents in Criminal Matters for the Sachsenhausen Concentration Camp Trials, Indictment, Copy: The Senior Public Prosecutor for the Regional Court to the Regional Court in Düsseldorf, June 12, 1959," 5.1/82298844/ITS Digital Archive, USHMM. (followed by translation).

DOCUMENT 2.5. Niederlahnstein Cemetery map including graves of French, Dutch, Polish, Russian, and Italian citizens, 5.3.5/101105363/ITS Digital Archive, USHMM. No date provided.

DOCUMENT 2.6. "Certified Copy from the Death Register of the Bureau of Vital Statistics in Kamp (Rhine)," 2.2.0.1/82447342/ITS Digital Archive, USHMM (followed by translation).

DOCUMENT 2.7. "Inquiry into the Whereabouts of Civilian and Military Members of the United [Allied] Nations (Italy), the Mayor, Dept. IV, Oberlahnstein, April 18, 1946," 2.1.3.1/70828180/ITS Digital Archive, USHMM.

DOCUMENT 2.8. "Report, Niederlahnstein, July 20, 1942," 2.1.3.1/ 70828194/ITS Digital Archive, USHMM (followed by translation).

DOCUMENT 2.9. "The Prosecutor-General, Frankfurt-Main, to the Reich Minister of Justice, Dresden, July 24, 1944," 1.2.2.0/82158434/ITS Digital Archive, USHMM (followed by translation).

DOCUMENT 2.10. Romanians incarcerated in the Niederlahnstein Court Prison, 1943. "Niederlahnstein Court Prison," 1.2.2.1/11369856/ITS Digital Archive, USHMM (followed by translation).

DOCUMENT 2.11. "Stalag XII A," 2.2.5.3/82363781/ITS Digital Archive, USHMM.

DOCUMENT 2.12. CM/1 form for Zygmunt Halas, 3.2.1.4/80998233/ITS Digital Archive, USHMM.

DOCUMENT 2.13. Handwritten interview notes, September 8, 1951, found in CM/1 form for Kálmán Abay, 3.2.1.1/78861855/ITS Digital Archive, USHMM (followed by transcription).

DOCUMENTS

DOCUMENT 2.1*

*Numbers 1 through 10 added for translation purposes.

1. **K.L. Buchenwald**: Buchenwald Concentration Camp
2. **First and last name**: Eichberg, Josef
3. **Prisoner number**: 26.207
4. **Date and place of birth**: May 10, 1889, in Niederlahnstein
5. **Transportation expenses**: [blank]
6. **Date**: December 3, 1938
7. **Received**: 60 RM [*Reichsmark*], 0 Rpf [*Reichspfennig*]
8. **Withdrawn**: 0 RM, 0 Rpf
9. **Assets**: 60 RM, 0 Rpf
10. **Brought forward**: [blank]

DOCUMENT 2.2

```
                                              132

    DUKES  FRIEDRICH                    VIENNE
    3 10 91

    DURLACHER  ELISA
    2 03 96

    DURLACHER  HERMANN                  MUNZESCHEIM
    12 08 93

    DZICK  ACHILLE                      PARIS
    17 06 31        10 PASSAGE DE ROUCE PARIS

    DZICK  GELA  FRIDMAN                KALUSZYN
           92    10 PASSAGE DE ROUCE PARIS

    DZICK  WACHIM                       KOLUSZYN
    25 01 90        10 PASSAGE DE ROUCE PARIS

    DZIZA  BERWA                        OFFENBACH
    9 09 97

    EBERD  CHAIM                        JASLOWIEC
    11 08 11

    ECKHAUS  KARL                       WASLEW
    30 03 92

    EHRENTHAL  KARL  16 avenue Roger Bonyelled.  VIENNE
    10 08 99

    EHRLICH  ALFRED                     ARNSTADT
    28 12 89

    EHRLICH  MAX  3 rue Amelot Paris 11°.  WIEDERSCHBACH
    12 06 84

    EICHBERG  JOSEPH                    NIEDERLAHNSTEIN
    10 05 89

    EICHBERG  EMMY LEWALD
    12 03 99

    EIFFELER  FRITZ                     MECHERLINCH
    1 07 05

    EINSTEIN  HILDE
    22 09 94

    EINTRACHT  TONY
    18 08 94

    EISEMANN  SAMUEL                    BINAU
    30 01 80
```

DOCUMENT 2.3*

BA - 1014

```
     1 B A E R, Emil Israel              196 837

                    -                        -

     2 12./17.4.1876    Oberlahnstein         -



     3 vermutl. i.KZ Sachsenhausen inhaft.
     4 Jan.1945   vermutl. umgekommen



     5 Staatsanwaltschaft b.Landgericht München        mi.
       8.6.67
                    File 209.372               30.6.67
```

1. **First and last name**: Baer, Emil Israel; **T/D file number**: 196 837
2. **Date and place of birth**: April 12/17, 1876, in Oberlahnstein
3. **Fate**: presumably incarcerated in the Sachsenhausen concentration camp
4. Jan. 1945   presumably perished
5. **Inquiring source**: Public Prosecutor's Office, Munich Regional Court

*Numbers 1 through 5 added for translation purposes.

DOCUMENT 2.4

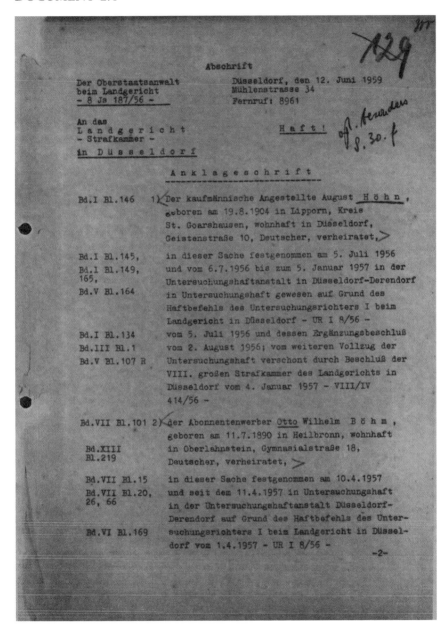

Abschrift

Der Oberstaatsanwalt
beim Landgericht
- 8 Js 187/56 -

Düsseldorf, den 12. Juni 1959
Mühlenstrasse 34
Fernruf: 8961

An das
L a n d g e r i c h t
- Strafkammer -
in D ü s s e l d o r f

H a f t !

A n k l a g e s c h r i f t

Bd.I Bl.146   1) Der kaufmännische Angestellte August H ö h n ,
               geboren am 19.8.1904 in Lippern, Kreis
               St. Goarshausen, wohnhaft in Düsseldorf,
               Geistenstraße 10, Deutscher, verheiratet,

Bd.I Bl.145,   in dieser Sache festgenommen am 5. Juli 1956
Bd.I Bl.149,   und vom 6.7.1956 bis zum 5. Januar 1957 in der
165,   Untersuchungshaftanstalt in Düsseldorf-Derendorf
Bd.V Bl.164   in Untersuchungshaft gewesen auf Grund des
               Haftbefehls des Untersuchungsrichters I beim
               Landgericht in Düsseldorf - UR I 8/56 -
Bd.I Bl.134   vom 5. Juli 1956 und dessen Ergänzungsbeschluß
Bd.III Bl.1   vom 2. August 1956; vom weiteren Vollzug der
Bd.V Bl.107 R Untersuchungshaft verschont durch Beschluß der
               VIII. großen Strafkammer des Landgerichts in
               Düsseldorf vom 4. Januar 1957 - VIII/IV
               414/56 -

Bd.VII Bl.101 2) der Abonnentenwerber Otto Wilhelm B ö h m ,
               geboren am 11.7.1890 in Heilbronn, wohnhaft
Bd.XIII   in Oberlahnstein, Gymnasialstraße 18,
Bl.219   Deutscher, verheiratet,

Bd.VII Bl.15   in dieser Sache festgenommen am 10.4.1957
Bd.VII Bl.20, und seit dem 11.4.1957 in Untersuchungshaft
26, 66   in der Untersuchungshaftanstalt Düsseldorf-
               Derendorf auf Grund des Haftbefehls des Unter-
Bd.VI Bl.169   suchungsrichters I beim Landgericht in Düssel-
               dorf vom 1.4.1957 - UR I 8/56 -
                                                      -2-

Copy

The Senior Public Prosecutor   Düsseldorf, June 12, 1959
for the Regional Court   Mühlenstrasse 34
—8 Js 187/56—   Telephone: 8961

To the
R e g i o n a l C o u r t   A r r e s t !
—Criminal Chamber—
in D ü s s e l d o r f

I n d i c t m e n t

Vol. I, p. 146	1)	The commercial clerk August H ö h n, born on August 19, 1904, in Lipporn, District of St. Goarshausen, residing in Düsseldorf, Geistenstrasse 10, German citizen, married,
Vol. I, p. 145		arrested in this matter on July 5, 1956, and in investigative custody from
Vol. I, pp. 149, 165		July 6, 1956, until January 5, 1957, in the detention center in Düsseldorf-Derendorf, based on the detention order of Examining Magistrate I at the
Vol. V, p. 164		Regional Court in Düsseldorf—UR I 8/56—
Vol. I, p. 134		of July 5, 1956, and his supplementary order of August 8, 1956; spared
Vol. III, p. 1		from further enforcement of investigative custody by order of the VIIIth
Vol. V, p. 107 R		Large Criminal Chamber of the Regional Court in Düsseldorf on January 4, 1957—VIII/IV 414/56—
Vol. VII, p. 101	2)	The subscriptions salesman <u>Otto</u> Wilhelm B ö h m, born on July 11, 1890, in Heilbronn, residing in Oberlahnstein, Gymnasialstrasse 18, German
Vol. XIII, p. 219		citizen, married,
Vol. VII, p. 15		arrested in this matter on April 10, 1957, and held since April 11, 1957, in
Vol. VII, pp. 20,		investigative custody in the detention center in Düsseldorf-Derendorf
26, 66		based on the detention order of Examining Magistrate I at the Regional
Vol. VI, p. 169		Court in Düsseldorf of April 1, 1957—UR I 8/56—

DOCUMENT 2.5

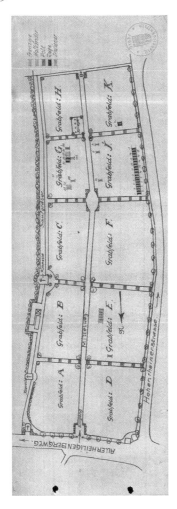

DOCUMENT 2.6

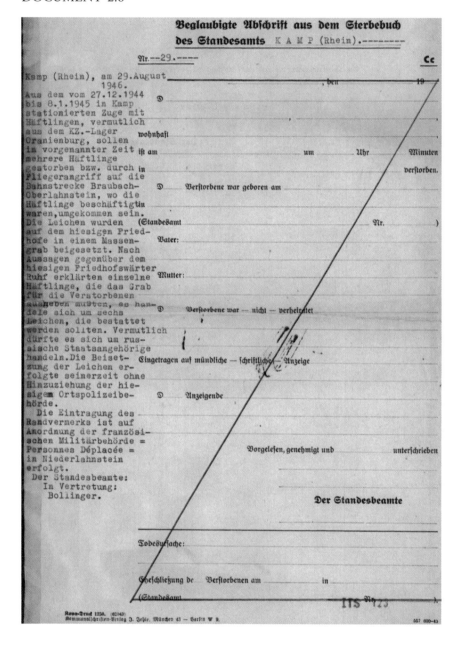

Beglaubigte Abschrift aus dem Sterbebuch
des Standesamts K A M P (Rhein).————

Nr.—29.———

Cc

Kamp (Rhein), am 29.August 1946.

Aus dem vom 27.12.1944 bis 8.1.1945 in Kamp stationierten Zuge mit Häftlingen, vermutlich aus dem KZ.-Lager Oranienburg, sollen in vorgenannter Zeit mehrere Häftlinge gestorben bzw. durch Fliegerangriff auf die Bahnstrecke Braubach-Oberlahnstein, wo die Häftlinge beschäftigt waren,umgekommen sein. Die Leichen wurden auf dem hiesigen Fried-hofe in einem Massen-grab beigesetzt. Nach Aussagen gegenüber dem hiesigen Friedhofswärter Ruhf erklärten einzelne Häftlinge, die das Grab für die Verstorbenen ausheben mußten, es han-dele sich um sechs Leichen, die bestattet werden sollten. Vermutlich dürfte es sich um rus-sische Staatsangehörige handeln.Die Beiset-zung der Leichen er-folgte seinerzeit ohne Hinzuziehung der hie-sigen Ortspolizeibe-hörde.
  Die Eintragung des Randvermerks ist auf Anordnung der französi-schen Militärbehörde = Personnes Déplacée = in Niederlahnstein erfolgt.
  Der Standesbeamte:
    In Vertretung:
    Bollinger.

..., den ..., 19...

𝔇 ...

wohnhaft ...

ist am ... um ... Uhr ... Minuten ... verstorben.

in ...

𝔇 Verstorbene war geboren am ...

(Standesamt ... Nr. ...)

Vater: ...

Mutter: ...

𝔇 Verstorbene war — nicht — verheiratet ...

Eingetragen auf mündliche — schriftliche — Anzeige ...

𝔇 Anzeigende ...

Vorgelesen, genehmigt und ... unterschrieben ...

Der Standesbeamte

Todesursache: ...

Eheschließung de Verstorbenen am ... in ...

(Standesamt ...).

ITS Nr.123

Revo-Druck 1250. (45343)
Kommunalschriften-Verlag J. Jehle. München 43 — Berlin W 9.

557 600–43

Die Übereinstimmung der umseitigen Abschrift mit den Eintragungen im Sterbebuch wird hiermit beglaubigt.

-K a m p (Rhein) , den 25. Oktober-- 19 46.

(Siegel)

Der Standesbeamte

In Vertretung :

Certified Copy from the Death Register
of the Bureau of Vital Statistics in K A M P (Rhine)

No. 29   Cc

Kamp (Rhine), August 29, 1946

From the train carrying prisoners, presumably from the Oranienburg concentration camp, that was positioned in Kamp from December 27, 1944, to
January 8, 1945, several prisoners are said to have died during that time, more
specifically to have lost their lives as a result of an air raid on the railroad line
between Braubach and Oberlahnstein, where the prisoners were working. The
bodies were interred in a mass grave in the local cemetery. According to statements made to the local cemetery custodian, Ruhf, several prisoners who were
made to dig the grave for the deceased declared that there were six bodies sched-
uled for burial. Presumably these were Russian citizens. The burial of the corpses
took place in due course without involving the local police authority.

The entry of the marginal note was made at the order of the French military
authority = Personnes Déplacées = in Niederlahnstein.

The Registrar:
By proxy:
Bollinger

[page 2]
It is hereby certified that the copy on the overleaf corresponds to the entries
in the Death Register.
   [seal]   *Kamp (Rhine), October 25, 1946*
                   The Registrar
                   By proxy: [signed] Bollinger

DOCUMENT 2.7

ITS 070

Der Bürgermeister
Abt.IV

Oberlahnstein, den 18. April 1946.

zu I b (126)

Betr.: Nachforschung über Verbleib von Zivil- und Militärangehörigen
der vereinten Nationen.

(I t a l i e n)

Lfd. Nr.	Name und Vorname		ungefähres Datum des Aufenthalts	beschäftigt während dieser Zeit bei:
1.	Amato	Antonio	Nov. 1943-März 1945	Stadtverw. Oberlahnstein
2.	Borgonovo	Giuseppe	Nov. 1943-März 1945	desgl.
3.	Bellone	Ester	Nov. 1943-März 1945	desgl.
4.	Barba	Angelico	Dez. 1943-März 1945	desgl.
5.	Brevi	Alfredo	Febr.1944-Aug. 1944	desgl.
6.	Cogliati	Pietro	Nov. 1943-Dez. 1943	desgl.
7.	Caldera	Angelo	Nov. 1943-März 1945	desgl.
8.	Campieri	Silvio	Nov. 1943-Dez. 1943	desgl.
9.	Corro	Giodano	Nov. 1943-Dez. 1943	desgl.
10.	Casadei	Mario	Nov. 1943-März 1945	desgl.
11.	Costalunga	Merito	Nov. 1943-Apr. 1944	desgl.
12.	Carlini	Ernesto	Dez. 1943-März 1945	desgl.
13.	Cornare	Giovanni	Apr. 1944-März 1945	Geschw. Helbach O.L.
14.	Damato	Leonardo	Nov. 1943-Jan. 1944	Stadtverw. Oberlahnstein
15.	de Domenico	Rosario	Nov. 1943-März 1945	desgl.
16.	de Rosa	Giovanne	Nov. 1943-März 1945	desgl.
17.	del Utri	Rosario	Dez. 1943-März 1945	desgl.
18.	Ferrari	Dino	Nov. 1943-März 1945	desgl.
19.	Faggiani	Edoardo	Nov. 1943-März 1945	desgl.
20.	Fulgenzi	Aurelio	Nov. 1943-Jan. 1944	desgl.
21.	Fontana	Giuseppe	Nov. 1943-März 1945	desgl.
22.	Fimiani	Enzo	Nov. 1943-März 1945	desgl.
23.	Fintani	Giuseppe	Apr. 1944-März 1945	Geschw.desgl Helbach O.L.
24.	Gonzotto	Eranquillo	Nov. 1943-Dez. 1943	Stadtverw. Oberlahnstein
25.	Grillo	Giulio	Nov. 1943-März 1945	desgl.
26.	Grasseli	Giovanni	Nov. 1943-März 1945	desgl.
27.	Lapi	Guerrino	Nov. 1943-März 1945	desgl.
28.	Lafelice	Felixe	Nov. 1943-Apr. 1944	desgl.
29.	Martini	Sabatino	Nov. 1943-März 1945	desgl.
30.	Moreschi	Giuseppe	Nov. 1943-März 1945	desgl.
31.	Marini	Saigi	Jan. 1944-März 1945	desgl.
32.	Negri	Aldo	Nov. 1943-Apr. 1944	desgl.
33.	Ongaro	Farasin	Jan. 1944-März 1945	desgl.
34.	Piera	Nelo	Nov. 1943-Jan. 1944	desgl.
35.	Paterlini	Valterno	Jan. 1944-März 1945	desgl.
36.	Quaglia	Luigi	Nov. 1943- März 1945	desgl.
37.	Scotto	Andrea	Nov. 1943-März 1945	desgl.
38.	Scacialippe	Dino	Apr. 1944-März 1945	Geschw. Helbach O.L.
39.	Todesco	Antonio	Dez. 1943-März 1945	Stadtverw. Oberlahnstein
40.	Vitali	Grazio	Nov. 1943-März 1945	desgl.

DOCUMENT 2.8

ITS 084·

F9-23

Niederlahnstein, den 20. Juli 1942.

M e l d u n g .

    Um 20 Uhr 45 des heutigen Abends rief der Ortsbauernführer
W e i n h e i m e r aus Koblenz-Horchheim an und gab folgendes
bekannt:

    "Jn Richtung nach dem Distrikt "Lag" in Niederlahnstein sind
9 litauische Arbeiter unterwegs, wahrscheinlich um Felddiebstähle
auszuführen."

    Pol.Oberw.Mstr. d.Res. Pabel und der Unterzeichnete begaben
sich mittels Fahrräder sofort nach dem Distrikt Lag. Wir haben dort
um 21 Uhr 30 vier litauische Arbeiter gestellt. Es handelt sich um
Leute, die sich seit einigen Wochen auf dem Didierwerk Niederlahn-
stein beschäftigt sind und auch auf diesem Werkgrundstück wohnen.
Da dieselben die deutsche Sprache nicht beherrschten, war eine Ver-
ständigung kaum möglich. Es handelt sich um folgende ausländische
Arbeiter:

	Zuname,	Vorname,	Geburtsdatum.	Geboren in:
1.	Ruksenhs,	Johann	26.5.1916	Lyngmiany Schwentschionys
2.	Bauzys,	Alfons	11.7.1923	Jgnalina Schwentschionys
3.	Paszun,	Bronislaus	10.5.1920	Kackany Schwentschionys
4.	Kardalis,	Johann	4.6.1922	Lynkmiany Schwentschionys

    Die unter Nr. 1 und 2 aufgeführten stehen in dringendem
Verdacht, die Gartentüre des Gartens Hoffeller aufgebrochen zu haben,
denn es waren an dieser Stelle frische, jedoch durch das Regenwetter
nicht vergleichbare Fussspuren vorhanden, die von der Gartentüre aus
quer durch den Garten führten und unten in dem Nachbarsgarten durch
ein Loch, das sich in dem Drahtgeflecht befand, auf den dort befind-
lichen Pfad hinausgingen. Jm Garten Hoffeller waren 2 Kartoffelstau-
den frisch ausgerupft. Die Kartoffeln lagen noch beim Kartoffelkraut.
Es ist mit Bestimmtheit anzunehmen, dass die unter 1 und 2 aufge-
führten Litauer die Kartoffeln ausgerupft haben, jedoch durch unser
plötzliches Erscheinen auf Fahrrädern auf dem oben beschriebenen
Weg verschwunden sind. Zu bemerken ist noch, dass die unter Nr. 1
und 2 Genan-nten ca. 2 Minuten vorher noch bei den unter Nr. 3 und
4 Genannten auf dem Lagweg vor dem Garten Hoffeller von uns gesehen
wurden. Wir sind erst nach dem plötzlichen Verschwinden der zwei
ersten auf die Stelle zugefahren und haben zuerst die zwei Letzt-
genannten im Lagweg und die zwei Erstgenannten etwas später im
Neugasser-Feldweg auch in unmittelbarer Nähe des Gartens Hoffeller
gestellt. Der unter Nr. 4 Genannte hatte eine alte, leere, lederne
Aktentasche um den Bauch undzwar unter der Hose unsichtbar festge-
bunden. Dass dieselben Diebstahlsabsichten hatten ging aus dem Ver-
halten klar hervor, indem dieselben des öfteren stehen blieben und
Einblick in die Gärten nahmen. Desweiteren spricht das schlechte
Wetter dafür (4 Regentage) und der auf dem Berg am Waldrand, in
ca. 1 km Entfernung vom Stadtbering einsam gelegene Distrikt "Lag",
wo dieselben gestellt wurden.

                                    Die

ITS 084

*Die 4 gestellten Personen wurden auf die Polizeiwache gebracht
und nach telefonischer Benachrichtigung des Meisters K l e i n
von den Didierwerken N.L., von diesem nach ihrer Wohnung gebracht.*

Noll,
Feldhüter.

Der Bürgermeister
als Ortspolizeibehörde
· Schutzpolizeidienstabteilung ·

Niederlahnstein, den 21. Juli 1942

Tagb.Nr.45
----------   An den

Herrn L a n d r a t

St. Goarshausen.

Landratsamt
22. JUL 1942

Betrifft: Felddiebstähle durch ausländische(litauische)Arbeiter.

Wie aus den beigefügten Anlagen ersichtlich,wurden am
Montag den 20.ds.Mts.sechs litauische Arbeiter,die hier bei der
Firma Didier-Werke N.L. beschäftigt und wohnhaft sind,bei Feld=
diebstählen gestellt.Nach Rücksprache mit der Werksleitung wurde
festgestellt,daß die beim genannten Werk beschäftigten Litauer
bisher noch zu keinen Klagen Anlaß gegeben hatten.Es wäre ange=
bracht wenn denselben zur Pflicht gemacht würde in Zukunft eine
Stunde vor Eintritt der Dunkelheit im Quartier zu sein.

Niederlahnstein, July 20, 1942

<u>R e p o r t</u>

At 8:45 this evening, the local farmers' leader, W e i n h e i m e r, telephoned from Koblenz-Horchheim and announced the following:

"Lithuanian workers are on the move, headed in the direction of the 'Lag' area in Niederlahnstein, probably to steal agricultural produce."

Reserve Police Senior Constable Pabel and the undersigned immediately went by bicycle to the Lag area. There, at 9:30 p.m., we apprehended four Lithuanian workers. These are men who have been working for several weeks at the Didier Works in Niederlahnstein and also live on the plant grounds. Since these men are not proficient in the German language, communication was barely possible. The persons in question are the following foreign workers:

	Surname	Given Name	Date of Birth	Born in:
1.	Ruksenhs	Johann	May 25, 1916	Lyngmiany Schwentschionys [Švenčionys]
2.	Bauzys	Alfons	July 11, 1923	Ignalina Schwentschionys
3.	Paszun	Bronislaus	May 10, 1920	Kackany Schwentschionys
4.	Kardalis	Johann	June 4, 1922	Lyngmiany Schwentschionys

The men listed above under 1 and 2 are strongly suspected of having forced open the garden gates of the Hoffeller garden, because there were fresh footprints at this site, though the rainy weather made them impossible to compare. They led from the garden gate straight through the garden and, down in the neighbor's garden, went out through a hole in the wire netting onto the path located there. In the Hoffeller garden, two potato plants had been freshly pulled out. The potatoes still lay next to the foliage. It must be assumed with certainty that the Lithuanians listed as 1 and 2 pulled up the potatoes but disappeared as a result of our sudden appearance on bicycles on the above-mentioned path. It must also be noted that the men listed as 1 and 2 were seen by us about 2 minutes earlier, still with the men listed as 3 and 4, in the Lag lane before we reached the Hoffeller garden. Only after the sudden disappearance of the former two did we ride to the site, and we first apprehended the latter two in the Lag lane and the former two somewhat later in the Neugasser farm lane, also in the immediate vicinity of the Hoffeller garden. Man No. 4 had tied an old, empty leather satchel around his abdomen, underneath his trousers, where it could not be seen. It was clear from their behavior that they had intentions of stealing, as they kept stopping and peering into the gardens. An additional indication is the bad weather (4 days of rain) and the isolation of the "Lag" area, located on a hill at the edge of the forest, about 1 km from the part of town inside the town walls.

[page 2]

The four apprehended persons were brought to the police station, and after Klein, the foreman at the Didier Works in <u>Niederlahnstein,</u> had been notified by telephone, they were taken by him to their lodgings.

[signed] Moll,
Field Watchman

[stamp]
The Mayor as Local Police Authority   Niederlahnstein, July 21, 1942

Uniformed Police

<u>Log No. 45</u>

To the Head A d m i n i s t r a t o r
<u>St. Goarshausen</u>

Regarding: <u>Thefts of Agricultural Produce by Foreign (Lithuanian) Workers</u>

As evident from the accompanying enclosures, on Monday, July 20, six Lithuanian workers who are employed here and live at the Didier Works in Niederlahnstein were apprehended while stealing agricultural produce. After consultation with the plant management, it was ascertained that the Lithuanians employed at the plant had given no previous cause for complaint. It would be advisable to require these men in the future to be in their quarters one hour before nightfall.

DOCUMENT 2.9

Der Generalstaatsanwalt

Frankfurt (Main), den _____24. Juli 143 19 44.
Gerichtsfache 2 – Sammelnummer: Panta 20 41

Geschäftsnummer: IV 1o . 75 (114)/44 g.

Geheim!

Bei Antwortschreiben bitte vorstehende Nummer angeben.

Betr.: Arbeitseinsatz der Gefangenen
in den kleineren Vollzugsanstalten.
Erlaß vom 26.5.1944 –V s $\frac{2}{=}$ 469 s/44 g–.
Vorbericht v. 1o.7.1944 –IV 1o. 75 (1oo)/44 g–.

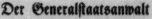

An den

Herrn Reichsminister der Justiz,

–oder Vertreter im Amt–,

Postleitstelle: D r e s d e n A.1.

    Von den kleineren Vollzugsanstalten meines Bezirks sind lediglich die
Gerichtsgefängnisse in Limburg/Lahn und Niederlahnstein und die Jugendarrest –
anstalt in Wetzlar/Lahn geöffnet. Die Belegung in den beiden Gefängnissen ist sehr
gering. Jm Gerichtsgefängnis in Limburg sitzen zur Zeit 2 männliche Strafge –
fangene ein, die ebenso wie die nur vorübergehend untergebrachten Untersuchungs –
gefangenen mit dem Zerkleinern von Holz für Holzgasgeneratoren beschäftigt werden.
Die wenigen weiblichen Gefangenen sind mit Waschen und Flicken der Anstaltskleidung
beschäftigt. Jm Gerichtsgefängnis in Niederlahnstein sitzen 3 männliche Gefangene
ein, die mit der Aufarbeitung von Eisenagraffen für die Aktiengesellschaft C.J.
Schmidt, einer wehrwirtschaftlich wichtigen Arbeit, beschäftigt sind. Neue Ar –
beiten konnten in diesen Anstalten bisher nicht aufgenommen werden.

    Die Jugendarrestanstalt in Wetzlar hatte im Juni eine Durchschnittsbe –
legung von 16, 1o. Die Jugendlichen werden, soweit sie nicht zu Hausarbeiten her –
angezogen werden, mit der Zusammensetzung von kleinen Blumentöpfen aus ge –
stanster Pappe für die Pflanzenzucht beschäftigt. Die Arbeiten werden für die
Kartonagenfabrik Bergmann in Wetzlar ausgeführt. Die zahlreichen Bemühungen,
für die Beschäftigung der Jugendlichen eine Rüstungsarbeit zu beschaffen, waren
bisher vergeblich und scheiterten insbesondere an der infolge der kurzen Strafzeit
schnell wechselnden Belegung der Anstalt.

                Jn Vertretung:
                (gez.):Wandel,
                Oberstaatsanwalt.

Beglaubigt:

Justizangestellte.

K 0906

The Prosecutor-General   Frankfurt (Main), July 24, 1944
Reference Number: IV 10—75 (114)/44 g—
                                   Gerichtsstrasse 2, Collective number:
                                                      [illegible]

To reply in writing, please use the Reference Number above.

<u>Re:</u> Labor Deployment of Prisoners in the Smaller Penal Institutions

Decree of May 26, 1944—V s—2 469 s/44 g—
Preliminary Report of July 10, 1944—IV 10. 75 (100/44 g—
                                                Secret! [stamp]

[various stamps and handwritten notes]

To the Reich Minister of Justice
or His Deputy
<u>Mail Routing Post Office D r e s d e n A.1</u>

Of the smaller penal institutions in my district, only the court prisons in Limburg/Lahn and Niederlahnstein and the juvenile detention center in Wetzlar/Lahn are open. Occupancy in the two prisons is very low. The court prison in Limburg now holds 2 male prisoners, who, like the pretrial detainees accommodated there only temporarily, are occupied in chopping wood for wood gas generators. The few female prisoners are busy with washing and mending the institutional clothing. The court prison in Niederlahnstein holds 3 male prisoners, who are involved in reconditioning iron clasps for the corporation C. J. Schmidt. This task is quite important to the wartime economy. Thus far, it has not been possible to take on new activities in these facilities.

In June, the juvenile detention center in Wetzlar had an average occupancy of 16 males, 10 females. The youths, unless involved in domestic work, are involved in making small flowerpots out of die-cut cardboard for plant breeding. The work is being done for the Bergmann Cardboard Factory in Wetzlar. The numerous attempts to secure armaments-related work for the youths to perform have been unsuccessful thus far, and they failed in particular because of the rapid turnover in the institution's occupancy due to the short detention time.

By proxy:
(signed): Wandel,
Senior Public Prosecutor

[official seal]
Certified:
[signature]
Clerk of the Court

DOCUMENT 2.10*

1. **Register** (excerpt from the register book of prisoners) of R o m a n i a n nationals incarcerated in the court prison here
2. **Serial number:** 1.
3. **Personal information and details of the offense**: K a r a s Thomas, miner, born on January 15, 1918, in Lupeni, Romania
4. **Time in prison or custody**: May 12, 1943, through June 5, 1943
5. **Sentence**: [Pol. Haft, *Polizei-Häftling*], police prisoner
6. **Enforcing authority**: Gestapo Frankfurt am Main
7. **Reason for discharge**: [Lt. Vfg., *Laut Verfügung*] transferred to Düsseldorf by order of the Gestapo

---

*Numbers 1 through 7 added for translation purposes.

DOCUMENT 2.11

hs   WEHRKREIS XII.

Stalag XII A.

DT	756/1	Supligen	(voir Stalag XI A.)
DT	485/65	Bodendorf	(Voir Stalag XI A.)
DT	429 B	Sirshahn	
DT	863	Sirshahn	
DT	1427	Limburg	
DT	872	Oberlahnstein	
DT	795	Wiederhustin	
DT	922	Bad Eme	
DT	636	Nassau Lahn	
DT	521	Zollhaus	
DT	1176	Limburg	
DT	937	Hanstatten	
DT	962	Montabaus	
Dt	1307	Wiederneisen	
DT	522	Hohheim	
DT	974	Hausein	
DT	987	Girod	
DT	513	Obernaisse	
DT	997	Languisen	
DT	508	Limburg	
DT	1294	Fachingen	
DT	1012	Diez-Lahn	
DT	969	Bad Schwalbach	
DT	936	Michelbach	
DT	1385	Limburg	
DT	1233	Limburg	
DT	1147	Guckingen	
DT	1737 B	Russelheim	
DT	1016	Schierstein	
DT	1088	Schierstein	
DT	900	Dotzheim	
DT	556	Holzappel	
DT	1203	Holzappel Hutte	
DT	321	Bingen	
DT	5/776	Bingen	
DT	313	Aspisheim	
DT	171	Nieersaultheim	
DT	815	Wiesbaden	
DT	437	Nieder-Olm	
DT	404 B	Nackenheim	
DT	1404	Dellfeld	
DT	1017	Worms	
DT	1331	Wiesbaden	
DT	1088		
DT	782		
DT	1116		
DT	818		
DT	900		
DT	1370		
DT	646		
DT	815		
DT	1088		
DT	1016		

DOCUMENT 2.12

RECOMMENDATION FOR EMPLOYMENT

Profession: **Agricultural labourer** *Saw mill worker*

Family name: **HALAS**

Country of origin or former citizenship: **Poland**

Religion: **Roman catholic**

Special features:

Present location: **French Zone, Germany.**

First names, age and relationship to head of family:
Zygmunt,   31, Head;
Antonina,   25, Wife;
Zygmunt,   2, Son.

PROFESSIONAL HISTORY:

1926 - 1933   Primary School at Rogusno, Poland.
1933 - 1936   Labourer in a sawmill at Jezierna, Poland.
1936 - 1938   Labourer in a quarry at Puluwy, Poland.
1938 - 1939   Apprenticed with a Baker at Warsaw.
1940 - 1945   Deported to Germany for forced labour. Employed on various farms.
1945   Inmate of the Displaced Persons' Camp at Niederlahnstein, without work.
1946   Camp-Guard in the Niederlahnstein Camp.
1947   Labourer, in the employ of Messrs.Ufer, Builders, Coblence.
1948 - 1949   Employed with Messrs. DAKIN, Forest exploitation company, Maisborn.
1949 - to   Labourer, in the employ of Messrs.Ufer, Builders, Coblence, until February 1950.
date.   Since then unemployed.

EMPLOYMENT POSSIBILITIES:

Mr. HALAS, Zygmunt, having worked as agricultural labourer for five years, in a saw-mill for four years, and in a quarry for two years, is suitable for a post as

(1) Agricultural labourer
(2) Labourer in a saw-mill, in a quarry, or on a building-site.

This family may be recommended from all points of view. Very neat and tidy. The husband is conscientious and fond of work and is bringing up his family in a correct and worthy manner. Will give entire satisfaction to his employers. Highly recommendable.

DOCUMENTS ENCLOSED:

Curriculum vitae.
Reference from Messrs.Ufer, Builders, Coblence, and English translation.
Reference from Messrs.Dakin, Forest Exploitation Company, Maisborn, and English translation.
Reference from Messrs.Ufer, Builders, Coblence, and English translation.
Testimony:IRO Vocational Testing Certificate No. 000 206 RP (farmhand)
Testimonial from IRO Agricultural Expert, and English translation.

DOCUMENT 2.13

Re-interviewed at the request of
US DP Commission.

ABAY Kalman, 4.1.49.

Applicant was a Hungarian rural-police
(gendarm) officer. - He was promoted to colonel on 1.11.
1944 (during the Szalasi regime) but he claims his
promotion had been prepared by the Horthy-regime
in July-August 1944 and it was a normal promotion
not an extra-ordinary one.

Appl. claims he was an expert of personell ~~cases~~
~~and di~~ and disciplinary cases. He had nothing
to do with Jewish cases.

He was not a member of any party. He claims
he was a mil. person and never took part in any
party movement.

After the war he was interned by US authorities.
His case was investigated for 1 and a half year
and discharged on 2.5.1947 without any charge.

There are no proofs and no signs that he ~~was~~ is
a war-criminal. - His service during the war cannot
be regarded as a voluntary ~~one~~.

As there is known no fact for exclusion from IRO
~~man~~ ~~~~. No change of WRO status.

Within the mandate of I.R.O.
Eligible for RESETTLEMENT SERVICES

4.5.77   W.G. REINDERS
Eligibility Officer
Date   US Zone, Germany

a Pürth
28.9.5~~~~

Re-Inteviewed at the request of
US DP Commission   ABAY Kálmán, January 4, 49

Applicant was a Hungarian rural police (gendarm) officer. He was promoted to Colonel on November 1, 1944 (during the Szálasi regime) but he claims his promotion had been prepared by the Horthy-regime in July–August 1944 and it was a normal promotion not an extra-ordinary one.

Applicant claims he was an expert of personnel and disciplinary cases. He had nothing to do with Jewish cases.

He was not a member of any party. He claims he was a military person and never took part in any party movement.

After the war he was interviewed by U.S. authorities. This case was investigated for one and a half year[s] and discharged on May 2, 1947 without any charge.

There are no proofs and no signs that he is a war-criminal. His sercice during the was cannot be regarded as voluntary.

As there is known no fact for exclusion from IRO mandate I support: No change of IRO status.

A. Pásztor
September 28, 51

CHAPTER 3

JEWISH VOICES

TO SHATTER the notion that collections held by the International Tracing Service (ITS) consist simply of "lists of names," this chapter samples the variety of documents in the ITS holdings in which Jews describe their experiences. These documents include postwar Allied questionnaires; letters to ITS in search of missing family members, often contained in tracing and documentation (T/D) files; applications for displaced person (DP) status; correspondence and interviews with relief agencies, caseworkers, and eligibility officers; and compensation applications and transcripts of interviews with German investigators. Jewish voices in the ITS holdings demonstrate the broad geographic reach of the archive. To illustrate this point, let us examine a selection of statements made by Lithuanian Jews born in Vilna,[1] all the sole survivors of their families

---

1. When German armed forces occupied Vilna on June 24, 1941, Jews in Vilna numbered approximately fifty-seven thousand, one-quarter of the city's population. German mobile killing units and Lithuanian volunteers murdered one-third of the Jewish population in Ponary before ghettos I and II were established on September 6, 1941. By the end of 1941, German and Lithuanian killers had murdered almost two-thirds of prewar Vilna Jews, including the inmates of ghetto I. German-led forces and their collaborators liquidated ghetto II in September 1943, sending approximately seven thousand inmates to Estonia for slave labor. Roughly twenty-five hundred Vilna Jews survived the war. See, among others, David Bankier, *Expulsion and Extermination: Holocaust Testimonials from Provincial Lithuania* (Jerusalem: Yad Vashem, International Institute for Holocaust Research, 2012); Christoph Dieck-

and put to slave labor in little-known and less discussed forced labor camps in Estonia[2] on the eastern rim of the Baltic Sea. From their collective voices, we glean detailed information about their families' experiences in the Vilna ghetto and their own subsequent experiences as slave laborers. These accounts were written or spoken as these individuals filled out restitution forms or responded to German prosecutors.[3]

Lejb Orbach, born in 1922 in Vilna, was taken from the Vilna ghetto in September 1943 to a series of forced labor camps in Estonia:[4] first Vaivara,[5] then

---

mann, *Deutsche Besatzungspolitik in Litauen, 1941–1944* (Göttingen: Wallstein Verlag, 2011); Vincas Bartusevičius, Joachim Tauber, and Wolfram Wette, eds., *Holocaust in Litauen: Krieg, Judenmorde und Kollaboration im Jahre 1941* (Cologne: Böhlau, 2003); Alvydas Nikžentaitis, Stefan Schreiner, and Darius Staliūnas, eds., *The Vanished World of Lithuanian Jews* (New York: Rodopi, 2004); Alfonsas Eidintas, *Jews, Lithuanians, and the Holocaust* (Vilnius: Versus Arueus Publishers, 2003); Christoph Dieckmann with Saulius Sužiedėlis, *The Persecution and Mass Murder of Lithuanian Jews during Summer and Fall of 1941* (Vilnius: Margi Raštai, 2006).

2. At the beginning of World War II, the three Baltic countries, Latvia, Lithuania, and Estonia, had a combined Jewish population of approximately 350,000: 250,000 in Lithuania, including refugees from Poland, 95,000 in Latvia, and 4,500 in Estonia. In the summer of 1944, German forces retreated from the Baltic countries and transferred those Jews still alive to concentration camps in Germany. Approximately 6 percent of the prewar Jewish population survived. See, among others, Wolfgang Curilla, *Die deutsche Ordnungspolizei und der Holocaust im Baltikum und in Weissrussland, 1941–1944* (Paderborn: F. Schöningh, 2006); David Gaunt, Paul A. Levine, and Laura Palosuo, eds., *Collaboration and Resistance during the Holocaust: Belarus, Estonia, Latvia, Lithuania* (New York: Peter Lang, 2004). For a history of the Holocaust in Estonia, see Ruth Bettina Birn, *Die Sicherheitspolizei in Estland, 1941–1944: Eine Studie zur Kollaboration im Osten* (Paderborn: Schöningh, 2006); Anton Weiss-Wendt, *Murder without Hatred: Estonians and the Holocaust* (Syracuse, NY: Syracuse University Press, 2009), especially ch. 10, "Jewish Forced Labor Camps, 1943–1944," 273–300.

3. These documents are in 5.1 (folder 0110) and are copies from another archive, though the source of these copies and their date of transfer to ITS are not specified. They appear to be a combination of two different types of documents: first, statements made to German investigators from the Central Office of State Justice Administrations in Ludwigsburg, established in 1958; second, standard forms required of applicants for restitution following the September 1953 Bundesergänzungsgesetz (BErgG/BGBl. I S. 1387), effective October 1, 1953, and the broader June 1956 law, Bundesgesetz zur Entschädigung für Opfer der nationalsozialistischen Verfolgung, or Bundesentschädigungsgesetz (BEG/BGBl. I S. 562). See the 39-page brochure *Entschädigung von NS-Unrecht* published by the German Finance Ministry in November 2012 and available on their website. Restitution forms point to the utility of compensation applications as a source for studying Jewish slave labor.

4. Akt Nr. 5412, Eidliche Erklärung, Identitätskarte Nr. 07209, Lejb Orbach, Kiriat Borochow, Tel Aviv, Israel, April 24, 1955, 5.1/82326164–5/ITS Digital Archive, USHMM.

5. Vaivara was established on September 19, 1943, as the result of a labor shortage combined with Heinrich Himmler's desire to murder the remaining Jewish population in the Baltic countries. The primary purpose of Vaivara and its subcamps was oil shale production.

Goldfields,[6] Narva-Ost,[7] Aseri,[8] and finally Vivikonna.[9] In his recollection, all of the camps were enclosed in barbed wire. Prisoners wore striped uniforms with numbers and were forced by their German and Estonian overseers to work until their transfer to Germany in June 1944.[10] Sam (Schachner) Hamburg, also born in Vilna in 1922 and also taken from the Vilna ghetto to a string of forced labor camps in Estonia, was more descriptive about the work he was forced to perform and detailed clearly the damage done to his health. (See document 3.1.[11])

> Before the beginning of the persecution measures [. . .] I was a strong, healthy young man [. . .] a mechanic[. . . . W]hen the [Vilna] ghetto was

---

Many players were involved in its establishment and administration: the civil administration and SS-police in Estonia; the German army; the company Baltische Öl GmbH (Baltöl); the Organisation Todt (OT); Einsatzgruppe Russland-Nord; and Einsatz Baltöl. Camp personnel were provided by the SS-Business Administration Main Office (Wirtschaftsverwaltungshauptamt, WVHA) in Berlin, with the WVHA in Riga in charge locally. Jewish inmates were segregated from the multiethnic inmate population. Camps were guarded by the Estonian Schutzmannschaftsbataillon 287 and the Russian Schutzmannschaftsbataillon 290. Foremen were mostly taken from the OT. See Ruth Bettina Birn, "Vaivara Main Camp," in *The United States Holocaust Memorial Museum Encyclopedia of Camps and Ghettos, 1933–1945*, vol. 1: *Early Camps, Youth Camps, and Concentration Camps and Subcamps under the SS-Business Administration Main Office (WVHA)*, ed. Geoffrey P. Megargee (Bloomington: Indiana University Press in association with USHMM, 2009), 1:1490–95.

   6. In the written protocol, Orbach calls this subcamp of Vaivara "Goldfilz." Opened in February 1944, Goldfields was run by Baltöl. See Ruth Bettina Birn, "Goldfields," in Megargee, *The United States Holocaust Memorial Museum Encyclopedia of Camps and Ghettos*, 1:1498–99. See also Weiss-Wendt, *Murder without Hatred*, 299–300.

   7. Narva-Ost was an OT-run subcamp of Vaivara and operated from the fall of 1943 to February 1944. Work there consisted of "building fortifications and digging anti-tank trenches for the so-called Pantherstellung, an army defensive network; roadwork; woodcutting," as well as OT-run construction projects. See Ruth Bettina Birn, "Narva," in Megargee, *The United States Holocaust Memorial Museum Encyclopedia of Camps and Ghettos*, 1:1503–4.

   8. Aseri (also called Organisation Todt Ostländer Lager) was a subcamp of Vaivara established May 8, 1944. It held 225 inmates monitored by twenty-three guards. Its inmates "either worked in a quarry or laid down railway tracks." See Ruth Bettina Birn, "Aseri," in Megargee, *The United States Holocaust Memorial Museum Encyclopedia of Camps and Ghettos*, 1:1496.

   9. Orbach calls this camp "Fifikoni." It actually consisted of three camps: the main camp, Vivikonna OT, and Vivikonna Baltöl. Vivikonna was primarily a mining camp; inmates "mined shale in open pits." Ruth Bettina Birn, "Vivikonna," in Megargee, *The United States Holocaust Memorial Museum Encyclopedia of Camps and Ghettos*, 1:1508.

   10. Akt Nr. 5412, Eidliche Erklärung, Identitätskarte Nr. 07209, Lejb Orbach, Kiriat Borochow, Tel Aviv, Israel, April 24, 1955, 5.1/82326164–5/ITS Digital Archive, USHMM.

   11. Eidliche Erklärung, Sam Hamburg, July 19, 1966, 5.1/82326167/ITS Digital Archive, USHMM.

liquidated, I was transferred to the Waiwara [Vaivara] forced labor camp. In this camp, I was made to perform hard labor again, building railroad lines, and I was also used for excavation work. My working time totaled 14 hours daily. Our food was meager and very poor. I developed a serious case of typhus and, sick and completely weakened, dragged myself back to work because I was terribly afraid of being killed. In October 1943, I was taken to Fifikoni [Vivikonna], and from there to the Kiviolo [Kiviõli],[12] Narwa [Narva], Aseri, and Goldfilz [Goldfields] camps.[13]

The document goes on to describe the work he performed in this series of camps, his second major illness and a resulting primitive operation, and his transfer to Germany in the summer of 1944. It is an intense and painful rendering of his experience as a Jewish slave laborer.

The list of camps and types of labor in Estonia grows longer with each affidavit (*Eidliche Erklärung*). Josef Mielnik,[14] born in 1928 in Vilna, upon liquidation of the Vilna ghetto, was sent to the Ereda camp[15] to work as slave labor in low-depth oil-shale mining; in December 1943, to Narva to dig antitank ditches; in early 1944, to Aseri to work in the quarry; and in July 1944, to Kiviõli to work again in oil-shale mining before he too was transferred to Stutthof in October 1944.[16] In his 1965 interview with German investigators, he provided details about each camp: his dates of incarceration; the names of the camp commandant, camp elder (*Lagerältester*), and camp guards; names of fel-

---

12. Kiviõli was the headquarters of Baltöl; the Petroleum Command (Mineralölkommando); the general labor leader (*Generalarbeitsführer*) of the OT Industrial Protective Service (Werkschutz); a German gendarmerie post; the local headquarters (*Ortskommandantur*) of the German army; and the branch office of the Security Police in Estonia. Inmates worked at Baltöl construction sites. See Ruth Bettina Birn, "Kiviõli I and II," in Megargee, *The United States Holocaust Memorial Museum Encyclopedia of Camps and Ghettos*, 1:1500.

13. Eidliche Erklärung, Sam Hamburg, July 19, 1966, 5.1/82326166–7/ITS Digital Archive, USHMM.

14. German and Lithuanian troops arrested him, alongside his father and two brothers, on July 14, 1941, within three weeks of the arrival of German troops in Vilna. He escaped the column of arrested men and returned home; his father and brothers were murdered in Ponary. See *Vernehmungsniederschrift* [interrogation transcript], Josef Mielnik, Tivon, Israel, September 5, 1965, 5.1/82326170/ITS Digital Archive, USHMM.

15. Run by Baltöl, Ereda was one of the first Vaivara subcamps to be set up and consisted of lower and upper camps. It was particularly dangerous and known for the sadism of its overlords. See Ruth Bettina Birn, "Ereda," in Megargee, *The United States Holocaust Memorial Museum Encyclopedia of Camps and Ghettos*, 1:1497–98.

16. Eidliche Erklärung, Josef Mielnik, June 27, 1954, 5.1/82326168–9/ITS Digital Archive, USHMM.

low prisoners; the kind of work he performed; prisoner conditions; and whether he directly witnessed any murders in the camps.[17]

"IT ALL DEPENDED ON HIS MOOD"[18]

Through testimony provided to German investigators one can learn about the form murder took in the Vilna ghetto and subsequently in Estonian labor camps. We can turn the lens on perpetrators to see their actions and behaviors from the viewpoint of their Jewish victims[19]—an entirely different exercise from reading about what German and Estonian overlords did to their victims in camp after camp and case after case as detailed in perpetrator documents. Moses Nodel, born in Vilna in 1911, described the infamous liquidation of Ghetto I in October 1941, after which only those families with "yellow certificates" were allowed to remain alive.[20] "After a three-day *Aktion* of so-called yellow work permits, I did not receive a yellow work permit, but managed nonetheless to stay in the ghetto, in hiding. Three days later, after the people returned to the ghetto, I left my hiding place and tried to get a yellow work permit," he wrote. He was able to purchase one from a noncommissioned officer named Mack in the military administration headquarters (*Unteroffizier des Feldkommandos*) and subsequently worked there as an auto mechanic.[21] He could recall well his over-lord: "This Mack wore glasses, was of medium height, and was about 40 years old[. . . . H]is relationship with the other Jews with whom I worked in the military administration headquarters (*Feldkommando*) varied: one day he would hit them; another day he would bring them food; it all depended on his mood."[22]

Mielnik, when interviewed about Narva and asked whether he witnessed murders in that camp, described the fate of ill prisoners in the so-called *Schonun-*

---

17. *Vernehmungsniederschrift*, Josef Mielnik, Tivon, Israel, September 5, 1965, 5.1/82326171/ITS Digital Archive, USHMM.

18. Übersetzung, Nodel, Moses, Tel Aviv, May 25, 1961, 5.1/82326180/ITS Digital Archive, USHMM.

19. See Mark Roseman, "Holocaust Perpetrators in Victims' Eyes," in *Years of Persecution, Years of Extermination: Saul Friedländer and the Future of Holocaust Studies*, ed. Christian Wiese and Paul Betts (London: Continuum, 2010), 81–100.

20. By early 1942, ghetto II held approximately twenty thousand Jews (fifteen thousand Jews with "yellow certificates" and five thousand who managed to remain there illegally).

21. Übersetzung, Nodel, Moses, Tel Aviv, May 25, 1961, 5.1/82326180/ITS Digital Archive, USHMM.

22. Ibid.

gsblock ("convalescence block" for prisoners unable to perform hard labor), where he was a typhus patient.[23] (See document 3.2.[24]) After more than twenty years, he could still recount in vivid detail the arrival of an SS medical orderly (*Sanitäter/Sanitätsdienstgrad*, SDG)[25] with a pickax. "I can well recall how he screamed at the inmates to stand," said Mielnik, and three or four did so. The SDG proceeded to hack the inmates to death with such force that the pickax fully penetrated their bodies and was visible from the other side. The surviving inmates gathered the mutilated bodies and brought them to the crematorium. When further pressed about the incident by his interrogator, Mielnik's words exploded from him:

> They were Jews like me. They were completely exhausted and almost dead from starvation. When such utterly exhausted people are battered in that way, one can hardly imagine that they would survive. I saw with my own eyes how the tip of the pickax pierced the bodies of the prisoners. It was done in such a way that the tip of the pickax poked out on the other side. I also saw that the whole floor was wet with blood. When people are killed in that way, it is more than sadism. This man [. . .] stopped at nothing.[26]

The surviving prisoners gave this SDG the nickname "Pickax."[27] "I was fifteen years old," he noted. "At that age one is still a child."[28]

Accounts by Jews as young as he and younger are among the most moving documents to be found in the ITS holdings. The case files of the Child Tracing Branch (6.3.2) provide a rich source of such testimonies. Children's voices best capture the enduring human need for innocence and hope, still to be found, against all odds, in some Jewish children orphaned in the Holocaust. (See docu-

---

23. *Vernehmungsniederschrift*, Josef Mielnik, Tivon, Israel, September 5, 1965, 5.1/82326172/ITS Digital Archive, USHMM.

24. Ibid., 82326173–4.

25. For the role of the SDG, see Birn, "Vaivara Main Camp," 1492.

26. See document 3.2.

27. This is the spelling in the affidavit. Mielnik was likely referring to SS medic or SDG Erich Scharfetter, nicknamed "Kirkennik" and assigned to various Vaivara subcamps to "combat typhus epidemics." See Birn, "Goldfields," 1499. Weiss-Wendt cites a different execution as the source of the nickname "Kirkenik": in late February 1944, in the Kuremäe subcamp, Scharfetter murdered twenty-two elderly men with an ax and then sliced their throats with a knife. See Weiss-Wendt, *Murder without Hatred*, 283.

28. *Vernehmungsniederschrift*, Josef Mielnik, Tivon, Israel, September 5, 1965, 5.1/82326173–5/ITS Digital Archive, USHMM.

ment 3.3.[29]) "Dear Mrs. Hutton,"[30] wrote Lazar Kleinmann to an administrator at the Kloster Indersdorf children's rehabilitation home in Bavaria,[31] "I thank you very much for your kind and interesting letter and for the trouble you have taken for me. We are now learning English and arithmetics and some of us are learning music. I am playing the trumpet," he wrote from the Jewish Refugee Hostel on 17 Wellington Street in Salford, England. He penned this letter at the age of fifteen, having survived separation from his parents, four sisters, and three brothers in Birkenau, then subsequent incarceration in Buna, Oranienburg, and Flossenbürg. "I am feeling quite well here," he continued. "Every day I have lessons in English and Hebrew." Uncertainty as to the fate of his parents and siblings still clouded all these positive things.[32] In his case we know that he overcame these traumatic experiences to establish a business, raise a family, and, in 2011, return to Auschwitz to light nine candles for his murdered siblings and parents.[33]

"FRAGEN AN ALLE AUSCHWITZER"[34]

Subcollection 1.1.0.7 (ITS Compilation of Information Related to Various Detention Sites and Camps) contains extraordinary testimonies by Jews sent to the ITS in response to a set of questionnaires created in the first five years after the war ended in 1945. (See document 3.4.[35]) The responses, which number in the thousands, are organized by the camp to which they pertain, allowing

29. Letter from Lazar Kleinmann, Salford, England, to Marion Hutton, Kloster Indersdorf, 6.3.2.1/84313462/ITS Digital Archive, USHMM.

30. He is writing to Marion E. Hutton, acting director, DP Children's Center at Kloster Indersdorf. See Child Search Case File for Lazar Kleinmann, 6.3.2.1/84313466/ITS Digital Archive, USHMM.

31. For more on Kloster Indersdorf, see Anna Andlauer, *The Rage to Live: The International D.P. Children's Center Kloster Indersdorf, 1945–46*, first published in German as *Zurück ins Leben. Das internationale Kinderzentrum Kloster Indersdorf 1945–46* (Nuremberg: Antogo Verlag, 2011).

32. Letter from Lazar Kleinmann, Salford, England, to UNRRA Team 182, Indersdorf, Germany, December 21, 1945, ITS Child Search Case File for Lazar Kleinmann, 6.3.2.1/84313463/ITS Digital Archive, USHMM.

33. See Andlauer, *The Rage to Live*, 57.

34. "Questions to all 'Auschwitzers,'" a title on a form found in 1.1.0.7/87763878/ITS Digital Archive, USHMM. A linguist might study such forms to determine how descriptive language about the Holocaust has changed over decades; one would be unlikely to see a document phrased this way today.

35. Ibid.

researchers interested in prisoners' experiences in a particular camp to analyze their responses as a whole and draw out patterns.[36] For example, one can review the questionnaires completed by Jews from across Europe who spent anywhere from days to weeks to months in Auschwitz I, II, or III in 1943 or 1944. They reveal what Jews understood upon arrival; for those not immediately murdered, their treatment; what types of labor they were forced to perform; their clothing; their estimation of how many prisoners were in the camp; whether the camp was bombed, and if so, when and how many were wounded and killed; the camp's evacuation; and the names of other inmates, both living and deceased.[37] Imagine the social histories of sites of detention written for the first time based on aggregated studies of ITS-held questionnaires or, alternatively, offering a different lens on camp social histories generally thought of as understood and revealing that when such places are described in aggregate in victims' voices, there is still much to learn.

"I was in the Auschwitz-Birkenau transit camp only 14 days. Outside of nightly beatings by Kapos, there were no unusual occurrences during this time," wrote Jakob Klein, born in Sátoraljaújhely, Hungary.[38] He retained his civilian clothes, and for two of those fourteen days, he was forced to carry bricks.[39] Polish Jew Aron Zultowski had a different dominant memory of his three months in Auschwitz after he arrived by cattle car on July 31, 1944, with 1,614 other male Jews.[40] To the first question on this particular questionnaire, "Can you tell us about any unusual occurrences in the camp during your time of imprisonment," Zultowski, a labor, ghetto, and concentration camp veteran since 1940, wrote simply, "There were selections."[41] Unlike Klein, he arrived in

36. The questionnaires filled out by Jewish and non-Jewish victims in 1.1.0.7 are the subject of a planned monograph by Susanne Urban. These documents are originals. For the origins, content, and dissemination of these questionnaires, see Susanne Urban, "'Mein einziger Dokument ist der Nummer auf der Hand': Schriftliche Aussagen Überlebender im Archiv des ITS," in *Freilegungen: Überlebende—Erinnerungen—Transformationen*, ed. Rebecca Boehling, Susanne Urban, and René Bienert. Jahrbuch des International Tracing Service II (Göttingen: Wallstein Verlag, 2013), 173–97.

37. For the responses to the particular version of the 1950 questionnaire from Auschwitz survivors, see the thirty-two questionnaires mixed in with other restitution-related documentation in 1.1.0.7/87763857–908/ITS Digital Archive, USHMM.

38. Central Name Index (CNI) card for Jakob Klein, 0.1/52445614 and T/D file for Jakob Klein, 6.3.3.2/100480785–802/ITS Digital Archive, USHMM.

39. "Ermittlungsblatt betr. [betreffs] der Toten des Lagers Auschwitz-Birkenau," completed by Jakob Klein, DP Camp Feldafing, May 24, 1950, 1.1.0.7/87763859/ITS Digital Archive, USHMM.

40. Martin Dean, "Bliżyn," in Megargee, *The United States Holocaust Memorial Museum Encyclopedia of Camps and Ghettos*, 881.

41. "Ermittlungsblatt betr. [betreffs] der Toten des Lagers Auschwitz-Birkenau," com-

Auschwitz I, would have been assigned a number,[42] and spent his first two weeks in quarantine. He then worked in the potato storehouse (*Kartoffelbunker*) and with the so-called sewer squad (*Kanalisation*) of the Auschwitz Central Construction Office (Zentralbauleitung der Waffen-SS und Polizei Auschwitz) and wore prisoners' clothing. He cited the German Labor Front–owned Deutsche Bau AG (German Construction Corporation) as the private company for which his fellow prisoners worked.[43] When asked about "unusual occurrences in the camp during [his] time of imprisonment," Polish Jewish shoemaker Salomon Danielski, an inmate of Auschwitz III–Monowitz (Buna)[44] with tattooed number 144218, simply responded, "No." Nor did he give a long answer with regard to the seventh question on the questionnaire: "Was the camp bombed? If so, when? How many wounded or dead?" He answered simply, "Yes, 1944,"[45] with regard to what has become one of the most contested points of the Allied response to the Holocaust.[46]

Some wrote directly about murder by gas.[47] To the question "Can you tell

---

pleted by Aron Zultowski, Schulstrasse 49/II, Munich, May 24, 1950, 1.1.0.7/87763861/ ITS Digital Archive, USHMM. Zultowski was born in Poland on February 15, 1913. His Holocaust odyssey began in April 1940 in the Lublin labor camp. In October 1940, he was transferred to the labor camp in Tomaszów Mazowiecki; from there he was sent to the ghetto in Tomaszów in March 1941; to Bliżyn, a forced labor camp for Jews, in May 1943; and to Auschwitz in July 1944. He remained in Auschwitz for three months and was transferred to Oranienburg in October 1944. He was liberated on April 26, 1945, in Ohrdruf. See the T/ D file for Aron Zultowski, 6.3.3.2/101124787–812/ITS Digital Archive, USHMM.

42. Dean, "Bliżyn," 881.

43. "Ermittlungsblatt betr. [betreffs] der Toten des Lagers Auschwitz-Birkenau,'' completed by Aron Zultowski, Schulstrasse 49/II, Munich, May 24, 1950, 1.1.0.7/87763861/ ITS Digital Archive, USHMM.

44. For further information about Buna, see Florian Schmaltz, "Auschwitz III–Monowitz Main Camp," in Megargee, *The United States Holocaust Memorial Museum Encyclopedia of Camps and Ghettos*, 1:215–19.

45. "Ermittlungsblatt betr. [betreffs] der Toten des Lagers Auschwitz-Birkenau,'' completed by Salomon Danielski, Munich, May 24, 1950, 1.1.0.7/87763862/ITS Digital Archive, USHMM. Like Aron Zultowski, Danielski spent five years in the camps and ghettos system. Born in 1915 in Przedecz, Poland, between February 1940 and April 1945, he was in the ghetto in Przedecz; taken for forced labor in the district (*Regierungsbezirk*) Hohensalza; deported to Auschwitz-Buna; then sent to Oranienburg, Flossenbürg, and Trostberg. See T/ D file for Salomon Danielski, 6.3.3.2/85618442–65/ITS Digital Archive, USHMM.

46. See Joseph Robert White, "Target Auschwitz: Historical and Hypothetical Responses to Allied Attack," *Holocaust and Genocide Studies* 16, no. 1 (spring 2002): 54–76.

47. This subcollection also contains testimonies about gassing in Auschwitz II–Birkenau by non-Jewish prisoners. Ethnic German and Greek Catholic Theo Jurkiewitsch, born in 1915 in Złoczów, Poland (today Zolochiv, Ukraine), wrote, "As a member of the band [consisting of camp prisoners], I could see the gas chambers themselves and crates full of

us about any unusual occurrences in the camp during your time of imprison-ment," Chaim Grünberg, a Polish Jew, wrote, "People were often hanged or shot. Upon arrival, the weak, the old and the sick were sent directly to be gassed."[48] And then there was the response by Edgar Mannheimer, a Czech Jew: "[My] parents, two brothers, and a sister died there."[49] He and his family arrived in Birkenau via Theresienstadt in the first days of February 1943; he was eigh-teen years old when the crematoria in Birkenau made him an orphan.[50] Greek Jew Dinos (Daniel) Allaluf wrote of his family too, naming them all. (See docu-ment 3.5.[51]) "We came to the camp with the whole family [in March 1943]. My father, Israel Allaluf, my mother, Palomba, and my three sisters: Rachel with a daughter (1 month old), Klara, and Maria[. They] were sent to the crematorium right after arrival (except for Maria and Klara). Maria and Klara worked for a few months and then were killed."[52]

When one looks collectively at the questionnaires, Czech Jew Helene Isa-kowitz[53] was among the sharpest with her pen. To the third question on the questionnaire form, "What kind of work did the prisoners do? For what firms?" she wrote, "All the dirty work in the camp" (*Alle Schmutzarbeit im Lager*). She

objects like jewelry, golden rings, and the like." Jurkiewitsch was in Auschwitz from January through May 1943. He played the accordion in Block 5. See "Ermittlungsblatt betr. [betreffs] der Toten des Lagers Auschwitz-Birkenau," completed by Theo Jurkiewitsch, Regensburg, May 19, 1950, 1.1.0.7/87763906, and the T/D file for Theo Jurkiewitsch, 6.3.3.2/99466607–30/ITS Digital Archive, USHMM.

48. "Ermittlungsblatt betr. [betreffs] der Toten des Lagers Auschwitz-Birkenau," com-pleted by Chaim Grünberg, Schwindegg, June 2, 1950, 1.1.0.7/87763908, and DP-2 card for Chaim Grynberg, 3.1.1.1/67262929/ITS Digital Archive, USHMM.

49. "Ermittlungsblatt betr. [betreffs] der Toten des Lagers Auschwitz II–Birkenau," com-pleted by Edgar Mannheimer, Munich, May 16, 1950, 1.1.0.7/87763905/ITS Digital Archive, USHMM.

50. CNI card for Edgar Mannheimer, 0.1/39904372–83, and T/D file for Edgar Mann-heimer, 6.3.3.2/100366084–117/ITS Digital Archive, USHMM.

51. "Ermittlungsblatt betr. [betreffs] der Toten des Lagers Auschwitz-Birkenau," Inquiry sheet concerning those who died in the camp at Auschwitz II–Birkenau, completed by Daniel Allalouf, DP Camp Landsberg am Lech, May 17, 1950, 1.1.0.7/87763894/ITS Digital Archive, USHMM.

52. Ibid. Though he did not mention him, Dinos also had a brother, Isakino, who was deported with the entire family to Auschwitz and given prisoner number 109425; Dinos was given number 109424, so they endured the tattooing process side by side. See T/D file for Isakino (Isaac) Allalouf (Hallalouf), 6.3.3.2/100012164–88/ITS Digital Archive, USHMM.

53. T/D file for Helene Isakowitz (Isakovic, Eisner; maiden name Storch), 6.3.3.2/100682524–47/ITS Digital Archive, USHMM.

was also the most descriptive about murder by gassing in Birkenau, writing, "There were 4 crematoria in Auschwitz, where most of the prisoners were burned. In addition, various prisoners were beaten to death, hanged, shot [etc.]."[54] Polish Jew Markus Kremer (Langsam) wrote, "The crematorium was operating day and night, as burnings [of bodies] were constantly carried out there."[55] Devastating and overwhelming, these are only some of the references to gassing in the thirty-two questionnaires in the "Auschwitz I–III" folder in subcollection 1.1.0.7. Their power is obvious when one thinks about thousands of responses like these addressing key aspects of Jews' experiences in all manner of camps, from labor camps to extermination camps like Auschwitz.

One must look beyond the incarceration and persecution collections in the ITS holdings (1.1 through 1.2.8.1) to appreciate the many Jewish voices found across the entire archive. The registrations and files of displaced persons, children, and missing persons (3.1 through 3.3.2.4) are no exception. International Refugee Organization (IRO) review board cases found in subcollection 3.2.1.5[56] are one source. (See document 3.6.[57]) These were petitions from individuals whose initial application for DP status was refused. The files contain the board's recommendation; the applicant's own narrative is not included. That said, the IRO review board's justification narratives reveal multiple facets of wartime

54. "Ermittlungsblatt betr. [betreffs] der Toten des Lagers Auschwitz-Birkenau," completed by Helene Isakowitz, Camp Ebelsberg bei Linz, Austria, May 24, 1950, 1.1.0.7/87763904/ITS Digital Archive, USHMM.

55. "Ermittlungsblatt betr. [betreffs] der Toten des Lagers Auschwitz-Birkenau," completed by Markus Langsam, Munich, May 22, 1950, 1.1.0.7/87763902/ITS Digital Archive, USHMM. While his biography is not the subject of this chapter, extensive documentation can be found in ITS on his fate. See CNI cards for Markus Kremer (Langsam), 0.1/28796401–2; CNI cards for Markus Langsam, 0.1/30142529–30; Auschwitz number index card for prisoner number 161335, 1.1.2.5/1099267–8; Buchenwald prisoner envelope for Markus Kremer, 1.1.5.3/6377808–15; Buchenwald number index card for prisoner number 120704, 1.1.5.5/9450712–6; and T/D file for Markus Langsam (Kremer), 6.3.3.2/104973365–85/ITS Digital Archive, USHMM.

56. These files are organized and searchable by name only and are located in 3.2.1.5 (CM/1 opposition proceedings, IRO Bureau Geneva). For an analysis of these petitions pertaining to non-Jewish cases, see Ruth Balint, "The Use and Abuse of History: Displaced Persons in the ITS Archive" in *Freilegungen: Spiegelungen der NS-Verfolgung und ihrer Konsequenzen, Jahrbuch des International Tracing Service*, Bd. 4, ed. Rebecca Boehling, Susanne Urban, Elizabeth Anthony, and Suzanne Brown-Fleming (Göttingen: Wallstein Verlag, 2015), 173–186.

57. Decision of the review board of the Preparatory Commission for the International Refugee Organization (PCIRO) for Jakob Abrahamovicz, 3.2.1.5/81288526/ITS Digital Archive, USHMM.

experiences of Jewish people; they often demonstrate that in the study of the Holocaust and immediate postwar years, truth can be stranger than fiction. For example, in the case of Italy-based Haim Abraam, IRO officers in Geneva wrote that the "petitioner is a Bulgarian Jew who left his country in July 1943 when the persecution of Jews started [there]. He arrived in Trieste [Italy] with his wife and three daughters, bearing Italian passports [. . .] obtained by bribery. They proceeded to Rome where they remained during the whole war."[58] Austria-based Jakob Abrahamovicz, a Czech Jew, is described as "from Carpatho-Ukraine [and] claims to have joined [a] Czech Legion in [the] USSR in May 1944. On his return to his country he was given the trusteeship of a butcher's business which formerly belonged to a German. In spite of his privileged position he came under suspicion after February 1948 as Western-oriented, and in June of 1948 he was obliged to flee."[59] Such summaries, written by the IRO review board, appear over and over again in subcollection 3.2.1.5.

Particularly rich are the already discussed IRO care and maintenance—welfare and support (CM/1) forms.[60] Each CM/1 form contained a set of questions to which applicants had to respond. While the forms were not 100 percent uniform across zones of occupation or year of issue, they all asked for basic biographical information for the applicant and his or her family (questions 1–9); places of residence for the last ten years (question 10); employment for the last ten years (question 11); education (question 12); languages (question 13); financial resources (question 14); relatives (question 15); record of previous assistance and documents (questions 16–18); present address (question 19); and a section concerning "future plans" (question 21). Question 21 included the following subquestions: "Do you wish to return to your country of former residence?" "Do you wish to remain in the country of current residence?" "Do you wish to emigrate to some other country, and if so, what is your country of

---

58. See decision of the IRO review board for Haim Abraam, 3.2.1.5/81255396–7/ITS Digital Archive, USHMM.

59. See decision of the PCIRO review board for Jakob Abrahamovicz, 3.2.1.5/81288525–6/ITS Digital Archive, USHMM.

60. The CM/1 forms, discussed in chapter 1, can be found in 3.2.1.1 (CM/1 forms originating in Germany), 3.2.1.2 (CM/1 forms originating in Italy), 3.2.1.3 (CM/1 forms originating in Austria), 3.2.1.4 (CM/1 forms originating in Switzerland), and 3.2.1.6 (CM/1 forms originating in England). Groups 3.2.1.1 and 3.2.1.2 were the subject of the aforementioned project by the USHMM, Yad Vashem, and the ITS in Bad Arolsen, supported by the Conference on Jewish Material Claims against Germany, to expand the set of fields by which the material in the CM/1 forms could be searched and aggregated (see chapter 1). Groups 3.2.1.3 to 3.2.1.6 are organized and searchable by name only.

preference?" "Do you have relatives there?" Finally, question 21 had a section on "other preferences to resettlement, and reasons."[61]

In answering these twenty-one or so questions, Jews who may or may not have experienced the wrath of the Nazi and Axis regimes, from across Europe and sometimes from Africa or the Middle East,[62] gave a variety of answers, short and long. Their voices echo across these forms. To question 21 ("Do you wish to return to your country of former residence?"), Szimon Abend of Tarnów, Poland, answered simply, "Family murdered and home destroyed."[63] Moses Abelansky, also from Poland, responded, "Because I have no one at home!"[64] Magda Aarts, from Holland, gave precisely the same answer,[65] as did thousands of others. Some CM/1 forms portray in stark relief the emotional lives of survivors who struggled through the first difficult decade after the murder of their loved ones.

"IN BUCHENWALD I SAID I AM A GREE[K] AND NOT [A] JEW"[66]

Let us return to Dinos Allaluf, separated from his parents, three sisters, and one-month-old niece in Auschwitz. (See document 3.7.[67]) Within the first few sheets of his 137-page CM/1 file, one finds the following assessment by American Jewish Joint Distribution Committee (AJDC) caseworker Deborah Levy, at that time based out of the Social Service Department in the AJDC emigration office at Siebertstrasse 3 in Munich:[68]

---

61. For example, see CM/1 form for Moses Abelansky, 3.2.1.1/78862255–8/ITS Digital Archive, USHMM.

62. See, for example, the CM/1 form for Joseph Abadi, 3.2.1.2/80304938/ITS Digital Archive, USHMM. Born to Iranian Jewish parents in Aleppo, Syria, he moved to Beirut, Lebanon, then to Haifa, Israel, and finally, in 1951, to Milan, Italy, in search of work. Because he was never "persecuted for religious reasons," he was found "not to be within the mandate of the IRO."

63. Original German: *Angehörige ermordet und Heim vernichtet.* See CM/1 form for Szimon Abend, 3.2.1.1/78862501/ITS Digital Archive, USHMM.

64. Original German: *Weil ich habe niemand Zuhause!* CM/1 form for Moses Abelansky, 3.2.1.1/78862255–8/ITS Digital Archive, USHMM.

65. CM/1 form for Magda Aarts, 3.2.1.1/78861667/ITS Digital Archive, USHMM.

66. Certificate of incarceration for Daniel Allaluf, part of the T/D file for Dinos Allaluf, 6.3.3.2/99000883/ITS Digital Archive, USHMM.

67. Notes on the Allaluf case are included in the CM/1 form for Dinos Allaluf, 3.2.1.1/ 78873841/ITS Digital Archive, USHMM.

68. In July 1953, both Allaluf cases were assigned to Miss Levy, and she appears to be the author of a lengthy summary report about the cases that is part of the CM/1 form for

Allaluf—10 March [1953] continued. He thinks that his life in this country [Germany] has only been a waste and covered his best years. He is now 30 years of age[69] and since he was 18, he was pushed around and lived in camps. Mr. Allaluf expressed the great desire to have a family of his own, he would like very much to have children but feels, as long as [he and his wife] are living in the camp, there is no place to bring up a child. He explained that he came from a large family, there were 5 children and he would like to carry on his family tradition and especially, to give the name of his deceased parents to their children[,] which is customary in his country [of Greece] and presents a sign of respect to the dead persons.[70]

Allaluf arrived in Auschwitz on March 20, 1943. Within two months, he was transferred to the Budy subcamp for agricultural labor on an SS farm,[71] then to Buchenwald as a political prisoner, where he claimed to be Greek but not Jewish, then to Tröglitz/Rehmsdorf, and finally to Flossenbürg, where the US Army liberated him.[72] Note that Allaluf did not differentiate between the extermination, concentration, and labor camps he experienced from 1943 to 1945 and the DP camps in Lechfeld, Landsberg, Feldafing, and Föhrenwald, where he lived from 1945 until the date of Levy's note in March 1953.

His attempts to resume some kind of a normal life did not go smoothly in those first years after liberation. In 1949, he married dressmaker Anna Meworach also Jewish, a survivor of Auschwitz and Bergen-Belsen, and also born in Greece.[73] At one point, they divorced because "they were told that a single

---

Dinos (Daniel, Dena) Allaluf (Allalouf), hereafter cited as CM/1 form for Dinos Allaluf, 3.2.1.1/78873838/ITS Digital Archive, USHMM.

69. Allaluf was born in Salonika on November 17, between 1921 and 1925. His birth date varies across ITS documentation. As was the case with many victims, his date of birth is difficult to determine; he likely added or subtracted years as necessary for survival when providing data first to the Nazis and then to the Allies and relief organizations responsible for determining his emigration eligibility.

70. Notes on the Allaluf case included in the CM/1 form for Dinos Allaluf, 3.2.1.1/78873841/ITS Digital Archive, USHMM.

71. "Ermittlungsblatt betr. [betreffs] der Toten des Lagers Auschwitz-Birkenau," completed by Daniel Allaluf, DP Camp Landsberg am Lech, May 17, 1950, 1.1.0.7/87763894/ITS Digital Archive, USHMM.

72. See CNI cards for Dinos Allaluf, 0.1/12953857 and 12953864–7; Auschwitz number index card for prisoner number 109424, 1.1.2.5/989991–2; Buchenwald number index card for prisoner number 120071, 1.1.5.5/9447512–6; and T/D file for Dinos Allaluf, 6.3.3.2/99000883/ITS Digital Archive, USHMM.

73. T/D file for Anna (Meworach, Meborach) Allaluf, 6.3.3.2/93515905–50/ITS Digital Archive, USHMM.

person would have a better chance to emigrate [to Canada]."[74] Their attempt to emigrate to Canada failed nonetheless. Dinos had already been barred from emigration to the United States because he "had been involved in a fight with the German police [in 1946]."[75] In later explaining this, he told AJDC case-workers that his "1946 troubles with the German police [. . .] did not represent a real crime[;] it was a natural outburst as a result of tensions that exist between German authorities and Jewish persons." Further, he believed his case had not subsequently been "presented properly" to the US consulate.[76] The conflict between Jewish DPs and Germans during the DP camp era is yet another fasci-nating issue into which ITS-held documents offer insight.[77]

By March 1953, Dinos and Anna, divorced in civil court but still a couple, lived in Missouri 15/a, DP Camp Föhrenwald, approximately fifteen miles south of Munich. Dinos could only come home "once a week" on his day off from his job as a dishwasher[78] at the US-run McGraw Kaserne in Munich.[79] The CM/1 file reveals a couple struggling first to survive several concentration camps and then, after liberation in 1945, to find their bearings after the murder of their families. Dinos and Anna were regulars at the AJDC emigration offices in Föhrenwald and Munich, asking for help, perhaps receiving it, and typically leaving unsatisfied. The Allalufs, of Sephardic origin and fluent in Spanish and Greek, felt frustration when trying to make themselves understood by the staff

---

74. She, too, had lost family in the Holocaust, telling her AJDC interviewer on March 2, 1953, that she lost "her mother and 3 sisters in the concentration camp." They considered their marriage "under Jewish rite" to be binding and continued to live as man and wife. See interview notes with Anna Allaluf dated March 2, 1953, Föhrenwald DP Camp, part of the CM/1 form for Dinos Allaluf, 3.2.1.1/78873849/ITS Digital Archive, USHMM.

75. A November 20, 1950, report noted that Allaluf "had been rejected by [the] US Consul [as a candidate for emigration to the United States] on 30.10.1950 [because] he [Allaluf] was sentenced by Military Court Augsburg in April 1946 for twelve months"; it also noted that Allaluf had been "advi[s]ed to lodge an appeal with [the] parole board [in] Munich, [or] will otherwise not be able to emigrate anywhere. Firm residual [DP] sent back to camp of origin. Should be processed to residual camp Feldafing." Counseling reclassifica-tion report by Field Welfare Officer F. Preziosi, Area 5, November 20, 1950, part of CM/1 form for Dinos Allaluf, 3.2.1.1/78873937/ITS Digital Archive, USHMM.

76. See interview notes with Allaluf dated March 10, 1953, part of CM/1 form for Dinos Allaluf, 3.2.1.1/78873848/ITS Digital Archive, USHMM.

77. See Grossmann, *Jews, Germans and Allies.*

78. See interview notes with Anna Allaluf dated March 2, 1953, Föhrenwald DP Camp, part of CM/1 form for Dinos Allaluf, 3.2.1.1/78873849/ITS Digital Archive, USHMM.

79. The McGraw Kaserne is located at the intersection of Tegernseer Landstrasse, Peter-Auzinger-Strasse, and Stadelheimer Strasse in the southern sector of Munich.

of the AJDC.[80] On March 16, 1953, Anna had fixed upon Greece as her desired destination for resettlement, and Dinos was to follow. Levy wrote, "Mrs. Allaluf came to the [AJDC] office [in Föhrenwald] and discussed the developments in her situation. She was skeptical whether AJDC could help her since so far she felt that she had never received anything positive."[81] (See document 3.8.[82]) In fact, Levy did follow up immediately to support her case, efforts recorded in painstaking detail and collected in this CM/1 file.[83] A few months later, on May 5, 1953, the Föhrenwald office noted, "Interview with Mrs. Allaluf, who reported that her husband had lost the job [at McGraw Kaserne] for lack of health. He is receiving unemployment assistance which covers his expenses. Mrs. Allaluf was very concerned about the developments and insisted on help to get out of the camp as quickly as possible, since she felt in that atmosphere she will be close to a breakdown."[84] Anna emigrated from Germany to Greece on September 21, 1953. The report by her AJDC caseworker shows her ambivalence about leaving Germany and Dinos behind and the frustration her wavering caused the AJDC. Dinos remained in Germany.[85]

Anger, depression, struggle, and loss are themes in this CM/1 file, and the Allalufs clearly confounded the caseworkers trying to help them. Following a visit by Dinos to the Munich AJDC emigration office on October 8, 1953, Levy wrote, "Allaluf had been offered the resettlement scheme in Norway in 1952, but since Mr. Allaluf refused to accept the conditions proposed by the Norwegian mission, he resigned from this project." She continued, "Then it came out

---

80. The report notes, "Mr. Allaluf came to the interview [with Anna Allaluf. He] is a small man, black hair and has a mustache which identifies him more closely to his Spanish-Jewish [Sephardic] origin. Mr. Allaluf started the interview in Spanish as he knew from his wife that [the case] worker could talk this language. Mr. Allaluf was very critical about AJDC and complained that he never has received help." See interview notes with Allaluf dated March 10, 1953, part of CM/1 form for Dinos Allaluf, 3.2.1.1/78873848/ITS Digital Archive, USHMM.

81. See interview notes with Anna Allaluf dated March 16, 1953, Föhrenwald DP Camp, part of CM/1 form for Dinos Allaluf, 3.2.1.1/78873845/ITS Digital Archive, USHMM.

82. Letter from M. Kohn, AJDC emigration officer, Föhrenwald, to Miss Gladys Roth, director of emigration services, Germany, March 18, 1953, 3.2.1.1/78873894/ITS Digital Archive, USHMM.

83. Ibid.

84. See interview notes with Anna Allaluf dated May 5, 1953, Föhrenwald DP Camp, part of CM/1 form for Dinos Allaluf, 3.2.1.1/78873845/ITS Digital Archive, USHMM.

85. Report by Rita Katz, October 8, 1953, part of CM/1 form for Dinos Allaluf, 3.2.1.1/78873842/ITS Digital Archive, USHMM.

that Mr. Allaluf was not very anxious to return to Greece since he became aware that at the moment he would be back in his country, he would have to serve in the [Greek] Army. He felt that he has been long enough in the Army during the war, and he did not consider it his duty to serve for this country [Greece]. We offered to help [him] further on his repatriation matter, but he declined this offer, saying that he can take care of himself and will go when he considers it appropriate."[86]

He must have angered Levy during this visit. On that same day, she wrote to her colleague, M. Einziger,

> We want to bring to your attention that Mrs. Anna Allaluf left for Greece on September 22, 1953. Her husband Mr. Dinos Allaluf has not yet completed his finalities to return also to Greece and this on his own choice. He has told me that he does not want us to work on the matter as he is very capable of taking care of himself. He furthermore does not get any relief from JDC. Considering all these facts, we wish to inform you that we close the case of Mr. Dinos Allaluf and so he is no longer the concern of [the] Social Services Department.[87]

Twelve days later, Dinos returned to the AJDC offices in Munich without an appointment. Levy was away from the office. "Mr. Allaluf appeared in my office in a very excited manner and said that he had to talk to me," wrote her coworker Rita Katz on October 20, 1953. When she explained that she had other appointments and could not accommodate him in that moment, "he started to make a lot of noise." When she responded in what she described as "a quiet and polite manner" and opened the door for him to depart, "he got into [a] rage and slam[m]ed the door with such a furious temper that the door hit my foot and the shoe was thrown in a corner." A policeman escorted him out.[88]

After another year of sending mixed signals to the AJDC staff,[89] Dinos

86. Report by Rita Katz, October 8, 1953, part of CM/1 form for Dinos Allaluf, 3.2.1.1/ 78873842/ITS Digital Archive, USHMM.

87. Letter from Deborah Levy, Social Services Department, AJDC, Munich, to Mr. M. Einziger, AJDC, Munich, October 8, 1953, part of CM/1 form for Dinos Allaluf, 3.2.1.1/ 78873887/ITS Digital Archive, USHMM.

88. Report by Rita Katz, October 8, 1953, part of CM/1 form for Dinos Allaluf, 3.2.1.1/ 78873842/ITS Digital Archive, USHMM.

89. On March 3, 1954, Jean Goldsmith in the Föhrenwald Emigration Department wrote to her colleagues in the AJDC's Athens (Greece) office, "In reply to your letter of February 9, 1954, we wish to inform you that [your] client appeared in our office only today and refused to give us the names of his parents required for issuance of a new birth certificate.

finally emigrated to Greece in October 1954, nine years after war's end.[90] As Deborah Levy described it, he "live[d] in a DP camp for eleven years and now return[ed] to a country where he ha[d] no house or job and no help from the Jewish community."[91] By December 1, 1954, he had returned to the Föhrenwald DP camp, much to the dismay of Deborah Levy, now assistant director of AJDC Föhrenwald Services.[92] By 1980, he was living in Munich and wrote to the ITS from his address at Erich-Kästner-Strasse 2 as late as 1987, asking for help locating his brother, Isakino (Isac).[93] Isac's fate remained unresolved, and ITS staff presumed him to be deceased.[94] But Dinos did not believe this to be so. (See document 3.9.[95]) In one of many attempts over decades to solicit information from ITS about his brother, in 1986 Dinos wrote that at war's end, three different persons at three different times told Dinos that his brother had survived. One of them kept a book in which he recorded the names of all those who had been liberated in Theresienstadt. "My brother's name was also listed there," wrote Dinos. Those who had perished had a cross by their names. "There was *no* cross next to my brother's name, and so I assume that he is still alive," he wrote.[96] Dinos's explanation for why Isac never looked for Dinos after

Mr. Allaluf stated that he did not want to be repatriated to Greece as he allegedly received unfavorable news on the economic situation in Greece. He did not want further action in this matter to be taken." See letter from Jean Goldsmith, Emigration Department, to AJDC, Athens, March 3, 1954, part of CM/1 form for Dinos Allaluf, 3.2.1.1/78873881/ITS Digital Archive, USHMM.

90. Notice of individual departure to Greece, United Hebrew Immigrant Aid Society Service, Munich, October 27, 1954, part of CM/1 file for Dinos Allaluf, 3.2.1.1/78873839/ITS Digital Archive, USHMM.

91. Notes on Dinos Allaluf by Deborah Levy, September 2, 1954, part of CM/1 file for Dinos Allaluf, 3.2.1.1/78873872/ITS Digital Archive, USHMM.

92. This is the date on a simple card stating only, "Allaluf, Dinos, back in camp, December 1, 1954," and a note in a "Case or Family Data" form stating, "Departed for Greece on 27 October 1954. Returned to Föhrenwald (file remains closed)," part of CM/1 file for Dinos Allaluf, 3.2.1.1/78873917 and 78873926/ITS Digital Archive, USHMM. For Deborah Levy's reaction, see letter from Deborah Levy, assistant director, Föhrenwald Services, to Haim Benrubi, AJDC, Athens, January 11, 1955, part of CM/1 file for Dinos Allaluf, 3.2.1.1/78873917 and 78873850/ITS Digital Archive, USHMM.

93. Letter from unidentified ITS staff member, Bad Arolsen, to Daniel Allalouf, Munich, April 8, 1987, part of T/D file for Anna (Meworach, Meborach) Allaluf, 6.3.3.2/93515933/ITS Digital Archive, USHMM.

94. ITS-generated name card, part of T/D file for Isakino Allaluf, 6.3.3.2/100012165/ITS Digital Archive, USHMM.

95. Letter from Daniel Allalouf, Munich, to ITS, Bad Arolsen, December 3, 1986, titled "Search for My Brother," 6.3.3.2/100012170/ITS Digital Archive, USHMM.

96. Ibid.

the war was equally wrenching: "My brother was assuming that I had been shot after an attempted escape and subsequent transfer to another camp. That explains why he is not looking for me."[97] Scholars of trauma and loss might study these files to determine patterns in how survivors wrote ITS multiple times over decades in search of particular loved ones, despite having or receiving no new information.

Why such an extensive rendering of this one file, aside from its particular breadth (137 pages) and range, from Greece to Auschwitz to Germany, to Greece again, back to Germany, and ending at Erich-Kästner-Strasse 2 in Munich? By aggregating CM/1 forms by category (e.g., religion, ethnicity, location, or another variable), scholars can study specific patterns in physical, psychological, and other difficulties faced by Jewish DPs. The Allaluf CM/1 form captures and chronicles the long and difficult road Jewish survivors faced after liberation. Some, like the Allalufs, seem never to truly recover from the sudden and traumatic loss of their families, the physical and psychological hardships of concentration camp life, and the irony of remaining in Germany for years while sputtering toward new lives. There to see, page by page, are the emotional strain, broken relationships, volatility, and even rejection by Jewish DPs of help from agencies and caseworkers whose almost superhuman efforts on their behalf jump from the pages of ITS-held documentation. Scholars studying the aftermath of genocide from a psychological perspective have much material to work with in the roughly 350,000 CM/1 forms in the ITS holdings.

"WE REGRET TO INFORM YOU . . ."[98]

In early October 1949, Felix Ries, a German Jew, sent a postcard from his postwar residence in Dinkelsbühl (Bavaria) to 3 Siebertstrasse, the Munich headquarters of the Central Committee of Liberated Jews for the US Zone of occupied Germany.[99] (See document 3.10.[100]) He wrote to ask for help in

---

97. Ibid.

98. A. J. Wittamer, chief, Records Branch, ITS, Bad Arolsen, to A. M. Apelbom & Kossoy, Law & Notorial Offices, Munich, April 27, 1951, 6.3.3.2/100159019/ITS Digital Archive, USHMM.

99. The Central Committee of Liberated Jews in the US Zone of Occupation (1945–1950) "considered itself responsible for rehabilitation and welfare of all Jewish DPs located there and as their sole representative vis-à-vis military authorities." See Arieh J. Kochavi, "Liberation and Dispersal," in *The Oxford Handbook of Holocaust Studies*, ed. Peter Hayes and John K. Roth (Oxford: Oxford University Press, 2010), 516.

100. Ibid.

obtaining a certificate of incarceration regarding his foster brother (*Pflegebruder*), Harry I. Müller, and Harry's wife, Theresia.[101] About two weeks later, he wrote the Central Committee again, but with a bit more detail. He explained that he already knew Harry and Theresia Müller had been "taken to the east" (*nach Osten gebracht*).[102] On October 28, 1944, Harry and Theresia Müller were put on transport "Ev" from Theresienstadt to Auschwitz—the very last of the ten autumn transports.[103] Felix claimed to have been incarcerated at Theresienstadt in October 1944 as well, and we can assume that is how he knew that Harry and Theresia were "taken to the east." But he did not say so in this letter. Rather, he wrote with regard to his "nephews."[104] "I would very much like to safeguard their reparations claims [*Wiedergutmachungsansprüche*] and for this purpose, I need official confirmation [of the deaths of their parents]," he wrote.[105]

A survivor himself, Ries was born in 1892 in Hennersdorf (Upper Silesia; today Czech Republic).[106] A self-employed merchant in Neisse (Upper Silesia; today Nysa, Poland), he claimed to have been arrested and incarcerated in Buchenwald from November 9, 1938, to February 18, 1939.[107] From there,

101. Postcard from Felix Ries, Dinkelsbühl, to the Central Committee of the Liberated Jews in Germany, Munich, October 15, 1949, 6.3.3.2/84797428/ITS Digital Archive, USHMM. For more on the fate of Müller and his family, see Suzanne Brown-Fleming, "'Wiedervereinigung Ersehnend': Gender and the Holocaust Fates of the Müller and Gittler Families," in *Different Horrors/Same Hell: Gender and the Holocaust*, ed. Myrna Goldenberg and Amy Shapiro (Seattle: University of Washington Press, 2013), 177–97.

102. Letter from Felix Ries, Dinkelsbühl, to the Central Committee of the Liberated Jews in Germany, Munich, October 28, 1949, 6.3.3.2/85371030/ITS Digital Archive, USHMM.

103. Presumably, they were murdered on arrival. See transport lists from the Theresienstadt ghetto, 28.10.1944 "Ev" to KL Auschwitz, 1.1.42.1/4959636/ITS Digital Archive, USHMM. This document is a copy received by ITS from the Staatsanwaltschaft bei dem Landgericht Frankfurt am Main in 1971.

104. While not naming them in the letter, Felix must have been referring to Harry and Theresia Müller's two sons, Hans Gert Müller (1908–1946) and Klaus Müller, still living in 1949. The Müllers also had two daughters, Lieselotte (b. 1910) and Ursula (b. 1913). The letter specifically refers, however, to Felix's "nephews" (*meine Neffen*). On the Müller children, see Brown-Fleming, "*Wiedervereinigung Ersehnend*," 179.

105. Letter from Felix Ries, Dinkelsbühl, to the Central Committee of the Liberated Jews in Germany, Munich, October 28, 1949, 6.3.3.2/85371030/ITS Digital Archive, USHMM.

106. CNI attributes for Felix Ries, 0.1/51813505, and CNI cards for Felix Ries, 0.1/33965273–89/ITS Digital Collection, USHMM. See also T/D file for Felix Ries, 6.3.3.2/85620076–101.

107. ITS staff could not locate documentation for his incarceration in Buchenwald; this was not uncommon for men imprisoned following *Kristallnacht*. See letter from A. J. Wittamer, chief, Documentation Division, ITS, Bad Arolsen, to the Bayerisches Landesentschädigungsamt, Munich, August 2, 1951, 6.3.3.2/85620092/ITS Digital Archive, USHMM.

Ries was transferred to a labor camp in Falkenberg (today Niemodlin, Poland) until July 1944, then to Theresienstadt until May 1945. He spent his first year as a liberated man in Petschau bei Karlsbad (today, Bečov nad Teplou, Czech Republic).[108] In 1946, he moved to Dinkelsbühl, where he died on November 12, 1951.[109] Felix Ries was relying, we can presume, on the November 10, 1947, Law #59 on the Restitution of Identifiable Property, promulgated by the US military government.[110] Writing within four years of the war's end, he was among the first wave of Jewish families to request restitution for material losses during the Holocaust.

While not explored in any depth in this volume, Jewish voices calling for justice in the form of restitution and compensation[111] are a key component of ITS-held T/D files. Like the evolving and global restitution and reparations process itself, T/D files span from 1945 until today. The quest for restitution and compensation, Jewish and non-Jewish, seen from the viewpoint of the inquirers writing to ITS, be they individuals, institutions, or governments, unfolds over decades, and the story still awaits telling from the vantage point of those doing the asking. Further, as Regula Ludi points out, Jewish thinkers played a key role in conceiving "alternative approaches" to reparations following a war that had "surpassed any catastrophe within living memory."[112] What is more, scholars have not treated at all the role the ITS itself played in the ability of survivors to receive restitution and compensation. Let us look at the illustra-

---

108. CM/1 form for Felix Ries, 3.2.1.1/79655412–14/ITS Digital Archive, USHMM. An attempt to find supporting documentation for his wartime history was unsuccessful; no documentation from either Buchenwald or Theresienstadt records in ITS references Ries.

109. ITS *Inhaftierungsbescheinigung/Krankenpapiere/Sterbeurkunde* form for Felix Ries, June 6, 1958, 6.3.3.2/85620084/ITS Digital Archive, USHMM. See also CM/1 form for Felix Ries, 3.2.1.1/79655412–14/ITS Digital Archive, USHMM. Anni (Babucke) Ries was born on November 5, 1905, in Neisse. She was foreman of a textile factory there until July 1944, when she, too, was sent from Neisse to Theresienstadt. Felix and Anni Ries did not apply for IRO assistance until September 1949. It is likely that Anni was not Jewish and that the Ries family owned the textile factory in Neisse, as both factors would explain her ability to run it until 1944.

110. For a thorough discussion of early Allied efforts with regard to restitution and subsequently compensation, see Regula Ludi, *Reparations for Nazi Victims in Postwar Europe* (Cambridge: Cambridge University Press, 2012), 87–102.

111. Restitution, or "restoration of a good and its equivalent value," referred specifically to property taken from Jews. Seen as separate by the victorious Allies, compensation was meant to redress "harm done to the lives, bodies and health, freedom, property, and professional and economic advancement of Holocaust survivors." See Peter Hayes, "Plunder and Restitution," in *The Oxford Handbook of Holocaust Studies*, 548–49.

112. Ludi, *Reparations for Nazi Victims in Postwar Europe*, 13, 19–23.

tive case of Abram (Abraham) Langer, a Polish Jew, to demonstrate the limitations of the ITS holdings and the folly of human error in relation to Jewish survivors and their advocates.

Langer was born in 1922 in Chrzanów, Poland.[113] Incarcerated in the Chrzanów ghetto from October 1939 to November 1941, he was then sent to a long list of forced labor camps in a series of smaller villages and towns:[114] first to St. Annaberg from November 2, 1941, to January 1942; then to Laurahütte from January to October 1942; from there to Sakrau (today Zakrzów) from October to December 1942; next to Brande (later Pradki) from December 1942 to February 1943; then to a place his legal representatives called "Gross-Masslowitz" (perhaps a reference to Łowicz) from March to August 1943; next to Görlitz from August 1943 to March 1944; and finally to Kretschamberg,[115] from where he and other Kretschamberg prisoners were marched to Buchenwald in February 1945. The survivors of this death march arrived in Buchenwald on April 4, 1945.[116]

Langer spent the next four years in DP camps in Bavaria. On March 15, 1949, he boarded El Al Flight Number 71 to Israel, leaving Europe behind for good, like so many other survivors.[117] Langer's thick T/D file chronicles his multiple attempts to receive documentation about his Holocaust odyssey from

---

113. See 3.2.1.1/79385445–7; 1.1.5.3/6440034–5; and 3.1.1.1/67972490/ITS Digital Archive, USHMM.

114. See letter from E. Kossoy, Apelbom & Kossoy Law & Notarial Offices, Munich Office, to ITS, Bad Arolsen, February 10, 1956, 6.3.3.2/100159011/ITS Digital Archive, USHMM. For further information on these sites of incarceration, see Aleksandra Namyslo, "Chrzanów," in *The United States Holocaust Memorial Museum Encyclopedia of Camps and Ghettos, 1933–1945*, vol. 2: *Ghettos in German-Occupied Eastern Europe*, Martin Dean ed. (Bloomington: Indiana University Press in association with USHMM, 2012, 146–47; on St. Annaberg, headquarters for the Organisation Schmelt camps, see Megargee, *The United States Holocaust Memorial Museum Encyclopedia of Camps and Ghettos*, 1:699; Stanislawa Iwaszko, "Laurahütte," in Megargee, *The United States Holocaust Memorial Museum Encyclopedia of Camps and Ghettos*, 1:261–62; and references to Görlitz in Megargee, *The United States Holocaust Memorial Museum Encyclopedia of Camps and Ghettos*, 1:1615.

115. In the document, Kretschamberg is misspelled as "Kretschenberg." Kretschamberg was a subcamp of Gross-Rosen in the town of Kretschamberg near Kittlitztreben (today Trzebień, Poland). Only put into operation in February or March 1944, "1,700 to 1,800" Jewish men, most from Poland and Hungary, were imprisoned there. See Danuta Sawicka, "Kittlitztreben," in Megargee, *The United States Holocaust Memorial Museum Encyclopedia of Camps and Ghettos*, 1:753–54.

116. Chapter 4 discusses Langer's testimony with regard to this death march.

117. ITS certificate of residence for Abraham Langer, March 22, 1956, 6.3.3.2/100159015/ITS Digital Archive, USHMM.

Bad Arolsen for restitution/compensation purposes. Represented by Apelbom & Kossoy Law & Notarial Offices (19 Rothschild Boulevard in Tel Aviv, with a Munich office on Zweibrückenstrasse), Langer requested a certificate of incarceration from ITS in February 1951.[118] He was able to supply a prisoner number, 19213, which he understood to be his Buchenwald prisoner number.[119] Not surprisingly, given the late date of Langer's arrival and the still nascent organization of records at ITS, nothing could be found. "We regret to inform you that the original concentration camp documents, held by the International Tracing Service, do not contain sufficient information to enable us to issue the requested certificate," A. J. Wittamer, chief of the ITS Records Branch, wrote to Apelbom & Kossoy.[120] Imagine the immense frustration that Langer must have felt, given his experiences. But he did not give up. In 1955, Apelbom & Kossoy wrote to the ITS again, asking that they recheck their records.[121]

The response was slow but more fruitful than in the first go-round. This time, ITS staff located both a displaced person registration record (DP-2) card and also documentation from Langer's stay in Garmisch (Bavaria) from 1945 to 1949, before his emigration to Israel. Based on this, the ITS issued a certificate of residence confirming that Langer registered at the Mittenwald DP camp on April 3, 1946, and lived on Ludwigstrasse 35 and then Rathausstrasse 6 in Garmisch until departing for Israel. No documentation from Buchenwald could be located still, but ITS staff noted that Langer's DP-2 card contained the notation "Buchenwald prisoner number 19213."[122] Langer persisted. (See document 3.11.[123]) His attorney wrote yet again to ITS the following year, 1956, again specifying the long list of sites where Langer had suffered.[124] Finally, their

---

118. Request for certificate of incarceration from A. M. Apelbom & Kossoy Law & Notarial Offices, Munich, to ITS Headquarters, February 21, 1951, 6.3.3.2/100159020/ITS Digital Archive, USHMM.

119. This prisoner number appears on the DP-2 card for Abraham Langer, 3.1.1.1/67972490/ITS Digital Archive, USHMM.

120. A. J. Wittamer, chief, Records Branch, ITS, Bad Arolsen, to A. M. Apelbom & Kossoy, Law & Notarial Offices, Munich, April 27, 1951, 6.3.3.2/100159019/ITS Digital Archive, USHMM.

121. Dr. F. Kosak, Apelbom & Kossoy Law & Notarial Offices, Munich Office, to ITS, Bad Arolsen, September 23, 1955, and E. Kossoy to ITS, November 9, 1955, 6.3.3.2/100159012–13/ITS Digital Archive, USHMM.

122. Certificate of residence, Abraham Langer, March 22, 1956, 6.3.3.2/100159015/ITS Digital Archive, USHMM.

123. E. Kossoy, Apelbom & Kossoy Law & Notarial Offices, Munich Office, to ITS, Bad Arolsen, February 10, 1956, 6.3.3.2/100159011/ITS Digital Archive, USHMM.

124. Ibid.

efforts met with success. This time, ITS staff managed to locate a single infirmary card (*Revierkarte*) dated May 7, 1945, for a "Langer" with prisoner number 19213.[125] This was the crucial document that the Bayerisches Landesentschädigungsamt (BLEA) needed. Yet, one key omission in the list of sites supplied by Langer's attorneys meant the process still failed.

In their March 22, 1956, letter to Apelbom & Kossoy, ITS staff expressed reservations and caution with regard to the infirmary card, which they described as follows: "Langer, no further personal data, former prisoner number 19213, was brought to the Buchenwald concentration camp, no date given. On the infirmary card is noted: admission to infirmary—date admitted: May 7, 1945." Maddeningly, the letter continues, "Because the personal information is incomplete, we cannot determine whether the [. . .] report pertains to the above-mentioned individual. According to an April 4, 1945, report on changes [in the number of prisoners] at the Buchenwald concentration camp, a transport arrived from the Gross-Rosen concentration camp/Kittlitz-Treben [Kittlitztreben near Kretschamburg] [work] detachment with 746 prisoners, who never got registered at the Buchenwald concentration camp." In their February 1956 letter, Apelbom & Kossoy never included Kittlitztreben/Kretschamburg on the long list of sites of incarceration (!).[126] Yet, we know Langer was in Kretschamburg due to his testimony given to the US Army in June 1945, a copy of which arrived at ITS in 1956.[127] Neither ITS nor, apparently, Apelbom & Kossoy made this connection. As a result, nearly ten years later, when BLEA wrote to ITS asking for a copy of the Buchenwald infirmary card,[128] ITS staff sent it as requested, but with the following caveat: "We note that the Buchenwald concentration camp was liberated on April 11, 1945, and that the infirmary admission of the person in question took place on May 7, 1945. No other patient documents or relevant information is available."[129] ITS documents do

125. ITS, Bad Arolsen, to Apelbom & Kossoy, Munich, March 22, 1956, 6.3.3.2/100159022/ITS Digital Archive, USHMM. For the infirmary card, see 1.1.5.3/6440034–5/ITS Digital Archive, USHMM.

126. Even so, fellow Jewish survivor of this death march, Leon Nass, also assigned a number upon arrival in Buchenwald and also sent to the infirmary after liberation, lost the slip of paper given to him on his release from the infirmary. He too had difficulty obtaining the necessary paperwork for reparation/compensation. See T/D file for Leon Nass, 6.3.3.2/90754910/ITS Digital Archive, USHMM.

127. Sworn statement of Abram Langer, Buchenwald, June 17, 1945, 1.1.5.0/82065532/ITS Digital Archive, USHMM.

128. Letter from the Bayerisches Landesentschädigungsamt, Munich, to ITS, Bad Arolsen, March 10, 1964, 6.3.3.2/100159009/ITS Digital Archive, USHMM.

129. Letter from G. Pechar, ITS, Bad Arolsen, to Bayerisches Landesentschädigungsamt, Munich, June 15, 1964, 6.3.3.2/100159017/ITS Digital Archive, USHMM.

not tell us whether Langer ever managed to prove his long history of incarceration so as to receive restitution and/or compensation.

An introductory volume like this one cannot hope to provide more than a taste of what ITS holdings will offer scholars of the Holocaust and its aftermath in the decades ahead. This volume's aim is far more modest: to give color and a voice to those who experienced the Holocaust. In the case of Jewish voices, ITS-held documents assembled here tell stories with few happy endings. We began this chapter in Estonia, where orphaned Vilna Jews labored in places few students in the modern Holocaust classroom have heard of: Aseri, Ereda, Goldfields, Kiviõli, Narva-Ost, Vivikonna, and others. Jewish victims are allowed the dignity of describing their tormenters and their (few) saviors in the first person: Mack, who "one day would hit" Vilna ghetto inmates and "another day bring them food [depending] on his mood"; SS medic Eric Scharfetter, who liked to murder Jewish inmates with a pickax; and Marion Hutton, acting director of Kloster Indersdorf, whose humanity helped to save young Lazar Kleinmann's innocence.

With the best of intentions, even the most skilled scholars and professors teaching this subject can struggle to impart the human voice of Jewish victims in their books and courses on Nazi and Axis ideology, machinery, bureaucracy, and brutality. Yet students instinctively understand somehow that they cannot relate to mass numbers or descriptions of a Jewish people acted upon, rather than acting and speaking for themselves. And as the rich documents in the ITS holdings show us, Jewish voices offer a perspective the world needs. Students of psychology and linguistics will find much material here with which to try to explain how human beings process and put words to the unimaginable. The most (in)famous and described episode of the Holocaust, mass murder by gassing at Auschwitz II–Birkenau, is made new again by ITS-held questionnaires answered within five years after war's end—and with no intention by their authors of providing a future pedagogical tool.

CM/1 files tell us of the less triumphant endings for many Jewish survivors who never fully readjusted. Today, we hear stories of hope from survivors who have lived rich lives, and we would be dishonest to say this is not comforting, even easy on some level. Yet so many either did not survive at all or, like Dinos Allaluf never really left the selection ramp in Birkenau in their imaginations and memories. Finally, very promising indeed are the ITS-held T/D files for conveying a better understanding of how individuals, institutions, and nations struggled to apply old standards of restitution and compensation to an unprecedented event like the Holocaust. So many vantage points are possible here: that of the inquiring victims and their families; of nations struggling with practical realities that conflicted and conflict with the moral imperatives raised by the Holocaust; of institutions like the ITS itself; and of Jewish offices and agencies seeking elusive justice.

DOCUMENT LIST

DOCUMENT 3.1. Sworn statement, Sam Hamburg, July 19, 1966, 5.1/ 82326167/ITS Digital Archive, USHMM (followed by translation).

DOCUMENT 3.2. Interrogation transcript, Josef Mielnik, Tivon, Israel, September 5, 1965, 5.1/82326173–4/ITS Digital Archive, USHMM (followed by translation).

DOCUMENT 3.3. Letter from Lazar Kleinmann, Salford, United Kingdom, to Marion Hutton, Kloster Indersdorf, 6.3.2.1/84313462, ITS Digital Archive, USHMM (followed by transcription).

DOCUMENT 3.4. "Questions to all 'Auschwitzers,'" 1.1.0.7/87763878/ ITS Digital Archive, USHMM.

DOCUMENT 3.5. Inquiry sheet concerning those who died in the camp at Auschwitz II-Birkenau, completed by Daniel Allaluf, DP Camp Landsberg am Lech, May 17, 1950, 1.1.0.7/87763894/ITS Digital Archive, USHMM (followed by translation).

DOCUMENT 3.6. Decision of the Preparatory Commission for the International Refugee Organization review board for Jakob Abrahamovicz, 3.2.1.5/ 81288526/ITS Digital Archive, USHMM.

DOCUMENT 3.7. Notes on Allaluf case included in the CM/1 form for Dinos Allaluf, 3.2.1.1/78873841/ITS Digital Archive, USHMM.

DOCUMENT 3.8. Letter from M. Kohn, AJDC emigration officer, Föhrenwald, to Miss Gladys Roth, director of emigration services, Germany, March 18, 1953, 3.2.1.1/78873894/ITS Digital Archive, USHMM.

DOCUMENT 3.9. Letter, titled "Search for My Brother," from Daniel Allalouf, Munich, to ITS, Bad Arolsen, December 3, 1986, 6.3.3.2/100012170/ ITS Digital Archive, USHMM (followed by translation).

DOCUMENT 3.10. Postcard from Felix Ries, Dinkelsbühl, to the Central Committee of the Liberated Jews in Germany, Munich, October 15, 1949, 6.3.3.2/84797428/ITS Digital Archive, USHMM (followed by translation).

DOCUMENT 3.11. E. Kossoy, Apelbom & Kossoy Law & Notarial Offices, Munich Office, to ITS, Bad Arolsen, February 10, 1956, 6.3.3.2/100159011/ITS Digital Archive, USHMM (followed by translation).

DOCUMENTS

DOCUMENT 3.1

Vor Beginn der Verfolgungsmassnahmen lebte ich zusammen mit meiner Mutter - mein Vater war bereits im Jahre 1923 verstorben - und meinen fuenf Geschwistern in Wilno. Ich war ein kraeftiger, gesunder junger Mann und kann mich - ausser an die ueblichen Kinderkrankheiten - an keine ernstliche Krankheit erinnern. Ich war als Mechaniker beschaeftigt und verdiente ausreichend.

Nach dem Einmarsch der deutschen Truppen in Wilno war ich schweren Verfolgungsmassnahmen ausgesetzt.

Im September 1941 wurde ich in das Ghetto meiner Heimatstadt eingeliefert Die Verhaeltnisse waren niederdrueckend. Wir waren auf engstem Raum zusammengepfercht, hatten nicht genug zu essen und ich wurde zu schwerer Zwangsarbeit im Minitionslager herangezogen.

Als das Ghetto im September 1943 liquidiert wurde, ueberstellte man mich in das Zwangsarbeitslager Waiwara. In diesem Lager zog man mich wieder zu harten Arbeiten beim Bau von Eisenbahnlinien heran, auch zu Erdarbeiten wurde ich eingesetzt. Meine Arbeitszeit betrug taeglich 14 Stunden. Unser Essen war knapp und sehr schlecht. Ich erkrankte an einem schweren Typhusfieber und schleppte mich noch krank und vollkommen abgeschwaecht wieder zur Arbeit, da ich furchtbare Angst vor einer Vernichtung hatt

Im Oktober 1943 schleppte man mich in das Zwangsarbeitslager Fifikoni, von da aus in die Lager Kiviolo, Narwa, Aseri und Goldfilz. Ueberall musste ich schwer arbeiten, zuerst liess man mich wieder Bahnbauarbeiten verrichten, spaeter hatte ich in einer Oelfabrik zu arbeiten, wurde zu Lastarbeiten und Reinigungsarbeiten genommen und im Saegewerk eingesetzt. Im Lager Fifikoni bekam ich ein Abszess am rechten Oberschenkel. Man operierte mich unter primitivsten Bedingungen. Ich litt unter entsetzlichen Schmerzen.

Im Sommer1944 kam ich ueber Tallin und Danzig in das Konzentrationslager Stutthof. Zu dieser Zeit war ich schon voellig abgeschwaecht. Trotzdem hatte ich auch dort wieder verschiedene Schikanearbeiten zu verrichten.

State of New York)
County of New York) ss.   - 2 -

On the _____19th_____ day of __July 1966__ before me appeared the person who stated under oath that he signed the foregoing statement and that the contents of it are true to his own knowledge and belief.

ELISABETH KEYSER

Before the beginning of the persecution measures, I lived together with my mother—my father had already died in 1923—and my five siblings in Wilno [Vilna]. I was a strong, healthy young man and cannot remember any serious illness, apart from the usual childhood diseases. I was employed as a mechanic and earned good money.

After the German troops marched into Wilno, I was exposed to severe measures of persecution.

In September 1941, I was taken to the ghetto of my native city. The conditions were depressing. We were crowded together in the tightest space, did not have enough to eat, and I was used for hard forced labor in the munitions dump.

When the ghetto was liquidated in September 1943, I was transferred to the Waiwara [Vaivara] forced labor camp. In this camp, I was made to perform hard labor again, building railroad lines, and I was also used for excavation work. My working time totaled 14 hours daily. Our food was meager and very poor. I developed a serious case of typhus and, sick and completely weakened, dragged myself back to work because I was terribly afraid of being killed.

In October 1943, I was taken to the Fifikoni [Vivikonna] forced labor camp and from there to the Kiviolo [Kiviõli], Narwa [Narva], Aseri, and Goldfilz [Goldfields] camps. Everywhere, I had to do heavy work; first I was made to do railroad construction work again, and later I had to work in an oil plant and was used for carrying loads and doing cleaning jobs and working in a sawmill. In the Fifikoni camp, I got an abscess on my right thigh. I was operated on under the most primitive conditions. I suffered terrible pain.

In the summer of 1944, I came via Tallinn and Danzig to the Stutthof concentration camp. By this time, I was completely weakened. Nevertheless, I had to do various tasks there again, as a form of harassment.

[remainder of page in English]

DOCUMENT 3.2

- 4 -

        Herr Mielnik, Sie sagen so sicher, daß es sich hierbei um
Leichen gehandelt hat. Haben Sie gesehen, wie diese Leute
ablebten und wissen Sie genau, daß diese 3 oder 4 Erschlagenen zum Verbrennungsofen gebracht wurden? Überlegen Sie
sich Ihre Beantwortung bitte genau, bitte äußern Sie sich
jetzt hierzu.

Bei diesen erschlagenen Personen hat es sich ebenfalls um typhuskranke
gehandelt. Es waren Juden wie ich. Sie waren völlig entkräftet und
standen vor dem Hungertode. Wenn solche, völlig entkräfteten Menschen
derart geschlagen werden, so ist kaum anzunehmen, daß sie davon über-
lebten. Ich habe mit eigenen Augen gesehen, wie die Spitze vom Pickel
die Körper der Häftlinge durch-bohrt hat. Es war so, daß die Spitze
durxxm des Pickels auf der anderen Seite herausschaute. Ich habe auch
gesehen, daß der ganze Fußboden voll von Blut war. Wenn man Personen
so erschlägt, so ist dies schon mehr als Sadismus. Dieser Mann war
völlig verroht und schreckte vor nichts zurück. Wenn er den Schonungsblock betreten hat, hatten wir immer alle Angst, daß wir nun an die
Reihe kämen.

Auf Grund dieser bestialischen Ermordung hat man diesem Sanitäter den
Namen " K i r k o n i k " (Übersetzt: Spitzhacke) gegeben.

        Herr Mielnik, was sagt Ihnen der Name R u n d e und um was
für eine Person hat es sich hierbei gehandelt?

Der Name R u n d e ist mir geläufig. Ich weiß, daß dieser Mann ein
deutscher SS-Mann war. Soweit ich mich erinnern kann, hatte er einen
kleinen SS-Dienstgrad. Ich glaube, daß er einen oder höchstens 2 Winkel
am Arm hatte. Nach meiner Erinnerung war dieser Mann etwa 27-30 Jahre
alt; 175 cm groß, normal entwickelter Statur. Irgendwelche Besonder-
heiten sind mir an ihm nicht aufgefallen. Mir wurden jetzt mehrere Licht-
bilder vorgelegt. Von den fotografierten Personen kenne ich niemanden.
Wenn mir jetzt gesagt wird, daß sich unter diesen Personen R u n d e
befindet, so hilft mir dies auch nichts. Jetzt wurde mir das Bild des
R u n d e vorgelegt und ich muß wiederum ein Nichterkennen bestätigen.
Es sind immerhin 20 Jahre bereits vergangen und das einwandfreie er-
kennen ist nicht unbedingt einfach. Ich will niemanden belasten und habe
mir vorgenommen, nur absolut Richtiges zu bestätigen. Wenn in Narva der
Sanitäter R u n d e geheißen haben soll, so kann es sich nur um den

- 5 -

2379

138

- 5 -

von mir genannten Sanitäter handeln. Ich weiß sicher, daß in
Narva nur ein Sanitätsdienstgrad tätig war und dieser Mann
wurde von uns " K i r k o n i k " genannt.

Andere Tötungshandlungen von "Kirkonik" habe ich selbst nicht
gesehen, auch sind mir solche nicht bekannt.
Mir ist noch dunkel erinnerlich, daß dieser Sanitäter einen
Transport alter und kranker Häftlinge von Narva nach Wilna ge-
leitet hat. Man hat dann erzählt, man habe diese Leute fertig-
gemacht. Ich meine damit, sie wurden erschossen oder sonstwie
umgebracht. Ich bin sicher, daß ich zu dieser Zeit nicht mehr
im Schonungsblock lag. Ich weiß auch nicht, ob die abtransportierten
Häftlinge aus dem Schonungsblock kamen oder aus dem Lagerbereich
ausgesondert wurden.

Auf die Frage hin, ob ich weiß, daß während meiner Zeit in Narva
der Lagerführer P a n n i c k e einmal erkrankt war, kann ich
antworten, daß dies der Fall war. Ich kann weiter sagen, da die
Vertretung für den erkrankten P a n n i c k e der S c h n a b e l
übernahm.

Zu der mir gestellten Hauptfrage, ob gleichzeitig mit S c h n a -
b e l ein Sanitäter in dieser Vertretungszeit mitgekommen ist,
so kann ich nur sagen, daß ich dies nicht 100 %-ig bestätigen kann.

Mit absoluter Sicherheit weiß ich jedoch, daß in Narva nur ein
Sanitäter tätig war.

<u>Betrifft:</u> Ersuchen der StA Stuttgart -16 Js 326/62- von 13. Juli 1965
           aus Hechingen

Der Zeuge konnte zu den 5 aufgeführten Punkten keinerlei Beantwortung
geben.

Der Zeuge gibt nun an, keinerlei Angaben über Narva mehr machen zu
können und schildert seinen weiteren Leidensweg von Narva nach Kiviöli II.

Mr. Mielnik, you say with such certainty that this involved corpses. Did you see these people die, and do you know for certain that these 3 or 4 men who had been beaten to death were taken to the incinerator? Please consider your answer very carefully, and please speak now.

These people who were beaten to death were also typhus patients. They were Jews like me. They were completely exhausted and almost dead from starvation. When such utterly exhausted people are battered in that way, one can hardly expect them to survive it. I saw with my own eyes how the tip of the pickax pierced the bodies of the prisoners. It was done in such a way that the tip of the pickax poked out on the other side. I also saw that the whole floor was wet with blood. When people are killed in that way, it is more than sadism. This man was completely brutal and stopped at nothing. Whenever he entered the convalescence block, we all were afraid that now it would be our turn.

Because of this bestial murder, this medical orderly was given the name "K i r k o n i k" (meaning "pickax").

Mr. Mielnik, what does the name R u n d e mean to you, and what sort of person was this?

I'm familiar with the name R u n d e. I know that this man was a German SS man. As far as I can recall, he had a low SS rank. I think he had one or at most two triangles on his sleeve. As I recall, this man was between twenty-seven and thirty years old, 175 cm [5 feet, 7 1/2 inches] tall, of normal build. No specific features of his caught my attention. Several photos were shown to me just now. I know none of the people in the photographs. If I am now told that R u n d e is one of the people pictured, this does not help me either. Just now I was shown a photo of R u n d e, and once again I must confirm that I do not recognize him. After all, twenty years have passed now, and recognition beyond a shadow of a doubt is not necessarily easy. If the medical orderly in Narva is said to have been named R u n d e, then it can be

[second page]

only the medical orderly I mentioned. I know for certain that only one medical orderly was working in Narva, and this man was called "Kirkonik" by us.

I myself did not witness other acts of killing by "Kirkonik"; nor do I know of any.

I can still vaguely remember that this medical orderly led a transport of old and sick prisoners from Narva to Wilna. It was subsequently said that these people had been killed. By that, I mean they were shot or murdered in some other way. I am certain that I was no longer a patient in the convalescence block at this time. I also do not know whether the prisoners on the transport came from the convalescence block or were selected from the camp area.

In reply to the question whether I know that Camp Leader [head SS officer] P a n n i c k e once fell ill during my time in Narva, I can say that this was the case. In addition, I can say that S c h n a b e l stood in for P a n n i c k e while he was ill.

Regarding the main question put to me, whether a medical orderly came along simultaneously with S c h n a b e l in this period while he was standing in, I can only say that I cannot answer with 100 percent certainty.

With absolute certainty, however, I know that only one medical orderly was working in Narva.

Regarding: Request of the Stuttgart Public Prosecutor's Office—16 Js 326.62—of July 13, 1965, from Hechingen.

The witness now claims to be unable to give any additional information about Narva and describes his further painful experiences, from Narva to Kiviõli II.

DOCUMENT 3.3

Jewish Refugee Hostel.

Principal.
Rabbi C. Weingarten.

17. Wellington St. East.
Salford. 7.
Lancs.

Dear. Mrs. Hutton

I thank you very much for your kind and interesting letter and for the trouble you have taken for me.

We are now learning English and arithmetics and some of us are also learning music. I am playing the trumpet.

We have not yet started learning trades but hope to do so soon.

Best regards to all my friends at the center. Why don't the boys write to us here sometimes?

Kindest regards from B. Meisels and Brothers Klein. Please also give my regards to Miss Robbins and Mr. Max

I remain yours sincerely

Lazar Kleinmann

Jewish Refugee Hostel

Principal   17. Wellington St. East
Rabbi C. Weingarten   Salford, 7. Lancs.

Dear Mrs. Hutton,

I thank you very much for your kind and interesting letter and for the trouble you have taken for me.

We are now learning English and arithmetic and some of us are learning music. I am playing the trumpet.

We have not yet started learning trades but hope to do so soon.

Best regards to all of my friends at the center. Why don't the boys write to us here sometimes?

Kindest regards from B. Meivels and Brother Klein. Please also give my regards to Miss. Robbins and Mr. Max.

I remain yours sincerely,
Lazar Kleinmann

DOCUMENT 3.4*

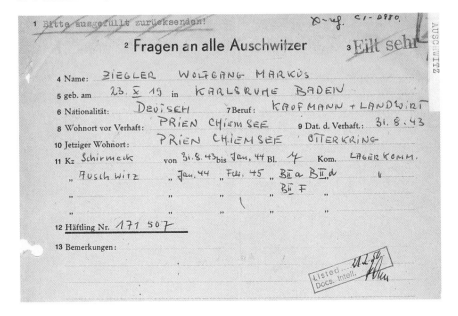

1. Please fill out and return!
2. Questions to all Auschwitzers
3. [stamp] "Eilt Sehr": very urgent
4. **Name**: Ziegler, Wolfgang Markus
5. **Date and place of birth**: October 23, 1919, in Karlsruhe Baden
6. **Nationality**: German
7. **Occupation**: businessman and farmer
8. **Place of residence before arrest**: Prien Chiemsee
9. **Date of arrest**: August 31, 1943
10. **Current place of residence**: Prien Chiemsee
11. **Concentration camp**: Schirmeck; **from**: August 31, 1943 **to**: Jan. 1944; **block**: 7; [**work**] detachment: *Lagerkommandant*: camp commandant; Auschwitz from January 1944 to February 1945; *block*: BIIA, BIID, BIIF
12. **Prisoner number**: 171 507
13. **Remarks**: blank

---

*Numbers 1 through 13 added for translation purposes.

DOCUMENT 3.5

Headquarters
= = = = = = = = = = = = = = = =

A13

Ermittlungsblatt betr. der Toten des Lagers: .....A.U.S.C.H.W.I.T.Z.................

1) Koennen Sie uns Angaben ueber besondere Vorkommnisse im Lager waehrend Ihrer
Haft machen? Wir kamen in das Lager mit der ganzen Familie.Mein Vater
Israel ALLALUF, meine Mutter Palomba,und meine 3 Schwestern:Rachel
mit einer Tochter(von 1 Monat alt),Klara und Maria wurden gleich nach
der Ankunft (ausser Maria und Klara)ins Krematorium geschickt.Maria
2) Welche Arbeit verrichteten Sie im Lager? und Klara arbeiteten einige Monate
Ich war dort nur im Quarantaene-Lager.38 Tage.   und wurden dann umge-
                                                    bracht.
3) Welche Arbeiten hatten sonst noch die Haeftlinge zu verrichten?Fuer welche Firma?
Weiss ich nicht,weil ich nicht lange dort war.

4) Trugen Sie KZ-Kleidung oder Zivilsachen?
K-Z-Kleidung.

5) Wie war die Gesamtstaerke des Lagers z.Zt. Ihrer Haft?
Ungefaehr 15-20,000 Menschen?

I.   MAIL OFFICE
T. DATE RECEIVED 31.5.57
S. REG. No.:   1656

6) Wieviel weibliche Gefangene befanden sich im Lager?
Wo ich war,waren keine Frauen.Daneben war ein Frauenlager,wieviel
Frauen weiss ich nicht.
7) Wurde das Lager bombardiert? Wenn ja, wann? Zahl der Toten und Verletzten?
Als ich dort war, nicht.

8) Wurde das Lager evakuiert? Wann? Wohin?
Als ich dort war,nicht. Unsere Gruppe von 180 Mann wurde Anfang
Mai 1943 nach Budy evakuiert.

9) Wie ging die Evacuierung vor sich?
Mit Dem Autobus mit Wache (SS).

1o) Besitzen Sie irgendwelche amtlichen Listen oder sonstigen Unterlagen ueber
Personen, die in diesem Lager gefangen waren oder darin starben?
Nein.

11) Kennen Sie irgendwelche Personen, die derartige Listen und sonstigen Unterlagen
im Besitz haben? Wenn ja, koennen Sie uns deren Adresse angeben?
Nein.

12) Ist Ihnen bekannt, wohin die Akten und sonstigen Unterlagen dieses Lagers
nach der Befreiung gekommen sind?
Nein. Ich war nicht bis zum Schluss dort.

13) Wissen Sie, wo gegebenenfall Akten dieses Lagers noch zu finden sind?
Nein.

14) Kennen Sie Namen und Adresse von noch lebenden Mitgefangenen?
1.Mordo TIANO,Griechenland,Saloniki, Pawlo Mella.
2.Jehoschua BENJAMIN,Griechenland,Saloniki.
3.Saul BENMAJOR, Israel.
15) Kennen Sie Namen und Adresse von im Lager verstorbenen Mitgefangenen? Wissen
Sie von dem Tod dieser Mitgefangenen aus eigener Kenntnis?
Nein.Genaues weiss ich nicht. Ausser von meinen Eltern und drei Geschwistern.(Namen unter Rubrik 1.)
16) Gehoeren Sie irgendeiner Vereinigung der ehemaligen Haeftlinge dieses Lagers an?
Wenn ja, welches ist die Anschrift dieser Vereinigung?
Nein.Ich weiss nichts von einem solchen Verein.

Daniel ALLALUF
DP Camp, Bl.4/37
L A N D S B E R G / Lech

Allaluf (Danos) Dania
(Unterschrift)

INTERNATIONAL TRACING SERVICE
Headquarters

May 17, 1950

Inquiry sheet concerning those who died in the camp at: A U S C H W I T Z

1) Can you give us information about specific occurrences in the camp during your imprisonment?

We came to the camp with the whole family. My father, Israel ALLA-LUF, my mother, Palomba, and my three sisters: Rachel with a daughter (1 month old), Klara, and Maria were sent to the crematorium right after arrival (except for Klara and Maria). Maria and Klara worked for a few months and then were killed.

2) What work did you perform in the camp?

I was only in the quarantine camp there. For thirty-eight days.

3) What kinds of work did the prisoners usually have to perform? For what company?

I don't know, because I wasn't there long.

4) Did you wear concentration camp clothing or civilian clothes?

Concentration camp clothing.

5) What was the overall prisoner strength of the camp at the time of your imprisonment?

Approximately 15,000 to 20,000 people.

6) How many female prisoners were in the camp?

Where I was, there were no women. Next to us was a women's camp, how many women, I don't know.

7) Was the camp bombed? If so, when? Number of dead and injured?

Not while I was there.

8) Was the camp evacuated? When? To where?

Not while I was there. Our group of 180 men was evacuated to Budy in early 1943.

9) How did the evacuation take place?

By bus, with guards (SS).

10) Do you possess any <u>official</u> lists or other documents concerning persons who were prisoners in this camp or died there?

No.

11) Do you know any persons who have such lists or other documents in their possession? If so, can you give us their addresses?

No.

12) Do you know what became of the records and other documents of this camp after it was liberated?

No. I was not there all the way to the end.

13) Do you know where records of this camp are possibly still to be found?

No.

14) Do you know names and addresses of fellow prisoners who are still alive?

1. Mordo TIANO, Greece, Thessaloniki, Pawlo Mello.

2. Jehoschua BENJAMIN, Greece, Thessaloniki.

3. Saul BENMAJOR, Israel.

15) Do you know names and addresses of fellow prisoners who died in the camp? Do you have <u>personal</u> knowledge of the death of these fellow prisoners?

No. I know nothing specific. Except about my parents and three sisters. (Names given above in 1.)

16) Do you belong to any association of former prisoners of <u>this</u> camp? If so, what is the address of this association?

No. I know nothing about any such organization.

Daniel ALLALUF
DP Camp, sheet 4/87
L A N D S B E R G / Lech   [Signature]

DOCUMENT 3.6

INTERNATIONAL REFUGEE ORGANIZATION

DECISION OF THE REVIEW BOARD   No. : Geneva *20434*
LB/8 ....

Zone : AUSTRIA II .... District : ...LINZ............ Case No. : 1,048,362

In accordance with the Provisional Constitution of the Review Board,

the undersigned have, on this ....25th........ day of ...April 1950........... sitting at

Linz.................., reviewed the appeal of .... Jakob ABRAHAMOVICZ................

against the decision taken on 4.1.50.... Petitioner was interviewed on 24.4.50.

Having examined the case-file and found it to be reasonably complete, the

Review Board has reached the following decision, which has been placed on the records

of the Board.

Petitioner is declared **within the mandate**
~~not within the mandate~~

Consulted : Dr. A. Bedo   _____ Chairman
M. de BAER

concurring .... Member

dissenting .... Member

.... Member

.... Recorder

Assistant   F. McAskell

Strictly confidential. The contents of this
copy should **NOT** be communicated to
the petitioner nor to any person outside
the Organization.

Petitioner is a Czechoslovak Jew from Carpatho Ukraine who
claims to have joined the Czech Legion in USSR in May 1944.   On
his return to his country he was given the trusteeship of a butcher's
business which formerly belonged to a German.

In spite of his privileged position he came under suspicion
after February 1948 as Western orientated, and in June 1948 he was
obliged to flee.

He has convinced the Board that his story is plausible and that
he fled for political reasons.

He is accepted as a genuine refugee who is within the mandate
of the Organization.

DOCUMENT 3.7

Allaluf — 10 Mar cont'd

He thinks that his life in this country had only been a waste and covered his best years. He is now 30 years of age and since he was 18, he was pushed around and lived in camps. Mr. Allaluf expressed the ggreat desire to have a family of his own, he would like very much to have children but feels, as long as they are living in the camp , there is no place to bring up a child. He explained that he came from a large family, there were 6 children and he would like to care on his family tradition and especially, to be able to give the name of his deceased parents to their children which is customary in his country and presents a sign of respect to the dead persons.

The worker asked Mr. Allaluf whether he has the intention to return to Greece. Mr. Allaluf said that he wanted to go there and emphasized that he is very fond of his wife. There is no reason for them to live apart in spite that they are officially divorced, which they got because they thought the divorce would help them to emigrate to the States. Mr. Allaluf stated that he wanted that his wife goes first because she is alone all the time in the camp and in Greece she will have a cousin with whom she could live after her arrival. He will wait another few months to join her, first because he is still employed at the McGraw Kaserne and he does not depend on anybody directly, and in the meantime he could be working on his restitution and he hopes to settle it fairly soon.

Mr. Allaluf is practically living out of camp and he only comes to Foehrenwald once a week on his day off. Mr. Allaluf said that as soon as his wife is able to leave he will start with the steps for himself. It seems not to be wise for both to leave together for reasons appearing in the past experience.

Mrs. Allaluf came, she already talked to her husband about the interview. She did come now to request that something will be done in order that she could get back the documents she had before on her Canadaian emigration. These documents were important for her to have. The worker told her that she would look after this matter.

The worker talked to the emigration officer in Foehrenwald and requested to get the documents from the Canadian Mission back for Mrs. Allaluf.

12 Mar 53   .   IL

The documents had arrived and Mrs. Allaluf was called to collect them back.

DOCUMENT 3.8

Foehrenwald,March 18th 1953

To : Miss Gladys Roth, Director of Emigration
Service Germany

From : AJDC Emigration Office
Foehrenwald

Re : Allaluf Anna

We were requested by Miss LEVY according to a discussion
she had with us in the above case to forward to you
the passport of the above named as well as application
forms completed in Greek language by Mrs. Allaluf
with English translations.

According to Miss Levy it would be advisable to try to
get an entry visa (visitor visa ?) with the possibility
of establishment for Mrs. Allaluf instead of handling
the repatriation to Greece which would take a very long
time. Mrs. Allaluf claimes that she has relatives in
Greece who would help her to settle down. Furthermore
Mrs. Allaluf stated that she already sent the same
questionnaire to the Greek Consulate in Frankfourt in
October or November 1952 together with her birth
certificate as proof of Greek citizenship.

Sincerely Yours

M.Kohn
AJDC Emigration Officer
Foehrenwald

c.c. Miss Deborah LEVY
f i l e

MK/bu

DOCUMENT 3.9

Daniel Allalouf
Erich-Kästner-Str. 2   3. Dez. 86
8ooo München 4o

Intern. Suchdienst
Große Allee 5-9
3548 Arolsen

Suche nach meinem Bruder

Sehr geehrte Damen und Herren,

seit der Befreiung aus dem Konzentrationslager Theresienstadt
Ende des Krieges ist mein Bruder verschollen.

Angaben zur Person:

Allalouf, Isac evtl. auch Hallalouf, Isakino
geb: 1.9.1922 in Saloniki, Griechenland
Tätowierte KZ-Nr.: 1o 94 25 (gegeben im Lager Auschwitz)
Kriegsende: Befreiung aus dem KZ Theresienstadt (ČSSR)

Kurz nach dem Kriege wurde mir von drei Personen (zu ver-
schiedenen Zeiten) gesagt, sie sind gemeinsam mit meinem
Bruder aus dem KZ-Lager Theresienstadt befreit worden.
Einer der drei war ein früherer Nachbar aus Saloniki. Er
lebte bis 1952 in Prag und wanderte dann aus in die USA
über Deutschland. Dieser Mann führte ein Buch bei sich,
das all die Namen derer auflistete, die aus dem KZ Theresienstadt befreit worden waren.
Der Name meines Bruders war ebenfalls aufgeführt, allerdings
in falscher Schreibweise, nämlich mit einem vorgesetzten
"H": HALLALOUF.
Die Namen derer, die nach der Befreiung starben, waren mit
einem Kreuz versehen. Der Name meines Bruders führte kein
Kreuz, so daß ich annehme, daß er noch lebt.

Es besteht die Möglichkeit, daß der Familienname auch später
weiter falsch geschrieben wurde: außer dem vorgestellten "H"
evtl. auch mit verändertem Anfangsbuchstaben "E", "O"
oder "U".

Eine Möglichkeit zur Suche nach meinem Bruder, - er wäre
der einzige, der außer mir von unserer gesamten Familie
überlebte -, sehe ich in der Durchsicht der Namen der An-
träge zur Wiedergutmachung.
Mein Bruder ging damals davon aus, daß man mich nach einem
Fluchtversuch und anschließender Überführung in ein anderes
Lager erschossen hatte. - Das erklärt, daß er nicht nach
mir sucht.
Bitte teilen Sie mir mit, ob ich mich getrennt bei der Stelle
zur Wiedergutmachung erkundigen soll.

Besten Dank für Ihre Hilfe und
freundliche Grüße

i.A. Regler

Daniel Allalouf   December 3, 1986
Erich-Kästner-Str. 2
8000 Munich 40

International Tracing Service
Grosse Allee 5-9
3548 Arolsen

Search for my brother

Dear Sir or Madam:

Since liberation from the Theresienstadt concentration camp at the end of the war, my brother has been missing.

Personal data:

Allalouf, Isac, possibly also Hallalouf, Isakino
Born: September 1, 1922, in Thessaloniki, Greece
Tattooed concentration camp number: 10 94 25 (assigned in the Auschwitz camp)

Shortly after the war, I was told by three individuals (at different times) that they had been liberated along with my brother from the Theresienstadt concentration camp. One of the three was a former neighbor from Thessaloniki. He lived in Prague until 1952 and then immigrated via Germany to the United States. This man carried a book with him that listed all the names of those who had been liberated from the Theresienstadt concentration camp.

My brother's name was also listed there, though it was misspelled, specifically spelled with an "H" as the first letter: HALLALOUF.

The names of those who died after liberation were marked with a cross. There was *no* cross next to my brother's name, and so I assume that he is still alive.

The odds are that the surname continued to be misspelled later on as well: besides the "H" in front, perhaps also with "E," "O," or "U" as the first letter.

I see one possibility for tracing my brother—he would be the only one of our entire family, besides me, to survive—in searching through the names on the applications for reparations.

In those days, my brother was assuming that I had been shot after an attempted escape and subsequent transfer to another camp. That explains why he is not looking for me.

Please advise me whether I should independently make inquiries with the Office for Reparations.

Many thanks for your assistance, and with my kind regards,

DOCUMENT 3.10

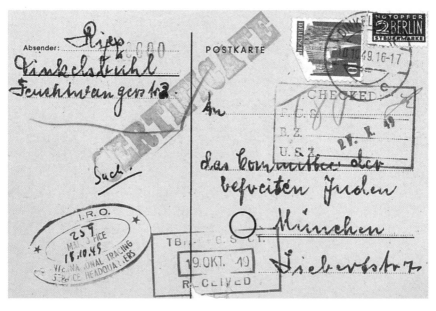

[1]
To the Committee of the Liberated Jews, Munich
My foster brother Harry Müller and his wife Resi, née Süssmann, from Leobschütz/S[ilesia] were imprisoned in Theresienstadt (ghetto town), and I am asking you for proof of confinement to that effect.
Yours respectfully,
Felix Ries

Dinkelsbühl, October 17, 1949

[2]
From: Ries
Dinkelsbühl
Feuchtwangerstr. 3[?]

To
The Committee of the Liberated Jews
Munich
Siebertstr. [?]

DOCUMENT 3.11

T 458 227 c_1 16 881   A

LAW & NOTARIAL OFFICES
APELBOM-KOSSOY

Büro München
München, St. Anna-Straße 6/I
Tel. 26476 - Cables: APEX München

An den

München, den ......lo.2.56....E. 1 3. FEB. 19

I.T.S.

A r o l s e n

Inhaft	Sterbeurk.
Aufenth	Such str.
Auswand.	Fotokopie
Dok.-Auszug	
DP-Dok.Auszug	

Betrifft: L a n g e r   Abraham
geb. 19.6.1916/1922 in Chrzanow
CI 16881

In obiger Entschädigungssache bitten wir um
nochmalige Überprüfung Ihrer Unterlagen.
Der Antragsteller gibt ergänzend an, in
folgenden Lagern inhaftiert gewesen zu sein:
lo.39-11.41 Chrzanow
2.11.41 - 1.42   KL Annaberg
1.42   - lo.42   KL Laurahütte
lo.42 - 12.42   KL Sakrau
12.42 - 2.43   KL Brande
3. 43 - 8.43   KL Gross- Masslowitz
8. 43 - 3.45   KL Görlitz
3.45 bis Befreiung KL Buchenwald

lo.45-1949 in Garmisch- Partenkirchen

Für baldige Bearbeitung wären wir dankbar
und zeichnen

                    hochachtungsvoll
                Law & Notarial Offices
                  Apelbom - Kossoy

                    E.Kossoy
                  Rechtsanwalt

hg

Law & Notarial Offices
APELBOM-KOSSOY

Munich Office
Munich, St. Anna-Strasse 6/1
Tel. 26476—Cables: APEX Munich

Munich, February 10, 1956

To the I.T.S.
A r o l s e n

Regarding: Abraham L a n g e r, born June 19, 1916/1922, in Chrzanów
CI 16881

In the above-mentioned compensation matter, we request another search of your documents. The applicant claims in addition to have been imprisoned in the following camps:

October 1939–November 1941	Chrzanów
November 2, 1941–January 1942	Annaberg concentration camp
January 1942–October 1942	Laurahütte concentration camp
October 1942–December 1942	Sakrau concentration camp
December 1942–February 1943	Brande concentration camp
March 1943–August 1943	Gross-Masslowitz concentration camp
August 1943–March 1945	Görlitz concentration camp
March 1945 to liberation	Buchenwald concentration camp

October 1945–1949 in Garmisch-Partenkirchen

We would appreciate your speedy handling.

Respectfully,

Law & Notarial Offices
Apelbom-Kossoy

[Signed]
E. Kossoy
Attorney at Law

CHAPTER 4

HOUR ZERO: THE YEAR 1945

O N JANUARY 1, 1945, Hans Heinrich Fuge, head (*Lagerleiter*) of the Dzierżązna subcamp, reported positive tidings regarding the state of affairs on this agricultural estate 15 kilometers (9.3 miles) from Łódź.[1] The Dzierżązna subcamp of the Polish Youth Custody Camp of the Security Police (*Polen-Jugendverwahrlager der Sicherheitspolizei*) in Litzmannstadt, opened in early 1943, held two hundred prisoners at its high point.[2] This small and little-known camp was still operational on the date of Fuge's report, New Year's Day 1945.[3]

---

1. For a brief description of the Dzierżązna subcamp, see Joseph Robert White, "Polish Youth Custody Camp of the Security Police Litzmannstadt," in *The United States Holocaust Memorial Museum Encyclopedia of Camps and Ghettos, 1933–1945*, Vol. 1: *Early Camps, Youth Camps, and Concentration Camps and Subcamps under the SS-Business Administration Main Office (WVHA)*, ed. Geoffrey P. Megargee (Indianapolis: Indiana University Press in association with USHMM, 2009), 1528.

2. Martin Weinmann, *Das Nationalsozialistische Lagersystem* (Frankfurt am Main: Zweitausendeins, 1990), 322.

3. Bericht über die Bewirtschaftung des Hofes Dzierżązna (Arbeitsbetrieb des Polenjugendverwahrlagers der Sicherheitspolizei in Litzmannstadt), 1.1.22.0/82115751–6/ITS Digital Archive, USHMM. This report is a copy received by ITS in 1984 from Michael Hepp of the Verein zur Erforschung der nationalsozialistischen Gesundheits- und Sozialpolitik e.V. in Hamburg. Hepp is author of "Denn ihrer ward die Hölle. Kinder und Jugendliche im Jugendverwahrlager Litzmannstadt," in *Mitteilungen der Dokumentationsstelle zur NS-Sozialpolitik* 11/12 (April 1986): 49–71.

"In the residential building of farm II, all the stairways were fixed and the house freshly painted. The heating system for the chicken coop, laundry room, and workshop was repaired and the flooring replaced in all the areas referred to," wrote Fuge. "We did all the above-mentioned work by ourselves, without any outside help," he added, meaning, we can presume, the adolescent Polish inmates of the camp performed the described labor.[4] At the time of his report, with the war lost and the Third Reich months from collapse,[5] Fuge seemed blissfully or perhaps willfully unaware of how bankrupt the racial ideals of the Third Reich had become. In condescendingly describing his so-called pupils (*Zöglinge*), he noted (twice) that the Polish people suffered from a disinclination to work (*Arbeitsunlust*) and that his "pupils" were no different. "One must bear in mind," he wrote, "that the workers involved are only Poles, who accomplish nowhere near what a German worker does. The Polish pupils also are not to be rated as full-fledged workers, as they are youngsters (girls) twelve to fifteen years old."[6]

HOUR ZERO

The year 1945 marked the demise of the Nazi and Axis regimes and a rebirth for liberated nations and peoples caught up in World War II and the Holocaust. Thus far, scholars have paid great attention to the notion of a *Stunde Null*, or "hour zero," for Germany as a nation and for former Nazi sympathizers, collaborators, and Germans not targeted by the Nazi regime.[7] Documents held

4. Bericht über die Bewirtschaftung des Hofes Dzierżązna (Arbeitsbetrieb des Polenjugendverwahrlagers der Sicherheitspolizei in Litzmannstadt), 1.1.22.0/82115751/ITS Digital Archive, USHMM.

5. After the German defeat during the Battle of the Bulge (the German offensive campaign launched through the Ardennes region of Wallonia in Belgium, France, and Luxembourg from December 16, 1944, to January 25, 1945), the western Allied troops rapidly approached the German border from the west, while Soviet troops advanced from the east.

6. As of January 1, 1945, he reported thirty inmates in the Dzierżązna subcamp, down from 150 at some point in 1944. See Bericht über die Bewirtschaftung des Hofes Dzierżązna, 1.1.22.0/82115753 and 82115755/ITS Digital Archive, USHMM.

7. Extensive literature on the ways in which 1945 represented continuities and discontinuities in German political, economic, and cultural practices exists: Bernt Engelmann, *Wir haben ja den Kopf noch fest auf dem Hals: Die Deutschen zwischen Stunde Null und Wirtschaftswunder: 1945–1948* (Göttingen: Steidl, 1997); Geoffrey Giles, ed., *Stunde Null: The End and the Beginning Fifty Years Ago* (Washington, DC: German Historical Institute, 1997); Nina Grontzki, Gerd Niewerth, and Rolf Potthoff, *Die Stunde Null im Ruhrgebiet. Kriegsende und Wiederaufbau: Erinnerungen* (Essen: Klartext, 2005); Shane Brian Stufflet, "No 'Stunde Null': German Attitudes toward the Mentally Handicapped and Their Impact on the Postwar Trials of T4 Perpetrators" (PhD diss., 2006), inter alia.

by the International Tracing Service (ITS) allow us to view 1945 through a variety of lenses, not just from the perspective of a vanquished Germany or of humbled former Nazis and their beneficiaries. As we have seen in previous chapters, what Daniel Blatman terms "the Nazi oppression machine"[8] produced victims among all the nationalities in Europe, Jewish and non-Jewish, caught up in all manner of camps and prisons, forced military service or forced labor, or in hiding. The year 1945 saw the liberation of all these sites of terror, unjust punishment, and utter brutality. Millions of victims in poor mental, physical, and emotional health fell to the care of bewildered Allied forces, governments, and aid organizations. The year also saw the first efforts to recover, rebuild, return, and consider retribution. The period from January 1 to December 31, 1945, is a remarkable analytical lens through which to view a Europe in the remaking.

MURDER AND COLLABORATION AT WAR'S END

In a secret January 3, 1945, report provided to Supreme Headquarters/Allied Expeditionary Forces (SHAEF) by the British War Office, a "Polish officer," never identified by name, tried to describe what he had heard about the gas chambers in Auschwitz.[9] In what we now know is an inaccurate account, he wrote, "The condemned prisoners, usually Jews, are first given a hot bath to open the pores of the skin and are then herded into a large room equipped with overhead sprays."[10] The author had never been in the Auschwitz camp complex himself, and the War Office was skeptical about the reliability of the details in the report. A cover letter remarked, "No attempt has been made to evaluate the information contained in it and no guarantee of its accuracy can be given."[11]

---

8. Daniel Blatman, *The Death Marches: The Final Phase of Nazi Genocide* (Cambridge, MA: Belknap Press, 2011), 1.

9. Peter Hayes writes, "The grisly story of Zyklon B as a murder instrument is traced from its testing in barracks basements of the main camp in August-September 1941, through its application first in the crematorium there until December 1942, then in two converted farm houses at Birkenau (Bunkers I–II) from early 1942 to the spring of 1943, and finally in four specially built brick crematoria (II–V), which until the gassing stopped in early November 1944 consumed more than half the people who ever died at Auschwitz." Peter Hayes, "Auschwitz, Capital of the Holocaust," *Holocaust and Genocide Studies* 17, no. 2 (2003): 337–38.

10. Report on German concentration camps, January 3, 1945, 1.1.0.6/82328950–55/ITS Digital Archive, USHMM. This document is original and was received by ITS in 1956 from an unidentified source.

11. Ibid, 82328951.

The report is not historically valuable for its accuracy, as the reference to Jews being given a "hot bath" before their murder in the gas chambers of Birkenau already tells us it is flawed. However, the manner in which this anonymous Polish officer described the so-called *Sonderkommandos*[12] of Auschwitz, at this late date in the extermination process, is fascinating:

> The bodies are cleared from the room by a special squad of prisoners [. . .] composed of Jewish men selected for their strength and physique. They serve a three months [*sic*] tour on gas chamber duties and during that time receive excellent treatment. Working hours are short, discipline lax, food and tobacco in abundance. At the end of the 3 months they in turn go into the gas chambers and in due course their successors tumble their bodies into the furnace. Nevertheless in spite of this grim condition, there is never any lack of volunteers for the gas chamber squad and the camp guards can pick or choose at their will from the innumerable applicants.[13]

This inaccurate report—out of context and even accusatory, with its mention of no "lack of volunteers for the gas chamber squad" and guards who could "pick or choose at their will from the innumerable applicants"—was disseminated to a long list of SHAEF[14] offices in sets of multiple copies in the first days of 1945.[15] It gives us a sense of the distinct lack of empathy Jews who managed to survive the Holocaust would face in the long months ahead.

In the last days of January, forty-year old Gertrud Leppin worked at the

---

12. In the context of Auschwitz II–Birkenau, *Sonderkommandos* consisted of Jewish prisoners who worked around the gas chambers and crematoria. Their duties included removing the murdered from the gas chambers, retrieving valuables from the dead, and burning the dead in the crematoria or open pits. For an accurate rendering, see, among other rare and important memoirs, Jadwiga Bezwinska and Danuta Czech, *Amidst a Nightmare of Crime: Manuscripts of Members of Sonderkommando*, trans. Krystyna Michalik (Oświęcim: Auschwitz State Museum, 1973), and Filip Müller, *Eyewitness Auschwitz: Three Years in the Gas Chambers*, trans. and ed. Susanne Flatauer (Chicago: Ivan R. Dee, 1979).

13. Report on German concentration camps, January 3, 1945, 1.1.0.6/82328955/ITS Digital Archive, USHMM.

14. SHAEF is the term for the headquarters of the commander of the Allied forces in northwestern Europe from late 1943 until the end of World War II. US General Dwight D. Eisenhower commanded SHAEF throughout its existence. SHAEF's "wartime mission ended on V-E Day. The last residual mission, the redisposition into the zones, was completed on July 10, 1945, and the Supreme Command terminated on the 14th." Earl F. Ziemke, *The U.S. Army in the Occupation of Germany, 1944–1946* (Washington, DC: US Army Center for Military History, 1990), 317.

15. Report on German concentration camps, January 3, 1945, 1.1.0.6/82328951/ITS Digital Archive, USHMM.

post office in the small German village of Sonnenburg (today, Słońsk, Poland). A Berliner by birth, as a so-called *Mischling* (person of "mixed race") born to a Jewish mother, she moved to Sonnenburg in November 1943 because her former home was "bombed out" and she "did not want to get into trouble" on account of her racial status. She lived at Münzstrasse 21, "200 meters [656 feet]" from the town's prison. "Sonnenburg is a small place in which the prison played a large role," she testified.[16] Established in the early nineteenth century as a royal Prussian penitentiary, it was located 600 meters [1,969 feet] outside the town on the major road leading to Poznań. Able to hold "637 inmates" and "economically significant for the town," the prison was closed in 1931 "due to catastrophic sanitary conditions." In early 1933, it became one of the first Nazi concentration camps; by 1945, it had returned to its function as a penitentiary.[17]

Leppin recollected the penitentiary as quite full that bitter winter. She guessed that approximately a thousand prisoners were incarcerated there and worked either in the town or in surrounding villages, sometimes with and sometimes without supervision. She thought it was the night of January 29 or 30 on which she heard gunfire and assumed Russian troops had arrived. But she did not hear machine-gun fire; rather, she heard single shots, one after another, over two or three hours. She opened her window and, hearing no more shots, walked out of her house toward the prison. "I could not hear any cries," she wrote, but

16. Erklärung unter Eid (affidavit), Gertrud Leppin (geb. Grünberger), 1.1.0.6/82326797–8/ITS Digital Archive, USHMM. Staff working in the Interrogation Branch, Evidence Division, Office of the Chief of Counsel for War Crimes (OCCWC), Office of Military Government–United States interviewed Gertrud Leppin on February 5, 1947, in Berlin, where she was living at that time. ITS staff received this document, a copy, in 1956. The original document is part of approximately fifteen thousand pretrial interrogation transcripts compiled by the OCCWC and used in the prosecution of 185 defendants in the so-called Nuremberg successor trials, twelve separate proceedings held before US military tribunals I–VI from 1946 to 1949 in Nuremberg. For the formation of the OCCWC and a broader background of US efforts to try Nazi criminals, see Donald Bloxham, *Genocide on Trial: War Crimes and the Formation of Holocaust History and Memory* (Oxford: Oxford University Press, 2001), 28–29. Specifically, Leppin's affidavit was part of case number 3, the "Justice Case" (*United States of America v. Josef Altstoetter et al.*, 1947). One of the sixteen defendants indicted was Herbert Klemm, undersecretary (*Staatssekretär*) in the Reich Ministry of Justice, who was responsible for Sonnenburg penitentiary in 1945. See the so-called Green series in *Trials of War Criminals before the Nuernberg Military Tribunals under Control Council Law No. 10*, Vol. 3: *Nuremberg: October 1946–April 1949* (Buffalo, NY: William S. Hein & Co., Inc., 1997), 1099.

17. The Nazis dissolved the Sonnenburg concentration camp in the spring of 1934, converting it to a penitentiary under the Reich Ministry of Justice. Kaspar Nürnberg, "Sonnenburg," in Megargee, *The United States Holocaust Memorial Museum Encyclopedia of Camps and Ghettos*, 1:163–65.

she verified that the shots were coming from the penitentiary. Upset, she went to her neighbors, then to her in-laws, but could learn nothing. So she went to another neighbor, one "Schenkwitz," a guard at the penitentiary, and asked him "what was going on" (*was los war*).[18]

Schenkwitz was packing. "SS," he told Leppin, were shooting political prisoners (*politische Gefangene*). In fact, he told her, the SS ordered the regular staff of the penitentiary to take part, and they (he claimed) "all refused." She was not able to ask Schenkwitz further questions as he was "very upset" (*sehr aufgeregt*) and in a hurry to leave (*wollte schnell weg*). She felt the need to add that Schenkwitz was "no National Socialist." On the following day, she heard that "all the SS together with the wives of the high-ranking regular prison staff" had fled. Local German Sonnenburgers would have been glad to go with them, she claimed, but the SS left them behind. Russian troops arrived on February 2, 1945. They told Leppin that "the SS" had "committed atrocities" in the penitentiary; bodies were piled up on the ground and in the cells. Not one prisoner survived, they said. Rumors circulated in the town that beyond the "815" "political" prisoners, the "SS [had] murdered women and children from Grodno." But Russian troops did not confirm this, Leppin noted in her affidavit.[19]

Leppin did not have it exactly right: in fact, the shootings took place on the night of January 30 and into the early hours of January 31, 1945. The victims were not women and children from Grodno but rather male detainees from Belgium, Denmark, France, Holland, Luxemburg, Norway, Poland, Russia, Ukraine, and Yugoslavia. The number of prisoners murdered on that night, as cited to Leppin by Russian soldiers, was approximately correct (in the neighborhood of eight hundred). Following the transfer of approximately eight hundred so-called Night and Fog prisoners[20] out of Sonnenburg to Oranienburg on November 11, 1944, prisoners sentenced by Wehrmacht military tribunals for desertion took their place. Gestapo men, who controlled the prison, did the

---

18. Erklärung unter Eid (affidavit), Gertrud Leppin (geb. Grünberger), 1.1.0.6/82326797–8/ITS Digital Archive, USHMM.

19. Ibid.

20. Night-and-Fog (*Nacht und Nebel*) prisoners were the remnant of those not immediately killed as a result of the Wehrmacht Night-and-Fog Decree. The decree, issued by General Wilhelm Keitel in December 1941, allowed the Gestapo and the SD to arrest "all those found guilty of 'undermining the effectiveness of the German Armed Forces' in occupied western territories." Intending to "deter anti-Nazi resistance in France, Belgium, the Netherlands, Denmark and Norway," German military courts "imposed death sentences or deportation to concentration camps" on resisters. See Geoffrey P. Megargee, *Inside Hitler's High Command* (Lawrence: University of Kansas Press, 2000).

shooting.[21] Leppin's testimony illustrates a different point: the brutality and chaos of that time and the response of local Germans to open murder in their midst, which, generally speaking, ranged from a lack of intervention to participation.

"BUT IT WAS NONE OF MY BUSINESS"[22]

ITS holdings are rich in material pertaining to gender and the Holocaust, including but not limited to the role of women from small towns, eager for opportunities and adventure that led to collaboration in the Nazi system.[23] In Ruth Kleinsteuber's experience, even in the early months of 1945, for Germans the Nazi oppression machine still brought career opportunities for those not targeted by the regime. Born in 1922 in the small town of Aschersleben (Saxony), Kleinsteuber began to work in the local textile factory, the Junkers Werke, as an embroiderer in 1936. She was fourteen. Eight years later, in December 1944, the factory manager asked her whether she might be interested in training as an *SS Aufseherin* (prison guard). She was indeed interested. Dressed in a grey SS uniform and trained for four days at the Ravensbrück concentration camp, in mid-December 1944 she was assigned to the work education camp (*Arbeitserziehungslager*)[24] Nordmark in Kiel (Schleswig-Holstein).[25] In February 1945, she was promoted from guard to platoon leader and, by her own testimony, essentially functioned as overseer of all the female guards (*Oberaufseherin*), with authority over approximately one hundred female inmates.[26] "Most of the

---

21. André Hohengarten, *Das Massaker im Zuchthaus Sonnenburg vom 30/31 Januar 1945* (Luxemburg: Verlag der St. Paulus Druckerei, 1979).

22. Deposition of Ruth Kleinsteuber, 5.1/82300809/ITS Digital Archive, USHMM.

23. See Wendy Lower, *Hitler's Furies: German Women in the Nazi Killing Fields* (Boston: Houghton Mifflin Harcourt, 2013); Elizabeth Anthony, "Representations of Sexual Violence in ITS Documentation: Concentration Camp Brothels" in *Freilegungen: Spiegelungen der NS-Verfolgung und ihrer Konsequenzen, Jahrbuch des International Tracing Service*, Bd. 4, ed. Rebecca Boehling, Susanne Urban, Elizabeth Anthony, and Suzanne Brown-Fleming (Göttingen: Wallstein Verlag, 2015), 49–60.

24. These were labor and disciplinary work camps.

25. For more about this camp, see, among other works, Fritz Bringmann, *Arbeitserziehungslager Nordmark: Berichte, Erlebnisse, Dokumente* (Kiel: VVN-Bund der Antifaschisten, 1982); Detlev Korte, "Vorstufe zum KZ: Das Arbeitserziehungslager Nordmark in Kiel, 1944–1945," in *Die vergessenen Lager*, ed. Barbara Distel and Wolfgang Benz (Munich: DTV, 1994).

26. Kleinsteuber testifies, and other sources confirm, that in April 1945, transports from other camps, especially from the Fuhlsbüttel penal complex, increased the prisoner population to five hundred (in her estimation). These new prisoners were Russian, Polish, French, Dutch, and German, and food supplies became insufficient. See deposition of Ruth Klein-

female prisoners had to work eight to ten hours per day with a mid-day break of one, and later one-half hour," she stated. As to mistreatment of prisoners in that camp, she had "never seen a female guard beat prisoners. But female guards, whose names I can no longer remember, told me they slapped faces of female prisoners," she added. As to her own behavior, she wrote, "I myself have boxed the ears of two prisoners slightly." She acknowledged that most of the guards, male or female, "carried wooden sticks in camp." She claimed not to have done so herself. In January 1945, within her first month at the camp, she saw a male guard "beat a female prisoner." "I believe," she added, "he had a stick in his hand. But it was none of my business."[27] British officials did not agree and tried her for war crimes in Hamburg in 1947. It is a case in point of a young and ambitious German woman who, even in early 1945, with the war lost and the Nazi regime weak and discredited, was willing to take part in its terror apparatus.

DEATH BY MARCH

On January 27, 1945, US Air Force Lieutenant John C. Brown was marched with other prisoners of war (POWs) from the famous Stalag (*Stammlager*) Luft III near Sagan[28] (now Żagań, Poland) to Spremburg "in the snow, rain and regular winter weather of Silesia."[29] "I arrived at Nure[m]berg with the first

steuber, 5.1/82300809/ITS Digital Archive, USHMM. These new prisoners also came from Mölln and Neustadt in Holstein, both subcamps of Neuengamme. See Christine Schmidt van der Zanden, "Mölln" and "Neustadt in Holstein," in Megargee, *The United States Holocaust Memorial Museum Encyclopedia of Camps and Ghettos*, 1:1164–65.

27. Deposition of Ruth Kleinsteuber, 5.1/82300809/ITS Digital Archive, USHMM. This deposition was taken on August 1, 1947, by Sergeant G. Goddard, Field Investigation Section, War Crimes Group, British Army of the Rhine. ITS contains a set of copies of documents related to Arbeitserziehungslager Kiel (5.1, folder 0021) sent to Bad Arolsen in the decades after the British Military Tribunal Kiel Hasse Case, which took place in Hamburg from October 29 to December 9, 1947. Kleinsteuber was acquitted. Very little secondary source literature exists on this trial.

28. About 160 kilometers (100 miles) southeast of Berlin, Stalag Luft III, a POW camp for captured air force servicemen run by the German Luftwaffe, is well known for two prisoner escapes. See Arthur A. Durand, *Stalag Luft III: The Secret History* (Baton Rouge: Louisiana State University Press, 1988).

29. Transcription, sworn statement of 2nd Lt. John C. Brown, 1.1.5.0/82065162/ITS Digital Archive, USHMM. Eleven thousand POWs were marched out of Stalag Luft III before midnight on January 27, 1945, due to the proximity of Soviet troops. Temperatures were below freezing, and six inches of snow lay on the ground. The march was a total of eighty kilometers (fifty miles), with a stop in Bad Muskau. See Durand, *Stalag Luft III*, 332–33.

group to set up the camp, and here I stayed until we marched out of there on the 4th of April," he wrote.[30] "In this time I had three showers, one of which was a delousing shower." "The conditions were rotten," he added, and one has to smile at his American euphemism. He went on to describe the lack of adequate food and shelter. In fact, prisoners "tore down outside washhouses to provide fuel for cooking and heating."[31] Abraham Langer (see document 4.1.[32]) was incarcerated in the forced labor camp for Jews in the forested village of Kretschamberg/Kittlitztreben in Silesia when he and other prisoners[33] were marched to Buchenwald in February 1945.[34] He had arrived in the Kretscham-

---

30. Durand explains that at Spremberg, the prisoners were divided; Americans from Stalag Luft III's West Compound "went to Stalag XIII D outside Nuremberg." Durand, *Stalag Luft III*, 335.

31. Transcription, sworn statement of 2nd Lt. John C. Brown, 1.1.5.0/82065162/ITS Digital Archive, USHMM.

32. Photograph of Abraham Langer contained in his CM/1 file, 3.2.1.1/79385447/ITS Digital Archive, USHMM.

33. A keyword search using the term 'Kretschamberg' in ITS across all archival units allows us to identify other Jewish prisoners also on this death march from Kretschamberg to Buchenwald. See the "Attributes" tab for Michael Potasch, 0.1/50585686; Leon Nass, 0.1/51393554; Baruch Brechner, 0.1/51835833; Fiszel Rabinowicz, 0.1/51904969; and Leib Goldman, 0.1/52206493/ITS Digital Archive, USHMM. Each has a T/D file as well, detailing efforts to obtain documentation for reparations/compensation.

34. Sworn statement of Abraham Langer, Buchenwald, June 17, 1945, 1.1.5.0/82065532/ITS Digital Archive, USHMM. This document is a copy of a set of sworn statements by former Buchenwald prisoners taken in June 1945 by the Judge Advocate Section, War Crimes Branch, US Third Army. ITS acquired copies in 1956. Ultimately, the statements were utilized for the US Army trial *United States of America v. Josias Prince of Waldeck et al.* (Case 000–50–9), the so-called Buchenwald Trial, which took place in Dachau from April to August 1947. In all, thirty-one defendants were indicted for war crimes related to the Buchenwald concentration camp and satellite camps, including Bad Arolsen's own Prince Josias zu Waldeck und Pyrmont (1896–1967). Heinrich Himmler had appointed Waldeck the *Höhere SS- und Polizeiführer* (higher SS and police chief) of Weimar, giving him "supervisory authority over the concentration camp at Buchenwald." General George Patton's forces captured Waldeck at Buchenwald on April 13, 1945, a little over two months before Langer gave his testimony. In the trial, Waldeck was found guilty and sentenced to life in prison. He was later amnestied under US High Commissioner John J. McCloy and released on November 29, 1950. He lived out the remainder of his life a wealthy man and died in his castle, Schloss Schaumburg (Diez an der Lahn), at the age of seventy-one. See Jonathan Petropoulos, "Prince zu Waldeck und Pyrmont: A Career in the SS and Its Murderous Consequences," in *Lessons and Legacies, Volume IX: Memory, History, and Responsibility: Reassessments of the Holocaust, Implications for the Future*, ed. Jonathan Petropoulos, Lynn Rapaport, and John K. Roth (Evanston, IL: Northwestern University Press, 2010), 169–84. Records relating to the Buchenwald and other US Army trials are available at the US National Archives in College Park, Maryland.

berg/Kittlitztreben camp in March 1944.[35] He was one of nearly one thousand prisoners on the long march to Buchenwald.[36] Due to the impending arrival of Russian troops, German inhabitants of Kittlitztreben were evacuated at 7 a.m. on the morning of February 9, amid the chaos of German aircraft firing on Russian tanks. Elderly villagers and women with small children were allowed to evacuate via train. One local villager's otherwise detailed account makes no mention of the huge column of prisoners who were also evacuated. The account does mention two villagers from Kittlitztreben who perished: Charlotte Glauer, the local butcher's daughter, and Berta Stammwitz, who both died of heatstroke in the train station.[37]

As to the Jewish prisoners, because of ITS documents, we can reconstruct this death march with some precision. (See documents 4.2 and 4.3.[38]) The death march from Kittlitztreben to Buchenwald, a distance of 325 kilometers (202 miles), consisted entirely of Jewish prisoners. The United Nations Relief and Rehabilitation Administration (UNRRA) Central Tracing Bureau investigations cite a start date of January 26 rather than February 9.[39] All sources agree that the prisoners reached Buchenwald on April 4, 1945. In all, the prisoners made sixteen stops after setting off from Kittlitztreben on foot: first Hennersdorf, then Penzig (Pieńsk), Ludwigsdorf (Ludwikowice Kłodzkie), Görlitz, Reichenbach (Dzierżoniów), Weissenberg, Bautzen, Bühlau, Radeberg, Brest, Kesseldorf, Lugau, Zwickau, Gera, Jena, and finally Buchenwald.[40] UNRRA investigators

---

35. He must have been among those two hundred prisoners transported from Görlitz to the camp in March 1944. See Danuta Sawicka, "Kittlitztreben," in Megargee, *The United States Holocaust Memorial Museum Encyclopedia of Camps and Ghettos*, 753.

36. Sawicka, "Kittlitztreben," 754.

37. Fragebogenberichte zur Dokumentation der Vertreibung der Deutschen aus Ost-Mitteleuropa (Gemeindeschicksalsberichte) VI. Schlesien, 1.2.7.11/82191577/ITS Digital Archive, USHMM. These materials are copies from the German Federal Archive (Bundesarchiv) acquired by ITS in 1972.

38. "Kittlitztreben-Buchenwald," 5.3.3/84619503/ITS Digital Archive, USHMM; hand-drawn map of the death march from Kittlitztreben to Buchenwald, 5.3.3/84619504/ ITS Digital Archive, USHMM.

39. The Commissariat Belge au Rapatriement created a map of this death march that is part of ITS holdings in Bad Arolsen. It gives a start date of January 21, 1945, for this death march. See Evacuation de Kittlitztreben à Buchenwald, Signatur (Reference Code) KP 12, ITS, Bad Arolsen.

40. Frustratingly, the questionnaires that the Allies sent to mayors across territories that had seen death marches (see "Investigations of the Allies," 5.3.1) do not include any reports or witness testimonies from these locations. For a clear and thorough explanation of why this was so, see Daniel Blatman, "On the Traces of the Death Marches: The Historiographical Challenge," in *Freilegungen: Auf den Spuren der Todesmärsche*, ed. Jean-Luc Blondel, Susanne

noted, "More than half the prisoners died on the way. The SS eliminated every morning the most feeble. Common graves [are] all along the way. The mayors [in these villages and towns] can furnish dates."[41]

The camp commandant at Kittlitztreben, recollected Langer, was SS Oberscharführer Otto Weingärtner.[42] Weingärtner was, said Langer, "about twenty-eight to thirty years of age, tall, slender, black hair, [with] a scar on [his] right cheek." Weingärtner "killed two Jews during the march on February 9, 1945. The name of the one was Berek Wellner, I saw it with my own eyes," Langer said. "Five weeks later I saw that [Weingärtner] shot [a prisoner named] Ziegler." The "prisoner chief of the barrack, Chaim Zylberberg," also behaved murderously, according to Langer, who said Zylberberg "was especially angry" with Hungarian Jews. "During the march from the camp [Kretschamberg] to Buchenwald [. . .] Zylberberg was in charge of barrack five, while I was assigned to the sixth barrack," Langer continued. "I saw that Zylberberg struck with a big stick chiefly those who fainted during the march. The mistreated persons were put on a wagon and brought to the next barn where we passed the night. Daily many of them died. Before we arrived at Buchenwald, he [Zylberberg] hurt the prisoner Leichter, who died the following day."[43]

LIBERATION

When Langer arrived at Buchenwald, the camp was days from liberation. Liberation was a moment no one could forget, and among the most poignant testimonies are those taken by Allied soldiers in the days immediately following their arrival in the camps. Captain Alfred T. Bogen Jr., assistant army inspector general, First US Army, took one such testimony at the 51st Field Hospital in Nordhausen[44] on April 14, 1945. Captain Bogen interviewed Christian Guy, a Belgian prisoner from Malines (Mechelen) brought from Gross-Rosen to Nord-

---

Urban, and Sebastian Schönemann. Jahrbuch des International Tracing Service I (Göttingen: Wallstein Verlag, 2012), 85–107.

41. "Kittlitztreben-Buchenwald," 5.3.3/84619503/ITS Digital Archive, USHMM.

42. Otto Weingärtner does not have the luxury of remaining anonymous in ITS. He can be found in a document ITS received in copy form from the Zentrales Staatsarchiv in Ludwigsburg. See p. 5 in the report "Übersicht über Verfahren wegen NS-Gewaltverbrechen: Stand vom 1.12.1961," 5.1/82301475/ITS Digital Archive, USHMM.

43. Sworn statement of Abraham Langer, Buchenwald, June 17, 1945, 1.1.5.0/82065532/ITS Digital Archive, USHMM.

44. For more on Nordhausen, see Michael J. Neufeld, "Mittelbau (Dora) Main Camp," in Megargee, *The United States Holocaust Memorial Museum Encyclopedia of Camps and Ghettos*, 1:965–72.

hausen via open railway car in February 1945, who had been there ever since.[45] In Guy's recollection, Allied bombs began to rain on Nordhausen "at 4:30 on April 3," and on April 4 he and several hundred other prisoners hid themselves in a cellar. Here they remained, subsisting on bread pilfered "from the German kitchens." On April 11, "in the morning, one of the boys came in and like a madman called, 'There is an American with a car against the gate.' All the comrades in the cell[ar] started yelling and weeping. They were mad. I could not move at the moment or believe it. I was astonished but a few hours later I had to accept it. The day after this we were taken away to city houses and then I was evacuated to this American field hospital." He then added, "I am glad you arrived and wish you all success and hope that you get as many Germans as you can. I am sorry I cannot help you boys to do my part."[46]

Stunned and disconcerted liberating armies and their helpers struggled first to size up the situation in a given camp and then to act. ITS-held documents contain many reports written by Allied authorities that summer, giving their impressions of those first days of liberation and the many problems that would follow. The report by Miss I. Hillers, active in the Prisoners of War and Displaced Persons Division of the British Red Cross Society at the Sandbostel camp,[47] is a case in point.[48] British troops liberated the camp on April 29, 1945. Hillers composed this particular report on the basis of "war diaries of all medical units operating in the British Liberation Army from April to June, 1945."[49]

45. Testimony of Christian Guy, civilian, Malines, Belgium, interviewed by Captain Alfred T. Bogen, Jr., assistant army inspector general, First US Army, 51st Field Hospital, Nordhausen, April 14, 1945, 1.1.27.0/82121869/ITS Digital Archive, USHMM. These testimonies are copies from the State Archive (Staatsarchiv) of Nuremberg made in 1978. See 1.1.27.0/82121642/ITS Digital Archive, USHMM.

46. Ibid., 82121870.

47. Sandbostel (Stalag X-B) was a POW and prisoner reception camp in Lower Saxony. However, Sandbostel was flooded with thousands of concentration camp prisoners in April 1945, sent from the Neuengamme subcamps. At the time of liberation, sixty-eight hundred prisoners among the eight- to nine-thousand-strong prisoner population remained alive. See Marc Buggeln, "Neuengamme Subcamp System," in Megargee, *The United States Holocaust Memorial Museum Encyclopedia of Camps and Ghettos*, 1:1081.

48. Report on missing persons for Sandbostel Camp, Miss I. Hillers, BRCS, POW and DP Division, Control Commission for Germany, 55 Search Bureau, Göttingen, BAOR, July 18, 1946, 1.1.13.0/82111873–77/ITS Digital Archive, USHMM. The report appears to be an original acquired by the ITS in 1956. Only the first eight pages of the report are in ITS.

49. Ibid., 82111874.

Father Dewar-Duncan, Medical Unit 10, Casualty Clearing Station, wrote, "As you can appreciate things in Sandbostel in May 1945 were rather chaotic and it may well be that a mistake in identity could have occurred. The patients in their weak state would very often change beds, and with an inadequate staff and the added difficulty of language it was sometimes impossible to keep track of who was who."[50]

"Typhus and open T.B. [tuberculosis] were rife," a member of the Medical Unit 11 Field Dressing Station wrote, adding that "typhus, T.B. and [the] unclassified sick were segregated and identified by the employment of yellow, blue and pink labels tied to the person. This proved very necessary owing to the wandering propensities of many patients who[,] in spite of their weak condition[,] would step out of bed and wander about in the nude."[51] Thousands of such testimonies and early reports, written from the viewpoints of both the liberated and the liberators in the days and weeks after liberation, span the range of sites of detention in the ITS holdings. The ambitious scholar might consider a monograph-length study of prisoners' impressions in these first days of liberation as portrayed in ITS-held documents.

"DEATHS WERE AVERAGING 500 PER DAY"[52]

ITS-held documents detail mass death and convalescence in the camps within the first month of liberation. A copy of the supplement to the *British Zone Review* titled "Belsen,"[53] available in the ITS holdings, is a case in point.[54] When British troops liberated Bergen-Belsen on April 15, 1945, they estimated that

---

50. Ibid., 82111875.

51. Ibid.

52. "Belsen," supplement to the *British Zone Review*, October 13, 1945, 1.1.3.0/ 82350807/ITS Digital Archive, USHMM.

53. For a summary of the Bergen-Belsen concentration camp, see Thomas Rahe, "Bergen-Belsen Main Camp," in Megargee, *The United States Holocaust Memorial Museum Encyclopedia of Camps and Ghettos*, 1:278–81.

54. "Belsen," supplement to the *British Zone Review*, October 13, 1945, 1.1.3.0/ 82350807–10/ITS Digital Archive, USHMM.

sixty thousand prisoners were in the camp.[55] (See document 4.4.[56]) "The conditions revealed on the British entry," notes the supplement, "were these: deaths were averaging 500 per day. More than half the total inmates needed immediate hospital treatment. There were ten thousand unburied bodies, typhus-infested, many in advanced stages of decomposition strewn about the ramp. Huts intended for 60 inmates housed 600. Feeding, toilet, and sanitary utensils and equipment were non-existent[. . . . T]here had been neither food nor water for five days preceding the British entry. Evidence of cannibalism was found. The inmates included men, women and children." We read, too, a not uncommon description of the prisoners themselves: "The inmates had lost all self-respect, were degraded morally to the level of beasts. Their clothes were in rags, teeming with lice, and both inside and outside the [prisoner] huts was an almost continuous carpet of dead bodies, human excreta, rags and filth," stated the supplement.[57]

From this chaos and human misery, Allied authorities began to create stability. Convalescence is an interesting and understudied aspect of that summer of 1945, and ITS-held documents are rich with material on this very specific aspect of prisoners' experience.[58] One way to approach this issue would be to study the voluntary agencies that approached UNRRA and subsequently the International Refugee Organization (IRO), offering their services. There were many such agencies, including national-level Red Cross offices and national and international Jewish, Catholic, and Protestant faith-based agencies such as the Church World Service,[59] the Young Men's Christian Association (YMCA)/

---

55. Ibid., 82350807.

56. Ibid.

57. Ibid., 82350807-8.

58. Postliberation hospital records, consisting mainly but not exclusively of lists of prisoners and biographical detail about them, abound in ITS. For example, see 2.1.3.2 (Hospital Files, French Zone), 2.1.4.3 (Lists of Inpatients of Hospitals in the Soviet Zone), 2.1.4.4 (Hospital Files, Soviet Zone), 2.1.5.2 (Lists of Inpatients of Hospitals in Berlin), 2.1.5.3 (Hospital Files, Berlin), 2.3.3.2 (Card file of Persecutees Treated in Hospitals on the Territory of the Later French Zone), 10.7.41 (American Hospitals Files/Prisons), and many other subunits in which the treatment and convalescence of child and adult victims can be found interspersed with other kinds of material.

59. The Church World Service was founded in 1946. Seventeen Catholic and Protestant denominations came together to form an agency to "feed the hungry, clothe the naked, heal the sick, comfort the aged, shelter the homeless." See "History," Church World Service, www.cwsglobal.org/about-us/history.html (accessed July 7, 2015).

Young Women's Christian Association (YWCA)[60] (see document 4.5.[61]), the Unitarian Universalist Service Committee (UUSC, formerly known as the Unitarian Service Committee),[62] and many others, such as the Jewish relief agencies referred to in chapters 1 and 3.

ITS holdings describing the work of the Child Projects Department of the UUSC capture well the mission of such voluntary agencies. "The time between [children's] liberation from Nazi terror and their final placement will be very decisive for the future development of displaced children, determining whether they will become healthy, happy individuals, delinquents or neurotic wrecks, and whether they will prove an asset or a danger to society," wrote Ernst Papanek, director of child projects for the UUSC in the summer of 1945.[63] (See document 4.6.[64]) Margaret J. Newton, child welfare specialist for UNRRA District Office No. 2 in Wiesbaden, was delighted and accepted the offer of help. "We have just received your letter informing us that staff would be available from the Unitarian Service Committee. We would be grateful for the services of six or seven workers, who would be used as case workers with United Nations[65] children living in German families or in German institutions. We have a real need for additional help," she wrote.[66]

In the summer of 1945, Jewish refugees, including Jewish children, faced antisemitism still. "The U.S. Zone has been working for several weeks on the location of unaccompanied children who might be eligible for haven under the

---

60. Headquartered in Geneva, the YMCA-YWCA was founded in 1844 with the mission "to bring social justice and peace to young people and their communities, regardless of religion, race, gender or culture." See "Who We Are," World YMCA, www.ymca.int/who-we -are (accessed June 17, 2014).

61. World YMCA-YWCA Organizational Chart, US Zone 1946, 6.1.2/82491687/ITS Digital Archive, USHMM.

62. The UUSC was founded in 1945 to support relief work in Europe. The USHMM holds archival records for the UUSC that would complement well the study of ITS documents pertaining to the UUSC. See RG 67.012 and 67.028, USHMM.

63. Statement by Ernst Papanek, director of child projects, Unitarian Service Committee, New York, 1945, 6.1.2/82491726/ITS Digital Archive, USHMM.

64. Margaret J. Newton, child welfare specialist, for Olive Biggar, relief services officer, UNRRA District Office No. 2, Wiesbaden, to G. K. Richman, assistant director, Relief Services Office, UNRRA, Pasing/Munich, July 19, 1946, 6.1.2/82491725/ITS Digital Archive, USHMM.

65. At that time, the term referred to the Allied powers that had fought against the Nazis and Axis powers in World War II.

66. Margaret J. Newton, child welfare specialist, for Olive Biggar, relief services officer, UNRRA District Office No. 2, Wiesbaden, to G. K. Richman, assistant director, Relief Services Office, UNRRA, Pasing/Munich, July 19, 1946, 6.1.2/82491725/ITS Digital Archive, USHMM.

invitation extended by the British government," wrote Vernon Kennedy, Director, American Zone Austria, to E. Rhatigan in UNRRA's Frankfurt office on August 16, 1945. "As you know," Kennedy continued, "the English offer includes 1,000 children under the age of 16 years who have been in concentration camps[. . . . A] high percentage of these children are Jewish. We want to be sure that this is understood by the British government before the children are moved." Kennedy was also sensitive to the needs of German Jewish children, adding, "First consideration should be given to children from concentration camps, including children of enemy nationality who were in concentration camps as a result of racial or political persecution."[67] Even after the Holocaust, Jewish children could still be hard to place and, when finally given a home, were not always welcomed.[68]

The summer months of 1945 saw the return of some of those children kidnapped by the Nazis and subjected to so-called Germanization as part of the Lebensborn program (see chapter 1).[69] In July 1945, Polish aid workers came to the home of Therese Grassler in Salzburg, Austria, to take ten-year-old Henderike Goschen[70] back to her native country.[71] Therese met Henderike in August 1943, when the latter was eight. On August 23, at the Regional Youth Office Salzburg, claimed Therese, "I picked out the eight and half year old girl Henderike Goschen." Therese was told, she claimed, that Henderike "was an orphan from the German east who had lost both parents." The little girl "looked quite

67. Letter from Vernon Kennedy, director, American Zone Austria, Salzburg, to E. Rhatigan, UNRRA, Frankfurt, August 16, 1945, 6.1.1/82502593–4/ITS Digital Archive, USHMM.

68. See, among others, Beth B. Cohen, *Case Closed: Holocaust Survivors in Postwar America* (New Brunswick, NJ: Rutgers University Press, 2007).

69. See also Johannes-Dieter Steinert, "Germanisierung, Kollaboration und militärische Aktionen," in *Deportation und Zwangsarbeit: Polnische und Sowjetische Kinder im Nationalsozialistischen Deutschland und im besetzten Osteuropa, 1939–1945* (Essen: Klartext, 2013), 97–108; Roman Hrabar, *"Lebensborn": Czyli, źródło życia* (Katowice: Wydawn. "Śląsk," 1980), and other works by Hrabar on the kidnapping of Polish children.

70. Her real name was Henryka Gozdowiak; she was born on either December 12 or November 16, 1934. See 6.3.2.1/84247777/ITS Digital Archive, USHMM.

71. Copy, affidavit of Therese Grassler, Document Book X for Max Sollmann in the proceedings against Ulrich Greifelt and others submitted to Military Court I by Dr. Paul Ratz, Nuremberg. Dr. Ernst Braune, assistant defense counsel, American Military Tribunal Case 8, took this affidavit in Grassler's home on Ganzhofstrasse 19 in Salzburg-Maxglan on December 26, 1947. See 4.1.0/82480770–73/ITS Digital Archive, USHMM. This is one in a set of copies pertaining to Nuremberg Successor Trial Number 8, *U.S. v. Ulrich Greifelt*, the so-called Rasse- und Siedlungshauptamt Case from October 10, 1947, to March 10, 1948. These documents are the original reproductions used in the case, given to ITS in 1956.

different from the children in this part of the country; she was short and squat, had dark blond hair, but her eyes were blue." When questioned about the child's Polish heritage, Therese responded, "Henderike told me that she came from the vicinity of Łódź [and] that she had been in an orphanage there."[72]

Henderike was a Polish child kidnapped and turned over to the Lebensborn. Therese acknowledged this in a roundabout way only, telling US Assistant Defense Counsel Ernst Braune, "Whilst the arrangements were being made for transferring the child to a foster home, I had no dealings with the Lebensborn society, and all arrangements were made by the Regional Youth Office [Salzburg] exclusively. Later on I was never approached by the Lebensborn but for one exception: I once received a letter from the Lebensborn asking how the child was behaving with me. I did not reply to this as I did not know what the Lebensborn really was, and since then I heard no more from them."[73] Their parting in July 1945 was a difficult one for Therese and, according to her foster mother at least, also for Henderike.[74] After being taken from her temporary home with Therese in Salzburg, Henderike was placed in a children's home in Łódź, where she was reunited with her brother.[75] As mentioned in chapter 1, the Nazi Lebensborn program is a new and growing subject of study by scholars, accompanied by memoir literature by Lebensborn children. These memoirs have yet to be systematically analyzed for the impact of the Lebensborn program on the children affected, their adoptive parents, their families of origin, and their own siblings and children when this family history is unearthed.[76]

CORC/P (45) 54

As loved ones sought one another, governments sought their missing nationals, and the Allies sought perpetrators and collaborators, practical frustrations and

---

72. Affidavit of Therese Grassler, 4.1.0/82480771/ITS Digital Archive, USHMM.

73. Ibid., 82480772. Other evidence in ITS-held documents confirm that Henderike was deported to the Lebensborn facility Hochland in Steinhöring, near Munich, on April 16, 1943. See 6.3.2.1/84247777/ITS Digital Archive, USHMM.

74. Affidavit of Therese Grassler, 4.1.0/82480773/ITS Digital Archive, USHMM.

75. See ITS Child Search Case Goschen, Henderike, 6.3.2.1/84247776–81/ITS Digital Archive, USHMM.

76. For example, see, among others, Anne-Maria Lenhart, *Eine Darstellung der Organisation "Lebensborn e.V."* (Hamburg: Diplomica, 2013); Per Meek and Arne Löhr, *Lebensborn 6210* (Kristiansund: Ibs Forlag, 2001); Dorothee Schmitz-Köster, *"Deutsche Mutter, bist du bereit—": Alltag im Lebensborn* (Berlin: Aufbau-Verlag, 1997); Dorothee Schmitz-Köster, *Kind L 364: Eine Lebensborn-Familiengeschichte* (Berlin: Rowohlt, 2007).

difficulties abounded. A mention of the various tracing service structures in existence by the end of 1945 is necessary here. In 1944, UNRRA (discussed in chapter 1) had already proposed both establishing national tracing bureaus (NTBs) like the existing British Red Cross Tracing Bureau and also setting up one central tracing bureau. No agreement on the proposal was reached until April 1945, and in the meanwhile some countries set up NTBs. Key NTBs included the British Red Cross Tracing Bureau in London; the Belgian Service d'Identification et de Recherches, established by the Commissariat Belge au Rapatriement in June 1944; the Commissariat au Rapatriement of Luxemburg, established in August 1944; the Polish Red Cross–founded Biuro Informacyjne, reopened in April 1945; the Bureau National Français des Recherches, established in the summer of 1945; the Informatiebureau van het Nederlandse Rode Kruis, established by the Netherlands Red Cross in September 1945; and the Central Location Index. Still others were established in 1946 and thereafter.[77]

On April 27, 1945, SHAEF "officially assumed the responsibility for the processing of tracing" and, the following month, established its Tracing and Locating Unit in Versailles. Then tiny, this unit was "supervised by a representative of the UNRRA liaison staff."[78] On June 28, US forces active in SHAEF moved to the headquarters of the US Forces, European Theater (USFET), located in Frankfurt am Main.[79] USFET headquarters opened on July 1, 1945.[80] SHAEF was dissolved in mid-July 1945 along with its Tracing and Locating Unit. Its responsibilities passed to the Combined Displaced Persons Executive (CDPX) of the Allied Control Council.[81] CDPX in turn comprised two parts:

---

77. Uwe Ossenberg, *The Document Holdings of the International Tracing Service* (Bad Arolsen: ITS, 2009), 2–3.

78. "The Tracing of Missing Persons in Germany on an International Scale, with Particular Reference to the Problem of UNRRA: Study Prepared by UNRRA Administration," June 1, 1946, 6.1.1/82492879/ITS Digital Archive, USHMM.

79. At the time of the transfer, "the UNRRA staff [of the CDPX Central Tracing Bureau] had increased to only five." "The Tracing of Missing Persons in Germany on an International Scale, with Particular Reference to the Problem of UNRRA: Study Prepared by UNRRA Administration," June 1, 1946, 6.1.1/82492879/ITS Digital Archive, USHMM.

80. Separate and distinct from SHAEF, USFET commanded only US troops. Under Eisenhower as theater commander, when it opened in Frankfurt on July 1, and "when its increments from European Theater of Operations, U.S. Army (ETOUSA), SHAEF, and the 12th Army Group were fully assembled," it consisted of 3,885 officers and 10,968 enlisted men. Its sphere of responsibility, notes Earl F. Ziemke, extended to US troops in "England, France, Belgium, Norway, and Austria." Two military government staffs governed the US Zone of Occupation: the US Group Control Council and the theater G-5 (Civil Affairs–Military Government Section). See Ziemke, *The U.S. Army in the Occupation of Germany*, 317, 458.

81. Established on August 30, 1945, the Allied Control Council (Allied Control Author-

the Central Records Office and the Central Tracing Bureau.[82] UNRRA staff worked within the CDPX.[83]

Lack of staffing was a grave problem. "On 26 June there were five members of the [CDPX-run Central Tracing Bureau] staff; to this number six were added on July 3, four from 4 July to 20 August, and eleven on 23 August," noted one report.[84] Further, the proliferation of different national offices and the near-constant mutation of a central tracing effort caused much confusion. Chaos often reigned supreme that first summer. On August 25, R. Oungre of the UNRRA office in Neuilly-sur-Seine (a western suburb of Paris) wrote to Colonel A. H. Moffitt in the USFET headquarters in Frankfurt. (See document 4.7.[85]) "I should like to take the opportunity of asking whether I should direct my enquiries regarding lost relatives to you or to Miss de la Pole who, we have been told, is in charge of the tracing bureau, but from whom we have never received any reply," wrote Oungre.[86] Even routine matters like mail delivery were problematic. "You will observe that this letter was written on the 17th of May [1945], posted through the US Army Postal Service on the 22nd of May. It does not appear to have reached this country until the 30th of July," wrote Colonel L. W. Charley, deputy chief programs officer, Displaced Persons (DP) German Planning Branch in the United States, writing to E. E. Rhatigan at UNRRA's Frankfurt office. "It will be interesting to know where this unconscionable delay has occurred," he added.[87] Challenges were far greater, of course, than the lack of a speedy postal system.

ity) was the military occupation governing body of the Allied occupation zones in Germany. The members were the Soviet Union, United States, and United Kingdom; France was later added with a vote but had no duties.

82. Ossenberg, *The Document Holdings of the International Tracing Service*, 3–4.

83. In July 1945, UNRRA had "2,656 persons in 332 DP teams deployed throughout the western zones." Ziemke, *The U.S. Army in the Occupation of Germany*, 318.

84. "The Tracing of Missing Persons in Germany on an International Scale, with Particular Reference to the Problem of UNRRA: Study Prepared by UNRRA Administration," June 1, 1946, 6.1.1/82492879–80/ITS Digital Archive, USHMM.

85. Letter from R. Oungre, 48 Boulevard Maillot, Neuilly-sur-Seine, France, to Colonel A. H. Moffitt, CDPX, c/o G-5 Division, USFET, August 25, 1945, 6.1.1/82496332/ITS Digital Archive, USHMM. This document is original to ITS.

86. Ibid.

87. Cable on postal service for displaced persons from Colonel L. W. Charley, deputy chief programs officer, DP German Planning Branch, to Mr. E. E. Rhatigan, UNRRA/CDPX, c/o G-5, USFET, Frankfurt, August 20, 1945, 6.1.1/82496301/ITS Digital Collection, USHMM. This document is original to ITS.

In August 1945, various actors hardly knew whom to write in their pursuit of the missing. By summer's end in 1945, the American, British, French, and Soviet counterparts of the Allied Control Council in Berlin-Schöneberg found they could agree on establishing a much-needed Central Tracing Service.[88] (See document 4.8.[89]) Issued September 13, 1945, directive CORC/P (45) 54 established such a service with four objectives: (1) "to search for and trace military and civilian missing of the United Nations"; (2) "to establish, where possible, the fate of those missing who cannot be found alive"; (3) "to locate, collect and preserve all available records regarding displaced persons in Germany"; and (4) "to serve as a link to bring interested persons into communications with each other."[90] The CDPX was to be dissolved on October 1, and UNRRA would then assume responsibility for the newly created Central Tracing Service.

Here was the size of it: "Although it had been clearly requested that a staff of 89 would be necessary before 1 October 1945 when UNRRA was to assume the entire responsibility for the operation, only 34 UNRRA employees were available at that time, assisted by six Class II employees and 18 displaced persons."[91] The UNRRA Central Tracing Bureau was formally established on November 16, 1945, subordinate to the Allied Control Council's Central Tracing Policy Board.[92] Then and in the years ahead, Allied authorities struggled to keep accurate lists of DPs, both inside and outside camps.[93] (See document 4.9.[94]) ITS-held documents leave one with a sense of the overwhelming nature of the task, at the level not only of heads of state or major international relief organizations but also of ordinary men and women facing this work daily. (See document 4.10.[95]) "Search activities in Belsen [. . .] began in December 1945,"

---

88. CORC/P (45) 54: Allied Control Authority Coordinating Committee for establishment of a Missing Persons Tracing Service, September 13, 1945, 6.1.1/82500219–22/ITS Digital Archive, USHMM.

89. Ibid., 82500220.

90. Ibid.

91. "The Tracing of Missing Persons in Germany on an International Scale, with Particular Reference to the Problem of UNRRA: Study Prepared by UNRRA Administration," June 1, 1946, 6.1.1/82492880/ITS Digital Archive, USHMM.

92. Ossenberg, *The Document Holdings of the International Tracing Service*, 6.

93. Ibid. Chapter 2 discusses the scholarly value of such lists.

94. "Displaced Persons and Foreign Workers Living Outside Camps," October 5, 1945, 2.2.0.1/82392576/ITS Digital Archive, USHMM.

95. Report on the search in Belsen for the [Allied] Control Commission for Germany, Search Bureau Department, Belsen, June 10, 1946, 1.1.3.0/82350833/ITS Digital Archive, USHMM.

wrote Lieutenant H. François Ponet, the French search officer in that camp. "Originally the number of enquiries [. . .] averaged thirty to forty a week," he wrote. They would quickly increase to over one hundred per week. "It soon became obvious that with the means at my disposal, that is two employees, I could not cope effectively with the number of enquiries I was receiving," he lamented. "The enquiries [. . .] necessitate a number of investigations and check[s], and it proves impossible for only three people to deal with more than three or four cases a day, if these are to be investigated with accuracy and thoroughness," he acknowledged.[96]

ITS-held documents illustrate the role of prisoners both in administering the Nazi concentration camp universe and, after war's end, in aiding the Allies to rehabilitate former prisoners. Not yet examined by scholars is the role that former prisoners themselves played in the tracing process. A case in point is the International Information Office (IIO) at Dachau.[97] Its amazing story begins with the so-called camp registration office (*Lagerschreibstube*), "as old as the camp itself, the first records [originating] in 1933."[98] As of November 1, 1944, the "first camp writer [clerk]" for the *Lagerschreibstube* was Dachau prisoner Jan Domagała. Working with him were "three camp messengers, one Pole, one German, and one Austrian." In the days before Dachau was liberated on April 29, 1945, these prisoners hid the original records from camp authorities to save them from destruction, an act of tremendous resistance and bravery given the violence of those last days of Nazi domination. A report on the history of the IIO describes this chain of events thusly: "At the camp's liberation, the first camp writer [Domagała] understood [the need] to save the records of the *Lagerschreibstube*, excluding only a few camp records [. . .] as the SS destroyed all files of other offices. The *Lagerschreibstube* was in possession of all the records concerning the strength and feeding of the camp. The concerned prisoners [Domagała and the camp messengers] were responsible for the total [reporting regarding] the strength [i.e., population] of the camp."[99]

96. Ibid. The author is Lieutenant H. François Ponet, the French search officer.

97. For broad analysis of the history of the Dachau site postwar, see Harold Marcuse, *Legacies of Dachau: The Uses and Abuses of a Concentration Camp, 1933–2001* (Cambridge: Cambridge University Press, 2001).

98. For the history of the Dachau *Schreibstube*, see "History of the International Information Office Dachau," 1.1.6.0/82089047–59/ITS Digital Archive, USHMM. The report is undated, and its author is not identified. This document is original.

99. "History of the International Information Office Dachau," 1.1.6.0/82089047–59/ITS Digital Archive, USHMM. See also Jan Domagała, *Ci, którzy przeszli przez Dachau* (Warsaw: Pax, 1957).

ITS holds the original copies of these saved cards, which include, as seen in chapter 1, prisoner category, previous and current prisoner number and block assignment, date and place of birth, religion, occupation, and transfer or death date. In aggregate, scholars might carry out a statistical analysis of the prisoner population (nationality, occupation, age, fate) or changes in the camp's administration and policies as evidenced by changes in these cards over time. More than that, scholars may discuss the development and operations of this fascinating prisoner-run tracing service, already functioning in the summer of 1945,[100] and those first months of what became the IIO, initially run by Domagała himself as camp secretary, with former prisoner Walter Cieslik as his deputy.[101]

Established in June 1945 by order of the US military government in the city of Dachau[102] and ultimately located on Schleissheimer Street,[103] the IIO was "the only place which was able to care for evidence, information about [the] camp and [its] prisoners, and transports."[104] Specifically, this meant distributing "cards enabling survivors to receive double rations for eight weeks and disburs [ing] sums of money and items of clothing based on individual need to [. . .] local

---

100. For an account of how these documents came to rest with the Central Tracing Bureau, see 6.1.1/82510716/ITS Digital Archive, USHMM. The accession notes for 1.1.6.7 (Office Cards Dachau) only make note of copies of a limited number of cards received from the Dachau memorial.

101. Marcuse (*Legacies of Dachau*, 66) is erroneous in calling Cieslik the first "head" of the IIO. In fact, Domagała was its first head, from June until September 1945, when he returned to Poland. He was succeeded by the head of the IIO press office, Mr. Husareck, who retired in May 1946. Only then did Cieslik assume this role. See "History of the International Information Office Dachau," 1.1.6.0/82089049/ITS Digital Archive, USHMM.

102. Ibid. According to the report on the IIO, "General Adams" confirmed the transformation of the *Schreibstube* into the IIO, as did the commanding officer stationed at Dachau at the time, Colonel Bill Joyce. IIO staff reported directly to the US Army camp officer, Lieutenant Rosenbloom, who was succeeded by Captain Schmitt and finally Captain Deal.

103. Ibid. Marcuse (*Legacies of Dachau*, 66) correctly notes the location of the IIO when it officially became known as such. An added detail from the ITS report is that during the operation of the camp, and at the time the records were preserved, the *Lagerschreibstube* was in "hut one" of the camp. After liberation, the nascent IIO was placed in the former Dachau commandant's building and only then moved to Schleissheimer Street.

104. Ibid., 82089048.

and traveling liberated inmates."[105] Given what we have seen concerning incredibly low numbers of staff engaged in tracing in those first fraught weeks and months,[106] staffing of the IIO was rather astounding, "consisting of forty-two block writers, forty evidence writers and twenty-nine office writers."[107] The results were hundreds of documents like that dated November 30, 1945, in English, German, and Polish: "We attest that Mr. Kalicki Izydor born on 8.4.1909 in Kikól [a village in Poland] was in our office as clerk from 5th of May till 15th of December 1945."[108] (See document 4.11.[109]) Prisoners turned office clerks like Kalicki worked "day and night"[110] and even created one of the first postwar exhibitions on the camp in its crematorium building in the fall of 1945.[111]

INSTEAD OF RETRIBUTION, JUSTICE

On November 20, 1945, the International Military Tribunal (IMT) opened in Nuremberg. Arguably the most famous and precedent-setting court of the twentieth century, the IMT consisted of the United States, Great Britain, France, and the Soviet Union. The IMT indicted twenty-four of the highest-ranking Third Reich leaders still alive and ultimately tried twenty-two select political leaders; eleven subsequent trials dealt with officers of the SS and Wehrmacht, policemen, judges, medical doctors, industrialists, and economists. The IMT charges against these defendants included crimes against peace, war crimes, crimes against humanity, and membership in criminal organizations.[112] ITS holds partial copies of the so-called Nuremberg successor trials, which frequently reference the precedent set by the IMT. For example, ITS holds a copy of the

105. Marcuse, *Legacies of Dachau*, 66.

106. As the report on the IIO put it, "At that time [June 1945] nobody cared, and there was no time for [tracing efforts]." "History of the International Information Office Dachau," 1.1.6.0/82089049/ITS Digital Archive, USHMM.

107. Ibid., 82089048.

108. Ibid.

109. Attestation for Izydor Kalicki, International Information Office, Dachau, November 30, 1945, 1.1.6.0/82097119/ITS Digital Archive, USHMM.

110. "History of the International Information Office Dachau," 1.1.6.0/82089048/ITS Digital Archive, USHMM.

111. See Marcuse, *Legacies of Dachau*, 170.

112. The literature on the IMT and its impact on legal practice is vast. Among the best sources are Lawrence Douglas, *The Memory of Judgment: Making Law and History in the Trials of the Holocaust* (New Haven, CT: Yale University Press, 2001), and Bloxham, *Genocide on Trial*, among many other excellent works by both authors.

opinion written by Robert M. Toms, presiding judge of Military Tribunal II
(*U.S. v. Oswald Pohl et al.*), titled "Treatment of the Jews." "This disgraceful
chapter in the history of Germany has been vividly portrayed in the judgment
of the International Military Tribunal," stated Judge Toms and his colleagues.
"Nothing can be added to that comprehensive finding of facts, in which this
Tribunal completely concurs. From it we see the unholy spectacle of six million
humans being deliberately exterminated by a civilized state whose only indictment was that its victims had been born in the wrong part of the world[,] to
forbearers whom the murderers detested. Never before in history has man's
inhumanity to man reached such depths."[113]

"STATISTICS"[114]

The year 1945 closed quietly, with the victims of the Nazi and Axis regimes
slowly recovering their physical health and struggling to take faltering steps
forward, with the Allies and the many agencies invested in aiding these steps
struggling to keep up with the volume of their needs, and with the perpetrators
of these criminal systems facing legal proceedings. The dramatic winter, spring,
and summer settled into a fall characterized by the routine but difficult work
that would face the Allies and their helpers for years to come. Scholars have not
yet studied at the day-to-day operational level the dedicated men and women
who carried out this work against enormous odds. The monthly report for the
Child Welfare Division, Eastern Military District, gives eight lines about the
work of Louise Pinsky in notes on December 7, 1945. Pinsky, regional child
welfare officer for Regensburg, "continues to give conscientious service," the
report states. "She has now transported her 200th unaccompanied child to Indersdorf." As 1945 came to a close, Pinsky worried, reporting that team regional
child welfare officers like herself suffered from a "lack of time [. . .] to devote
to [their] important work" and that, consequently, "many [officers were thus]
delegating this responsibility to DP interviewers."[115]

---

113. See "Excerpt from the Opinion and Judgment of United States Military Tribunals
Sitting in the Palace of Justice, Nuremberg, Germany, at a Session of Military Tribunal
II, Held 3 November 1947," 1.1.2.0/82349440–41/ITS Digital Archive, USHMM. This
document is a copy received by ITS in 1978 from the Staatsarchiv Nürnberg.
114. Memorandum from Louise Pinsky to Eileen Davidson, Regensburg, October 18,
1945, 6.1.2/82487052/ITS Digital Archive, USHMM.
115. Child Welfare Division monthly report, Eastern Military District, December 7,
1945, 6.1.2/82487236/ITS Digital Archive, USHMM. For documents confirming Pinsky's
role, see 6.1.2/82486994 and 82487011. For a report she wrote on differences she observed
between Jewish and non-Jewish children under her care, see letter from Pinsky to Eileen
Davidson, Regensburg, October 18, 1945, 6.1.2/82487052/ITS Digital Archive, USHMM.

ITS-held documents allow us to look through the lens of 1945 and see far beyond studies of the so-called Hour Zero up to this point. In early 1945, many Germans in the privileged position of not yet counting themselves among the regime's ever-increasing pool of victims did not understand or internalize that the war was lost, and with it, Nazism's false ideals. Hans Fuge could still report with relish on his "lazy" camp inmates—Polish girls not yet sixteen—and Ruth Kleinsteuber could still volunteer for SS guard duty, as it seemed more promising than working for a ninth year as an embroiderer. Jews still alive in January 1945 could look forward to little sympathy or understanding as to the unique set of "choiceless choices" they faced and to even more unimaginable abuse at the hands of Nazis and their collaborators on the increasingly documented death marches. Civilians and captured military from all over Europe, including the United States, experienced the last months of the war as the most brutal.

Liberation, thus, was an unbelievable moment for the persecuted and incarcerated. "I was astonished, but a few hours later I had to accept it," Christian Guy told Captain Alfred T. Bogen. Then came the shock—for the Allies, their helpers, and the world—of what they had managed to ignore or at least to view from a great distance until then: terrain formerly controlled by Germany, now littered with camps, mass graves, and murdered bodies. Everyone was disoriented, as captured in one British medic's comment that patients at Sandbostel, "in spite of their weak condition[,] would step out of bed and wander about in the nude." Death and disease still raged, and the Allies and charitable bodies of all sizes, denominations, and nationalities rushed to the scene. The work was desperate, and the need for some kind of centralized agency to trace missing persons and return the captured, kidnapped, and persecuted to their former homes (or new ones) became obvious almost immediately. Despite so many pressing concerns and human limitations, a Central Tracing Service was established. The many brave men and women, including former prisoners, who took up this work have yet to be studied and will be well worth attention in the future. The Allies and many victims of Nazism and its collaborators did not seek retribution in the end; rather, they hoped for justice. The IMT was a legal proceeding that forever changed the way the world would view the newborn concept of genocide.

For students and scholars, ITS-held documentation offers the opportunity to study the end phase of genocide and the beginning phase of recovery from the vantage point of every kind of actor, from perpetrator to witness to victim to rescuer. Any one aspect of that first year touched upon in this chapter merits

On Indersdorf, see chapter 3. For more on the activities of the Eastern Military District, see "Child Welfare Report on Activities in Eastern Military District," November 28 to December 9, 1945, 6.1.2/82486985–89/ITS Digital Archive, USHMM.

broader and more systematic study of ITS-held documentation relating to everyone from German perpetrators, collaborators, beneficiaries, and witnesses, to victims struggling to hang on for just one more day, to the Allied soldiers and aid workers who came upon them and had to rebuild a broken nation, society, and infrastructure. The role of religious and secular aid organizations, including their motivations and the impact of gender within these organizations on the roles they took on, remains an understudied topic. Further, because ITS-held documentation spans the years of the Third Reich until today, any of these questions may be studied not only for 1945 but across decades.

DOCUMENT LIST

DOCUMENT 4.1. Photograph of Abraham Langer contained in his CM/1 file, 3.2.1.1/79385447/ITS Digital Archive, USHMM.

DOCUMENT 4.2. "Extract from Report on Death Marches re: Kittlitztreben-Buchenwald," 5.3.3/84619503/ITS Digital Archive, USHMM.

DOCUMENT 4.3. Hand-drawn map of the death march from Kittlitztreben to Buchenwald, 5.3.3/84619504/ITS Digital Archive, USHMM.

DOCUMENT 4.4. Cover sheet, "Belsen," supplement to the *British Zone Review*, October 13, 1945, 1.1.3.0/82350807/ITS Digital Archive, USHMM.

DOCUMENT 4.5. World YMCA-YWCA organizational chart, US Zone, 1946, 6.1.2/82491687/ITS Digital Archive, USHMM.

DOCUMENT 4.6. Note by Margaret J. Newton, child welfare specialist, for Olive Biggar, relief services officer, UNRRA District Office No. 2, Wiesbaden, to G. K. Richman, assistant director, Relief Services Office, UNRRA, Pasing/Munich, July 19, 1946, 6.1.2/82491725/ITS Digital Archive, USHMM.

DOCUMENT 4.7. Letter from R. Oungre, 48 Boulevard Maillot, Neuilly-sur-Seine, France, to Colonel A. H. Moffitt, CDPX, c/o G-5 Division, USFET, August 25, 1945, 6.1.1/82496332/ITS Digital Archive, USHMM.

DOCUMENT 4.8. Extract from CORC/P (45) 54: Allied Control Authority Coordinating Committee for establishment of a Missing Persons Tracing Service, September 13, 1945, 1, 6.1.1/82500220/ITS Digital Archive, USHMM.

DOCUMENT 4.9. "Memorandum by US 3rd Army Military Government Regiment Regarding Displaced Persons and Foreign Workers Living Outside Camps," October 5, 1945, 2.2.0.1/82392576/ITS Digital Archive, USHMM.

DOCUMENT 4.10. Extract from the report on the search in Belsen for the [Allied] Control Commission for Germany, Search Bureau Department, Belsen, June 10, 1946, 1.1.3.0/82350833/ITS Digital Archive, USHMM.

DOCUMENT 4.11. Attestation for Izydor Kalicki, International Information Office, Dachau, November 30, 1945, 1.1.6.0/82097119/ITS Digital Archive, USHMM (in English, German, and Polish).

DOCUMENTS

DOCUMENT 4.1

DOCUMENT 4.2

109

- 38 -

KITTLITZTREBEN - BUCHENWALD

325 km.

Convoy of political prisoners, all Jewish, who were moved
from Kittlitztreben to Buchenwald in January-April 1945.

Place.	Map. ref.	Zone.	Km.	Date.	Remarks.
KITTLITZTREBEN	O 52/B 43	Poland		26.1.45.	Left on foot
			50		
HENNERSDORF	P 51/H 44	"			more than half the P.P. died on the way. The SS eliminated every morning the most feeble. Common graves all along the way. The burgomasters can furnish dates.
			7		
PENZIG	O 52/L 01	"			
			5		
LUDWIGSDORF	O 52/B 01	"			
			3		
GÖRLITZ	O 52/B 00	"			
			12		
REICHENBACH	O 52/A 79	"			
			12		
WEISSENBERG	O 52/A 81	USSR			
			17		
BAUTZEN	O 52/A 60	"			
			25		
BUHLAU	P 51/J 15	"			
			15		
RADEBERG	N 52/F 39	"			Turned around Brest and by-passed Langebruck
			8		
LANGENBRUCK	N 52/F 29	"			
			20		
KESSELDORF	N 52/F 18	"			
			40		
LUGAU	N 51/K 54	"			
			20		
ZWICKAU	N 51/K 34				
			35		
GERA	M 51/K 06	"			
			38		
JENA	M 51/J 66	"			
			18		
BUCHENWALD	M 51/J 57	"		4.4.45.	

325 km.

DOCUMENT 4.3

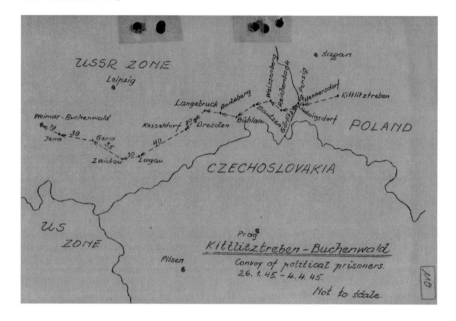

DOCUMENT 4.4

13 October, 1945

G.C.C. 1/24

Supplement to
BRITISH ZONE
R E V I E W

BELSEN

An account, based on Official Reports, of the uncovering by the British Army of the Belsen Concentration Camp and of the action taken during the vital days to minimise the suffering of the 60,000 inmates.

This is the scene which greeted the British troops when they arrived at the "sick camp". Seriously ill patients were lying with corpses in long huts littered with straw and filth. There was no medicine or doctors and the only relief offered to the inmates who entered this camp was death.

THE story of that greatest of all exhibitions of "man's inhumanity to man" which was Belsen Concentration Camp is known throughout the world. Therefore it is not intended to repeat it here except very briefly, and then only as a background for the story of what the British soldier did with the aid of British medical students and units of the British Red Cross to succour its tens of thousands of stricken inmates, to prevent the spread in epidemic form of the disease and infection there found, and finally to wipe Belsen off the face of the earth.

Belsen was not a new camp, not a wartime institution, but an established pre-war German concentration camp of a particular character and kind. It was an integral part of the Nazi regime and system. It was what the Germans called a "Krankenlager". Translated literally, a "sick camp", but the only cure offered the so-called sick who entered that camp was death. The inmates were not intended to recover and the arrival of death was accelerated by means of starvation, disease, physical degradation, slave conditions, work, and extreme cruelty.

The treatment was very effective. In fact, it was found that the turnover of inmates had been very rapid. No one has yet been found, except those liberated by British medical students, who has been able to claim to be a survivor of Belsen, while of the 60,000 found there by the British troops, none had been in the camp longer than eight to nine months, the great majority of them but three to four.

The conditions revealed on the British entry were these:

Deaths were averaging 500 per day. More than half the total inmates needed immediate hospital treatment. 10,000 unburied bodies, typhus-infested, many in an advanced stage of decomposition, lay about the camp. Huts intended for 60 inmates housed 600. Feeding, toilet and sanitary utensils and equipment were non-existent.

DOCUMENT 4.5

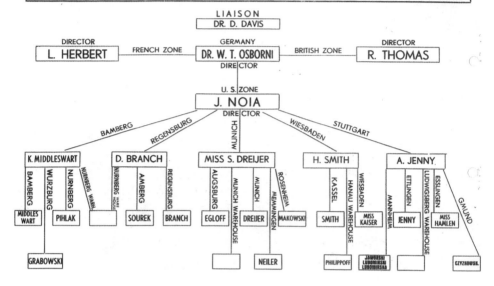

DOCUMENT 4.6*

UNITED NATIONS RELIEF AND REHABILITATION ADMINISTRATION

UNRRA District Office No. 2,
11, Paulinenstrasse,
Wiesbaden.   19th July, 1946.

To: Miss G.K.Richman, Assistant Director, Relief Services Office,
          UNRRA U.S.Zone, Pasing/Munich.

From;   Relief Services Office.

Attention: Child Welfare Specialist.

Subject: UNITARIAN SERVICE COMMITTEE.

          We have just received your letter informing us that staff would be
available from the Unitarian Service Committee.

          We would be grateful for the services of 6 or 7 workers, who would
be used as case workers with United Nations' children living in German families
or in German institutions.   We have a real need for additional help both in
this work and in the care of those children who have entered our district as
infiltrees.

          We shall be interested to hear when these persons will be available.

                                        OLIVE BIGGAR,
                                        Relief Services Officer.

                                        By MARGARET J.NEWTON,

MJN/81

---

*Original with hole punches and cut off at the bottom.

DOCUMENT 4.7

UNITED NATIONS ⸱IEF AND REHABILITATION ADMINISTRATIC
48 Boulevard Maillot,
Neuilly-sur-Seine

25th August, 1945

Your Ref:GE-CDPX 383.8(4.31)(4032)

Colonel A. H. Moffitt,
C.D.P.X.,
c/o G-5 Division,
UFSET

Dear Sir,

Mr. Martin Wainfeld

I wish to thank you for your reply to our enquiry
regarding Martin Wainfeld.

I should like to take this opportunity of asking
whether I should direct my enquiries regarding lost
relatives to you or to Miss de la Pole who, we have been
told, is in charge of the Tracing Bureau, but from whom
we have never received any reply.   I should be glad of
your advice on this point.

Yours truly,

R. Oungre

R. Oungre

DOCUMENT 4.8

CORC/P(45)54

DIRECTORATE OF PRISONERS OF WAR AND DISPLACED PERSONS

Recommendations of the Directorate regarding the Establishment of a
Central Tracing Service for United Nations' Nationals
Missing in Occupied Germany.

NOTE: This paper has been coordinated with the Political, Military,
and Internal Affairs and Communications Divisions of the four
National Elements of the Allied Control Authority and they
concur therein.

Objectives

1.   Recommended that the following should be the objectives of the
Tracing Service:

    (a)   to search for and trace military and civilian missing
of the United Nations;

    (b)   to establish, where possible, the fate of those missing
who cannot be found alive;

    (c)   to locate, collect and preserve all available records
regarding displaced persons in Germany;

    (d)   to serve as a link to bring interested persons into
communication with each other.

National Tracing Bureau

2.   Recommended that each interested United Nation that has not already
established a National Tracing Bureau within its own national boundaries
should be invited to establish such a Bureau, which should receive all
initial enquiries concerning missing of its own nationality.

Zonal Search Bureaux

3.   Recommended:

    (a)   that these Bureaux (which are already established in each
Zone) should assume responsibility for instituting searches
in their own Zones, including searches on all enquiries
passed to them by the Central Tracing Bureau;

    (b)   that each Zonal Bureau should operate under the complete jurisdiction
of its own ZonenCommander subject only to the general policies
of the Allied Control Council and the Central Tracing Policy Board.
(See below).

Central Tracing Bureau

4.   Recommended:

    (a)   that the Allied Control Council should be requested to invite
UNRRA to place the Central Tracing Bureau and Associated Central
Records Office, which it is already operating, at the Council's
disposal to be operated by UNRRA under policies and directives
issued by the Central Tracing Policy Board;

    (c)   that the Central Bureau should operate as a central clearing
house between the Zonal and National Bureaux and not as an
executive body; it should not, therefore, issue policies and
directives to the Zonal Bureaux, this being the task of the
Central Tracing Policy Board.

DOCUMENT 4.9

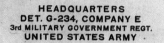

HEADQUARTERS
DET. G-234, COMPANY E
3rd MILITARY GOVERNMENT REGT.
UNITED STATES ARMY .

APO 403
DP/CJR/tf
5 October 1945

SUBJECT: Displaced Persons and Foreign Workers Living
Outside Camps

TO : Commanding General, Hq. Third U.S.Army,
G - 5 Section (Att: Displaced Persons Branch).

Submitted herewith are the lists of displaced persons
living outside Assembly Centers in Landkreis Altötting, prepared in accordance with letter, Detachment 201, dated 12 August 1945.

For the Military Government Officer:

CHARLES J.ROHR
CAPT   AUS
D P   Officer

1 Incl.:
Lists of Displaced Persons.

13 pages.

LK·ALTÖTTING.

DOCUMENT 4.10

II   ORGANIZATION OF THE SEARCH IN BELSEN

1.) Origin and development of the Search in Belsen :

Search activities in Belsen under the authority of Search Bureau began in December 1945.

The first officer in charge was Capt. BALME who was succeded by Capt. BLAKE, Capt. KADOMTZEF and myself.

Originally the number of enquiries received in Belsen averaged 3o to 4o a week but were soon increasing. As the result of an agreement between Capt. LATIMER, S.S.O. 3o Corps and Capt. DECATHALOGNE, French S.S.O. 3o Corps, I was asked in February 1946 to second Capt. KADOMTZEF in his duties as Search Officer. I carried on these duties alone when Capt. KADOMTZEF left Belsen in March 45.
46?

At that time, an average of 1oo enquiries were received every week, and this number has been maintained up to now. A total of 1.5oo enquiries have been sent to Belsen between the 15 th February and the 31 st of May, which re-presents about 4o % of all enquiries received in 3o Corps District from Search Bureau.

After Capt. KADOMTZEF's departure, it soon became obvious that with the means at my disposal, that is two employees, I could not cope efficiently with the number of enquiries I was receiving. The enquiries usually received in Belsen necessitates a number of investigation and checkings, and it proved impossible for only three people to deal with more than three our four cases a day, if these were to be investigated with accuracy and thoroughness.

DOCUMENT 4.11

International Information Office

D a c h a u

Dachau, 30th of November 1945

Attestation

We attest that Mr. Kalicki Izydor born at 8.4.1909 to Kikol was in our office as clerk from 5th of May till to 15th of December 1945 employed.

Bestätigung

Hiermit wird bestätigt, dass Herr Kalicki Izydor, geboren am 8.4.1909 in Kikol, in unserem Büro als Angestellter vom 5. Mai bis 15. Dezember beschäftigt war.

Zaswiadezenie

Niniejszym zaswiadcza sie, ze pan Kalicki Izydor urodzony dnia 8.4.1909 w Kikolowie. Byl w naszym biurze jako pracownik umyslowy od dnia 5. maja do 15. grudnia 1945 zatrudniony.

International Information Office

CHAPTER 5

Imagining the Displaced

O N DECEMBER 15, 1946, the United Nations adopted the constitution of the International Refugee Organization (IRO), which entered into force on August 20, 1948. The IRO was responsible for "care and maintenance" of displaced persons (DPs) and refugees, very specifically defined.[1] It had missions and offices in forty-nine countries all over the world[2] and defined DPs and refugees as those whose displacement resulted from the actions of or persecution by the National Socialist, Fascist, or "quisling" collaborator regimes, according to specific criteria outlined in Annex I (Definitions) of the IRO constitution.[3]

---

1. Supreme Headquarters/Allied Expeditionary Forces (SHAEF) defined refugees as those civilians "temporarily homeless within their own national boundaries" and DPs as "civilians outside of their national boundaries by reason of war." Within the DP category, the Allies considered two types: United Nations displaced persons, who were citizens of the Allied nations and those who could be given "equal status with them" (i.e., citizens of "neutral states"); and enemy or ex-enemy displaced persons, who were citizens of enemy states, for example, Germany, Austria, and Italy. See Gerald Steinacher, *Nazis on the Run: How Hitler's Henchmen Fled Justice* (New York: Oxford University Press, 2011), 3.

2. For a full list, see Louise W. Holborn, *The International Refugee Organization: A Specialized Agency of the United Nations. Its History and Work, 1946–1952* (Oxford: Oxford University Press, 1956), 763–64.

3. The IRO constitution replaced the Intergovernmental Committee for Refugees, in existence since 1938 to "help refugees from Germany and Austria," and also replaced the United Nations Relief and Rehabilitation Administration (UNRRA). The UN General

Most, but not all, who qualified for DP or refugee status were from Europe or other Axis-occupied or -controlled territories. Six categories of persons were defined as outside the concern of the IRO: (1) "war criminals, quislings and traitors," (2) those who had "assisted the enemy" in persecuting civilian popula-tions or "voluntarily assisted" enemy forces, (3) "ordinary criminals who [were] extraditable by treaty," (4) ethnic Germans,[4] (5) those with "financial support and protection from their country of nationality," and (6) those found to have "engaged in hostile behavior or activities against UN member nations" or to be "in the military or civil service" of a foreign state.[5]

"Who is a genuine, bona fide and deserving refugee?"[6] Gerard Daniel Cohen has so concisely explained the administrative process by which DPs and refugees were screened, who was determined to be within or outside the mandate and why, and the impact of the growing Cold War on this process that we need not revisit these topics here.[7] Documentation held by the International Tracing Service (ITS) gives color and life to the millions of individuals subject to the vagaries of Allied practices as relief agencies struggled to cope with the humani-tarian crisis described briefly in chapter 1. The geographical diversity of dis-placed persons and refugees in the ITS archive is one of its great potential strengths for drawing in those who might normally shy away from the study of the Holocaust, yet are drawn to the opportunity to study the wartime and

---

Assembly also established the Preparatory Commission for the International Refugee Organi-zation (PCIRO), "the activities of which started 31 January 1947." Eighteen states became full members of the IRO: Australia, Belgium, Canada, Denmark, the Dominican Republic, France, Guatemala, Iceland, Italy, Luxembourg, the Netherlands, New Zealand, Norway, the Republic of China, Switzerland, the United Kingdom, the United States, and Venezuela. Much has been written about the IRO already and will not be repeated in detail here. For a good summary, see Göran Melander, "International Refugee Organization," *Max Planck Encyclopedia of Public International Law* (MPEPIL), opil.ouplaw.com/home/EPIL (accessed September 26, 2015).

4. Ethnic Germans, or *Volksdeutsche*, included "German speakers and members of Ger-man cultural circles who were not German, Austrian, or Swiss citizens," living mostly in South Tyrol, Romania, Yugoslavia, Poland, and the Soviet Union. This category came to include so-called Reich Germans expelled from Silesia and eastern Prussia and Sudeten Ger-mans from Czechoslovakia. Steinacher, *Nazis on the Run*, 4.

5. Summary of annex I (definitions), part II, "Persons Who Will Not Be the Concern of the Organization," in Holborn, *The International Refugee Organization*, 586.

6. 1950 IRO Manuel for Eligibility Officers, 43AJ-1251, cited in Gerard Daniel Cohen, *In War's Wake: Europe's Displaced Persons in the Postwar Order* (New York: Oxford University Press, 2012), 35.

7. Ibid., 35–57.

postwar fates of their conationals as revealed by ITS-held material.[8] Thus, the aim of this chapter is threefold: first, to briefly consider new dimensions that ITS-held documents might bring to our understanding of predominantly European-born and Christian DPs and of European-born Jews; second, to bring to the fore some of the more unusual cases and highlight the presence in Nazi- and Axis-dominated Europe of prisoners, forced laborers, and even collaborators from Africa, Asia, the Middle East, and Latin America and/or belonging to ethnic or religious minorities; and third, to study the clues left behind in ITS-held documents recording the explanations collaborators gave and the paths they took to disappear into postwar, post-Holocaust societies in Germany and abroad.

FRESH APPROACHES TO DPs USING MASS DATA SETS

Many excellent studies of the predominantly European and Judeo-Christian DP population have recently become available.[9] Yet ITS holdings contained within Subunit Three (Registrations and Files of Displaced Persons, Children, and Missing Persons) still offer fresh possibilities for the study of DPs and refugees. Let us return to the largest body of material mentioned only briefly in chapter 1: the displaced person registration record (DP-2) card file, consisting of over 3.4 million digital images. Such mass data opens the door for quantitative studies of, for example, Polish, Ukrainian, or Jewish DPs. If one looks at Greinom Golub's DP-2 card (document 1.6), a study of any one of the more than twenty categories listed on his registration record, or several combined and then aggregated, could yield interesting results. For example, were particular towns or villages more heavily represented for "last permanent residence or residence [as of] January 1, 1938" (number 13)? If so, can such statistics provide clues as to towns and villages where Jewish survival patterns deserve further study? One might also run a statistical study of "desired destination" (number 12). What destinations were cited most frequently? One might sort by the "usual trade, occupation or profession" (number 14) or "languages spoken" (number 17) categories. Do predominant trades or languages come to the fore in a mass data study of DP-2 cards completed by Polish Jews? If so, what can these statistics tell us about a potential relationship between particular occupations or language skills and the ability to survive?

---

8. In the process of doing so, they will learn about and better understand the unique fate of Europe's Jews.

9. For a summary of these works and the predominant nationalites of the DP and refugee population, see chapter 1.

Golub was himself a so-called infiltree, as duly noted in the upper-left-hand corner of his registration card, meaning that he was one of "tens of thousands of Jewish 'infiltrees' who poured into the American zone from Eastern Europe." Atina Grossmann notes that those approximately two hundred thousand Polish Jewish DPs who had fled to the Soviet Union during World War II, returned to Poland postwar, and fled westward to escape antisemitism remain an understudied group.[10] A statistical analysis of DP-2 cards completed by Polish Jewish DPs might make a beginning toward better identifying these survivors and bringing to the fore any patterns that emerge when looking at their DP-2 cards in aggregate. Or researchers could examine material organized in ITS by specific infiltree centers.[11] This same model might be used for other specific DP and refugee subgroups to equal effect.

Geography is another lens through which to view the massive quantity of DP- and refugee-related data in the ITS holdings. One of the freshest recent approaches to the Holocaust has come from a group of geographers and historians who recognize it as a "profoundly geographical phenomenon."[12] For example, in their essay "Mapping the SS Concentration Camps," Anne Kelly Knowles and Paul B. Jaskot visually convey the four key stages in the "spatial-temporal development of the SS camps system."[13] A similar method might be employed using ITS-held documents on the DP camps and repatriation, resettlement, infiltree, and transient centers that exploded and then waned in Europe from May 1945 until the last camp closed in 1959. While we know about individual camps (though some remain understudied, especially in the French and Soviet zones), the ability to "map" them in relation to one another and over time will surely raise new questions. The same type of "mapping" of areas for "free living" DPs over time might also reveal patterns within survivor, refugee, and DP communities that were not as visible until scholars asked "spatial

---

10. These Polish Jewish infiltrees consisted of "three distinct but sometimes overlapping groups": survivors of concentration and labor camps and death marches who had initially returned to Poland to find family members or reclaim property; partisans and those in hiding; and, greatest in number, Jews who had fled to the Soviet Union and upon repatriation found rampant antisemitism in Poland. Atina Grossmann, *Jews, Germans and Allies: Close Encounters in Occupied Germany* (Princeton, NJ: Princeton University Press, 2007), 1–2.

11. See, for example, lists of infiltrees who registered at the Funkkaserne Infiltree Center in Munich, 3.1.1.2/82016408–500/ITS Digital Archive, USHMM.

12. Anne Kelly Knowles, Tim Cole, and Alberto Giordano, eds., *Geographies of the Holocaust* (Bloomington: Indiana University Press, 2014), 1.

13. Anne Kelly Knowles and Paul B. Jaskot with Benjamin Perry Blackshear, Michael De Groot, and Alexander Yule, "Mapping the SS Concentration Camps," in Knowles, Cole, and Giordano, *Geographies of the Holocaust*, 27.

questions" of the sources.[14] Spatial humanities methods might also allow for a closer look at the relationship of particular ports of exit from Europe taken by DPs and particular ports of entry in those countries accepting them. We have few effective visual tools to consider the path Holocaust survivors took, for example, from liberation to their new home countries. Researchers could also apply this line of inquiry to other groups of DPs, for which so much mass data can be found in the ITS holdings.

DPs BORN IN ASIA, AFRICA, THE MIDDLE EAST AND LATIN AMERICA

ITS-held documents demonstrate the international scope of World War II and the Holocaust in a way that allows us to see the intertwined fates of displaced persons, refugees, and those who claimed to be such from a staggering variety of ethnic and religious backgrounds from across Europe, Asia, Africa, the Middle East, and Latin America. (See document 5.1.[15]) Looking at such cases side by side, now possible due to the increasing search capability of the ITS digital archive, brings the war's long reach into sharp focus. One example is the project by the United States Holocaust Memorial Museum, the ITS in Bad Arolsen, and Yad Vashem to index the IRO's so-called care and maintenance (CM/1) forms by the categories of religion, nationality, and ethnicity (see chapter 1). In the course of the project, indexers discovered a surprisingly long and diverse list of nationalities, ethnicities,[16] and religious

14. Knowles and Jaskot with Blackshear, De Groot, and Yule, "Mapping the SS Concentration Camps," 1–3.

15. Supplement to summary of DP population "Others and Unclassified" by nationality, January 30, 1948, 3.1.1.0/82383977/ITS Digital Archive, USHMM.

16. The nationalities and ethnic groups captured as index terms (as entered into IRO CM/1 forms as "place of birth") are as follows: Abyssinian, Aegean Islands, Afghan, Albanian, Algerian, American, Andorran, Arab, Argentine, Armenian, Assyrian, Australian, Austrian, Avar, Azerbaijani, Banatian, Belgian, Belorussian, Bessarabian, Bohemian, Bolivian, Bosnian, Brazilian, British, Bulgarian, Burmese, Canadian, Chechen, Chilean, Chinese, Circassian, Columbian, Congolese, Costa Rican, Crimean, Croatian, Cuban, Cypriot, Cyrenaican, Czech, Dagestani, Daimatian, Danish, Dodecanese, Dominican, Dutch, Ecuadorian, Egyptian, English, Eritrean, Estonian, Ethiopian, Filipino, Finnish, French, Frisian, Georgian, German, Greek, Guatemalan, Hungarian, Icelander, Indian, Indochinese, Indonesian, Ingushetian, Iranian, Iraqi, Irish, Israeli, Italian, Japanese, Kabard, Kalmyk, Karaite, Karelian, Kazakhstani, Kenyan, Korean, Latvian, Lebanese, Liberian, Libyan, Lithuanian, Luxembourger, Macedonian, Maltese, Mexican, Moldavian, Monégasque, Mongolian, Montenegrin, Moroccan, Nicaraguan, Norwegian, Ossetian, Pakistani, Palestinian, Panamanian, Paraguayan, Persian, Peruvian, Polish, Portuguese, Rhodesian, Romanian, Russian, Salvadorian, Saudi, Scottish, Serbian, Siamese, Slovak, Slovene, South African, Soviet, Spanish,

affiliations.[17] Scholars interested in particular national, ethnic, or religious groups could use this search feature to begin investigating what ITS-held documents might yield. Further, scholars interested in the on-the-ground practices of the IRO in terms of whom it deemed to fall within or outside its mandate can efficiently select all CM/1 forms for a particular national, ethnic, or religious group and make a study of the patterns of who did or did not receive DP or refugee status and on what grounds.

The cases of European ethnic or religious minorities and individuals born in Asia, Africa, the Middle East, and Latin America were often less straightforward for IRO eligibility officers to evaluate. ITS-held documents allow us to investigate the experiences of those often marginalized or ignored in traditional World War II historiography. The cases presented here are on the periphery of the conventional boundaries of World War II experiences in the Western imagination, which has remained very Eurocentric in its analysis. Recently, Soviet and eastern European experiences have garnered more attention, and while this is a positive, important, and necessary development, Asian, African, Middle Eastern, and Latin American experiences, including those of Jews from these parts of the world, are vastly underresearched. Dozens of Western governments recruited refugees for their labor and reconstruction programs based on a strict hierarchy of races, as defined by ethnicity and physical attributes (i.e., "whiteness" and fitness).[18] The following cases demonstrate what practical evaluations looked like "on the ground" for these groups and how emergent nationalist movements created a set of applicants to the IRO impacted not only by World War II and the Holocaust but also by rapidly changing territorial and political realities in their homelands.

Sudanese, Surinamese, Swedish, Syrian, Tajik, Tanzanian, Thai, Tripolitanian, Tunisian, Turkestani, Turkish, Ugandan, Ukrainian, Uruguayan, from the USSR, Uzbek, Yemeni, Yugoslavian, Zairian, and, of course, "Undetermined," "Unknown," and "Stateless."

17. The religious affiliations captured as index terms (as written on IRO CM/1 forms) are as follows: Adventist, Albanian Orthodox, Anabaptist, Anglican, Anthroposophist, Armenian Apostolic, Armenian Catholic, Armeno Gregorian, Assemblies of God, Atheist, Augsburg Evangelical, Bahá'í, Baptist, Buddhist, Bulgarian Catholic, Byzantine Catholic, Calvinist, Catholic, Catholic Mariavite, Christian Scientist, Confessing Church member, Confucian, Coptic Orthodox Church, Czech Brethren, Deist, Dutch Reformed, Evangelical Lutheran, Free Thinker, Greek Orthodox, Hebrew, Hindu, Huguenot, Hussite, Jehovah Witness, Jewish, Mennonite, Methodist and United, Mormon, Muslim, New Apostolic, Old Believer, Orthodox Autocephalous, Pentecostal, Presbyterian, Quaker, Reformed, Russian Orthodox, Salvationist, Seventh Day Adventist, Shinto, Ukrainian Catholic, and Unitarian, among others.

18. For the Australian case, see Ruth Balint, "Industry and Sunshine: Australia as Home in the Displaced Persons' Camps of Postwar Europe," *History Australia* 11, no. 1 (2014): 102–27. See also Cohen, *In War's Wake*, ch. 5.

Jews and the Quest for "Due Protection"[19]

While for obvious reasons IRO eligibility officers determined most Jewish cases to fall within the mandate of the IRO, there were exceptions. (See document 5.2.[20]) Joseph Abadi,[21] born in 1927 in Aleppo, Syria, was one.[22] His parents were of Iranian Jewish origin.[23] The family moved to Syria before his birth but remained Iranian citizens. His mother tongue was French, and he was a trained pharmaceutical chemist, having studied for seven years at the prestigious American University of Beirut in Lebanon.[24] When he could not find work in Beirut after finishing his schooling, he moved to the still new state of Israel in March 1951.[25] He remained in Haifa for six months; then, still unable to find work, he went to Milan, Italy, to be with his brother, Ibrahim Abadi. In August 1951, Abadi applied for DP status, hoping to emigrate to Canada. He told his IRO

19. An IRO interviewer used this phrase in describing the meaning of Israel to Jewish applicants. See CM/1 form for Stella Hassan, 3.2.1.2/80385879 and 80385880/ITS Digital Archive, USHMM.

20. Extract from CM/1 form for "Abadi, Joseph," 3.2.1.2/80304938/ITS Digital Archive, USHMM.

21. Abadi was a prominent family name among Syrian Jews, and Aleppo was a major commercial conduit that "attracted Jews from all over the region." See Michael Menachem Laskier, "Syria and Lebanon," in *The Jews of the Middle East and North Africa in Modern Times*, ed. Reeva Spector Simon, Michael Menachem Laskier, and Sara Reguer (New York: Columbia University Press, 2003), 319.

22. CM/1 form for Joseph Abadi, 3.2.1.2/80304938/ITS Digital Archive, USHMM.

23. For more on the Jewish community in Iran, see Haideh Sahim, "Iran and Afghanistan," in Simon, Laskier, and Reguer, *The Jews of the Middle East and North Africa in Modern Times*, 367–86.

24. On the east coast of the Mediterranean Sea, Syria is today bordered by Turkey to the north and northeast, Iraq to the east and southeast, Jordan to the south, and Lebanon and Israel to the southwest. The 1920 Treaty of Sèvres granted Syria and Lebanon to the French as mandated territories. When World War II began, Vichy France controlled Syria and Lebanon. The Free French and British forces freed Syria in 1941, and Syria became fully independent in 1946, following the Allied withdrawal. See Laskier, "Syria and Lebanon," 316–18. For more on Syrian and Lebanese Jewish populations, see Laskier, "Syria and Lebanon," 318–23.

25. After the collapse of the Ottoman Empire in World War I, the 1920 Conference of San Remo placed Palestine under British mandate. The British partitioned Palestine to create the protectorate of Transjordan in 1923, which became the Kingdom of Jordan in 1946. See Ruth Kark and Joseph B. Glass, "Eretz Israel/Palestine, 1800–1948," in Simon, Laskier, and Reguer, *The Jews of the Middle East and North Africa in Modern Times*, 335. The British mandate ended and the modern state of Israel was established in 1948, following Zionist efforts in the late nineteenth and early twentieth centuries to "reestablish a Jewish national home in Palestine." See Boaz Cohen, "Israel," in *The Oxford Handbook of Holocaust Studies*, ed. Peter Hayes and John K. Roth (New York: Oxford University Press, 2010), 575–76.

interviewer that "the position of Jews in Syria and [Lebanon] became very difficult and dangerous because of persecutions of local authorities in connection [with] very strained relations between Israel and the Arab League."[26] "He says," added his interviewer, "that in the next future he foresees expulsion of all Jews from [the] Arab States of the Middle East." IRO eligibility officers evaluated the case as one would expect based on the IRO's constitution: a handwritten note stated that Abadi had "a valid passport of his government; was never persecuted for racial or religious reasons; [was] not a refugee; [was] not a DP."[27]

Mosé Habib, born in Tripoli, Libya, in 1931, filled out a CM/1 form on May 27, 1949. He must have noted dryly—and his interviewer duly recorded— that he was born an Italian subject, and his parents before him had been born Turkish subjects.[28] He lived in Tripoli with his father, mother, and nine siblings and attended an Italian school, which closed in June 1940 "because of [the] war."[29] The 1938 Italian racial laws,[30] passed when Habib was seven years old, prompted his family to go into hiding in Gharian (Gharyan), approximately 100 kilometers (62 miles) from Tripoli, in June 1940.[31] His father died of an unnamed illness while in hiding. Fascist and Nazi terror ended on January 23,

---

26. The Arab League began with a 1944 conference of the leaders of Iraq, Lebanon, Syria, and Transjordan in Alexandria and at the invitation of the Egyptian government. Together they issued a "Protocol of Alexandria," the foundation for the subsequent Arab League, formed in March 1945. It was "infused with the spirit of Pan-Arabism," though each member state retained full sovereignty. Its purpose was "economic, cultural and social cooperation," and specific clauses endorsed Lebanese independence, "the rights of the Arab people in Palestine," and "the need to establish an Arab state in Palestine." For further reading, see Howard M. Sachar, *Europe Leaves the Middle East, 1936–1954* (New York: Knopf, 1972), 398–406.

27. CM/1 form for Joseph Abadi, 3.2.1.2/80304938/ITS Digital Archive, USHMM.

28. Today, Libya is bordered by Tunisia and Algeria in the west, Egypt in the east, and Sudan, Chad, and Niger in the south. It consists of three regions: Tripolitania in the northwest, Cyrenaica in the northeast, and the Fezzan. The Ottoman Empire controlled parts of Tripolitania and Cyrenaica until 1911, when they came under Italian control. See Harvey E. Goldberg, "Libya," in Simon, Laskier, and Reguer, *The Jews of the Middle East and North Africa in Modern Times*, 431–32.

29. CM/1 form for Mosé Habib, 3.2.1.2/80384645–6/ITS Digital Archive, USHMM.

30. Benito Mussolini enacted the first racial laws in September 1938. They applied to both Italy and Libya. The laws prohibited Jews from attending public schools, revoked the citizenship of and expelled all Jews who had become Italian citizens after 1919, forbade so-called mixed marriages, and forbade residence to Jews in Italy, Libya, and the Aegean possessions, among other restrictions. Because of lax implementation, the laws impacted Libyan Jews "only slightly" in the first few years. See Maurice M. Roumani, *The Jews of Libya: Coexistence, Persecution, Resettlement* (Brighton, UK: Sussex Academic Press, 2008), 22–24.

31. In 1939, Libyan Jews numbered 30,387, most living in Tripolitania. After the out-

1943, commencing British military administration of Libya. Surviving members of the Libyan Jewish community "returned to find their homes ransacked and destroyed, their shops bombarded and left in ruins, and hardly any aspect of community life left."[32] The Habibs, too, returned to Tripoli, to "their previous address." Habib's mother died that year; he was twelve. Following his mother's death, Habib claimed to have "worked as [a] mechanic until 1946, when he returned to school to study the English, French, Hebrew, and Arabic languages." It was then that his brother, Saul, "escaped" to Palestine,[33] perhaps inspired by the anti-Jewish pogrom in Tripoli and neighboring towns the prior year.[34]

From this point on, Habib's questionnaire reads like a manifesto and is utterly captivating. Saul took a year to reach Palestine, as he was caught en route and sent to Cyprus. Only following escape from Cyprus did he manage to get to Palestine in 1948. Now sixteen, Habib left Tripoli for Italy in October 1947. He acknowledged in his 1949 interview that "he came to Italy [. . .] with the pretext to study in Italy, but the true reason was to emigrate to Palestine. He could not do it directly from Tripoli. When [he] reached Italy he preferred to stay here [in Italy] and attend school and wait until [he] could go regularly, as [a] refugee, [so as] not to meet [the] same troubles as his brother, who finished in Cyprus Island for more than a year."[35]

During his 1949 interview, when asked if he wanted to return to his home in Tripoli, Habib responded no. Was he "determined against repatriation"? He answered yes. In the section of the questionnaire requesting an explanation, Habib wrote, "First of all, all my brothers and sisters will emigrate to Palestine. It is only a question of time. I wish to stay in Palestine. I consider [it] my country. I don't know why we have to stay under foreign domination when there is a state for the Jews."[36] His sentiments were not uncommon among Libyan Jews. Maurice Roumani notes, "In less than 50 years, [Libyan] Jews had lived under three different powers [. . .] each with their own system of laws

---

break of World War II in September, Italy began to "rigorously uphold" the racial laws in Libya. The Jewish quarter in Tripoli suffered heavily from British and French bombing raids. The reference to Gharian is interesting in that following the second British withdrawal from Cyrenaica in January 1942, Mussolini ordered the "campaign of *sfollamento* [removal]" of Libyan Jews to detention camps in Algeria, Italy, and Tunis and to concentration camps in Tripolitania, including in Gharian. Roumani, *The Jews of Libya*, 28–29.

32. Roumani, *The Jews of Libya*, 38.
33. CM/1 form for Mosé Habib, 3.2.1.2/80384645/ITS Digital Archive, USHMM.
34. Roumani, *The Jews of Libya*, 48–51.
35. CM/1 form for Mosé Habib, 3.2.1.2/80384646/ITS Digital Archive, USHMM.
36. Ibid.

and regulations, expectations and dictates." Further, the persecution that the
community experienced from "1938 to 1943 [was] unprecedented in the modern history of Libyan Jewry,"[37] only to be followed by the pogrom of 1945 and
the anti-Jewish riots of 1948. For Libyan Jews and for Habib and his siblings,
"Israel became the solution."[38] Habib's interviewer did not classify him as
within IRO's mandate, however, writing, "[His] story [is] true-sounding, but
[he] seems more an emigrant than [a] refugee." The supervising officer was
unmoved, writing on June 8, 1949, "Not a refugee or DP; not within the
mandate of IRO; not eligible for any services."[39] ITS records do not tell us
whether Habib ever realized his dream of emigrating to Israel.

For Jews who had survived World War II in Europe, Israel made great sense
as a destination after they had seen their families murdered simply for being
Jewish. While excellent and extensive literature on European Jews seeking entry
to Palestine/Israel after World War II exists, ITS still offers poignant snapshots
of Jews like Stella Hasson, born in 1926 on the island of Rhodes.[40] (See document 5.3.[41]) "A very modest, intelligent, and good young girl," wrote her interviewer, Hasson was deported with her family to Auschwitz in July 1944. Russian
troops liberated her in Theresienstadt and repatriated her to Italy in September
1945. "Consider her being alone in the world apart from Rhodes friends [fellow
survivors] and [her] sister who are resettling [in Israel]," wrote her interviewer.
Of note here is how her interviewer described the new state of Israel: "She wants
to return to the old country of Israel to live together with her co-nationals and
find there due protection." IRO officers declared her "eligible" on November
18, 1948, but revoked her eligibility on April 27, 1949, due to a "failure to

---

37. Roumani, *The Jews of Libya*, 38.

38. Ibid., 68.

39. CM/1 form for Mosé Habib, 3.2.1.2/80384646/ITS Digital Archive, USHMM.

40. After World War I, Italy gained control of the Dodecanese Islands, which were subject to the already discussed 1938 Italian racial laws. See Arielli, *Fascist Italy and the Middle
East*, 10. In 1944, approximately seventeen hundred Italian-speaking Jews remained in by
then German-occupied Rhodes. In July 1944, German armed forces arrested the remaining
Jewish population, forced them onto "3 crowded boats," and subjected them to an eight-day
crossing to mainland Greece. Incarcerated briefly in the Haidari camp, they were deported to
Auschwitz. Fewer than two hundred survived. See Steve B. Bowman, "Greece," in *The Holocaust Encyclopedia*, ed. Walter Laqueur and Judith Tydor Baumel-Schwartz (New Haven, CT:
Yale University Press, 2001), 269, and the website of the Jewish Museum of Rhodes (www
.rhodesjewishmuseum.org, accessed June 8, 2014.)

41. Extract from CM/1 form for "R 6914 HASSON, Stella F., 15 NOV 48," 3.2.1.2/
80385879/ITS Digital Archive, USHMM.

report," presumably to her place of employment,[42] on March 11, 1949.[43] ITS-held records do not tell us more.

Muslims as Forced Laborers

In April 1944,[44] Crimean Tatar Ibrahim Abdurahman was living in Kosdegir-men (Predusel'noe) when the German army captured him and sent him to the Reich for forced labor in agriculture. (See document 5.4.[45]) Abdurahman spent two months, from April to June 1944, en route to Germany via Romania, Hungary, and Austria.[46] On arrival, he described himself as a "gardener" for "K. Becker" in the vicinity of Kassel, which IRO review board officials noted as "land work." Members of the review board of the Preparatory Commission for the International Refugee Organization (PCIRO)[47] described Abdurahman, born in the Bakhchisarai district of Crimea,[48] as "Mohammedan in religion [. . .] illiterate, speaks only Turkish, and [due to his age of fifty-six] is not considered eligible for military service in any form."[49] The PCIRO review board granted Abdurahman DP status,[50] surely having the 1944 expulsion of Crimean Tatars by Josef Stalin in mind.[51] "He is accepted as a DP who is unwilling to

---

42. See Holborn, *The International Refugee Organization*, 212, 273, 277, 376.

43. CM/1 form for Stella Hasson, 3.2.1.2/80385879 and 80385880/ITS Digital Archive, USHMM. She was reported "missing" as early as February 15, 1949 (see 3.2.1.2/80385878).

44. This particular date is likely related to fighting between the Red Army and five divisions of the 17th German Army, which, alongside seven Romanian divisions, had been cut off in the fall of 1943 in Crimea. On April 8–9, 1944, the Red Army crossed into Crimea and defeated German and Romanian forces by mid-May. See Gerhard L. Weinberg, *A World at Arms: A Global History of World War II* (Cambridge: Cambridge University Press, 1994), 670–71. For Crimea under German occupation, see Norbert Kunz, *Die Krim unter deutscher Herrschaft, 1941–1944: Germanisierungsutopie und Besatzungsrealität* (Darmstadt: Wissenschaftliche Buchgesellschaft, 2005); Andrej Angrick, *Besatzungspolitik und Massenmord: Die Einsatzgruppe D in der südlichen Sowjetunion, 1941–1943* (Hamburg: Hamburger Edition, 2003).

45. International Refugee Organization Decision of the Review Board, Case No. 263, appeal of Ibrahim Abdurahman, 3.2.1.5/81278186/ITS Digital Archive, USHMM.

46. CM/1 form for Ibrahim Abdurahman, 3.2.1.1/78862055/ITS Digital Archive, USHMM.

47. Recall that the PCIRO began operations months earlier than the IRO.

48. CM/1 form for Ibrahim Abdurahman, 3.2.1.1/78862055/ITS Digital Archive, USHMM.

49. Because one job of IRO interviewers was to identify those who had "voluntarily assisted enemy forces," placing them outside IRO's mandate, this reference to Abdurahman's age may have been an attempt to place him outside Crimean Tatars in the German army. See Antonio J. Munoz, "Crimean Tartar Volunteer Formations in the German Armed Forces,"

return [to Crimea] because of his fear of persecution as a Moslem Tartar minority, and his appeal is upheld," wrote the review board. He hoped to emigrate to Turkey.[52] There are other such cases from this region of Europe, including that of Iskak Seilhan, who in June 1942 was studying in Romania.[53] He claimed to have been sent to Karlsbad, Germany, for forced labor on a farm in 1942. His CM/1 form identifies him as a Turkish citizen born in Afghanistan in 1923 and an adherent of the Muslim religion. In his case, too, IRO officers determined him to be eligible for legal and political protection, despite the rather unclear circumstances of his deportation to Germany.[54]

Others were deemed to be outside the mandate, despite being able to prove they had at some point been put to forced labor for or incarcerated by the German or Axis regimes. German forces captured Djamie Karredian in Bordeaux on the southwest coast of France in July 1944[55] and transported him to Darmstadt, Germany, for forced labor. The type of labor is not specified; his employer is listed as the "German Army." Born in 1924 in Alexandria, Egypt, Karredian was deemed to fall outside the IRO mandate and sent to the Luitpold Kaserne in Munich. The basis for this decision was the fact that he had voluntarily moved to Vichy France in 1943.[56] Mohamed El-Mekki fared no better. Axis

in *The East Came West: Muslim, Hindu, and Buddhist Volunteers in the German Armed Forces, 1941–1945*, ed. Antonio J. Munoz (Bayside, NY: Axis Europa Books, 2001), 85–108; Klaus-Michael Mallmann and Martin Cüppers, *Nazi Palestine: The Plan for the Extermination of the Jews in Palestine* (New York: Enigma Books in association with USHMM, 2005), 186. For a fascinating set of documents original to ITS involving court-martial proceedings against non-Germans (of a wide variety of ethnic backgrounds) in the Wehrmacht, see the aforementioned 1.2.8.1/ITS Digital Archive, USHMM.

50. Decision of the PCIRO review board for Ibrahim Abdurahman, Geneva, November 5, 1949, 3.2.1.5/81278185/ITS Digital Archive, USHMM. See also 0.1/13709116–23 and 3.2.1.1/78862053–9.

51. For the 1944 expulsion of Tatars by Josef Stalin, see Refik Muzafarov, *Anatomiia deportatsii krymskikh tatar* (Simferopol': Tarpan, 2011).

52. CM/1 form for Ibrahim Abdurahman, 3.2.1.1/78862055/ITS Digital Archive, USHMM.

53. While the name of the place where he attended school is not recognizable, he may have been studying in the southeastern corner of Romania, near the Black Sea, the Danube, and Bulgaria, where more Muslim citizens remained from the days of the Ottoman Empire. The circumstances of his capture are not available in the file.

54. CM/1 form for Iskak Seilhan (Seilchan), 3.2.1.1/79204472–5/ITS Digital Archive, USHMM.

55. Heavy fighting between German and Allied forces commenced in the area after the Allied landing at Normandy. See Weinberg, *A World at Arms*, 686–95.

56. CM/1 form for Djamie Karredian, 3.2.1.1/79265737/ITS Digital Archive, USHMM. See also 0.1/27175820–26 and 3.2.1.5/812948735/ITS Digital Archive,

forces captured El-Mekki in Mersa Matruh, Egypt, in 1942.[57] Born in 1922 in Iraq, he had worked, following his schooling, in the port city of Mersa Matruh since 1940. According to one account in his CM/1 file, he was placed in a work detachment and sent to Germany to perform forced labor for the Reichsbahn (National Railway) in Württemberg and then, in December 1944, to do farm labor in Weinsberg. According to another account, in December 1944 he went from Württemberg to a work camp (*Arbeitslager*) on the Bahnhofstrasse in Stuttgart and was briefly imprisoned there. As an Iraqi citizen, El-Mekki was determined to be outside the mandate of the IRO on the presumption that he could return to Iraq.[58]

In completing a CM/1 form in 1948, Muhamed Abdulkadir, born in 1913 in Cairo, claimed to have been impressed into forced labor by the Italian army in Cairo in 1942, whereupon he was sent to Rome to work in ship building and then to Leipzig, Germany, for factory work, where he remained until the end of the war. According to the notes in the file, in Rome he worked six days per week and was paid; in Leipzig he was also paid, lived with a German family, and went to the movies and theater on Sundays. This account sounds fantastical and probably was: two years earlier, he had claimed a completely different wartime history. In filling out his June 1946 US Army questionnaire for DPs, he stated that he was in Marseilles at the outbreak of World War II, worked as a mechanic, and was swept up by the Germans in Paris in 1942 for forced labor.[59]

We are unlikely ever to know Abdulkadir's precise wartime history; his file better illustrates a different point. His interviewer, Emilian Rejnarowycz, described him as making "an impression of a very sly man who wants to play a stupid and blockhead. He speaks very bad German and French languages." Rejnarowycz suspected Abdulkadir of joining the Italian and German armies voluntarily and coming to Germany via this route. In any case, as an Egyptian citizen, Abdulkadir was "not a concern of the IRO," wrote Rejnarowycz's superior.[60] The role of the interviewer, usually a fellow DP, is another area in which

---

USHMM. Karredian was a highly educated man, fluent in Arabic, English, French, Italian, and Spanish.

57. Axis forces captured Fuka and Mersa Matruh, Egypt, on June 28, 1942. See Sachar, *Europe Leaves the Middle East*, 248.

58. CM/1 form for Mohamed El-Mekki, 3.2.1.1/79469440–42/ITS Digital Archive, USHMM. For more on his interviewer, see CM/1 file for Jozef Furmanski, 3.2.1.1/79100903–6.

59. CM/1 form for Muhamed Abdulkadir, 3.2.1.1/78861967/ITS Digital Archive, USHMM.

60. Ibid., 78861966–9.

ITS documents allow for a systematic study of the function, prejudices, and influence of these interviewers, who were in practice evaluating fellow DPs with whom they were competing for resources and emigration opportunities. In this case, Emilian Rejnarowycz, born in 1896 in Trijczyci, Galicia (Poland), had been swept up in 1944 and sent to the town of Suhl in Thuringia (Germany) for forced labor in agriculture. He most likely qualified as an interviewer because of his command of the Czech, German, Polish, Russian, and Ukrainian languages.[61]

Two more examples of Muslims born in the Middle East, put to forced labor or incarcerated in Germany during the war, and ultimately determined to be outside the IRO mandate follow. Some cases offer so few details that it is difficult to discern a precise wartime narrative. German forces captured Mohamed Achmed, for example, in Libya in 1942.[62] Born in 1918 in Beirut, Lebanon, he was thus determined after the war to be a French citizen. His CM/1 form provides few details as to why or precisely when he was in Libya in 1942. According to his account, after his father was killed in an air attack in Libya, German forces captured him and sent him to Berlin, via Naples, for labor. At least briefly in March 1945, he was registered as living in Leipzig.[63] Due to his temporary stay in the DP camp in Donauwörth, Bavaria,[64] Achmed hoped to emigrate to Australia. On September 8, 1949, IRO Area Welfare Officer F. Preziosi declared him ineligible.[65] Achmed registered in the Augsburg DP camp on September 13, 1949, and there his trail goes cold.[66] Even more puzzling is

---

61. Rejnarowycz identified himself as Greek Catholic. See CM/1 form for Emilian Rejnarowycz, 3.2.1.1/79649770–4/ITS Digital Archive, USHMM.

62. CM/1 form for Mohamed Achmed, 3.2.1.1/79496592–3/ITS Digital Archive, USHMM. For more on the Allied offensive and fighting in North Africa in 1942, see Weinberg, *A World at Arms*, 431–47.

63. See 2.2.2.1/73804387/ITS Digital Archive, USHMM.

64. Donauwörth DP camp was the location of the so-called Arab Committee, tasked with "cater[ing] for the social needs of those Arabs who came to Germany in the course of the last war [World War II] from all over the Arab world to join the Mufti Muhammad Amin Husaini and the former Prime Minister of Iraq, Rashid Ali al-Gailani and who are now living in refugee camps in southern Germany." See Muhammad Aman Hobohm, "Islam in Germany," *Islamic Review* (August 1951): 11–17. The article refers to the grand mufti of Jerusalem, Haj Muhammad Amin el-Husseini, so appointed on May 9, 1921. He and al-Gailani were both Axis allies during World War II. See Mallmann and Cüppers, *Nazi Palestine*.

65. CM/1 form for Mohamed Achmed, 3.2.1.1/79496593/ITS Digital Archive, USHMM.

66. DP-2 card for Mohamed Achmed, 3.1.1.1/68324276 and CNI cards for Mohamed Achmed, 0.1/42070205–7/ITS Digital Collection, USHMM.

the case of Ali Bourzam, born in 1909 in Sidi Aïch, Algeria. He was living and working in Paris, first for the Moulin Rouge and then as a mechanic, when Gestapo agents arrested him in 1943 and sent him to the Zittau subcamp of Gross-Rosen in Saxony. Despite his status as a former inmate of the Zittau subcamp, he was determined to be outside the IRO mandate. His CM/1 form does not indicate a reason.[67] The presence of individuals like Karredian, El-Mekki, Achmed, and Bourzam in German DP camps is a fascinating and understudied aspect of the ITS holdings. Researchers examining such cases in aggregate might determine patterns in how these individuals came to be in Germany during the war, how many remained there afterward to settle in a largely Christian society steeped in western European traditions, and how those who returned to their countries of origin fared.

"In Saigon I Have My Father"[68]

Some applying for refugee or DP status desperately wanted to return home rather than remain in Europe. Wilnguven Van Ut, a Roman Catholic born in Saigon in 1922, found himself betwixt and between in February 1949 when applying for IRO assistance.[69] As he was a French subject due to his birth in French Indochina,[70] his interviewers struggled with how to classify his citizenship. "Applicant born in Saigon, Indo-China," wrote his interviewer. "His citizenship of this country or of France is undecided, because they are presumably in war," he added.[71] In 1940, at age eighteen, Van Ut was conscripted to military labor service in Bergerac in southwest (Vichy) France and remained there until

---

67. CM/1 form for Ali Bourzam, 3.2.1.1/78960568–9/ITS Digital Archive, USHMM. For more on the Zittau camp, see Hans Brenner, "Zittau," in Megargee, *The United States Holocaust Memorial Museum Encyclopedia of Camps and Ghettos*, 1:811–12. See also 0.1/ 16750462–4 and 6.3.3.2/107881377–390/ITS Digital Collection, USHMM. His T/D file indicates that as of 1949 he was living in Munich.

68. CM/1 form for Wilnguven Van Ut, 3.2.1.2/79877527–8/ITS Digital Archive, USHMM.

69. Ibid.

70. French Indochina, the peninsula in Southeast Asia lying roughly southwest of China and east of India, was part of the French colonial empire in Southeast Asia (today, Burma, Cambodia, Laos, Malaysia, Thailand, and Vietnam). After the fall of France during World War II, the colony was administered by Vichy France and was under Japanese supervision until a brief period of full Japanese control between March and August 1945. Revolt against French rule began in 1941, and these territories were still in flux in 1949.

71. CM/1 form for Wilnguven Van Ut, 3.2.1.2/79877527–8/ITS Digital Archive, USHMM.

1944.[72] He was "discharged" on June 13, 1944, within a week of the Allied landing at Normandy. He then "accompanied the American Army through Germany until [reaching the city of] Asch and [then returning to] Roth bei Gelnhausen."[73] He remained in the picturesque village of Roth bei Gelnhausen (Hesse), employed by the American army. In approaching the IRO in 1949, he aimed to be repatriated to Saigon or the United States with his child, Berth-Hans Meisner, born out of wedlock to a German mother in 1949.[74] "I want to go to the United States, or, if it is not possible, I will go back to my native country. In Saigon I have my father," he wrote. Van Ut was found to be "neither a refugee nor a DP [and] not within the mandate."[75] As late as 1951, he still sought emigration and was again declared ineligible on May 4, 1951.[76]

Other cases from applicants born in Asia are much simpler. Buddhist Juen Tschang Al, born in 1903 in Chekiang province, China, "came [to Hamburg, Germany] as [a] cook with the Chinese consulate in July 1937."[77] He briefly opened his own shop from 1938 to 1940 and then became a butcher. By the time of his application to the IRO on April 6, 1949, he was still thus employed and offered no explanation for how he managed to survive the war years in heavily bombed Hamburg without any mention of difficulties with Nazi authorities.[78] Al had left a homeland embroiled in hostilities with an aggressive Japan since 1931, though neither he nor the IRO interviewing officer mentioned this.[79] During that time, the United States backed the Nationalist government of Chiang Kai-shek against Japan. In April 1949, the IRO declared Al "within the mandate of the IRO [and] eligible for legal and political protection, including repatriation,"[80] surely because of the Cold War, in full bloom by 1949.[81] As

---

72. Ibid.

73. Ibid., 79877528. In a later account completed on February 23, 1949, he told IRO officials that he became a prisoner of war of the US Army and did not arrive in Germany until May 1945.

74. Berth-Hans Meisner was born on May 28, 1949, in Roth.

75. CM/1 form for Wilnguven Van Ut, 3.2.1.2/79877527/ITS Digital Archive, USHMM.

76. CNI cards for Wilnguven Van Ut, 0.1/48414220–3/ITS Digital Archive, USHMM.

77. CM/1 form for Juen Tschang Al, 3.2.1.2/78870145/ITS Digital Archive, USHMM.

78. Ibid.

79. Nazi Germany attempted without success to mediate the conflict between Chiang Kai-shek's Nationalist regime in China and Japanese aggression. Weinberg, *A World at Arms*, 78–79.

80. CM/1 form for Juen Tschang Al, 3.2.1.2/78870145/ITS Digital Archive, USHMM.

81. On October 1, 1949, Chinese Communist Party leader Mao Zedong established the People's Republic of China in Beijing. Chiang and thousands of his troops fled to Taiwan. The United States continued to back Chiang's exiled Republic of China government in

of April 1949, he still wanted "to return home,"[82] having little idea what that would mean only six months later.

Il Duce

ITS-held documents reveal the impact of the Italian invasion of Ethiopia on the lives and destinies of ordinary Ethiopians. Abballagi Abbagiru, born in 1912 in Gimma, Ethiopia, had recently turned twenty-three when Benito Mussolini invaded in October 1935. When filling out his questionnaire from the Fraschette DP camp in Casilina, Italy, on April 5, 1948, he described himself as a peasant by trade, Catholic by religion, and illiterate. He claimed to have volunteered for the Polizia Africa Italiana (PAI) in 1935, remaining in Gimma in this capacity until 1940. His parents, he noted, had both been "killed by [the] Italians in 1935." He claimed to have been part of the Italian forces that "withdrew to Italy through Africa" in 1940[83] and by 1943 to have been living in a PAI camp in Rome, to which his interviewer adds, "Statement true!" When German forces occupied northern and central Italy in September 1943, Abbagiru claimed, he had "deserted with other Italian troops" to "join the Italian partisans" in the Marche mountains of Italy to fight against Germany.

After the liberation of Rome in July 1944, he married a local peasant girl, Elvira Buggiarda. He worked in her family's farmhouse, and they had a daughter. And so life continued until Italian police arrested him for living illegally in Italy and sent him to Fraschette in October 1947.[84] Abbagiru had no desire to return to Ethiopia. To the question in his CM/1 form "Do you want to return [to your home]," he responded that he would like to remain in Italy and in fact "was afraid to return because [he had] collaborated with [the] Italians and his [fellow] nationals would kill him or his wife and child." As Abbagiru had fought both for the Axis (in the Italian army) and then against Nazi Germany (as a partisan), it is not surprising that his interviewer and the supervising officer

---

Taipei. See "U.S. Relations with China," Council on Foreign Relations, www.cfr.org/china/us-relations-china-1949—-present/p17698 (accessed June 8, 2014).

82. CM/1 form for Juen Tschang Al, 3.2.1.2/78870145/ITS Digital Archive, USHMM.

83. In the winter of 1940 and 1941, British forces defeated Italy, liberated Ethiopia and British Somaliland, and occupied Eritrea and Italian Somaliland. For the British defeat of Italian forces in Italian East Africa in early 1941 and the "return of Ethiopian ruler Haile Selassie to his throne," see Weinberg, *A World at Arms*, 211, 503, 1129. See also Nir Arielli, *Fascist Italy and the Middle East, 1933–40* (New York: Palgrave Macmillan, 2010).

84. CM/1 form for Abballagi Abbagiru, 3.2.1.2/80304944/ITS Digital Archive, USHMM.

came to different conclusions. His interviewer wrote, "Subject is an honest, illiterate peasant [who] volunteered in 1935 for the Italian Army [and] is therefore eligible for repatriation." The supervising officer crossed this recommendation out and wrote, "Not a genuine refugee [and] ineligible for IRO assistance." The questionnaire was stamped "ineligible."[85] Abbagiru's CM/1 form does not tell us whether he was ultimately allowed to stay in Italy.[86]

Zamu Segai, born in 1921 in Eritrea[87] and therefore an Ethiopian citizen after World War II, fared even more poorly. (See document 5.5.[88]) His PCIRO application for assistance, completed in April 1948 at the Fraschette DP camp, is stark. For the section on family, his caseworker wrote, "None." For his education, "No education." For his financial resources, "No resources." For his relatives, friends, previous employers, documents, former organizations, and assistance since January 1, 1947: "No family; no documents; none; no assistance."[89] He spent 1938 to 1941 in the Italian navy in Eritrea. His time in the military ended with his capture and eight months in a British prisoner of war camp. In British-occupied Eritrea, he worked as a servant for an American firm in Ghinda in 1942, as a mechanic in Eritrea's capital, Asmara, from 1943 to 1945, and as a cook in Massawa in 1946. In March 1948, he embarked illegally on the *Carbonella*, a ship heading to Venice, hoping to escape "great misery" and hunger in his home country. Italian police captured him in Venice and sent him to Fraschette.[90] Despite Segai's explanation that he had come to Italy to find "the work and the bread" and that in Eritrea he was "always hungry," his PCIRO interviewers were not moved. "This is not a political refugee," one wrote. The supervising officer

85. Ibid.

86. There is an Italian registration card for Abballagi Abbagiru, but it indicates only that the Italian government sent an inquiry to ITS in the 1980s. See 3.1.1.8/98462752/ITS Digital Archive, USHMM.

87. Today, Eritrea is a country in the horn of Africa, bordered by Sudan to the west and Ethiopia in the south, with part of its coastline on the Red Sea across from Saudi Arabia and Yemen. The British occupied Eritrea in the winter of 1941 and established a British military administration there until the end of the war. At war's end, the British turned Eritrea over to Ethiopia. Italian Somaliland became independent and, together with British Somaliland, became the country of Somalia. See Weinberg, *A World at Arms*, 503.

88. PCIRO application for assistance, Zamu Segai, 3.2.1.2/80491149–53/ITS Digital Archive, USHMM.

89. Ibid.

90. Ibid.

simply wrote, "Collaborated," due to his stint in the Italian armed forces. He was found ineligible.[91] (See document 5.6.[92])

Waldemariam Tegeni (Teghenie), born in 1927 in Asmara, Eritrea, shared a similar biography. From 1938, he "was employed as a mechanic and driver by the Italians [in] Massawa" until he was drafted into the Italian army in 1939 at the age of twelve. He performed "guard duties" on the Isle of Durgam (off the coast of the Red Sea) near Massawa. When British forces occupied Eritrea in the winter of 1941, they did not take Tegeni prisoner "because he was young [fourteen years old]," noted his interviewer. And so he remained in Massawa working as a mechanic for American forces until their withdrawal in 1942. According to his account, he found work where he could in the British fort in Massawa until March 1948, when, like Segai, he went to Venice illegally, via the *Carbonella*. The Italian police were "waiting for him," and so he too found himself in Fraschette in April 1948.

Orphaned at some point during the war,[93] he answered, when asked why he left Eritrea, that "there nobody helped him and he was always hungry." The IRO supervising officer in Fraschette determined him, like Segai, to be ineligible.[94] In his case, we have some indication of what happened next, because he filed an appeal to the IRO review board in Geneva. In December 1948, he filled out a questionnaire in the Lipari (Italy) DP camp.[95] When his case came up in Geneva on September 2, 1949, he had disappeared. "Petitioner submitted an appeal against the decision of ineligibility, but information has been submitted to the Board that he/she has now left the country and/or has failed to keep the [IRO] informed of his/her whereabouts[. . . . T]he appeal must be considered as withdrawn," wrote IRO officials.[96] And there his trail goes cold.

One does not normally think of East African children when considering the long reach of World War II and Axis ambitions; yet Tegeni was no exception. (See document 5.7.[97]) On September 1, 1949, officers in the Naples Intake

---

91. Ibid.

92. Handwritten letter by Waldemariam Tegeni, Fraschette, April 7, 1948, 3.2.1.2/80524994/ITS Digital Archive, USHMM.

93. CM/1 form for Waldemariam Tegeni, 3.2.1.2/80524992/ITS Digital Archive, USHMM.

94. Ibid.

95. Ibid.

96. Decision of the IRO review board for Waldemariam Tegeni, 3.2.1.5/81264048, ITS Digital Archive, USHMM.

97. Photograph of Abraham Abaj, 3.2.1.2/80304954/ITS Digital Archive, USHMM.

Center interviewed Abraham Abaj, born in Asmara like Tegeni in 1929. He told his interviewer that he had "left home in 1943 [at the age of fourteen], clandestinely, on board the ship Sestra [and come] to Italy to find some work." He wished to return to Ethiopia "as he could not find work" in Italy.[98] These are but four examples of CM/1 forms for refugee hopefuls from Ethiopia and Eritrea, all poor, illiterate, and often very young East Africans whose fates hinged on that of Mussolini's regime. No current study addresses this particular group as part of World War II and postwar European history.

"Kalmook—Not Eligible for any Scheme"[99]

As already discussed briefly, ITS-held documents make painfully clear that physical appearance mattered to the degree that it could determine one's chances for repatriation or emigration. So-called unaccompanied children Vera Scharapowa (Abuschinow[a]) and her brother Stojan,[100] born in Bulgaria in 1932 and 1936, respectively, to a father of Kalmyk descent[101] and a Bulgarian mother, are a case in point.[102] The family fled Sofia, Bulgaria, in 1944 at the approach of the Red

---

98. CM/1 form for Abraham Abaj, 3.2.1.2/80304950/ITS Digital Archive, USHMM. Once in Italy, he was interned in the Fuorigrotta DP camp from 1943 to 1946 and again in 1949, and in the Lipari DP camp from 1946 to 1949 (see 3.2.1.2/80304949).

99. IRO Children's Village Bad Aibling, case audit and progress report, Vera Abuschinow, July 15, 1949, 6.3.2.1/84140144/ITS Digital Archive, USHMM.

100. Athough they are initially referred to in the documents as Sofia and Stojan Abuschinow, we later learn that their real names are Vera Scharapowa and Nikolai Scharapow. The name Abuschinow was used when the children registered at the DP camp in Krumbach because they lived with their uncle at that time. See note in addition to DP-2 A form, International Children Center on Chiemsee, July 17, 1948, 6.3.2.1/84140137 and 84140139/ITS Digital Archive, USHMM. The text refers to them as Vera and Stojan because these are the names they used as adults.

101. Nikolai fled Russia as a holder of a Nansen passport. Nansen passports were internationally recognized refugee travel documents, first issued by the League of Nations to stateless refugees and originally provided to refugees from the Russian civil war. See Holborn, *The International Refugee Organization*, 322. He was part of a first wave of Kalmyks from Kalmykia who, generally speaking, collaborated with the Whites during the Russian Civil War, most of whom came to Sofia and Belgrade. For a discussion of this "first wave" and Kalmyks in Eastern Europe after the Russian Revolution, see Elsa-Bair Guchinova, "Kalmyks in America," *Anthropology & Archeology of Eurasia* 41, no. 2 (2002): 7–22. Readers should also note that in document 5.1, the vast majority (11,389) had or claimed Nansen status. Nansen passport holders in the ITS holdings deserve further research.

102. Both children were born in Sofia and then baptized into the Greek Orthodox Church. See Child Tracing Branch file for Stojan and Vera Abuschinow, 6.3.2.1/84140127–77/ITS Digital Archive, USHMM.

Army because father Nikolai feared persecution. (See document 5.8.[103]) They reached Krumau am Kamp in Lower Austria, where Stojan and Vera became separated from their parents on an undetermined date in the spring of 1945. The file contains differing accounts of how this occurred. In one account, when German forces began the evacuation of Krumau in early 1945, "the children were sent with a car in the direction [of] Salzburg. The father stayed behind and promised to come with the next car. The mother stayed in a hospital in Krumau as she was very sick [with] TB [tuberculosis]. The children left and never saw their parents again."[104] According to a report from the Czech Red Cross, Wasilka Scharapowa (actually the children's stepmother) was released from the hospital in Krumau on May 16, 1945, and then disappeared.[105] Accounts agree that the children reached Salzburg, then differ again as to the circumstances of their admission to the International Children's Center near Prien am Chiemsee in Bavaria on November 12, 1946.[106]

Because of their Kalmyk blood and appearance, no country wanted them. Child Case Officer Joan W. Aitken described them this way: "Both children are undoubtedly of Kalmook descent. Vera is decidedly oriental in her appearance with slant eyes, yellow skin and straight, dark hair. Her brother[,] who looks only slightly oriental, could perhaps adjust into a white community with less feeling of difference than Vera."[107] By June 1949, attempts to send the children to Russia[108] and the United States had failed. "I regret to say," wrote Theodora Allen to their case supervisor in Bad Aibling,[109] "that according to U.S. immi-

---

103. Photograph of Vera Abuschinow[a], 3.2.1.1/84140130/ITS Digital Archive, USHMM.

104. See 6.3.2.1/84140136/ITS Digital Archive, USHMM.

105. Letter from R. Průchová, Leiterin des Suchdienstes, to IRO Area I Headquarters, Salzburg, March 21, 1949, 6.3.2.1/84140141–2/ITS Digital Archive, USHMM.

106. Supplementary record face sheet for Stojan Scharapow-Abuschinow, 6.3.2.1/ 84140134/ITS Digital Archive, USHMM. Another account states, "From Krumau they were sent to Salzburg where they stayed [a] few days [and were then] transferred to [a Kalmyk US-run DP] camp in Krumbach near Salzburg. They found their uncle [. . .] and lived with him nearly 1 year in Krumbach" (see 6.3.2.1/84140136).

107. Jean M. Aitken, "Social History, Scharapow (Abuschinow) Stojan and Scharapow (Abuschinow) Vera," 6.3.2.1/84140146/ITS Digital Archive, USHMM.

108. "Jean Reilly, Child Welfare Consultant, has informed us that [. . .] Scharapow-Abuschinow, Stojan and Scharapow-Abuschinow, Vera [. . .] have been rejected by the Russian Liaison Officer for repatriation to Russia." M. J. Henshaw to International Children's Center on Chiemsee/UNRRA Team 1069 at Prien, March 21, 1947, 6.3.2.1/84140131/ITS Digital Archive, USHMM.

109. In November 1948, the children moved from the Chiemsee center to the Bad Aibling Children's Village, a transit camp for DP orphans and homeless children near

gration laws they are not admissible to the U.S. However, if it is proved that they are not pure Kalmook we could present their case to the American Consulate to see if they could be admitted."[110]

Another July 1949 report—the first in the file to refer to the children as Buddhist Orthodox, despite the recognition in earlier notes that they had been baptized in the Greek Catholic tradition in Sofia—was even more plain. Aitken answered part II of the form, posing the question "If no plan for reestablishment has yet been formulated give reason why," as follows: "Kalmook—not eligible for any scheme." To the final question on the form, "What is workers' plan for dealing with child's or youth's feelings in response to above question?" Ms. Gitken wrote, "Possibility of children being adopted by a Kalmook family in a Kalmook camp."[111] A 1950 attempt to emigrate to the Netherlands failed due to lack of funds.[112] Later that fall, Vera and Stojan, along with two other Kalmyk "unaccompanied children," moved to Ingolstadt and then to DP camp Munich-Schleissheim under the guardianship of a Kalmyk couple. Together, the six were to emigrate to Paraguay. This plan too fell through, and circumstances in their temporary household were far from ideal.[113]

By January 1951, the Paraguay scheme had failed and the children were subject to neglect at the hands of their unstable guardians.[114] Among all this, extremely detailed reports by caseworkers on the physical and mental manifesta-

Munich. Jean M. Aitken, "Social History, Scharapow (Abuschinow) Stojan and Scharapow (Abuschinow) Vera," 6.3.2.1/84140146/ITS Digital Archive, USHMM.

110. Theodora Allen, European representative, US Committee for the Care of European Children, European Headquarters, Munich-Pasing, to Mrs. E. G. Lefsen, case supervisor, IRO Children's Village, Bad Aibling, June 1, 1949, 6.3.2.1/84140143/ITS Digital Archive, USHMM.

111. IRO Children's Village Bad Aibling, case audit and progress report, Vera Abuschinow, July 15, 1949, 6.3.2.1/84140144/ITS Digital Archive, USHMM.

112. Dr. H. M. L. H. Sark, chief, Netherlands Mission, IRO, to Mrs. G. H. A. Frank, area child care officer, IRO Children's Village Bad Aibling, June 28, 1950, 6.3.2.1/84140154/ITS Digital Archive, USHMM.

113. In one letter, Leon Lefson writes, "You will be interested to know that Mrs. Dambinow is now back with her husband and that the two of them have apparently 'buried the hatchet' for the moment (and not, fortunately, in anyone's head!)[. . . .] Thanks to the speed, efficiency and scintillating clarity with which arrangements between [the] IRO and the Paraguayan government regarding the Kalmook resettlement scheme were concluded, the children will probably depart [. . .] for South America with the next appearance of Haley's Comet!" See Leon Lefson, welfare officer, Subunit Ingolstadt, to Mr. Douglas Dean, director, Children's Village Bad Aibling, December 5, 1950, 6.3.2.1/84140164/ITS Digital Archive, USHMM.

114. Leon Lefson, welfare officer, Subunit Ingolstadt, to Miss Deiglmayr, child care officer, Munich, January 22, 1951, 6.3.2.1/84140165/ITS Digital Archive, USHMM.

tions Stojan and Vera both suffered by this point are the most devastating of all. Incredibly, their father, Nikolai, reemerged in April 1951, when Stojan received a card from him. He had remained in Krumlow (now Český Krumlov, Czech Republic) since their separation. Nikolai "ask[ed] the children to come to him to [Czechoslovakia]." They refused.[115] The last letter in the file, dated 1952, is a request that the World Council of Churches consider taking interest in the case, together with the council's refusal.[116] Stojan's tracing and documentation (T/D) file places him still in Munich in 1953, but no longer in the Schleissheim DP camp.[117] As for Vera, the last available report places her in Pestalozzi Children's Village in Stockach-Wahlwies, close to the German border with Switzerland.[118] There is great irony in the fact that as Nazism and its quest for an "Aryanized" Germany collapsed in 1945, German armed forces sent two children of Kalmyk descent toward Salzburg in a cart, after which they ended up in Germany. As with other refugees viewed as undesirable for their race or religion, no one wanted them. And so they remained in Germany, a permanent reminder of the folly of the Nazi racial enterprise and of the tremendous population upheaval on the European continent in the wake of Nazi and Axis ambitions.

COLLABORATORS AND PERPETRATORS IN ITS

Only briefly alluded to in the case of Ivan Demjanjuk (chapter 1), the presence of perpetrators and collaborators in the DP and refugee population has received increased scholarly attention in recent years. As Gerald Steinacher points out, "SS members and Nazi war criminals [. . .] lived in the same camps and accommodations and made the same journeys overseas" as other refugees and DPs and "were able to escape with the help of the IRO" and other international aid

---

115. "However the children, especially Stojan, definitely refuse repatriation. Their aim is to be resettled in the USA," wrote Paul Jansons. See "Social History. Scharapowa, Wera," Munich, October 15, 1951, by Paul Jansons, child welfare officer, 6.3.2.1/84140169/ITS Digital Archive, USHMM.

116. Josef Danko, child welfare office, IRO, Munich, to the World Council of Churches, Funkkaserne, Munich, March 11, 1952, 6.3.2.1/84140174/ITS Digital Archive, USHMM.

117. His address is listed as Saphirstrasse 11, Munich-Ludwigsfeld. See T/D file for Stojan Scharapow, 6.3.3.2/93552364–84/ITS Digital Archive, USHMM.

118. See T/D file for Vera (Veronica) Scharapowa, 6.3.3.2/93552387–403/ITS Digital Archive, USHMM. The first of its kind in Germany, the charity Pestalozzi Children's and Adolescents' Village Wahlwies e.V. was founded in 1947 in order to offer a home to orphans and fugitives after World War II. See the Pestalozzi Kinder- und Jugenddorf Wahlwies e.V website (www.pestalozzi-kinderdorf.de/aktuelles/englisch) (accessed May 31, 2014).

organizations such as the International Red Cross.[119] Specific high-profile cases studied by Steinacher include those of Adolf Eichmann, Josef Mengele, and leader of fascist Croatia Ante Pavelić. No less interesting is documentation about ordinary men and women whom we would today understand to be collaborators. In ITS-held documents, we read their invented war stories.

Let us look, for example, at the case of Mac Dünzl, born in 1912 in Manila, Philippines, one of thousands of collaborators who hoped to use the DP system to escape less than savory wartime histories. Roman Catholic and claiming to be a dual citizen of the United States and the Philippines, in his initial application for IRO assistance completed from Darmstadt, Germany, on March 31, 1948, he claimed to have been working in Hamburg, Germany, as an insurance expert, and then for the Hapag-Lloyd steamship line until the fall of 1940. According to his story, he next moved to Berlin to work in life insurance until 1943, when he went "into hiding." He claimed to have been captured in 1944, sent to a forced labor camp in Trieste, Italy, until March 1945, and liberated in Salzburg, Austria, in April 1945. To the next question on the June 1946 version of the "Questionnaire for DPs" (*Fragebogen für DPs*) regarding former organizations to which the applicant belonged, he wrote simply "inapplicable" (*entfällt*). His family left Manila for Germany in 1921 to inherit his grandfather's estate, he wrote. He did not want to become a German citizen (question 19) and wished to return to the Philippines (question 17).[120]

Things really become interesting when one reads his answer to question 20, "Were you persecuted in Germany for reasons of race, religion, or political views"? Yes, he answered. When asked for details, he answered, "I was often looked upon as a Jew [and] persecuted [and] fled as [a person] with American citizenship."[121] His initial interviewer seemed convinced. The notes read, "Applicant claims to be [a] citizen of [the] USA born in Manila. Has no documents but has a certificate from an American camp in Austria. During the war was hiding throughout Bavaria and Austria. It was possible because of knowledge of [the German] language. In 1944 [. . .] he passed [in]to Italy but there was taken into forced labor[. . . . He] escaped and went to Austria to find American troops. May be eligible for refugee status."[122]

---

119. Steinacher, *Nazis on the Run*, 3, 14. See also, among others, Richard Breitman and Norman J. W. Goda, *Hitler's Shadow: Nazi War Criminals, U.S. Intelligence, and the Cold War* (Washington, DC: US National Archives and Records Administration, 2010).

120. CM/1 form for Mac Dünzl, 3.2.1.1/79050409/ITS Digital Archive, USHMM.

121. Original German: *Ich würde vielfach als Jude betrachtet—verfolgung beziehungsweise Flücht als Amerikanische Staatsangehöriger.*

122. CM/1 form for Mac Dünzl, 3.2.1.1/79050410/ITS Digital Archive, USHMM.

While ITS records do not reveal what triggered her inquiry, in January 1951, A. W. Hawksley in the IRO's Frankfurt office requested a records check with the US Army Document Center in Berlin, from which she learned that Max (not Mac) Dünzl was born in Munich (not Manila). (See document 5.9.[123]) That was not all. He enrolled in the Nazi Party in September 1932, earning himself the spectacularly low party number 1,316,381. The Nazi Party expelled him in March 1933 for failing to pay his membership dues but revoked this decision on January 13, 1934. Further, the Nazi Party was his employer: he worked in various capacities for the party's Munich office of the Reich treasurer (*Reichsschatzmeister*) from 1933 to 1943.[124] Specifically, Dünzl worked in Main Office V, Legal Matters in the Office for Members (Rechtswesen im Amt für Mitgliedsschaftswesen). After 1941, he moved to Main Office VII, Insurance and Social Welfare Office (Versicherungs- und Sozialamt). Main Office VII served as an insurance agency and benefits office for Nazi Party members and members of the Schutzstaffel (SS), Sturmabteilung (SA), and National Socialist Motor Transport Corps (Nationalsozialistisches Kraftfahrkorps).[125]

As of April 16, 1951, he was living in Augsburg, which we know because he married, resulting in a record of this change at IRO headquarters in Geneva.[126] When confronted with his Nazi Party file the prior month by IRO officers, he acknowledged that he had falsified his CM/1 form. His interviewer, G. Loustalot, recorded the remainder of the interview as follows: "He is a German born [citizen] and has never been to Manila. He is an early NSDAP member and worked for the Party, etc. From now on [the] applicant told the story as it is written in the Party's file[,] trying to excuse himself for the lies[, those] told and [those] lived. He does not feel ashamed because he did not believe any more in Nazi ideal[s] and all his lies were because he wanted to start a new life." Dünzl then revealed details about his personal situation, causing his interviewer to comment, "What is true in this confession is hard to tell." Not so hard to make out was Max's manner, which his interviewer described as follows: "Mr. Dünzl is a clever man who, while he is speaking to you, tries to find what can be said to please you. With me he talks of his wife[. . . . With] Mr. Kauffmann

123. [Berlin] Document Center Records Check for Max Dünzl, 3.2.1.1/79050413/ITS Digital Archive, USHMM.

124. The Office of the Reich Treasurer was responsible for all financial matters pertaining to the Nazi Party. See Robert Ley, *Organisationsbuch der NSDAP* (Munich: F. Eher Nachf., 1943).

125. CM/1 form for Mac Dünzl, 3.2.1.1/79050413/ITS Digital Archive, USHMM.

126. Change of IRO status form for Mac Dünzl, April 16, 1951, 3.2.1.1/79050412/ITS Digital Archive, USHMM.

it was a question of [discussing] acts of noble work [by] Jewish DP doctors."[127] Max's IRO status was to be decided the following day, and his CM/1 file does not contain the outcome. Likely Max slipped back into postwar German society without notice or pause.

As in the Dünzl case, IRO interviewers were sensitive to the need to identify collaborators as best they could, often with limited resources and information. (See document 5.10.[128]) Roman Catholic Valentin Antonio Caballero, born in Buenos Aires in 1908, lived in Lwów, then in Poland, and was thirty-one years old when World War II broke out. University educated in Prague,[129] he had an engineering degree (*Diplomingenieur*) and owned a metal refinement factory.[130] Soviet forces occupied Lwów in September 1939, arrested Caballero in October, and sent him east as a so-called capitalist.[131] On December 20, 1940, he escaped to German-occupied Przemyśl, where, as he put it, his choices were to join the Ogranisation Todt (OT) or to be sent either to an internment camp or back to Soviet captivity. On December 28, he chose the OT.[132] The interview notes do not detail his precise activities in the OT as a lieutenant (first grade) and engineer from December 1940 until April 1942.[133] He described himself as posted in "many places in the Generalgouvernement [General Government]"[134] from

127. CM/1 form for Mac Dünzl, 3.2.1.1/79050414/ITS Digital Archive, USHMM. Presumably "Mr. Kauffmann" was another IRO official with whom Max came into contact.
128. "Extract from CM/1 form for Valentin Antonio Caballero, p. 8," 3.2.1.1/78984124/ITS Digital Archive, USHMM.
129. He studied engineering in Prague and had facility in the Czech, French, German, Polish, Slovak, Spanish, Ukrainian, and Russian languages.
130. "Extract from CM/1 form for Valentin Antonio Caballero, p. 8," 3.2.1.1/78984124/ITS Digital Archive, USHMM.
131. Caballero lists the following locations and situations for his Soviet captivity from October 1939 to December 1940: in Murmansk (October 1939); then internment at a forced labor camp in Pechora (November 1939 to July 1940); then work as an engineer in an oil refinery in Siberia (July 1940, until the 28th of that month); then en route to Poland via Moscow from July 28 to December 20, 1940; and finally escape to a German-run refugee camp in Przemyśl on December 20, 1940. See CM/1 form for Valentin Antonio Caballero, 3.2.1.1/78984124/ITS Digital Archive, USHMM.
132. Original German: *gelang es ihm über die Grenze in die [das] von Deutschen besetzte Gebiet von Przemyśl zu flieh[en]. Er trat dann in OT ein, als Ingineur [Ingenieur], weil [er] nur [die] Auswahl zwischen Intern[ierungs] Lager u[nd] zurückschicken hätte. In OT hätte [er] den Grad Lieutenant (erste Stufe) gehabt u[nd] trug OT Uniform.* See Ibid.
133. For further ITS records on the OT, see 2.2.3.0 to 2.2.3.3/ITS Digital Archive, USHMM.
134. The General Government, the civilian administrative unit established by the Germans in October 1939, comprised German-occupied eastern Poland and was not incorporated into the Third Reich. It included the districts of Warsaw, Kraków, Radom, Lublin, and

December 1940 until June 1941, including Przemyśl, Kraków, and Lwów. From June 1941 to April 1942, he was posted, as he put it, "in many places in" Ukraine.[135] He told his interviewer that he became openly disenchanted with Nazism, and so Gestapo agents arrested him in April 1942 in Kharkiv, Ukraine, sending him to Berlin and then to Oranienburg.[136] In thick red pencil, his interviewer underlined his time in the OT and wrote, "Collaborator."[137]

Yet, if one were to look only at his T/D file, one would never know he collaborated with the Nazi terror machine before he claimed to have been caught in its jaws himself. His T/D file contains nothing of his stint in the OT. Rather, it details his (uncorroborated) account of his time in the concentration camp system from April 1942 until April 1945.[138] An alternate last name, "Stepanenko," appears in the T/D file as well.[139] He claimed to have been incarcerated in Oranienburg from April until late August 1942 and then in the punishment camp (*Straflager*) in the IG Farben Leuna-Werke in Saxony-Anhalt (August 22, 1942, to February 10, 1945); then he claimed to have been put to forced labor in fortification building near Saarbrücken (Saarland). According to his statement in his T/D file, he was liberated in Krauchenwies (Baden-Württemberg). In Caballero's CM/1 form, his interviewer also underlined in thick red pencil

Lwów. See, among others, Jan T. Gross, ed., *The Holocaust in Occupied Poland: New Findings and New Interpretations* (Frankfurt am Main: Peter Lang, 2012).

135. CM/1 form for Valentin Antonio Caballero, 3.2.1.1/78984124/ITS Digital Archive, USHMM.

136. Original German: *Als Mitglied dieser Organization war bis Apr. 42 u[nd] würde in Bälde über Nazi - Politik sehr enttäuscht. Seine Meinungen Ausdruck gebracht u[nd] deswegen in IV. 42 verhaftet u[nd] in KZ-Lager Oranienburg geschickt.* See Ibid.

137. Another interesting feature of this CM/1 form is that it appears to have been filled out in Geneva, Switzerland, and quite late (August 1951). See Ibid.

138. In the fall of 1954, the Landesamt für Wiedergutmachung (State Office for Restitution) in Freiburg im Breisgau requested documentation of Caballero's incarceration in the concentration camp system (a so-called *Inhaftierungsbescheinigung*). ITS staff created one of the cards in the T/D file in response to the *Inhaftierungsbescheinigung* request. See T/D file for Antonio Caballero, 6.3.3.2/98868487–8 and 98868494/ITS Digital Archive, USHMM. Presumably he was refused as ITS staff included copies of his August 1951 IRO application for assistance, marked, as already noted, with the word "collaborator" in thick red pencil (see 6.3.3.2/98868497). Further, in checking their available files on the noted sites, they could find none (see 6.3.3.2/98868498 with notations "neg.[ative]" and 6.3.3.2/98868492 with the reply "A repeated check of our documentation offered no supplementary information").

139. A plausible explanation for the appearance of the last name "Stepanenko" in the T/D file is that at some point, when asked if he had ever used a different last name, he provided the name "Stepanenko."

Caballero's admission that he had worked at the Leuna-Werke "as an engineer," controlled, Caballero told his interviewer, "by the Gestapo" and living in the camp (*Unterkunft im Lager*).[140] In 1956, still in Germany and living in Friedrichshafen am Bodensee, he requested admission to Canada. His CM/1 form does not indicate what became of his application, stating only that in response to a request for information, ITS staff sent his 1951 CM/1 form to the Canadian Government Immigration Mission on Redtenbacherstrasse 11 in Karlsruhe (Baden).[141]

The utility of ITS-held documents to retrace the paths that those accused of war crimes took from Europe to welcoming shores worldwide reaches into our own day. Consider the case of Johann Breyer (1925–2014), born in the ethnic German farming village of Neuwalldorf, Czechoslovakia (now Nová Lesná, Slovakia). At the age of seventeen, as a member of the Waffen-SS, he performed guard duties in Buchenwald and Auschwitz.[142] In 1952, he emigrated to the United States under section 12 of the 1948 DP Act, which was favorable to ethnic Germans.[143] (See document 5.11.) The US Department of Justice Office of Special Investigations (today called the Human Rights and Special Prosecutions Section) first began to investigate Breyer in the early 1990s[144] and

---

140. CM/1 form for Valentin Antonio Caballero, 3.2.1.1/78984124/ITS Digital Archive, USHMM.

141. See 6.3.2.1/98868492–3.

142. Eric Lichtblau, "US Arrests Philadelphia Man Who Worked at Nazi Death Camp," *New York Times*, June 18, 2014, www.nytimes.com/2014/06/19/us/johann-breyer-accused -of-working-at-auschwitz-and-buchenwald.html?_r = 0 (accessed March 30, 2015).

143. Additional amendment to nominal roll of resettlement movement USNS "General Hersey" EX Bremerhaven, May 3, 1952, 3.1.3.2/81686733/ITS Digital Archive, USHMM. Public Law 774, known as the DP Act of 1948, increased the total number of DPs to be admitted to the United States to 205,000 per year. Qualified DPs had to be in Germany, Austria, or Italy by December 22, 1945; 50 percent of the visas were to be reserved for agricultural workers, and 50 percent of immigrating DPs were to come from Estonia, Latvia, and Lithuania. The DP Act of 1948 benefitted ethnic Germans in that after 1946, few Jewish displaced persons seeking emigration had arrived in Germany, Austria, or Italy prior to December 1945 or came from the Baltic countries. Section 12 of the DP Act of 1948 gave preference to ethnic Germans: of the 205,000 total DP population approved for emigration to the United States annually, 13,500 were to be exclusively *Volksdeutsche*, who had to arrive in the US Zone only by July 1948 (not December 1945). The DP Act of 1948 was amended in 1950, largely to correct its antisemitic nature, increasing the total number of displaced persons to be granted entry to 415,744 and removing restrictions applying disproportionally to Jewish DPs. See Suzanne Brown-Fleming, *The Holocaust and Catholic Conscience: Cardinal Aloisius Muench and the Guilt Question in Germany* (South Bend, IN: University of Notre Dame Press in association with USHMM, 2006), 116–17.

144. CNI card for Johann Breyer, 0.1/51497890/ITS Digital Archive, USHMM.

filed a denaturalization action against him in 1992. For reasons not to be detailed here, the case did not succeed, and he remained in the United States. In 2013, the district court of Weiden, Germany, issued an arrest warrant for Breyer, and in June 2014, US federal officials arrested him at his home in Philadelphia. His death prevented his extradition to Germany to stand trial.

ITS holdings reveal important details regarding Breyer's path to the United States. We can begin to trace Breyer only as early as 1948.[145] A list of "Czechs registered [as living] in Upper Austria out of camp" includes Breyer and his address as of October 1948: Gaumeberg 1 in Linz.[146] He appears to have moved from there to the Neustadt an der Waldnaab district in Bavaria,[147] then by February 1952 to Munich, where he registered at the Funkkaserne.[148] Among those ethnic Germans supported by the Provisional Intergovernmental Committee for the Movement of Migrants from Europe (PICMME),[149] he was able to leave Munich within a few months. As of April 1952, Breyer was one of ninety-nine migrants departing from Munich to Bremen by train on April 17, for emigration to the United States "via Bremen under the auspices of the PICMME and the German Liaison Office of the Resettlement Center Funkkaserne."[150]

Breyer then appears in the Intergovernmental Committee for European Migration (ICEM) correspondence and nominal rolls completed at Bremen-Grohn,[151] which recorded transport by ship of approximately fourteen hundred ethnic Germans and DPs to New York Harbor on USAT *General M. L. Hersey*.[152]

---

145. Further information may be contained in Breyer's T/D file, #1370236, accessible at this time in Bad Arolsen, Germany, and, in the future, in the digital repositories.

146. List of Czechs registered in Upper Austria out of camp, F-6–1654, 3, 3.1.1.2/82048760/ITS Digital Archive, USHMM. A card generated by ITS staff gives the date of October 7, 1948, and lists the source of information as the UNRRA Austria Bureau. See 0.1/66301321/ITS Digital Archive, USHMM.

147. Today, this area is bounded by the districts of Schwandorf, Amberg-Sulzbach, Bayreuth, and Tirschenreuth and by the Czech Republic. It is close to the town of Weiden.

148. Auswandererlager Funkkaserne München-Freimann, Meldkarte, 3.1.1.1/66693321–23/ITS Digital Archive, USHMM.

149. This organization underwent a succession of name changes, from the PICMME, to the Intergovernmental Committee for European Migration in 1952, the Intergovernmental Committee for Migration in 1980, and finally the International Organization for Migration (IOM) in 1989. See "IOM History," IOM, www.iom.int/iom-history (accessed March 30, 2015).

150. Nominal Roll No. 52–17 B (26 B), 3.1.3.2/81756202–3/ITS Digital Archive, USHMM.

151. The US Army military base and DP camp on the outskirts of Bremen, Germany, was called Camp Grohn (1945–1954).

152. Recapitulation page to nominal role of resettlement movement USNS "General

Nominal rolls provide a wealth of information about each emigrant: first and last name, nationality, religion, marital status, sex, age, country of birth, occupation, sponsoring individual or agency, destination, length of stay in a DP camp, and zone of origin.[153] For Breyer, then, as of May 3, 1952, this ITS-held nominal roll tells us that he was Czech, Protestant, single, male, age twenty-six, and born in Czechoslovakia; it lists his occupation as "factory laborer." His sponsor was George A. Barry Jr. of 330 South Country Road, Crystal Lake, Illinois.[154] Breyer is listed as having been in a DP camp for fifteen months in the American Zone.[155] With the benefit of hindsight concerning Breyer's wartime role as a teenage guard in two of the most notorious concentration and extermination camps of the Holocaust, interesting for us today is the wording of the certificates for ethnic Germans appearing at the end of the nominal roll.[156]

CONCLUSION

IRO workers must have been overwhelmed by cases in which World War II, the Holocaust, and a rapidly changing postwar political landscape, complete with the creation of entire new territories and countries, created dramatic difficulty for applicants. The IRO constitution was not written or equipped to account for nationalist movements in countries that struggled with independence or even existence for the first time in a world still awash with antisemitism, racism, nationalism, and xenophobia. As Ruth Balint notes, in this scenario, "the answers DPs gave to authorities and the testimonies and petitions they wrote

---

Hersey" EX Bremerhaven, May 3, 1952, for New York, NY, 3.1.3.2/81686727/ITS Digital Archive, USHMM.

153. For example, for the first page of the roll on which Breyer appears stipulating these categories, see recapitulation page to nominal role, 3.1.3.2/81686789/ITS Digital Archive, USHMM.

154. Nominal roll p. 55, USA 34, 3.1.3.2/81686790, and amendment to nominal roll, 3.1.3.2/81686729/ITS Digital Archive, USHMM.

155. Nominal roll p. 55, USA 34, 3.1.3.2/81686790/ITS Digital Archive, USHMM.

156. At the end of the nominal roll, verified by B. S. Galitsen (documentation officer, Migration Committee) and certified by Gerald A. Daley (senior officer, United States Displaced Persons Commission–Bremen), the following standard statement appears: "I hereby certify that this nominal roll has been examined by me and lists the identifying data and other appropriate information for 415 migrants (persons of German ethnic origin) who have been issued visas for emigration to [the] USA under section 12 of the US DP Act as amended, under the terms agreed between the Provisional Intergovernmental Committee for the Movement of Migrants from Europe and US to the DPC [Displaced Persons Commission] for the costs of processing and sea transportation to the USA," 3.1.3.2/81686813/ITS Digital Archive, USHMM.

were crafted for a certain purpose and a specific audience." She adds, and examples in this chapter bear out, that "what people wrote was not necessarily the truth."[157]

But truths emerge nonetheless. These forms offer a snapshot of the *zeitgeist* of the first five to six years after one of the most cataclysmic wars the world has ever seen. The ITS holdings illustrate several broader, lesser-known themes. The first includes both the precarious position of Jews born in the Middle East during its remaking after World War II and the birth of Israel. More than a state, Israel was an idea long held in the Jewish imagination that caught fire in the wake of the Holocaust. As one IRO interviewer put it, the new state of Israel offered hope for "due protection." Another theme is the presence of forced laborers not just from western, central, and eastern Europe but also from the Middle East and North and East Africa. While certainly a minority, they too formed a part of the history of Nazi forced and slave labor that should not be overlooked. On this score, this chapter hardly scratches the surface of what ITS-held documents offer the diligent researcher. Future students of the Nazi and Axis empires have here new and absorbing material. Another understudied area is that of poor, often illiterate, and frequently very young men and boys from French-occupied parts of Asia and Italian-occupied parts of North and East Africa, confronted with a choice between joining Axis forces or facing starvation or imprisonment. While Axis forces certainly used them ill, American and British forces offered them no protection on entering and then exiting Axis territories. One gets the sense that for such people, DP camps offered at least some relief and protection—temporarily. ITS-held documents do not reveal what happened to them after the DP system closed, and this deserves further attention.

Unsurprisingly, ITS-held documents have much to tell us about collaborators—about their lies, about their excuses, about how they gamed the system and remained undetected for years and even decades. This very cursory sampling demonstrates that age and education impacted one's choices: an illiterate East African teenager did not have the same options as an Argentinean-born, highly educated engineer. One could become caught up in menial and often dangerous frontline labor, fighting, or even guard duty; the latter was more likely to supervise slave laborers himself—or become one if he refused. Nor did education

---

157. Ruth Balint, "The Use and Abuse of History: Displaced Persons in the ITS Archive" in *Freilegungen: Spiegelungen der NS-Verfolgung und ihrer Konsequenzen, Jahrbuch des International Tracing Service,* Bd. 4, ed. Rebecca Boehling, Susanne Urban, Elizabeth Anthony, and Suzanne Brown-Fleming (Göttingen: Wallstein Verlag, 2015), 173–186.

mean individuals made more selfless choices, as we see in the case of Valentin Antonio Caballero. Or was it Valentin Antonio Stepanenko? No systematic study exists of the reabsorption of the huge number of people identified as "not within the [IRO] mandate" on the grounds of collaboration. ITS-held documents are a gold mine for the researcher ready to take up this unsavory task. Nor should we take lightly one IRO interviewer's comment regarding Munich-born Max Dünzl: he tried "to excuse himself for the lies told and lived. He [did] not feel ashamed." There were millions of Max Dünzls, and they felt no remorse. The process of ferreting out collaborators also deserves further study, as the "first line of defense," if you will, was usually a fellow DP interviewer. The interviewer's own nationality and ethnicity, political and personal views and experiences, and material needs likely colored, at least to some degree, each and every interview. This too needs to be studied. How were interviewers chosen? Can we find patterns in specific interviewers' recommendations? If so, what were the long-term implications for applicants and, ultimately, for a remade world absorbing them?

Finally, and most striking of all, when the war ended, millions of uprooted people who had behaved in every possible human way, from the noblest to the basest, now had to try to get home and resume their lives. Nationalism, new political realities, flight westward from the Soviet Union, racism, antisemitism, and a host of other complicating factors meant that some would never return to their homelands. Many Nazis, like Max Dünzl, stayed right where they were and faded into "normal" postwar lives. Ironically, however, many of those they and their collaborators had persecuted so viciously stayed too, because no one else would take them in. The role of these last refugees and DPs, the "hard core" that no one wanted, a living and visible reminder to the postwar German conscience, is a story that needs telling.

DOCUMENT LIST

DOCUMENT 5.1. Supplement to summary of DP population "Others and Unclassified" by nationality, January 30, 1948, 3.1.1.0/82383977/ITS Digital Archive, USHMM.

DOCUMENT 5.2. Extract from CM/1 form for "Abadi, Joseph," 3.2.1.2/ 80304938/ITS Digital Archive, USHMM.

DOCUMENT 5.3. Extract from CM/1 form for "R 6914 HASSON, Stella F., 15 NOV 48," 3.2.1.2/80385879/ITS Digital Archive, USHMM.

DOCUMENT 5.4. International Refugee Organization Decision of the Review Board, Case No. 263, appeal of Ibrahim Abdurahman, 3.2.1.5/ 81278186/ITS Digital Archive, USHMM.

DOCUMENT 5.5. PCIRO application for assistance, Zamu Segai, 3.2.1.2/80491150/ITS Digital Archive, USHMM.

DOCUMENT 5.6. Handwritten letter by Waldemariam Tegeni, Fraschette, April 7, 1948, 3.2.1.2/80524994/ITS Digital Archive, USHMM (followed by translation).

DOCUMENT 5.7. Photograph of Abraham Abaj, 3.2.1.2/80304954/ITS Digital Archive, USHMM.

DOCUMENT 5.8. Photograph of Vera Abuschinow[a], 6.3.2.1/ 84140130/ITS Digital Archive, USHMM.

DOCUMENT 5.9. [Berlin] Document Center records check for Max Dünzl, 3.2.1.1/79050413/ITS Digital Archive, USHMM.

DOCUMENT 5.10. "Extract from CM/1 form for Valentin Antonio Caballero, p. 8," 3.2.1.1/78984124/ITS Digital Archive, USHMM (followed by translation).

DOCUMENT 5.11. CNI card for Johann Breyer, 0.1/51497890/ITS Digital Archive, USHMM.

DOCUMENTS

DOCUMENT 5.1

SUPPLEMENT TO SUMMARY OF DP POPULATION

"OTHERS AND UNCLASSIFIED"

BY
NATIONALITY.

30th January, 1948.

(Based on Team Reports 17th Jan. 1948).

736

NATIONALITY	AREA NO.1	AREA NO.2	AREA NO.3	AREA NO.4	AREA NO.5	AREA NO.6	AREA NO.7	TOTAL
Albanian		1						1
Argentinian						65		65
Australian						6		6
Austrian	7	13		7		1	13	41
Belgian		3					1	4
Brazilian	1						6	7
Bulgarian	2	30	3				4	39
Byelo-Russian	2	1						3
Chilian							1	1
Chinese					1	1		2
Columbian	1							1
Czechoslovakian	14	17	4	14	1	4	77	131
Czech-Ukrainian	13	3	49	22	10	48	45	190
Danish		1					1	2
Dutch		1				1	2	4
Egyptian						13	1	14
Ecuadorian		1						1
Finnish					1		3	4
French	3	4			1		6	14
German	28	143		1	1		32	205
Greek	2	79		2		8	7	98
Guatemalan	1							1
Hungarian	5	9	9	43	5	6	38	115
Iranian		17			1	6		24
Irakian						2		2
Italian		2					3	5
Lebanese						1		1
Luxembourger	1							1
Mexican					1			1
Nansen & Claimed Nansen	968	354	740	2228	713	666	5720	11389
Norwegian		6						6
Portuguese		1						1
Roumanian		124	1	90	22	4	48	289
Saudi-Arabian						1		1
Spanish	1	4	1	4		1	69	80
Swedish		3						3
Swiss							1	1
Syrian						7		7
Turkish	2	17		2	1	69	1	92
U.K.			1				4	5
U.S.A.	90	2	1	1	2	2	25	123
Uruguayan							1	1
Undetermined Armenian	3	10			1	1		15
Undetermined Ukrainian	60	10	274				7	351
Undetermined	31	7					3	41
Venezuelan							1	1
TOTAL:	1235	863	1083	2416	759	849	6184	13389

BREAKDOWN OF JEWISH POPULATION								
Polish	31055	10791	8567	10585	10637	9422	7701	88738
Hungarian	400	371	782	580	675	585	788	4181
German	928	151	400	481	677	1254	327	4218
Others	1378	1221	1649	1246	1392	2275	2100	11261
TOTAL:	33741	12534	11398	12892	13381	13536	10916	108398

DOCUMENT 5.2

A B A D I   JOSEPH

Subject was born on 4.8.27 at Alep, Syria. His parents were both of Iranian Jewish origin. His mother tongue is French.

Education   : 5 years of School of Pharmacy of the American University of Beirut

Profession   : Pharmaceutical Chemist.

Subject's parents settled over from Iran to Syria before Subject's birth and lived there as the Iranian citizens.

1936   Subject is still living at Alep, Syria, attending there a local high school, which he finished in

1943   Applicant moved to Beirut, Liban, for to continue there his studies on the American University of Beirut, School of Pharmacy, he attended that school until

6.50   and afterwards he lived there jobless, being unable to get the permission for work, until

3.51   Subject left Beirut for Israel hoping to be able to establish there. Through Turkey-Istambul he came to Haifa and tried to find there some employement, but remained jobless till

9.51   Having a brother - Ibrahim Abadi- living in Milan, Italy and an uncle - Safdie Zaki- living also at Milan Subject got the Italian entry visa with a stay permit for 2 months and came to Italy. He is still living at Milan with his brother.

Subject declares that he has left Beirut for Israel desiring to try to establish there, but was unable to find some job there. He claims also that position of Jews in Syria and Liban became very difficil and dangerous because of persecutions of local authorities in connextion of very stretched relations between Isral and Arab Lique. He says that in the next future he forsee expultion of all Jews from Arab States of Middle East.
either
Being unable to establish in Israel or in Italy, Subject would like to emigrate to anada. With assistance of his brother is will be able to pay his travel exprences.
c
Applies for All Services.
s

The factual information has been read to me and Icertify it corresponds with the facts I have related.

Subject's Signature *Josef Abag* :   Interviewer *A. V. Miller*

Has a valid passport
of his Government. Was
never persecuted for racial
or religious reasons.
Not a Refugee not a D.P.

NOT WITHIN THE MANDATE OF IRO
6-9-51

P. A. Raman

DOCUMENT 5.3

R / 6914   HASSON   Stella   F   15 NOV 48

1938- Aged 12. Living with family in Rhodes. Attending the elem. school
1939- Was exempt from study as Jewess. Continued living with family. Father dealing in sale
    of bottles etc. (petty-commerce).
AUG 44-Aged 18 . All departed to Auschwitz A-24263 (tattoed no. corresponding o the real
    situation at that time i.e. group A). Was severed from family. No trace since.
OCT 44- Transferred to Wülistadt,near Berlin,then to Teresienstadt where she was liberated
    by the Russians in
MAY 45-Was taken to Vienna by Russians,then repatriated to Italy by URSS Auth.
SEP 45-Entered Italy , Milan and remained there with t e group of the Rhodes Jews assisted
    by UNRRA,HIAS ETC.
4 MAR 46-Transferred to Rome , Hachsharah ,Via Condotti.Remained there until
AUG 48-when she obtained a modest job as house-asst. with CUGNO family,Monte Verde,
    35,Pzza.Roselino Pilloe,Rome for board and allodgement only.

LEFT THE COUNTRY : Departed as Jewess to Auschwitz in 1944.
DOES NOT RETURN : Has nobody there , as all family and friends were departed and disappear
ed during the war . Intended before to return together with all others, but now, she wishes
resettle again with all others from the Rhodes group , that are her only friends and
relatives (sister) in this world who are able and willing to assist her. She wants to return to the old country of Israel to live together with her co-nationals and find there
due protection. In case this is impossible for whatever reason, she would resettle to
USA for security .
REMARK : Main evidence given (Auschwitz). A very modest ,intelligent and good young girl.
    Consider her being alone in the world apart from Rhodes friends and sister who are
    resettling. Story true.

Butkovic

ELIGIBLE   18 NOV 1948

Victim I A 1 (a)
V. obj.
Mewsner

Suspended eligibility revision.
Failed to report. Authority: letter,
E/171, 11.3.49, Elig. of Irish Annelies,
signed Tohighem. certified by
R. Lydon.

2 7 APR 1949   R. M. LYDON
Chief of Statistics and
Operational Reports

DOCUMENT 5.4

INTERNATIONAL REFUGEE ORGANIZATION

DECISION OF THE REVIEW BOARD   No. : Geneva ___15017___

_____K.0237._____

Zone : _____GUZ_____   District : _____Augsburg_____   Case No. : __263__

In accordance with the Provisional Constitution of the Review Board, the undersigned have, on this __5th_____ day of __November_____ 1949, sitting at _____Geneva_____, reviewed the appeal of __A B D U R A H M A N   Ibrahim_____

against the decision taken on __11.10.48.____ Petitioner was interviewed on __26.10.49.__

Having examined the case-file and found it to be reasonably complete, the Review Board has reached the following decision, which has been placed on the records of the Board.

Petitioner is declared within the mandate
/n̶o̶t̶/ w̶i̶t̶h̶i̶n̶/ t̶h̶e̶/ m̶a̶n̶d̶a̶t̶e̶/

Consulted :   Chairman

  concurring _____   Member
                                        E.S. KENNEDY.

  dissenting _____   Member

                      _____   Member

                      _____   Recorder

Assistant _____

Petitioner is a Crimean Tartar, Mohammedan in religion, born in 1893, who was deported to Germany for forced labour in 1944. He was employed as a land worker according to a certificate accepted as genuine. He declared that his statements in the first instance were false, because he feared forcible repatriation to the USSR. Petitioner is illiterate, speaks only Turkish, and is not considered to have been eligible for military service in any form. He is accepted as a DP who is unwilling to return because of his fear of persecution as a Moslem Tartar minority, and his appeal is upheld. He is considered to be a Displaced Person with valid objections under Part I, Section B.

Petitioner is within the Mandate of the Organization.

DOCUMENT 5.5

DOCUMENT 5.6

Bi Ografia.

TEGAHIE UALDIMARIAM   · Matricola 23. 81/6

Fraschette 7. 4 - 48

. Dal 1937 il 1° gennaio sotto la REGIA MARINA
sino 1940. dopo prigioniero dall' Inglesi. sino
all 1941, campo prigioniero Sudan. Doppo
sono rimasto a MASSAUA. dove lavoravo.
in porto. Pendente la guerra ho perso
tutti i genitore. Il giorno 3. marzo. 1948
imbarcato clandestino. sulla nave "Carbonnella"
sbarcato a Venezia diretto sul campo.
di Fraschette. internato il 21. 3. 48 -

Chiedo a questa commissione di rimanere
in Italia nel caso contrario emigrare

per l'America del . SUD.

Ringrazie Anticipate.

TEGANIE

NOT WITHIN THE
MANDATE OF IRO

NOT WITHIN THE
MANDATE OF IRO

Teganie Waldemariam   Register 23.81/6

Fraschette   April 7, 1948

I was in the Royal Navy from the 1st of January 1937 until 1940. After imprisonment by the English until 1941 in a prison camp in Sudan, I remained in Massawa (city in Eritrea) where I worked at the harbor. During the war, I lost my entire family. On March 3, 1948, I secretly embarked aboard the ship "Carbonnella" and disembarked in Venice on March 21, 1948, where I was immediately imprisoned in the Fraschette camp.

I am asking this commission (permission) to remain in Italy or else to emigrate to South America.

Thanks in anticipation

Teganie

DOCUMENT 5.7

DOCUMENT 5.8

DOCUMENT 5.9

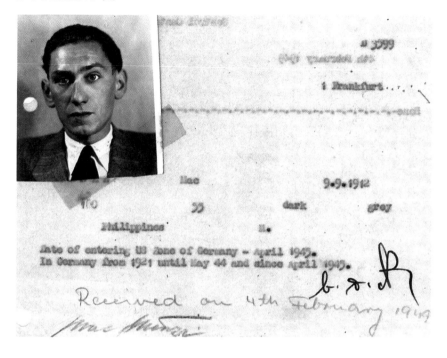

```
                7771 DOCUMENT CENTER
                APO 742.        US ARMY
                    Berlin, Germany
```

SUBJECT: Document Center Records Check:
         DUENZL, Max.

                                                    R e c o r d
TO   : IRO Frankfurt Office   DCS
         Control Center APO 757'
         Attn.: Miss A.W. HAWKSLEY

    1. Reference telephone conversation with your office
as of 18 Febr 1951 and your request dated 25 Jan 1951 the
following information is submitted:

         DUENZL, Max
         Born: 9 Sept 12 at Muenchen
         Occupation: Kaufmann
         Party No:·1 316 381
         entered : ·1 Sept 32
         Address: Muenchen, Tal 48
                  Braunes Haus Reichsltg.
         Was expelled from the party prior to March 1933
         as reported to NSDAP Reichsleitung by Party Gau,
         Oberbayern on that date.
         Expulsion revoked by decision of 13 Jan 1934.
         (NSDAP Master File)

         From March 1933 - 13 Jan 34 his Party membership
         was cancelled as he failed to pay membership-dues.
         Since 1 Nov 33 he was employed by the NSDAP:
         "Reichskarteiamt"   (1933 - Dec 41)
         "Schiedsamt"   (1942)
         "Hauptamt VII Versicherungs-u. Sozialamt" (1943).
         Held the post of a "Blockwart" and was "Sturmmann"
         in the SA.
         Place of birth: Muenchen.
         Occupation: Kaufm.Angestellter
         Address: Muenchen 9, Teutoburgerstr.3 (1943)
         Nationality: not given
         Folder closes in 1943.
         Picture available.
         (Partei Kanzlei Correspondence)
```

I. R. O.
DOC MENTS
Central-Section

RECEIVED
ON .26. 2. 57.
No. 3/.3.26.7/2.4.
REG.:

                                                    p.t.o.
```

DOCUMENT 5.10

— 8. — T ID-378940

T ID-494 932

Er. sei ein Argentinische St.-A., geb. 12.8.08 in Buenos-Aires, verheiratet seit 1935, von Beruf Dipl. Ing. Chemie, ausgewiesen durch:

die D.K.K. ausgest. 17.4.51 in Heidelberg.

Hat Argentinien schon im Jahre 1918 verlassen, als er mit d. Familie seines Pflegevaters mit ordentl. Reisepapieren nach Poland gekommen, wo sein Pflegevater ein Nachlass in Lemberg erhalten. So blieben sie alle in Poland als Argent. St.-A. bis 1939 und A. studierte inzwischen die Hochschule in Prag 1929–35. Während der Sowjets-Okupation in 1939 würde er als "Kapitalist" aus Lemberg nach Osten verbannt, – sieh 11.), aber in Dez. 1940 gelang es ihm über die Grenze in die von Deutschen besetzte Gebiet von Przemysl zu flieh. Er trat dann in O.T. ein, als Ingenieur, – weil nur Auswahl zwischen Intern. Lager u. Zurückschicken hätte. In O.T. hätte den Grad Lieutenant (erste Stufe) erhalt u. trug O.T. Uniform. Als Mitglied dieser Organisation war bis Apr. 42 u. würde in Bälde über Nazi-politik sehr enttäuscht. Seine Meinung zum Ausdruck gebracht u. deswegen in IV. 42 würde verhaftet u. in KZ-Lager Oranienburg geschickt – bis Aug. 42. Dann zur Arbeitseinsatz geschickt u. bestellt in Leuna-Werke in Merseburg b/Leipzig, als Dipl. Ing. – bis II. 45. Stand unter Kontrolle Gestapo, – mit Unterkunft in Lager. In II. 45 zur Schanzenarbeiten nach Saarbrücken geschickt – bis IV. 45. Dann ging nach Konstanz. Bis Okt. 49. wohnte in d. Französische Zone.

Bestätigt durch 1) Bescheinigung d. Fa. Usine – Leuna, 10. II. 45 – in Fotocopy d. Übersetzung
2) Geschein. d. Franz. Armee v. 1. 6. 1945 (Copie)

Über die ganze Zeit bis heute sei er Argentische St.-A. Nach dem Kriegsausgang bemüht sich

./. Fortsetzung sieh – 9 –

A. says he is an Argentine citizen, born on August 12, 1908, in Buenos Aires, married since 1935, by profession a chemical engineer with a university degree, with identification papers from the German Red Cross, issued on April 17, 1951, in Heidelberg.

He left Argentina as early as 1918, when he went with the family of his foster father, with proper travel documents, to Poland, where his foster father had received an inheritance in Lemberg. Thus they all remained in Poland as Argentine citizens until 1939, and A. studied in the meantime at the university in Prague from 1929 to 1935. During the Soviet occupation in 1939, he was expelled from Lemberg as a "capitalist" and sent eastward (see 11), but in December 1940 he managed to flee across the border into the German-occupied region of Przemyśl. He then joined OT [Organisation Todt] as an engineer— because he had only the choice between an internment camp and being sent back. In OT, he had the rank of lieutenant (first rank) and wore the OT uniform. He was a member of this organization until April 1942 and was soon very disappointed in Nazi policy. He expressed his opinion and therefore, in April 1942, was arrested and sent to the Oranienburg concentration camp—until August 1942. Then he was sent for labor deployment and assigned to the Leuna Works in Merseburg near Leipzig, as an engineer, until February 1945. He was under Gestapo control and lived in quarters in the camp. In February 1945, he was sent to Saarbrücken to work on trenches until April 1945. Then he went to Konstanz. Until October 1949, he lived in the French zone.

Throughout the entire time, to this day, he has been an Argentine citizen. After the end of the war

Continuation follows—9—

[Notes in left margin]
[In English] Collaborator
[In German] Corroborated by 1) confirmation by the firm Usine—Leuna, February 10, 1945, in a photocopy of the translation, and 2) confirmation by the French army, June 1, 1945 (copy)

DOCUMENT 5.11

BREYER, Johann　　　　　　　*137*02 *36*

30.5.1925 Neuwalddorf

vermutlich in Deutschland aufgehalten

Dep.of Justice, Washington
E: 18.9.1991
　　　　　　　　　　　23.9.91 Hed.

APPENDIX: THE INTERNATIONAL TRACING SERVICE HOLDINGS BY SUBUNIT

F OR a complete list and description of all items contained within this appendix, please refer to the "General Inventory" on the International Tracing Service (ITS) website (www.its-arolsen.org/en/archives/collections/general-inventory/index.html).

0. Global Finding Aids

0 consists of three units (0.1 through 0.3) including the Central Name Index (58,427,102 digital documents); the inventory card file War Time Documents, 1945–1951 (37,876 digital documents); and partial carding of archival unit 2.1.1.1 (3,084 digital documents).

1. Incarceration and Persecution

1.1 Camps and Ghettos

1.1.0 General Issues

1.1.0 consists of seven units (1.1.0.1 through 1.1.0.7) relating to the Wirtschafts- und Verwaltungshauptamt (SS-Business Administration Main Office) (3,271 digital documents); the Reichssicherheitshauptamt (Reich Security Main Office) (3,357 digital documents); so-called work reeducation camps (414 digital documents); Nazi extermination policy (1,756 digital documents); the "Night and Fog" decree (221 digital documents); and general correspondence relating to sites of persecution (approximately 16,838 digital documents).

1.1.1 Police Transit Camp Amersfoort

1.1.1 consists of three units subdivided into list material (32 digital documents); individual documents (105,311 digital documents); and a number index (26,366 digital documents).

1.1.2 Concentration and Extermination Camp Auschwitz

1.1.2 consists of three units (1.1.2.0 through 1.1.2.5) subdivided into general information (4,947 digital documents); list material (145,612 digital documents); and a number index (562,425 digital documents).

1.1.3 Concentration Camp Bergen-Belsen

1.1.3 consists of four units (1.1.3.0 through 1.1.3.6) subdivided into general information (388 digital documents); list material (8,150 digital documents); a number index (8,816 digital documents); and prisoners' cards without names (730 digital documents).

1.1.4 Transit Camp Breendonk

1.1.4 consists of three units (1.1.4.0 through 1.1.4.5) subdivided into general information (517 digital documents); list material (198 digital documents); and a number index (197 digital documents).

1.1.5 Concentration Camp Buchenwald

1.1.5 consists of ten units (1.1.5.0 through 1.1.5.10) subdivided into general information (24,268 digital documents); list material (137,013 digital documents); individual documents relating to male prisoners (2,134,375 digital documents); individual documents relating to female prisoners (264,103 digital documents); a number index (1,737,305 digital documents); prisoners' cards without names (15,729 digital documents); a number and name index for male prisoners (283,687 digital documents); a number and name index for female prisoners (54,183 digital documents); employment cards (26,862 digital documents); and a registry of prisoner numbers (1,620 digital documents).

1.1.6 Concentration Camp Dachau

1.1.6 consists of nine units (1.1.6.0 through 1.1.6.10) subdivided into general information (18,152 digital documents); list material (64,819 digital documents); individual documents (444,338 digital documents); a number index (217,658 digital documents); prisoners' cards without names (3,685 digital documents); camp registration office cards (187,635 digital documents); the so-called Messerschmittkartei card file (4,612 digital documents); a malaria card file (694 digital documents); and hospital files (50,578 digital documents).

1.1.7 Concentration Camp Esterwegen

1.1.7 consists of one unit (1.1.7.1) of list material (10 digital documents).

1.1.8 Concentration Camp Flossenbürg

1.1.8 consists of six units (1.1.8.0 through 1.1.8.6) including documents related to general information (3,278 digital documents); list material (16,811 digital documents); individual documents relating to males (244,263 digital documents); individual documents relating to females (38,868 digital documents); a number index (68,868 digital documents); and prisoners' cards without names (16,606 digital documents).

1.1.9   Camps in France

1.1.9 consists of seven units (1.1.9.1 through 1.1.9.13) including documents related to list material (6,689 digital documents); an index card file from Drancy (1 digital document); list material from Drancy (3,998 digital documents); list material from Beaune-la-Rolande, Pithiviers (612 digital documents); list material from Gurs (390 digital documents); list material from Montluc (Lyon) (21 digital documents); and list material from Rivesaltes (272 digital documents).

1.1.10   Labor Education Camp Grossbeeren

1.1.10 consists of one unit (1.1.10.1) including documents related to list material (54 digital documents).

1.1.11   Concentration Camp Gross-Rosen

1.1.11 consists of five units (1.1.11.0 through 1.1.11.7) including documents related to general information (1,342 digital documents); list material (26,248 digital documents); a number index (165,868 digital documents); prisoners' cards without names (7,218 digital documents); and hospital cards (340 digital documents).

1.1.12   Concentration Camp Herzogenbusch-Vught

1.1.12 consists of four units (1.1.12.0 through 1.1.12.5) including documents related to general information (107 digital documents); list material (582 digital documents); individual documents (97,380 digital documents); and a number index (21,198 digital documents).

1.1.13   Special SS Camp Hinzert

1.1.13 consists of four units (1.1.13.0 through 1.1.13.5) including documents related to general information (2,189 digital documents); list material (365 digital documents); individual documents (8,940 digital documents); and a number index (573 digital documents).

1.1.14   Camps in Italy and Albania

1.1.14 consists of two units (1.1.14.1 and 1.1.14.6) including documents related to list material (2,536 digital documents) and an Italian card file (16,399 digital documents).

1.1.15   Camps in Yugoslavia

1.1.15 consists of one unit (1.1.15.1) including documents related to list material from Yugoslavia (199 digital documents).

1.1.16   Concentration Camp Kislau

1.1.16 consists of two units (1.1.16.0 and 1.1.16.1) including documents related to general information (1,338 digital documents) and list material (1,722 digital documents).

1.1.17   Concentration Camp Klooga (Vaivara)

1.1.17 consists of three units (1.1.17.1 through 1.1.17.5) including documents related to list material (106 digital documents); individual documents (6,471 digital documents); and a number index (1,752 digital documents).

1.1.18   Ghetto Kauen (Kaunas, Kowno)

1.1.18 consists of two units (1.1.18.1 and 1.1.18.5) including documents related to list material (134 digital documents) and a number index (575 digital documents).

1.1.19   Concentration Camp Cracow-Plaszow

1.1.19 consists of three units (1.1.19.0 through 1.1.19.5) including documents related to general information (147 digital documents); list material (509 digital documents); and a number index (2,625 digital documents).

1.1.20   Concentration Camp Lichtenburg

1.1.20 consists of three units (1.1.20.0 through 1.1.20.5) including documents related to general information (194 digital documents); list material (576 digital documents); and a number index (625 digital documents).

1.1.21   Labor Education Camp Liebenau

1.1.21 consists of one unit (1.1.21.6) including documents related to prisoners' cards (670 digital documents).

1.1.22   Ghetto Litzmannstadt (Łódź)

1.1.22 consists of two units (1.1.22.0 and 1.1.22.1) including documents related to general information on the Litzmannstadt ghetto and detention camp for Polish adolescents (387 digital documents) and list material (2,877 digital documents).

1.1.23   Concentration Camp Lublin (Majdanek)

1.1.23 consists of five units (1.1.23.0 through 1.1.23.7) including documents related to general information (361 digital documents); list material (2,820 digital documents); individual documents (28,125 digital documents); a number index (32,766 digital documents); and a memorial book (421 digital documents).

1.1.24   SS Deportation Camp Mechelen (Malines)

1.1.24 consists of one unit (1.1.24.1) including documents related to list material (8,519 digital documents).

1.1.25   Concentration Camp Mauritius

1.1.25 consists of one unit (1.1.25.1) including documents related to list material (44 digital documents).

1.1.26   Concentration Camp Mauthausen

1.1.26 consists of seven units (1.1.26.0 through 1.1.26.7) including documents related to general information (2,988 digital documents); list material (46,662 digital documents); individual documents relating to males (541,463 digital documents); individual documents relating to females (18,015 digital documents); a number index (622,378 digital documents); prisoners' cards without names (26,796 digital documents); and war crime investigations (1,854 digital documents).

1.1.27   Concentration Camp Mittelbau (Dora)

1.1.27 consists of four units (1.1.27.0 through 1.1.27.5) including documents related to general information (1,161 digital documents); list material (11,432 digital documents); individual documents (221,925 digital documents); and a number index (358,332 digital documents).

1.1.28   Concentration Camp Moringen

1.1.28 consists of two units (1.1.28.0 and 1.1.28.1) including documents related to general information (998 digital documents) and list material (6,078 digital documents).

1.1.29   Concentration Camp Natzweiler (Struthof)

1.1.29 consists of five units (1.1.29.0 through 1.1.29.6) including documents related to general information (7,755 digital documents); list material (12,524 digital documents); individual documents (111,091 digital documents); a number index (129,800 digital documents); and prisoners' cards without names (11,671 digital documents).

1.1.30   Concentration Camp Neuengamme

1.1.30 consists of seven units (1.1.30.0 through 1.1.30.8) including documents related to general information (15,477 digital documents); list material (14,661 digital documents); individual documents (65,279 digital documents); a number index (117,973 digital documents); cards without names (28,484 digital documents); a card file of deceased persons (25,606 digital documents); and a so-called Bad Nenndorf card file (1,226 digital documents).

1.1.31   Concentration Camp Niederhagen (Wewelsburg)

1.1.31 consists of four units (1.1.31.0 through 1.1.31.5) including documents related to general information (106 digital documents); list material (152 digital documents); individual documents (13,751 digital documents); and a number index (3,518 digital documents).

1.1.32   Camps in Norway

1.1.32 consists of one unit (1.1.32.1) including documents related to list material (11 digital documents).

1.1.33   Concentration Camp Oranienburg

1.1.33 consists of one unit (1.1.33.1) including documents related to list material (21,999 digital documents).

1.1.34 "Emsland" Camps (Papenburg)

1.1.34 consists of two units (1.1.34.0 through 1.1.34.1) including documents related to general information on prisoner of war camps in the "Emsland" (2,615 digital documents) and list material from Papenburg (56,891 digital documents).

1.1.35 Concentration Camp Ravensbrück

1.1.35 consists of five units (1.1.35.0 through 1.1.35.6) including documents related to general information (674 digital documents); list material (9,338 digital documents); individual documents (28,047 digital documents); a number index (262,812 digital documents); and prisoners' cards without names (6,770 digital documents).

1.1.36 Concentration Camp Riga (Kaiserwald)

1.1.36 consists of two units (1.1.36.1 and 1.1.36.5) including documents related to list material (131 digital documents) and a number index (341 digital documents).

1.1.37 Concentration Camp Sachsenburg

1.1.37 consists of three units (1.1.37.0 through 1.1.37.5) including documents related to general information (593 digital documents); list material (5,903 digital documents); and a number index (2,683 digital documents).

1.1.38 Concentration Camp Sachsenhausen

1.1.38 consists of four units (1.1.38.0 through 1.1.38.6) including documents related to general information (2,345 digital documents); list material (61,683 digital documents); a number index (240,103 digital documents); and prisoners' cards without names (17,106 digital documents).

1.1.39 Reception Camp Sandbostel

1.1.39 consists of one unit (1.1.39.1) including documents related to list material (518 digital documents).

1.1.40 Concentration Camp Schirmeck-Vorbruck

1.1.40 consists of two units (1.1.40.0 through 1.1.40.1) including documents related to general information (79 digital documents) and list material (1,023 digital documents).

1.1.41 Concentration Camp Stutthof

1.1.41 consists of five units (1.1.41.0 through 1.1.41.6) including documents related to general information (1,458 digital documents); list material (11,425 digital documents); individual documents (289,388 digital documents); a number index (238,179 digital documents); and prisoners' cards without names (18,145 digital documents).

1.1.42   Ghetto Theresienstadt

1.1.42 consists of five units (1.1.42.0 through 1.1.42.7) including documents related to general information (85 digital documents); list material (5,494 digital documents); a card file (177,478 digital documents); a memorial book (899 digital documents); and postwar documents (5,844 digital documents).

1.1.43   Extermination Camp Treblinka

1.1.43 consists of one unit (1.1.43.1) including documents related to list material (14 digital documents).

1.1.44   Ghetto and Concentration Camp Warsaw

1.1.44 consists of two units (1.1.44.0 through 1.1.44.1) including documents related to general information (76 digital documents) and list material (12 digital documents).

1.1.45   Concentration Camp Welzheim

1.1.45 consists of one unit (1.1.45.1) including documents related to list material (179 digital documents).

1.1.46   Reception Camp Westerbork

1.1.46 consists of two units (1.1.46.1 and 1.1.46.7) including documents related to list material (10,537 digital documents) and copies of transport lists (2,269 digital documents).

1.1.47   Various Camps

1.1.47 consists of four units (1.1.47.0 through 1.1.47.9) including documents related to general information (1,576 digital documents); list material (28,705 digital documents); a postwar compilation of Buchenwald-related documents (78,193 digital documents); and a catalogue of concentration camp cemeteries (449 digital documents).

1.1.48   Concentration Camp Bad Sulza

1.1.48 consists of one unit (1.1.48.1) including documents related to list material (41 digital documents).

1.1.49   Concentration Camp Colditz

1.1.49 consists of one unit (1.1.49.1) including documents related to list material (420 digital documents).

1.1.50   Protective Custody Camp Hohnstein

1.1.50 consists of two units (1.1.50.0 and 1.1.50.1) including documents related to general information (42 digital documents) and list material (428 digital documents).

1.1.51   Concentration Camp Sonnenburg

1.1.51 consists of one unit (1.1.51.1) including documents related to list material (19 digital documents).

1.1.52   Concentration Camp "Columbia-Haus," Berlin-Tempelhof

1.1.52 consists of one unit (1.1.52.0) including documents related to general information (45 digital documents).

1.1.53   Concentration Camp Eutin

1.1.53 consists of one unit (1.1.53.0) including documents related to general information (87 digital documents).

1.1.54   Concentration Camp Heinersdorf

1.1.54 consists of one unit (1.1.54.0) including documents related to general information (5 digital documents).

1.1.55   Concentration Camp Heuberg

1.1.55 consists of one unit (1.1.55.0) including documents related to general information (9 digital documents).

1.1.56   Concentration Camp Kemna

1.1.56 consists of one unit (1.1.56.0) including documents related to general information (119 digital documents).

1.1.57   Concentration Camp Kuhlen

1.1.57 consists of one unit (1.1.57.0) including documents related to general information (12 digital documents).

1.1.58   Concentration Camp Osthofen

1.1.58 consists of one unit (1.1.58.0) including documents related to general information (11 digital documents).

1.1.59   Concentration Camp Rosslau

1.1.59 consists of one unit (1.1.59.0) including documents related to general information (7 digital documents).

1.1.60   Concentration Camp Wittmoor

1.1.60 consists of one unit (1.1.60.0) including documents related to general information (54 digital documents).

1.1.61   Children's Detention and Education Camp Lebrechtsdorf

1.1.61 consists of one unit (1.1.61.0) including documents related to general information (145 digital documents).

1.2   Miscellaneous

1.2.1   Transports

1.2.1 consists of four units (1.2.1.1 through 1.2.1.4) including documents related to Gestapo transport lists (32,972 digital documents); an American Jewish Joint Distribution Committee (AJDC) Berlin card file (44,632 digital documents); reference lists of transports (531 digital documents); and a card file of Berlin transports to the east (5,036 digital documents).

1.2.2   Prisons

1.2.2 consists of nine units (1.2.2.0 through 1.2.2.10) including documents related to general information (9,029 digital documents); list material (958,001 digital documents); a Gestapo Berlin card file (1,384 digital documents); a Bonn Prison card file (4,563 digital documents); a Butzbach Prison card file (2,426 digital documents); a Darmstadt Prison card file (2,270 digital documents); a Jauer [now Jawor, Poland] Women's Jail card file (1,239 digital documents); a Recklinghausen Court Prison card file (2,276 digital documents); and a Ziegenhain Jail card file (20,752 digital documents).

1.2.3   Gestapo

1.2.3 consists of fifteen units (1.2.3.0 through 1.2.3.14) including documents related to files of and information on the Gestapo (2,922 digital documents); a Frankfurt card file (137,607 digital documents); a Hamburg card file (7,151 digital documents); a Koblenz card file (101,278 digital documents); a Lenne card file (384 digital documents); a Luxembourg card file (1,160 digital documents); a Münster card file (525 digital documents); a Neustadt card file (57,797 digital documents); an Osnabrück card file (56,359 digital documents); a Trier card file (140 digital documents); a Wiesbaden card file (1,466 digital documents); a collection of Würzburg individual documents for German Jews (19,166 digital documents); a collection of Würzburg files (101,883 digital documents); a collection from Luxembourg, containing a subsection of the Diekirch card file (759 digital documents); and files from the Gestapo in Düsseldorf (2,949 digital documents).

1.2.4   Various Organizations

1.2.4 consists of three units (1.1.4.1 through 1.1.4.3) including documents related to the so-called Reichsvereinigung der Juden card file (32,270 digital documents); a Dutch wartime card file of Jews (167,023 digital documents); and a Service Watson card file (2,139 digital documents).

1.2.5   Postwar Compilations

1.2.5 consists of one unit (1.2.5.1) including documents related to local lists of Jewish residents (5,537 digital documents).

1.2.6   Archival References

1.2.6 consists of three units (1.2.6.1 through 1.2.6.3) including documents related to the national archive in Düsseldorf (6,120 digital documents); collections from various archives (1,242 digital documents); and collections from the Regional Finance Office of Cologne (478 digital documents).

1.2.7   Persecution Actions Outside of the German Reich

1.2.7 consists of twenty-six units (1.2.7.1 through 1.2.7.26) including documents related to the persecution of Jews in general (2,138 digital documents); the persecution of Polish Jews in newspaper cuttings (1,312 digital documents); the persecution actions in the "occupied Eastern territory" in general (1,035 digital documents), in the Baltic states (2,527 digital documents), in Ukraine

(948 digital documents), in the former USSR (1,736 digital documents), in the General Government as a part of former Poland (10,071 digital documents), in the General Government within the District of Galicia (2,190 digital documents), in Reichsgau Wartheland as part of former Poland (1,067 digital documents), in Reichsgau Danzig as part of western Prussia (1,066 digital documents), in the territory of the Reich (1,956 digital documents), in District Białystok (299 digital documents), in Austria (452 digital documents), in the Protectorate of Bohemia and Moravia and in the Sudetenland (1,098 digital documents), in Hungary (879 digital documents), in Slovakia (376 digital documents), in Alsace and Lorraine (637 digital documents), in France and Monaco (4,000 digital documents), in the Benelux countries (2,511 digital documents), in the former USSR (3,002 digital documents), in North African states (117 digital documents), in Denmark and Norway (1,798 digital documents), in Serbia (2,414 digital documents), in Romania and Bulgaria (1,003 digital documents), and in Greece, Italy, and Spain (671 digital documents); and persecution actions directed against "gypsies" (218 digital documents).

1.2.8   Court-Martial Proceedings (17,905 digital documents)

2.   Registration of Foreigners and German Persecutees by Public Institutions, Insurance Companies, and Firms (1939–1947)

2.1   Implementation of Allied Forces' Orders to List All Foreigners and German Persecutees, and Related Documents

2.1.1   American Zone of Occupation in Germany

2.1.1 consists of three units (2.1.1.1 through 2.1.1.3) including documents related to the lists of all persons of the Allied nations and other foreigners, German Jews, and stateless persons within the American Zone of Bavaria and Hesse who were considered adults (701,609 digital documents); within the American Zone of Bavaria, Württemberg-Baden, and Bremen (115,419 digital documents); and within the American Zone of Bavaria and Hesse who were considered children (31,870 digital documents).

2.1.2   British Zone of Occupation in Germany

2.1.2 consists of one unit (2.1.2.1) including documents relating to the lists of all persons of the Allied nations and other foreigners, German Jews, and stateless persons within the British Zone (248,731 digital documents).

2.1.3   French Zone of Occupation in Germany

2.1.3 consists of two units (2.1.3.1 and 2.1.3.2) including documents relating to the lists of all persons of the Allied nations and other foreigners, German Jews, and stateless persons within the French Zone (56,118 digital documents) and hospital files (79,106 digital documents).

2.1.4   Soviet Zone of Occupation in Germany

2.1.4 consists of four units (2.1.4.1 through 2.1.4.4) including documents relating to the lists of all persons of the Allied nations and other foreigners, German Jews, and stateless persons within the Soviet Zone pt. 1 (38,332 digital documents) and pt. 2 (196,907 digital documents); the lists of patients in hospitals (373 digital documents); and hospital files (39,872 digital documents).

2.1.5   Berlin, All Sectors

2.1.5 consists of three units (2.1.5.1 through 2.1.5.3) including documents relating to the lists of all persons of the Allied nations and other foreigners, German Jews, and stateless persons within Berlin (33,970 digital documents); the lists of patients in hospitals (14 digital documents); and the hospital files (57,943 digital documents).

2.1.6   Austria, All Zones of Occupation

2.1.6 consists of one unit (2.1.6.1) including documents relating to the lists of all persons of the Allied nations and other foreigners, German Jews, and stateless persons within Austria (18,854 digital documents).

2.1.7   Other Countries

2.1.7 consists of five units (2.1.7.1 through 2.1.7.5) including documents relating to the lists of all persons of the Allied nations and other foreigners, German Jews, and stateless persons from those parts of Poland that had been territory of the German Reich until 1945 (9,504 digital documents); from those parts of Russia that had been territory of the German Reich until 1945 (164 digital documents); interned by German administration in Czechoslovakia (1,002 digital documents); interned by German administration in Yugoslavia (704 digital documents); and interned by German administration in various other countries (885 digital documents).

2.1.8   Various and Unknown Zones

2.1.8 consists of two units (2.1.8.1 and 2.1.8.2) including documents relating to lists of all persons of the Allied nations and other foreigners, German Jews, and stateless persons within various zones (1,592 digital documents) and within unknown zones (13,304 digital documents).

2.2   Documents on the Registration of Foreigners and the Employment of Forced Laborers, 1939–1945

2.2.0   Forced Labor

2.2.0 consists of two units (2.2.0.1 and 2.2.0.2) including documents relating to correspondence and records on forced labor (57,579 digital documents) and individual companies (5,677 digital documents).

2.2.1   Generalbauinspektor für die Reichshauptstadt

2.2.1 consists of three units (2.2.1.0 through 2.2.1.2) including documents relating to correspondence and records on foreign workers (524 digital documents); files with names of civilian foreign workers (3,143 digital documents); and lists concerning the payment of wages to foreign workers of the "Baustab Speer" in Berlin (4,077 digital documents).

2.2.2   Various Public Administrations and Companies (Documents Related to Single Persons)

2.2.2 consists of ten units (2.2.2.1 through 2.2.2.10) including documents relating to a wartime card file containing registration cards, employees' record books, and individual correspondence (6,282,692 digital documents); official marriage and death certificates for the western zones (232,255 digital documents); birth certificates from the Child Tracing Branch (156,051 digital documents); death certificates of children from the Child Tracing Branch (32,383 digital documents); official marriage and death certificates for the Soviet Zone pt. 1 (18,654 digital documents) and pt. 2 (3,298 digital documents); official certificates obtained from the national archive in Leipzig (1,280 digital documents); official marriage and death certificates obtained from the Russian Red Cross (29,410 digital documents); lists of unknown dead, compiled mostly from certificates without names (6,366 digital documents); and registration data of medical insurance plans in Osterode (30,252 digital documents).

2.2.3   Organisation Todt

2.2.3 consists of four units (2.2.3.0 through 2.2.3.3) including documents relating to general information (4,844 digital documents); a card file (23,264 digital documents); lists of employment in Norway (1,989 digital documents); and lists of employment in Germany (185 digital documents).

2.2.4   Employment Office Warsaw

2.2.4 consists of one unit (2.2.4.1) including documents relating to the lists of the Warsaw employment office concerning Polish forced agricultural laborers in Germany (19,410 digital documents).

2.2.5   Prisoners of War

2.2.5 consists of three units (2.2.5.1 through 2.2.5.3) including documents relating to administration in connection with POWs (936 digital documents); deceased POWs (1,211 digital documents); and POW camps (840 digital documents).

2.3   Postwar Evaluations of Various Organizations

2.3.1   Amt für die Erfassung der Kriegsopfer (Berlin)

2.3.1 consists of two units (2.3.1.1 and 2.3.1.2) including documents relating to correspondence and lists of names from the Office for the Registration of War Victims (2,662 digital documents) and a card file of the Office for the Registration of War Victims (68,012 digital documents).

2.3.2   Deutsche Dienststelle (Wehrmachtsauskunftstelle für Kriegerverluste und Kriegsgefangene [WASt, German Armed Forces Information Office for War Losses and Prisoners of War])

2.3.2 consists of two units (2.3.2.1 and 2.3.2.2) including documents relating to lists of graves of Soviet nationals obtained from the WASt (3,685 digital documents) and lists of graves of Soviet nationals obtained from the Russian Red Cross, Moscow (7,174 digital documents).

2.3.3   Haut-Commissariat de la République Française en Allemagne

2.3.3 consists of five units (2.3.3.1 through 2.3.3.5) including documents relating to a card file of persecutees in the later French Zone and of French persecutees in other areas (672,522 digital documents); a card file of persecutees treated in hospitals in the territory of the later French Zone (107,031 digital documents); a card file of deceased persecutees (78,454 digital documents); a card file of the French Liaison Office in Berlin (284,421 digital documents); and a French catalogue of concentration and forced labor camps in Germany and German-occupied territory (643 digital documents).

2.3.4   Miscellaneous

2.3.4 consists of one unit (2.3.4.1) including documents relating to registration of former persecutees by various tracing bureaus from 1945 to 1946 (2,939 digital documents).

2.3.5   Kingdom of Belgium Ministries

2.3.5 consists of one unit (2.3.5.1) including documents relating to a Belgian catalogue of concentration and forced labor camps in Germany and German-occupied territory (13,101 digital documents).

2.3.6   Kingdom of the Netherlands Ministries

2.3.6 consists of one unit (2.3.6.1) including documents related to a Dutch catalogue of concentration and forced labor camps in Germany and German-occupied territory (4,657 digital documents).

3.   Registrations and Files of Displaced Persons, Children, and Missing Persons

3.1   Evidence of Abode and Emigration

3.1.1   Registration and Care of DPs inside and outside Camps

3.1.1 consists of ten units (3.1.1.0 through 3.1.1.9) including documents relating to general information: camps, correspondence, service regulations (3,252 digital documents); a displaced person registration record card file (3,440,058 digital documents); the DP registration lists for DP camps (102,916 digital documents); the registration of liberated former persecutees at various locations (55,031 digital documents); the registration of former persecutees deceased at various locations, predominantly after the war (456 digital documents); index cards of the Central Location Index, New York (1,014 digital documents); a card file of refugees in Stade (674 digital documents); registrations in Denmark (29,029 digital documents); registrations in Italy (5,542 digital documents); and registrations in England (197,983 digital documents).

3.1.3   Emigration

3.1.3 consists of two units (3.1.3.1 and 3.1.3.2) including documents related to an AJDC Paris emigration card file (30,266 digital documents) and the passenger lists and further compilations regarding emigrated persons (149,193 digital documents).

3.2   Relief Programs of Various Organizations

3.2.1   International Refugee Organization "Care and Maintenance" Program

3.2.1 consists of six units (3.2.1.1 through 3.2.1.6) including documents related to International Refugee Organization (IRO) care and maintenance—welfare and support (CM/1) form files originating in Germany (1,111,760 digital documents), Italy (246,025 digital documents), Austria (341,414 digital documents), and Switzerland (357,946 digital documents); CM/1 opposition proceedings from the IRO Bureau in Geneva (60,670 digital documents); and CM/1 files originating in England (48,993 digital documents).

3.2.2   Intergovernmental Committee for European Migration. 3.2.2 consists of one unit (3.2.2.1) including documents related to ICEM files. (130,801 digital documents)

3.2.3   United Nations High Commissioner for Refugees

3.2.3 consists of three units (3.2.3.0 through 3.2.3.2) including documents related to correspondence and evaluations in connection with United Nations High Commissioner for Refugees (UNHCR) Hong Kong files (1,093 digital documents); UNHCR files (64,069 digital documents); and files of UNHCR Hong Kong (90,608 digital documents).

3.3   Child Tracing Branch

3.3.1   The Limited Registration Plan

3.3.1 consists of four units (3.3.1.1 through 3.3.1.4) including documents related to Limited Registration Plan (LRP) investigation results (55,066 digital documents); Hollerith cards of the LRP (669,978 digital documents); evaluation of Hollerith cards by dates of birth (6,782 digital documents); and various evaluations of Hollerith cards (679 digital documents).

3.3.2   Material Used for Tracing Work

3.3.2 consists of four units (3.3.2.1 through 3.3.2.4) including documents related to correspondence (37,590 digital documents); individual documents related to child tracing (1,366 digital documents); a child tracing index file

(154,042 digital documents); and a card file of foundlings sorted by location (3,742 digital documents).

4. Special Nazi Party Organizations and Actions

4.1 Lebensborn e.V.

4.1 consists of three units (4.1.0 through 4.1.2) including documents related to files of institutions of the Lebensborn e.V. (35,530 digital documents); a Lebensborn card file (7,929 digital documents); and lists of the Child Tracing Branch (3,035 digital documents).

4.2 Medical Experiments and "Euthanasia" (7,211 digital documents)

5. Miscellaneous

5.1 Nazi Trials (33,889 digital documents)

5.3 Death Marches/Identification of Unknown Dead (Investigations of the Allies, Routes, Identification of Unknown Dead, etc.)

5.3 consists of six units (5.3.1 through 5.3.6) including documents related to investigations of the Allies (5,785 digital documents); attempted identifications (16,123 digital documents); death marches and identification of unknown deceased individuals (13,425 digital documents); cartographical material from investigations (1 digital document); grave investigations/cemetery maps (7,513 digital documents); and a card file of death march locations (3,437 digital documents).

6. Records of the ITS and Its Predecessors

6.1 Administration and Organization

6.1 consists of two units (6.1.1 and 6.1.2) including documents related to predecessor organizations (31,519 digital documents) and the child tracing service under the United Nations Relief and Rehabilitation Administration and IRO (5,938 digital documents).

6.2 Information Material

6.2 consists of one unit (6.2.1) including documents related to compensation paid by the Federal Republic of Germany (541 digital documents).

6.3 Inquiry Processing

6.3.1 Searching for Missing Persons

6.3.1 consists of two units (6.3.1.1 and 6.3.1.2) including documents related to tracing inquiries from 1945 to 1946 (715,016 digital documents) and search lists (1,053 digital documents).

6.3.2 Case Files of the Child Tracing Branch, 1947–1951

6.3.2 consists of two units (6.3.2.1 and 6.3.2.2) including documents related to files of children identified by name (455,629 digital documents) and the Child Tracing Branch's files of foundlings (1,447 digital documents).

6.3.3 ITS Case Files as of 1947

6.3.3 consists of three units (6.3.3.2 through 6.3.3.4) including documents related to repository of tracing and documentation (T/D) cases (9,419,440 digital documents); deposit of inquiries filed under a *Briefnummer* (945,176 digital documents); and inquiries related to Stiftung "Erinnerung, Verantwortung und Zukunft" (Foundation "Remembrance, Responsibility, and Future") compensation efforts (1,133,559 digital documents).

10. Documentary Fonds of the Archival Management Section

10.1 Security Films

10.1 consists of two units (10.1.1 and 10.1.2) including films (1,767 films, 35 negatives) and fiche (45,727 fiches).

10.2 Microfilms (6,092 films, 60 glass tops, 1 file with negatives, 109 envelopes with negatives, 1 envelope with negative and positive photos)

10.3 Microfiche (5,571 fiches, 15 cardboard boxes, 77 boxes)

10.4 Disks (65 disks)

10.5 CDs and DVDs (616 CDs/DVDs)

10.6 Special Depot

10.6 consists of fifty-one units (10.6.1 through 10.6.51) including documents, correspondence, personal items, and media related to twenty-four specific concentration and forced labor camps; lists of extracts and photocopies sent to Belgian, French, Italian, Luxembourgian, and Dutch National Tracing Bureaus; transports from Gestapo areas in various cities in Germany; non-inventoried documents held in original form from six concentration camps; locations and cemeteries of deceased Soviet nationals; Group P.P.; Records Library; Service Watson; activity reports of the ITS; files for exchange with the Auschwitz State Museum; register of arriving and departing collective transports; foreign records seized; old films; escapees; a Messerschmitt index; Drancy; Montluc; Information Bureau of the Netherlands Red Cross; an inventory; files relating to Italians; circular letters distributed by the United Restitution Organization; a permanent index of dead persons; and miscellaneous holdings (59 archival boxes, 2 archival files, 26 pads, 1 stitched booklet, 17 spools of film, 72 sheets, 31 cardboard boxes, 142 books, 41 boxes, 61 briefcases, 1,161 folders total). For a complete list of units, please refer to the "General Inventory" on the ITS website (www.its-arolsen.org/en/archives/collections/general-inventory/index .html).

10.7 Finding Aids, Help Card Files, Labor Card Files, Papers

10.7 consists of 163 units (10.7.1 through 10.7.163) including documents and media related to various card indexes for concentration camps, prisoners, places, inventory, addresses, birthdays, DPs, civilians, and other wartime information; preparatory work for catalogues of prisons; reports concerning hostilities, evacuation, transports, and DPs; ITS history, postwar concentration camp evaluations by Allied forces, Nazi experiments, "Gypsy" treatment, ghetto locations, and other assorted wartime information; prison catalogues and information; finding aids in the form of various help card files, guides to German records, photographs of office buildings and war information, archival fonds, lists of prisoner numbers and other finding-aid information (1 archival file, 1 pad, 36 sheets, 68 envelopes, 4 photographs, 4 plates, 11 posters, 267 boxes, 484 stitched booklets, 116 books, 12,697 briefcases, 389 folders total). For a complete list of units, please refer to the "General Inventory" on the ITS website (www.its-arolsen.org/en/archives/collections/general-inventory/index.html).

10.8   Liaison Missions

10.8 consists of four units (10.8.1 through 10.8.4) including documents related to liaison missions in Belgium (7 archive boxes, 3 cards, 9 folders); Italy (7 books, 1 cardboard box, 354 folders); Israel (2 briefcases); and France (22 brochures, 11 books, 140,000 cards, 1,263 folders).

10.9   Documents Not Yet Inventoried

10.9 consists of two units (10.9.1 and 10.9.2) including nonpersonal documents (883 sheets, 12 boxes, 6 stitched booklets, 7 cardboard boxes, 4 boxes, 24 briefcases, 190 folders, 2 plates) and personal documents (18 work cards, 11 archive cardboard boxes, 2 archive files, 18,435 sheets, 1 wallet, 278 books, 670 CDs/DVDs, 7 disks, 3,500 fiches, 2,498 films, 85 photos, 540 cardboard boxes, 22 boxes, 4 briefcases, 12 metal plates).

10.10   Personal Effects

10.10 consists of two units (10.10.1 and 10.10.2) including documents related to correspondence on personal effects (19 archive boxes, 4 folders) and personal effects (3,306 envelopes).

10.11   File Deposit of HIST and "Sachnummern" (item code numbers: the reference codes of the nonpersonal documents) (14 books, 19 boxes, 31 briefcases, 443 folders)

10.12   Documents That Do Not Fall within the ITS Mandate

10.12 consists of ten units (10.12.1 through 10.12.10) including documents related to payrolls of German nationals employed in Sundhausen (7 stitched booklets); registration cards from Ahlen relating to Jewish persons; various sorted documents (1 archive box, 2 boxes); self-sufficiency of the entourage in Sundhausen (1 book); labor books of German nationals (2 books); passport of a Slovak national (1 book); ration coupons of German nationals from Waldeck (1 briefcase); military paybook, doctor's report on results, tracing cards, ownership testimony of a Hungarian national (1 envelope); various Romanian files from fonds of the United States Holocaust Memorial Museum; and photos showing various signs (8 photos).

10.13   Documents' Depot after Digital Inventorying

10.13 consists of two units (10.13.1 and 10.13.2) including digitized original documents (1 file, 787 sheets, 7 books, reenlargements of microfilm [42 boxes]).

10.14   Institutional File Deposit of All Departments (1 archive box, 23 books, 13 briefcases, 64 folders)

10.15   Maps and Plans (835 cards)

10.16   File Deposit Research

10.16 consists of four units (10.16.1 through 10.16.4) including documents related to projects (22 folders); archival requests; data media (11 CD boxes); and educational material (5 folders).

10.17   Any Other Items

10.17 consists of four units (10.17.1 through 10.17.4) including facsimile documents (1 archive box); the movement of the T/D correspondence files (11 books); documents taken from correspondence files (1 briefcase); and business travel reports (12 folders).

10.18   Indemnification UNHCR (2,590 cardboard boxes, 423 folders)

10.19   Medical Papers (1,103 cardboard boxes, 492 folders)

10.20   Nonidentified Concentration Camps

10.21   Requests Filed with the ITS

10.21 consists of nine units (10.21.1 through 10.21.9) including documents related to requests filed by the chief of police (12 folders), for which the ITS was not the competent office (60 folders), and regarding which the ITS checked back with the inquirer (64 folders); certificates of incarceration (71 folders); correspondence files (2,071,999 T/D correspondence cases); file 209 (55 cardboard boxes); microfilmed correspondence files (625 T/D correspondence cases); workflow requests (1 archive cardboard box); and the Central Register of Foreign Persons (5 folders).

10.22   Bulletins (8 folders)

10.23   File Deposit Inventorying Section (83 folders)

10.24   Press (1,718 articles, 1 stitched booklet)

10.25   Not Yet Digitized Documents on Forced Laborers and Postwar Documents, Files on Incarceration (1 archive box, 153 sheets, 8 books, 2 briefcases, 10 folders, 720 envelopes)

11.   Institutional File Deposit for All Departments

11.1   ITS Texts (3 boxes, 30 folders)

11.2   Liaison Mission (10 archive boxes, 7 cardboard boxes, 6 boxes, 31 books, 31 folders)

11.3   General Correspondence (1 box, 433 folders, 212 suspension files)

11.4   Statistics (2 boxes, 127 folders, 11 suspension files)
11.5   Data Protection (2 boxes, 22 folders, 13 suspension files)
11.6   Documents (4 boxes, 1 folder)
11.7   Case Requests (35 folders)
11.8   Document Acquisition (5 boxes, 436 folders, 56 suspension files)
11.9   Holocaust Deniers (2 folders)
11.10   ITS Reports (1 box, 22 folders)
11.11   Agreements (14 folders)
11.12   Conservation Work (7 folders, 10 suspension files)
11.13   Security Films (3 folders)
11.14   Archives (34 folders, 6 suspension files)
11.15   Public Prosecution (32 folders)
11.16   Research (6 boxes, 95 folders, 73 suspension files)
11.17   Methods of Treatment (2 boxes, 6 folders, 9 suspension files)
11.18   Commemorative Book (1 box, 15 folders, 17 suspension files)
11.19   Indemnification Funds (122 folders, 4 suspension files)
11.20   Memorial (13 folders)
11.21   Red Cross (39 folders, 1 suspension file)
11.22   Business Trip (16 folders, 178 suspension files)
11.23   Visitors to the ITS (11 books, 10 folders, 251 suspension files)
11.24   Press/Communication (93 folders, 60 single activities)
11.25   Director (2 folders)
11.26   Internal Issues (10 CDs/DVDs, 180 folders, 164 suspension files)
11.27   Minutes (27 folders, 3 suspension files)
11.28   Finances (686 folders, 24 suspension files)
11.29   Human Resources (1 file, 4 boxes, 851 folders, 3 suspension files)
11.30   Information Technology (82 folders, 31 suspension files)
11.31   Buildings (2 boxes, 12 folders, 4 suspension files)
11.32   Events (2 folders)
11.33   Personal Effects (11 suspension files)
11.34   Transmission of Copies (1 box, 37 suspension files)
11.35   Description Work (35 suspension files)
11.36   Processing of Requests (1 box, 42 books, 62 folders)
11.37   Budget (1 box, 2 folders)
11.38   Predecessor Organizations (1 archive box, 2 cardboard boxes, 1 box, 5 folders)
11.39   General Facts (9 boxes)
11.40   Indemnification (1 archive box, 1 box)
12.   Institutional File Deposit of the Directorate

12.1   International Committee of the Red Cross

12.1 consists of twenty units (12.1.1 through 12.1.20) including documents related to general correspondence (40 folders); evaluation and research (1 archive box); evaluation and research data protection (1 folder); processing of requests (7 folders); visitors (5 folders); events (3 folders); the Executive Council (1 folder); financial issues (7 folders); building (1 single activity); the International Commission (1 folder); inventory (2 archive boxes); direction and administration (10 folders); public relations work (16 folders); organizational strategies (2 folders); human resources (1 folder); legal issues (2 archive boxes, 10 folders); the Special Registry Office; miscellaneous (6 folders); cooperative projects (1 folder); and liaison missions.

12.2   International Commission

12.2 consists of twenty-one units (12.2.1 through 12.2.21) including documents related to general correspondence (82 folders); processing of requests (5 folders); regulations for access (2 folders); visitors (1 folder); data protection (1 folder); data transfer (4 folders); personal effects; events (2 folders); financial issues; rules regarding fees and tariffs; rules of procedure; direction and administration (1 folder); public relations work (1 folder); organizational strategies; the annual meeting (8 archive cardboard boxes, 37 folders); subcommission (14 folders); the United Nations Educational, Scientific, and Cultural Organization (1 archive box, 1 folder); liaison missions (1 folder); agreement papers (3 archive boxes, 10 folders); and cooperative projects.

13.   Library

13.1   Objects Captured in the Internal Database (FAUST) (10,609 books, 125 journals)

13.2   Correspondence (10 folders)

13.3   DVDs/Videos (100 CDs/DVDs)

13.4   Publications (7,000 books)

Bibliography

Andlauer, Anna. *Zurück ins Leben. Das internationale Kinderzentrum Kloster Indersdorf 1945–46.* Nuremberg: Antogo Verlag, 2011.

Angrick, Andrej. *Besatzungspolitik und Massenmord: Die Einsatzgruppe D in der südlichen Sowjetunion, 1941–1943.* Hamburg: Hamburger Edition, 2003.

Anthony, Elizabeth. "Representations of Sexual Violence in ITS Documentation: Concentration Camp Brothels." In *Freilegungen: Spiegelungen der NS-Verfolgung und ihrer Konsequenzen,* edited by Rebecca Boehling, Susanne Urban, Elizabeth Anthony, and Suzanne Brown-Fleming. Jahrbuch des International Tracing Service IV. Göttingen: Wallstein Verlag, 2015.

Arad, Yitzak. *Belzec, Sobibor, Treblinka: The Operation Reinhard Death Camps.* Bloomington: Indiana University Press, 1987.

Arielli, Nir. *Fascist Italy and the Middle East, 1933–40.* New York: Palgrave Macmillan, 2010.

Arnsberg, Paul. *Die jüdischen Gemeinden in Hessen: Anfang, Untergang, Neubeginn.* Frankfurt: Landesverband der Jüdischen Gemeinden in Hessen/Societäts-Verlag, 1971.

Balint, Ruth. "Industry and Sunshine: Australia as Home in the Displaced Persons' Camps of Postwar Europe." *History Australia* 11, no. 1 (2014): 102–27.

———. "The Use and Abuse of History: Displaced Persons in the ITS Archive." In *Freilegungen: Spiegelungen der NS-Verfolgung und ihrer Konsequenzen,* edited by Rebecca Boehling, Susanne Urban, Elizabeth Anthony, and Suzanne Brown-Fleming. Jahrbuch des International Tracing Service IV. Göttingen: Wallstein Verlag, 2015.

Bankier, David. *Expulsion and Extermination: Holocaust Testimonials from Provincial Lithuania.* Jerusalem: Yad Vashem, International Institute for Holocaust Research, 2012.

Bartov, Omer. "Wartime Lies and Other Testimonies: Jewish-Christian Relations in Buczacz, 1939–1944." *East European Politics and Societies* 25, no. 3 (2011): 486–511.

Bartusevičius, Vincas, Joachim Tauber, and Wolfram Wette, eds. *Holocaust in Litauen: Krieg, Judenmorde und Kollaboration im Jahre 1941.* Cologne: Böhlau, 2003.

Bauer, Yehuda. *Out of the Ashes: The Impact of American Jews on Post-Holocaust European Jewry.* Oxford, UK: Pergamon Press, 1989.

Baumann, Angelika, and Andreas Heusler, eds. *Kinder für den "Führer": Der Lebensborn in München*. Munich: Franz Schiermeier Verlag, 2013.

Belkin, Paul. "Opening of the International Tracing Service's Holocaust-Era Archives in Bad Arolsen, Germany." CRS Report for Congress, Order Code RS22638, April 5, 2007.

Benz, Angelika. *Der Henkersknecht: Der Prozess gegen John (Iwan) Demjanjuk in München*. Berlin: Metropol, 2011.

Bernhardt, Zvi, and Kinga Frojimovics. "The Synergy of Documents: Making Shards into a Whole." In *Freilegungen: Auf den Spuren der Todesmärsche*, edited by Jean-Luc Blondel, Susanne Urban, and Sebastian Schönemann, 19–25. Jahrbuch des International Tracing Service I. Göttingen: Wallstein Verlag, 2012.

Bezwinska, Jadwiga, and Danuta Czech. *Amidst a Nightmare of Crime: Manuscripts of Members of Sonderkommando*, translated from the Polish by Krystyna Michalik. Oświęcim: Auschwitz State Museum, 1973.

Birn, Ruth Bettina. "Aseri." In *The United States Holocaust Memorial Museum Encyclopedia of Camps and Ghettos, 1933–1945*, Vol. 1: *Early Camps, Youth Camps, and Concentration Camps and Subcamps under the SS-Business Administration Main Office (WVHA)*, edited by Geoffrey P. Megargee, 1496. Bloomington: Indiana University Press in association with USHMM, 2009.

———. *Die Sicherheitspolizei in Estland, 1941–1944: Eine Studie zur Kollaboration im Osten*. Paderborn: Schöningh, 2006.

———. "Ereda." In *The United States Holocaust Memorial Museum Encyclopedia of Camps and Ghettos, 1933–1945*, Vol. 1: *Early Camps, Youth Camps, and Concentration Camps and Subcamps under the SS-Business Administration Main Office (WVHA)*, edited by Geoffrey P. Megargee, 1497–98. Bloomington: Indiana University Press in association with USHMM, 2009.

———. "Goldfields." In *The United States Holocaust Memorial Museum Encyclopedia of Camps and Ghettos, 1933–1945*, Vol. 1: *Early Camps, Youth Camps, and Concentration Camps and Subcamps under the SS-Business Administration Main Office (WVHA)*, edited by Geoffrey P. Megargee, 1498–99. Bloomington: Indiana University Press in association with USHMM, 2009.

———. "Kiviõli I and II." In *The United States Holocaust Memorial Museum Encyclopedia of Camps and Ghettos, 1933–1945*, Vol. 1: *Early Camps, Youth Camps, and Concentration Camps and Subcamps under the SS-Business Administration Main Office (WVHA)*, edited by Geoffrey P. Megargee, 1500. Bloomington: Indiana University Press in association with USHMM, 2009.

———. "Narva." In *The United States Holocaust Memorial Museum Encyclopedia of Camps and Ghettos, 1933–1945*, Vol. 1: *Early Camps, Youth Camps, and Concentration Camps and Subcamps under the SS-Business Administration Main Office (WVHA)*, edited by Geoffrey P. Megargee, 1503–4. Bloomington: Indiana University Press in association with USHMM, 2009.

———. "Vaivara Main Camp." In *The United States Holocaust Memorial Museum Encyclopedia of Camps and Ghettos, 1933–1945*, Vol. 1: *Early Camps, Youth Camps, and Concentration Camps and Subcamps under the SS-Business Administration Main Office (WVHA)*, edited by Geoffrey P. Megargee, 1490–95. Bloomington: Indiana University Press in association with USHMM, 2009.

———. "Vivikonna." In *The United States Holocaust Memorial Museum Encyclopedia of*

Camps and Ghettos, 1933–1945, Vol. 1: *Early Camps, Youth Camps, and Concentration Camps and Subcamps under the SS-Business Administration Main Office (WVHA)*, edited by Geoffrey P. Megargee, 1508. Bloomington: Indiana University Press in association with USHMM, 2009.

Black, Peter. "Foot Soldiers of the Final Solution: The Trawniki Training Camp and Operation Reinhard." *Holocaust and Genocide Studies* 25, no. 1 (2011): 1–99.

Blatman, Daniel. *The Death Marches: The Final Phase of Nazi Genocide*. Cambridge, MA: Belknap Press, 2011.

———. "On the Traces of the Death Marches: The Historiographical Challenge." In *Freilegungen: Auf den Spuren der Todesmärsche*, edited by Jean-Luc Blondel, Susanne Urban, and Sebastian Schönemann, 85–107. Jahrbuch des International Tracing Service I. Göttingen: Wallstein Verlag, 2012.

Bloxham, Donald. *Genocide on Trial: War Crimes and the Formation of Holocaust History and Memory*. Oxford: Oxford University Press, 2001.

Boehling, Rebecca, Susanne Urban, Elizabeth Anthony, and Suzanne Brown-Fleming, eds. *Freilegungen: Spiegelungen der NS-Verfolgung und ihrer Konsequenzen*. Jahrbuch des International Tracing Service IV. Göttingen: Wallstein Verlag, 2015.

Boehling, Rebecca, Susanne Urban, and René Bienert, eds. *Freilegungen: Displaced Persons— Leben im Transit: Überlebende zwischen Repatriierung, Rehabilitation und Neuanfang*. Jahrbuch des International Tracing Service III. Göttingen: Wallstein Verlag, 2014.

———. *Freilegungen: Spiegelungen der NS-Verfolgung und ihrer Konsequenzen*. Jahrbuch des International Tracing Service IV. Göttingen: Wallstein Verlag, 2015.

———. *Freilegungen: Überlebende—Erinnerungen—Transformationen*. Jahrbuch des International Tracing Service II. Göttingen: Wallstein Verlag, 2013.

Bowman, Steve B. "Greece." In *The Holocaust Encyclopedia*, edited by Walter Laqueur and Judith Tydor Baumel-Schwartz, 269. New Haven, CT: Yale University Press, 2001.

Braiter, Leslaw, et al. "Gross Rosen." In *The United States Holocaust Memorial Museum Encyclopedia of Camps and Ghettos, 1933–1945*, Vol. 1: *Early Camps, Youth Camps, and Concentration Camps and Subcamps under the SS-Business Administration Main Office (WVHA)*, edited by Geoffrey P. Megargee, 693–812. Bloomington: Indiana University Press in association with USHMM, 2009.

Breitman, Richard, and Norman J. W. Goda. *Hitler's Shadow: Nazi War Criminals, U.S. Intelligence, and the Cold War*. Washington, DC: US National Archives and Records Administration, 2010.

Brenner, Hans. "Zittau." In *The United States Holocaust Memorial Museum Encyclopedia of Camps and Ghettos, 1933–1945*, Vol. 1: *Early Camps, Youth Camps, and Concentration Camps and Subcamps under the SS-Business Administration Main Office (WVHA)*, edited by Geoffrey P. Megargee, 811–12. Bloomington: Indiana University Press in association with USHMM, 2009.

Brenner, Michael. *After the Holocaust: Rebuilding Jewish Lives in Postwar Germany*, translated by Barbara Harshav. Princeton, NJ: Princeton University Press, 1997.

Bringmann, Fritz. *Arbeitserziehungslager Nordmark: Berichte, Erlebnisse, Dokumente*. Kiel: VVN-Bund der Antifaschisten, 1982.

Browder, George C. *Foundations of the Nazi State: The Formation of Sipo and SD*. Lexington: University of Kentucky Press, 1990.

———. *Hitler's Enforcers: The Gestapo and the SS Security Service in the Nazi Revolution*. Oxford: Oxford University Press, 1996.

Brown-Fleming, Suzanne. *The Holocaust and Catholic Conscience: Cardinal Aloisius Muench and the Guilt Question in Germany*. South Bend, IN: University of Notre Dame Press in association with USHMM, 2006.

———. "*Wiedervereinigung Ersehnend*: Gender and the Holocaust Fates of the Müller and Gittler Families." In *Different Horrors/Same Hell: Gender and the Holocaust*, edited by Myrna Goldenberg and Amy Shapiro, 177–97. Seattle: University of Washington Press, 2013.

Browning, Christopher. *Ordinary Men: Reserve Police Battalion 101 and the Final Solution in Poland*. New York: HarperCollins, 1992.

Bryant, Thomas. *Himmlers Kinder: Zur Geschichte der SS-Organisation "Lebensborn" e.V. 1935–1945*. Wiesbaden: Marixverlag, 2011.

Buggeln, Marc. "Neuengamme Subcamp System." In *The United States Holocaust Memorial Museum Encyclopedia of Camps and Ghettos, 1933–1945*, Vol. 1: *Early Camps, Youth Camps, and Concentration Camps and Subcamps under the SS-Business Administration Main Office (WVHA)*, edited by Geoffrey P. Megargee, 1081. Bloomington: Indiana University Press in association with USHMM, 2009.

Cohen, Boaz. "Israel." In *The Oxford Handbook of Holocaust Studies*, ed. Peter Hayes and John K. Roth, 575–76. Oxford: Oxford University Press, 2010.

Cohen, Gerard Daniel. *In War's Wake: Europe's Displaced Persons in the Postwar Order*. New York: Oxford University Press, 2012.

Crew, David F. *Germans on Welfare: From Weimar to Hitler*. New York: Oxford University Press, 1998.

Curilla, Wolfgang. *Die deutsche Ordnungspolizei und der Holocaust im Baltikum und in Weiss-russland, 1941–1944*. Paderborn: F. Schöningh, 2006.

D'Inka, Werner, Berthold Kohler, Günter Nonnenmacher, Frank Schirrmacher, and Holger Steltzner. "Es Ist Nie Vorbei." *Frankfurter Allgemeine Zeitung*, March 18, 2013.

Dean, Martin. "Bliżyn." In *The United States Holocaust Memorial Museum Encyclopedia of Camps and Ghettos, 1933–1945*, Vol. 1: *Early Camps, Youth Camps, and Concentration Camps and Subcamps under the SS-Business Administration Main Office (WVHA)*, edited by Geoffrey P. Megargee, 881. Bloomington: Indiana University Press in association with USHMM, 2009.

Decker, Jo-Ellyn. "Lazar Kleinman Identified." Interview with Lazar Kleinman. USHMM "Remember Me" Project. rememberme.ushmm.org/updates/entry/lazar-kleinman -identified (accessed May 30, 2014).

Decker, Jo-Ellyn, with Sara-Joelle Clark. "CNI Cards." Unpublished document, Holocaust Victims and Survivors Resource Center, USHMM, July 2012.

Department of State. "Constitution of the International Refugee Organization, August 20, 1948." In *Germany, 1947–1949: The Story in Documents*. Washington, DC: Department of State, Division of Public Affairs, 1950.

Dieckmann, Christoph. *Deutsche Besatzungspolitik in Litauen, 1941–1944*. Göttingen: Wallstein Verlag, 2011.

Dieckmann, Christoph, with Saulius Sužiedėlis. *The Persecution and Mass Murder of Lithuanian Jews during Summer and Fall of 1941*. Vilnius: Margi Raštai, 2006.

Domagała, Jan. *Ci, którzy przeszli przez Dachau*. Warsaw: Pax, 1957.

Douglas, Lawrence. *The Memory of Judgment: Making Law and History in the Trials of the Holocaust*. New Haven, CT: Yale University Press, 2001.

———. *The Right Wrong Man: John Demjanjuk and the Last Great Nazi War Crimes Trial.* Princeton, NJ: Princeton University Press, 2016.

Doulot, Alexandre. "'No Number Tattooed': The Cosel Convoys from France in the ITS Holdings." In *Freilegungen: Spiegelungen der NS-Verfolgung und ihrer Konsequenzen*, edited by Rebecca Boehling, Susanne Urban, Elizabeth Anthony, and Suzanne Brown-Fleming. Jahrbuch des International Tracing Service IV. Göttingen: Wallstein Verlag, 2015.

Dreyfus, Jean-Marc. "Neckarelz I and II." In *The United States Holocaust Memorial Museum Encyclopedia of Camps and Ghettos, 1933–1945*, Vol. 1: *Early Camps, Youth Camps, and Concentration Camps and Subcamps under the SS-Business Administration Main Office (WVHA)*, edited by Geoffrey P. Megargee, 1045–47. Bloomington: Indiana University Press in association with USHMM, 2009.

Dreyfus, Jean-Marc, Evelyn Zegenhagen, Christine Glauning, Immo Opfermann, Alfred Hoffmann, and Therkel Straede. "Natzweiler-Struthof." In *The United States Holocaust Memorial Museum Encyclopedia of Camps and Ghettos, 1933–1945*, Vol. 1: *Early Camps, Youth Camps, and Concentration Camps and Subcamps under the SS-Business Administration Main Office (WVHA)*, edited by Geoffrey P. Megargee, 1003–71. Bloomington: Indiana University Press in association with USHMM, 2009.

———. "Vaihingen/Enz." In *The United States Holocaust Memorial Museum Encyclopedia of Camps and Ghettos, 1933–1945*, Vol. 1: *Early Camps, Youth Camps, and Concentration Camps and Subcamps under the SS-Business Administration Main Office (WVHA)*, edited by Geoffrey P. Megargee, 1065. Bloomington: Indiana University Press in association with USHMM, 2009.

Durand, Arthur A. *Stalag Luft III: The Secret History.* Baton Rouge: Louisiana State University Press, 1988.

Eckert, Astrid. *The Struggle for the Files: The Western Allies and the Return of German Archives after the Second World War*, translated by Dona Geyer. New York: Columbia University Press, 2012.

Eidintas, Alfonsas. *Jews, Lithuanians, and the Holocaust.* Vilnius: Versus Aureus Publishers, 2003.

Engelmann, Bernt. *Wir haben ja den Kopf noch fest auf dem Hals: Die Deutschen zwischen Stunde Null und Wirtschaftswunder: 1945–1948.* Göttingen: Steidl, 1997.

Feinstein, Margaret Myers. *Holocaust Survivors in Postwar Germany, 1945–1957.* Cambridge: Cambridge University Press, 2010.

Fings, Karola. "SS-Baubrigaden and SS-Eisenbahnbaubrigaden." In *The United States Holocaust Memorial Museum Encyclopedia of Camps and Ghettos, 1933–1945*, Vol. 1: *Early Camps, Youth Camps, and Concentration Camps and Subcamps under the SS-Business Administration Main Office (WVHA)*, edited by Geoffrey P. Megargee, 1353–59. Bloomington: Indiana University Press in association with USHMM, 2009.

Frei, Norbert. *Adenauer's Germany and the Nazi Past: The Politics of Amnesty and Integration*, translated Joel Golb. New York: Columbia University Press, 2002.

Gaunt, David, Paul A. Levine, and Laura Palosuo, eds. *Collaboration and Resistance during the Holocaust: Belarus, Estonia, Latvia, Lithuania.* New York: Peter Lang, 2004.

Gentiloni, Umberto, and Stefano Palermo, *16.10.43 Li hanno portati.* Rome: Fandango Libri, 2012.

Gil, Idit. "Jewish Slave Laborers from Radom in the Last Year of the War: Social Aspects of

Exploitation." In *Freilegungen: Spiegelungen der NS-Verfolgung und ihrer Konsequenzen*, edited by Rebecca Boehling, Susanne Urban, Elizabeth Anthony, and Suzanne Brown-Fleming. Jahrbuch des International Tracing Service IV. Göttingen: Wallstein Verlag, 2015.

Giles, Geoffrey, ed. *Stunde Null: The End and the Beginning Fifty Years Ago*. Washington DC: German Historical Institute, 1997.

Goldberg, Harvey E. "Libya." In *The Jews of the Middle East and North Africa in Modern Times*, edited by Reeva Spector Simon, Michael Menachem Laskier, and Sara Reguer, 431–32. New York: Columbia University Press, 2003.

Greiser, Katrin. "Grabstätten und Sterbeorte in Bayern: Eine Suche nach den Opfern der Todesmärsche." In *Freilegungen: Auf den Spuren der Todesmärsche*, edited by Jean-Luc Blondel, Susanne Urban, and Sebastian Schönemann, 300–313. Jahrbuch des International Tracing Service I. Göttingen: Wallstein Verlag, 2012.

Grontzki, Nina, Gerd Niewerth, and Rolf Potthoff, *Die Stunde Null im Ruhrgebiet. Kriegsende und Wiederaufbau: Erinnerungen*. Essen: Klartext, 2005.

Gross, Jan T., ed. *The Holocaust in Occupied Poland: New Findings and New Interpretations*. Frankfurt am Main: Peter Lang, 2012.

Grossmann, Atina. *Jews, Germans and Allies: Close Encounters in Occupied Germany*. Princeton, NJ: Princeton University Press, 2007.

Gruner, Wolf. *Jewish Forced Labor under the Nazis: Economic Needs and Racial Aims*, translated by Kathleen M. Dell'Orto. Cambridge: Cambridge University Press, 2006.

Guchinova, Elsa-Bair. "Kalmyks in America." *Anthropology & Archeology of Eurasia* 41, no. 2 (2002): 7–22.

Hachtmann, Rüdiger. *Das Wirtschaftsimperium der Deutschen Arbeitsfront 1933–1945*. Göttingen: Wallstein Verlag, 2012.

Hammerschmidt, Peter. *Die Wohlfahrtsverbände im NS-Staat: Die NSV und die konfessionellen Verbände Caritas und Innere Mission im Gefüge der Wohlfahrtspflege des Nationalsozialismus*. Opladen: Leske & Budrich, 1999.

Harder, Jürgen, and Joseph Robert White. "Youth Protection Camp Moringen." In *The United States Holocaust Memorial Museum Encyclopedia of Camps and Ghettos, 1933–1945*, Vol. 1: *Early Camps, Youth Camps, and Concentration Camps and Subcamps under the SS-Business Administration Main Office (WVHA)*, edited by Geoffrey P. Megargee, 1530–32. Bloomington: Indiana University Press in association with USHMM, 2009.

Hayes, Peter. "Plunder and Restitution." In *The Oxford Handbook of Holocaust Studies*, edited by Peter Hayes and John K. Roth, 548–49. New York: Oxford University Press, 2010.

Heinemann, Isabel. *Rasse, Siedlung, deutsches Blut: Das Rasse- und Siedlungshauptamt der SS und die rassenpolitische Neuordnung Europas*. Göttingen: Wallstein Verlag, 2003.

Hepp, Michael. "Denn ihrer ward die Hölle. Kinder und Jugendliche im Jugendverwahrlager Litzmannstadt." In *Mitteilungen der Dokumentationsstelle zur NS-Sozialpolitik* 11/12 (April 1986): 49–71.

Herbert, Ulrich. "Forced Laborers in the Third Reich: An Overview." *International Labor and Working-Class History* 58, no. 1 (2000): 192–93.

———. *Hitler's Foreign Workers: Enforced Foreign Labor in Germany under the Third Reich*, New York: Cambridge University Press, 1997.

Hilton, Laura J., and John J. Delaney. "Forced Foreign Laborers, POWs and Jewish Slave Workers in the Third Reich: Regional Studies and New Directions." *German History* 23, no. 1 (2005): 83–95.

Hobohm, Muhammad Aman. "Islam in Germany." *Islamic Review* (August 1951): 11–17.

Hohengarten, André. *Das Massaker im Zuchthaus Sonnenburg vom 30/31 Januar 1945.* Luxemburg: Verlag der St. Paulus Druckerei, 1979.

Holborn, Louise W. *The International Refugee Organization: A Specialized Agency of the United Nations: Its History and Work, 1946–1952.* Oxford: Oxford University Press, 1956.

Holian, Anna. *Between National Socialism and Soviet Communism: Displaced Persons in Postwar Germany.* Ann Arbor: University of Michigan Press, 2011.

Hrabar, Roman. *"Lebensborn": Czyli, źródło życia.* Katowice: Wydawn. "Śląsk," 1980.

Huebner, Todd. "Sachsenhausen Main Camp." In *The United States Holocaust Memorial Museum Encyclopedia of Camps and Ghettos, 1933–1945*, Vol. 1: *Early Camps, Youth Camps, and Concentration Camps and Subcamps under the SS-Business Administration Main Office (WVHA)*, edited by Geoffrey P. Megargee, 1256. Bloomington: Indiana University Press in association with USHMM, 2009.

Hugo, Victor. *The Rhine.* Boston: Dana Estes, 1902.

Hummel, Karl-Joseph, and Christoph Kösters. *Zwangsarbeit und katholische Kirche 1939–1945: Geschichte und Erinnerung, Entschädigung und Versöhnung. Eine Dokumentation.* Patterborn: Verlag Ferdinand Schöningh, 2008.

Huth, Arno. "Die Auflösung des KZ Natzweiler und seines Aussenlagerkomplexes." In *Freilegungen: Auf den Spuren der Todesmärsche*, edited by Jean-Luc Blondel, Susanne Urban, and Sebastian Schönemann, 184–97. Jahrbuch des International Tracing Service I. Göttingen: Wallstein Verlag, 2012.

Iwaszko, Stanisława. "Laurahütte." In *The United States Holocaust Memorial Museum Encyclopedia of Camps and Ghettos, 1933–1945*, Vol. 1: *Early Camps, Youth Camps, and Concentration Camps and Subcamps under the SS-Business Administration Main Office (WVHA)*, edited by Geoffrey P. Megargee, 261–62. Bloomington: Indiana University Press in association USHMM, 2009.

Jaskot, Paul B. *The Architecture of Oppression: The SS, Forced Labor and the Nazi Monumental Building Economy.* London: Routledge, 2000.

Jockusch, Laura. *Collect and Record! Jewish Holocaust Documentation in Early Postwar Europe.* New York: Oxford University Press, 2012.

John-Stucke, Kirsten. "Wewelsburg Main Camp (Niederhagen)." In *The United States Holocaust Memorial Museum Encyclopedia of Camps and Ghettos, 1933–1945*, Vol. 1: *Early Camps, Youth Camps, and Concentration Camps and Subcamps under the SS-Business Administration Main Office (WVHA)*, edited by Geoffrey P. Megargee, 1517–21. Bloomington: Indiana University Press in association with USHMM, 2009.

Kark, Ruth, and Joseph B. Glass. "Eretz Israel/Palestine, 1800–1948." In *The Jews of the Middle East and North Africa in Modern Times*, edited by Reeva Spector Simon, Michael Menachem Laskier, and Sara Reguer, 335. New York: Columbia University Press, 2003.

Kerenji, Emil. *Jewish Responses to Persecution, Volume IV, 1942–1943.* Lanham, MD: Rowman & Littlefield in association with USHMM, 2015.

Knowles, Anne Kelly, Tim Cole, and Alberto Giordano, eds. *Geographies of the Holocaust.* Bloomington: Indiana University Press, 2014.

Kochavi, Arieh J. "Liberation and Dispersal." In *The Oxford Handbook of Holocaust Studies*, edited by Peter Hayes and John K. Roth, 516. New York: Oxford University Press, 2010.

Königseder, Angelika, and Juliane Wetzel. *Waiting for Hope: Jewish Displaced Persons in Post–World War II Germany.* Evanston, IL: Northwestern University Press, 2001.

Koop, Volker. *"Dem Führer ein Kind schenken": Die SS-Organisation Lebensborn e.V.* Cologne: Böhlau, 2007.

Korte, Detlev. "Vorstufe zum KZ: Das Arbeitserziehungslager Nordmark in Kiel, 1944–1945." In *Die vergessenen Lager*, edited by Barbara Distel and Wolfgang Benz. Munich: DTV, 1994.

Kovács, András Zoltán. "A Szálasi-kormány belügyminisztériuma." PhD diss., University of Pécs, 2008.

Kring, Karin, et al. *Wie war das damals in Lahnstein? Herausfordernde Geschichten aus den Jahren 1933–1945.* Lahnstein: Imprimatur Verlag, 2010.

Kruszyński, Piotr. "Riese/Wolfsberg." In *The United States Holocaust Memorial Museum Encyclopedia of Camps and Ghettos, 1933–1945*, Vol. 1: *Early Camps, Youth Camps, and Concentration Camps and Subcamps under the SS-Business Administration Main Office (WVHA)*, edited by Geoffrey P. Megargee, 796–97. Bloomington: Indiana University Press in association with USHMM, 2009.

Kunz, Norbert. *Die Krim unter deutscher Herrschaft, 1941–1944: Germanisierungsutopie und Besatzungsrealität.* Darmstadt: Wissenschaftliche Buchgesellschaft, 2005.

Laskier, Michael Menachem. "Syria and Lebanon." In *The Jews of the Middle East and North Africa in Modern Times*, edited by Reeva Spector Simon, Michael Menachem Laskier, and Sara Reguer, 318–23. New York: Columbia University Press, 2003.

Lavsky, Hagit. *New Beginnings: Holocaust Survivors in Bergen-Belsen and the British Zone in Germany, 1945–1950.* Detroit, MI: Wayne State University Press, 2002.

Lenhart, Anne-Maria. *Eine Darstellung der Organisation "Lebensborn e.V."* Hamburg: Diplomica, 2013.

Lewinsky, Tamar. *Displaced Poets: Jiddische Schriftsteller im Nachkriegsdeutschland, 1945–1951.* Göttingen: Vandenhoeck & Ruprecht, 2008.

Lilienthal, Georg. *Der Lebensborn e.V.: Ein Instrument nationalsozialistischer Rassenpolitik.* Frankfurt am Main: Fischer Verlag, 1993.

Lohse, Alexandra. "Forced Labor in ITS." Unpublished paper delivered at the "Introduction to Holocaust Studies" ITS seminar for undergraduate, master's, and early doctoral students, USHMM, July 2013.

———. "Landkreis Sankt Goarshausen." In *The United States Holocaust Memorial Museum Encyclopedia of Camps and Ghettos.* Vol. 6, edited by Martin Dean. Bloomington: Indiana University Press in association with USHMM, forthcoming.

Longerich, Peter. *Heinrich Himmler*, translated by Jeremy Noakes and Lesley Sharpe. New York: Oxford University Press, 2012.

Lower, Wendy. *Hitler's Furies: German Women in the Nazi Killing Fields.* Boston: Houghton Mifflin Harcourt, 2013.

Ludi, Regula. *Reparations for Nazi Victims in Postwar Europe.* Cambridge: Cambridge University Press, 2012.

Lumans, Valdis O. *Himmler's Auxiliaries: The Volksdeutsche Mittelstelle and the German National Minorities of Europe, 1933–1945.* Chapel Hill: University of North Carolina Press, 1993.

Maier, Franz. *Biographisches Organisationshandbuch der NSDAP und ihrer Gliederungen im Gebiet des heutigen Landes Rheinland-Pfalz.* Mainz: Hase & Koehler, 2007.

Mallmann, Klaus-Michael, and Martin Cüppers, *Nazi Palestine: The Plan for the Extermination of the Jews in Palestine.* New York: Enigma Books in association with USHMM, 2005.

Mankowitz, Zeev W. *Life between Memory and Hope: The Survivors of the Holocaust in Occupied Germany*. Cambridge: Cambridge University Press, 2002.

Marcuse, Harold. *Legacies of Dachau: The Uses and Abuses of a Concentration Camp, 1933–2001*. Cambridge: Cambridge University Press, 2001.

Maspero, Julia. "French Policy on Postwar Migration of Eastern European Jews through France and the French Occupation Zones in Germany and Austria." *Jewish History Quarterly* no. 2 (June 2013): 319–39.

Matthäus, Jürgen, and Mark Roseman, *Jewish Responses to Persecution, Volume I, 1933–1938*. Lanham, MD: AltaMira Press in association with USHMM, 2010.

Matthäus, Jürgen, with Emil Kerenji, Jan Lambertz, and Leah Wolfson, *Jewish Responses to Persecution, Volume III, 1941–1942*. Lanham, MD: Alta Mira Press in association with USHMM, 2013.

Meek, Per, and Arne Löhr. *Lebensborn 6210*. Kristiansund: Ibs forlag, 2001.

Megargee, Geoffrey P. "Editor's Introduction to the Series and Volume I." In *The United States Holocaust Memorial Museum Encyclopedia of Camps and Ghettos, 1933–1945*, Vol. 1: *Early Camps, Youth Camps, and Concentration Camps and Subcamps under the SS-Business Administration Main Office (WVHA)*, edited by Geoffrey P. Megargee, xxiii–xxxvi. Bloomington: Indiana University Press in association with USHMM, 2009

———. *Inside Hitler's High Command*. Lawrence: University of Kansas, 2000.

Melander, Göran. "International Refugee Organization." *Max Planck Encyclopedia of Public International Law (MPEPIL)*, Oxford Public International Law, opil.ouplaw.com/view/10.1093/law:epil/9780199231690/law-9780199231690-e512?rskey = wdNet3&result = 3&prd = EPIL&print (accessed June 2, 2014).

Meyer, Beate. *A Fatal Balancing Act: The Dilemma of the Reich Association of Jews in Germany, 1939–1945*. New York: Berghahn Books, 2013.

Müller, Filip. *Eyewitness Auschwitz: Three Years in the Gas Chambers*, edited by Susanne Flatauer. Chicago: Ivan R. Dee, 1979.

Müller, Ingo. *Hitler's Justice: The Courts of the Third Reich*. Cambridge, MA: Harvard University Press, 1991.

Munoz, Antonio J. "Crimean Tartar Volunteer Formations in the German Armed Forces." In *The East Came West: Muslim, Hindu, and Buddhist Volunteers in the German Armed Forces, 1941–1945*, ed. Antonio J. Munoz, 85–108. Bayside, NY: Axis Europa Books, 2001.

Musial, Bogdan, ed. *Aktion Reinhardt: Der Völkermord an den Juden im Generalgouvernement 1941–1944*. Osnabrück: Fibre, 2004.

Muzafarov, Refik. *Anatomiia deportatsii krymskikh tatar*. Simferopol': Tarpan, 2011.

Namysło, Aleksandra. "Chrzanów." In *The United States Holocaust Memorial Museum Encyclopedia of Camps and Ghettos, 1933–1945*, Vol. 2: *Ghettos in German-Occupied Eastern Europe*, edited by Geoffrey P. Megargee and Martin Dean, 146–47. Bloomington: Indiana University Press in association with USHMM, 2012.

Neufeld, Michael J. "Mittelbau (Dora) Main Camp." In *The United States Holocaust Memorial Museum Encyclopedia of Camps and Ghettos, 1933–1945*, Vol. 1: *Early Camps, Youth Camps, and Concentration Camps and Subcamps under the SS-Business Administration Main Office (WVHA)*, edited by Geoffrey P. Megargee, 965–1002. Bloomington: Indiana University Press in association with USHMM, 2009.

Nikžentaitis, Alvydas, Stefan Schreiner, and Darius Staliūnas, eds. *The Vanished World of Lithuanian Jews*. New York: Rodopi, 2004.

Nürnberg, Kaspar. "Sonnenburg." In *The United States Holocaust Memorial Museum Encyclopedia of Camps and Ghettos, 1933–1945*, Vol. 1: *Early Camps, Youth Camps, and Concentration Camps and Subcamps under the SS-Business Administration Main Office (WVHA)*, edited by Geoffrey P. Megargee, 163–65. Bloomington: Indiana University Press in association with USHMM, 2009.

Ossenberg, Uwe. *The Document Holdings of the International Tracing Service*. Bad Arolsen: ITS, 2009.

Otte, Hans, and Thomas Scharf-Wrede, eds. *Caritas und Diakonie in der NS-Zeit: Beispiele aus Niedersachsen*. Hildesheim: Georg Olms Verlag, 2001.

Patt, Avinoam. *Finding Home and Homeland: Jewish DP Youth and Zionism in the Aftermath of the Holocaust*. Detroit, MI: Wayne State University Press, 2008.

Patt, Avinoam, and Michael Berkowitz, eds. *"We Are Here": New Approaches to Jewish Displaced Persons in Postwar Germany*. Detroit, MI: Wayne State University Press, 2010.

Petropoulos, Jonathan. "Prince zu Waldeck und Pyrmont: A Career in the SS and Its Murderous Consequences." In *Lessons and Legacies, Volume IX: Memory, History, and Responsibility: Reassessments of the Holocaust, Implications for the Future*, edited by Jonathan Petropoulos, Lynn Rapaport, and John K. Roth, 169–84. Evanston, IL: Northwestern University Press, 2010.

Pine, Lisa. *Hitler's "National Community": Society and Culture in Nazi Germany*. London: Hodder Arnold, 2007.

Pohl, Dieter, and Tanja Sebta. *Zwangsarbeit in Hitlers Europa: Besatzung, Arbeit, Folgen*. Berlin: Metropol, 2013.

Rahe, Thomas. "Bergen-Belsen Main Camp." In *The United States Holocaust Memorial Museum Encyclopedia of Camps and Ghettos, 1933–1945*, Vol. 1: *Early Camps, Youth Camps, and Concentration Camps and Subcamps under the SS-Business Administration Main Office (WVHA)*, edited by Geoffrey P. Megargee, 278–81. Bloomington: Indiana University Press in association with USHMM, 2009.

Reese, Dagmar. *Growing Up Female in Nazi Germany*. Ann Arbor: University of Michigan Press, 2006.

Reinisch, Jessica. *The Disentanglement of Populations: Migration, Expulsion and Displacement in Postwar Europe, 1944–1949*. New York: Palgrave Macmillan, 2011.

Retzlaff, Birgit, and Jörg-Johannes Lechner, *Bund Deutscher Mädel in der Hitlerjugend: fakultative Eintrittsgründe von Mädchen und jungen Frauen in den BDM*. Hamburg: Kovač, 2008.

Rodgers, Jennifer. "From the 'Archive of Horrors' to the 'Shop Window of Democracy': The International Tracing Service and the Transatlantic Politics of the Past." PhD diss., University of Pennsylvania, 2014.

Roseman, Mark. "Holocaust Perpetrators in Victims' Eyes." In *Years of Persecution, Years of Extermination: Saul Friedländer and the Future of Holocaust Studies*, edited by Christian Wiese and Paul Betts, 81–100. London: Continuum, 2010.

Roumani, Maurice M. *The Jews of Libya: Coexistence, Persecution, Resettlement*. Brighton, UK: Sussex Academic Press, 2008.

Rummel, Walter. "Ein Ghetto für die Juden im Tal der Verbannten. Die Umwandlung der ehemaligen Bergarbeitersiedlung in Friedrichssegen (Lahn) zum Wohnlager für jüdische Zwangsarbeiter und—arbeiterinnen, 1938-1942." *Jahrbuch für westdeutsche Landesgeschichte* 30 (2004): 419–507.

———. "Zwangsarbeitereinsatz im Gebiet des heutigen Rheinland-Pfalz: Die bürokratische Dokumentation und ihr Verbleib." In *Zwangsarbeit in der Rheinland-Pfalz während des Zweiten Weltkriegs*, edited by Hedwig Brüchert and Michael Matheus, 8–9. Stuttgart: Franz Steiner Verlag, 2004.

Rüter, C. F., and D. W. de Mildt. *Die westdeutschen Strafverfahren wegen nationalsozialistischer Tötungsverbrechen 1945–1997: Eine systematische Verfahrensbeschreibung mit Karten und Registern.* Munich: K. G. Saur Verlag, 1998.

Sachar, Howard M. *Europe Leaves the Middle East, 1936–1954.* New York: Knopf, 1972.

Safrian, Hans. *Eichmann's Men.* New York: Cambridge University Press in association with USHMM, 2010.

Sahim, Haideh. "Iran and Afghanistan." In *The Jews of the Middle East and North Africa in Modern Times*, edited by Reeva Spector Simon, Michael Menachem Laskier, and Sara Reguer, 367–86. New York: Columbia University Press, 2003.

Sawicka, Danuta. "Kittlitztreben." In *The United States Holocaust Memorial Museum Encyclopedia of Camps and Ghettos, 1933–1945*, Vol. 1: *Early Camps, Youth Camps, and Concentration Camps and Subcamps under the SS-Business Administration Main Office (WVHA)*, edited by Geoffry P. Megargee, 753–54. Bloomington: Indiana University Press in association with USHMM, 2009.

Schelvis, Jules. *Sobibor: A History of a Nazi Death Camp.* New York: Berg in association with USHMM, 2007.

Schmaltz, Florian. "Auschwitz III Monowitz Main Camp." In *The United States Holocaust Memorial Museum Encyclopedia of Camps and Ghettos, 1933–1945*, Vol. 1: *Early Camps, Youth Camps, and Concentration Camps and Subcamps under the SS-Business Administration Main Office (WVHA)*, edited by Geoffry P. Megargee, 215–19. Bloomington: Indiana University Press in association with USHMM, 2009.

Schmeling, Anke. *Josias Erbprinz zu Waldeck und Pyrmont. Der politische Werdegang eines hohen SS-Führers.* Kassel: Verlag Gesamthochschule-Bibliothek Kassel, 1993.

Schmidt van der Zanden, Christine. "Mölln." In *The United States Holocaust Memorial Museum Encyclopedia of Camps and Ghettos, 1933–1945*, Vol. 1: *Early Camps, Youth Camps, and Concentration Camps and Subcamps under the SS-Business Administration Main Office (WVHA)*, edited by Geoffry P. Megargee, 1164–65. Bloomington: Indiana University Press in association with USHMM, 2009.

———. "Neustadt in Holstein." In *The United States Holocaust Memorial Museum Encyclopedia of Camps and Ghettos, 1933–1945*, Vol. 1: *Early Camps, Youth Camps, and Concentration Camps and Subcamps under the SS-Business Administration Main Office (WVHA)*, edited by Geoffry P. Megargee, 1165–66. Bloomington: Indiana University Press in association with USHMM, 2009.

Schmitz-Köster, Dorothee. *"Deutsche Mutter, bist du bereit—": Alltag im Lebensborn.* Berlin: Aufbau-Verlag, 1997.

———. *Kind L 364: Eine Lebensborn-Familiengeschichte.* Berlin: Rowohlt, 2007.

Schönemann, Sebastian. "'Accounting for the Dead': Humanitäre und rechtliche Motive der alliierten Ermittlungsarbeit zu den Todesmärschen." In *Freilegungen: Auf den Spuren der Todesmärsche*, edited by Jean-Luc Blondel, Susanne Urban, and Sebastian Schönemann, 122–51. Jahrbuch des International Tracing Service I. Göttingen: Wallstein Verlag, 2012.

Schulte, Jan Erik. *Zwangsarbeit und Vernichtung: Das Wirtschaftsimperium der SS: Oswald Pohl und das SS-Wirtschafts-Verwaltungshauptamt 1933–1945*. Paderborn: Verlag Ferdinand Schöningh, 2001.

Seibert, Hubertus, with Judith Sommer, eds. *Vom kurfürstlichen Ort zur grossen kreisangehörigen Stadt: Die Geschichte Lahnsteins im 19. und 20. Jahrhundert.* Lahnstein: Görres-Druckerei, 1999.

Shapiro, Paul A. "Exploring the Newly Opened ITS Archives." Keynote address delivered at the Seventh Stephen S. Weinstein Holocaust Symposium at Wroxton College, Oxfordshire, England, July 2008.

———. "History Held Hostage." *Reform Judaism* (winter 2009), http://www.reform judaism.org/history-held-hostage.

———. "Vapniarka: ITS and the Holocaust in the East." In *Freilegungen: Auf den Spuren der Todesmärsche*, edited by Jean-Luc Blondel, Susanne Urban, and Sebastian Schönemann, 26. Jahrbuch des International Tracing Service I. Göttingen: Wallstein Verlag, 2012.

———. "Vapniarka: The Archive of the International Tracing Service and the Holocaust in the East." *Holocaust and Genocide Studies* 27, no. 1 (spring 2013): 114–37.

Spörer, Mark. *Zwangsarbeit unter dem Hakenkreuz: Ausländischer Zivilarbeiter, Kriegsgefangene und Häftlinge im Deutschen Reich und im besetzten Europa, 1939–1945.* Stuttgart: Deutsche Verlags-Anstalt, 2001.

Steinacher, Gerald. *Nazis on the Run: How Hitler's Henchmen Fled Justice.* New York: Oxford University Press, 2011.

Steinert, Johannes-Dieter. *Deportation und Zwangsarbeit: Polnische und Sowjetische Kinder im Nationalsozialistischen Deutschland und im besetzten Osteuropa, 1939–1945.* Essen: Klartext, 2013.

Steinhart, Eric C. "The Chameleon of Trawniki: Jack Reimer, Soviet *Volksdeutsche*, and the Holocaust." *Holocaust and Genocide Studies* 23, no. 2 (fall 2009): 239–62.

———. "Displaced by War and Conquest: New Findings on DPs from Eastern Europe and the Soviet Union." Paper delivered at the 2012 "Beyond Camps and Forced Labour" conference, Imperial War Museum, London, January 2012.

———. "Toiling for the Reich: New Findings on Soviet Laborers in Nazi Germany from the International Tracing Service Digital Archive." Unpublished paper delivered at the American Association for the Advancement of Slavic Studies annual conference, Los Angeles, California, November 2010.

Stolleis, Michael. *The Law under the Swastika: Studies on Legal History in Nazi Germany.* Chicago: University of Chicago Press, 1998.

———. *Recht im Unrecht: Studien zur Rechtsgeschichte des Nationalsozialismus.* Frankfurt am Main: Suhrkamp, 1994.

Strebel, Bernhard. "Ravensbrück." In *The United States Holocaust Memorial Museum Encyclopedia of Camps and Ghettos, 1933–1945*, Vol. 1: *Early Camps, Youth Camps, and Concentration Camps and Subcamps under the SS-Business Administration Main Office (WVHA)*, edited by Geoffrey P. Megargee, 1187–228. Bloomington: Indiana University Press in association with USHMM, 2009.

Stufflet, Shane Brian. "No 'Stunde Null': German Attitudes toward the Mentally Handicapped and Their Impact on the Postwar Trials of T4 Perpetrators." PhD diss., University of Florida, 2006.

Tooze, Adam. *The Wages of Destruction: The Making and Breaking of the Nazi Economy.* London: Allen Lane, 2006.

US Government Printing Office. *Trials of War Criminals before the Nuernberg Military Tribunals under Control Council Law No. 10*, Volume 3: *Nuremberg: October 1946–April 1949*. Buffalo, NY: William S. Hein & Co., 1997.

Ulbricht, Josephine. "Die Untersuchungen der UNRRA zu den Todesmärschen des KZ Flossenbürg." In *Freilegungen: Auf den Spuren der Todesmärsche*, edited by Jean-Luc Blondel, Susanne Urban, and Sebastian Schönemann, 152–68. Jahrbuch des International Tracing Service I. Göttingen: Wallstein Verlag, 2012.

Urban, Susanne. "'Mein einziger Dokument ist der Nummer auf der Hand': Schriftliche Aussagen Überlebender im Archiv des ITS." In *Freilegungen: Überlebende—Erinnerungen—Transformationen*, edited by Rebecca Boehling, Susanne Urban, and René Bienert, 173–97. Jahrbuch des International Tracing Service II. Göttingen: Wallstein Verlag, 2013.

———. "'Vernehmungsunfähig': Registraturen nach der Ankunft von Räumungstransporten in KZ." In *Freilegungen: Auf den Spuren der Todesmärsche*, edited by Jean-Luc Blondel, Susanne Urban, and Sebastian Schönemann, 262–81. Jahrbuch des International Tracing Service I. Göttingen: Wallstein Verlag, 2012.

Vági, Zoltán, László Csősz, and Gábor Kádár, *The Holocaust in Hungary: Evolution of a Genocide*. Lanham, MD: Alta Mira Press in association with USHMM, 2013.

Wachsmann, Nikolaus. "The Dynamics of Destruction: The Development of the Concentration Camps, 1933–1945." In *Concentration Camps in Nazi Germany: The New Histories*, edited by Jane Caplan and Nikolaus Wachsmann, 32–33. New York: Routledge, 2010.

———. *Hitler's Prisons: Legal Terror in Nazi Germany*. New Haven, CT: Yale University Press, 2004.

Waltzer, Kenneth. "Opening the Red Cross International Tracing Service Archives." *John Marshall Journal of Computer and Information Law* 26, no. 1 (fall 2008): 166.

Weinberg, Gerhard L. *A World at Arms: A Global History of World War II*. Cambridge: Cambridge University Press, 1994.

Weinmann, Martin. *Das Nationalsozialistische Lagersystem*. Frankfurt am Main: Zweitausendeins, 1990.

Weiss, Petra. "Die Koblenzer Lager für Displaced Persons, 1945–1947." *Jahrbuch für westdeutsche Landesgeschichte* no. 29 (2003): 467–507.

———. "Eine Kaserne als Wartesaal: Displaced Persons in der Horchheimer Gneisenau-Kaserne." *Kirmes: Das Horchheimer Magazin* (2005): 82–89.

Weiss-Wendt, Anton. *Murder without Hatred: Estonians and the Holocaust*. Syracuse, NY: Syracuse University Press, 2009.

Welter, Beate. "Die Zusammenarbeit der Gedenkstätte SS-Sonderlager/KZ Hinzert mit dem ITS Bad Arolsen." In *Freilegungen: Auf den Spuren der Todesmärsche*, edited by Jean-Luc Blondel, Susanne Urban, and Sebastian Schönemann, 50, 52–53. Jahrbuch des International Tracing Service I. Göttingen: Wallstein Verlag, 2012.

White, Joseph Robert. "Polish Youth Custody Camp of the Security Police Litzmannstadt." In *The United States Holocaust Memorial Museum Encyclopedia of Camps and Ghettos, 1933–1945*, Vol. 1: *Early Camps, Youth Camps, and Concentration Camps and Subcamps under the SS-Business Administration Main Office (WVHA)*, edited by Geoffrey P. Megargee, 1528. Bloomington: Indiana University Press in association with USHMM, 2009.

———. "Target Auschwitz: Historical and Hypothetical Responses to Allied Attack." *Holocaust and Genocide Studies* 16, no. 1 (spring 2002): 54–76.

Wilbricht, Stefan. "'Dem KZL. Moringen zugeführt worden': Ergebnisse der Personenrecherche zu den Moringer KZ." In *Freilegungen: Auf den Spuren der Todesmärsche*, edited by Jean-Luc Blondel, Susanne Urban, and Sebastian Schönemann, 57. Jahrbuch des International Tracing Service I. Göttingen: Wallstein Verlag, 2012.

Wildt, Michael. *An Uncompromising Generation: The Nazi Leadership of the Reich Security Main Office*, translated by Tom Lampert. Madison: University of Wisconsin Press, 2009.

Winter, Martin Clemens. "Frühe Ermittlung zu den Todesmärschen: Quellen im Vergleich." In *Freilegungen: Auf den Spuren der Todesmärsche*, edited by Jean-Luc Blondel, Susanne Urban, and Sebastian Schönemann, 136. Jahrbuch des International Tracing Service I. Göttingen: Wallstein Verlag, 2012.

Woodbridge, George. *UNRRA: The History of the United Nations Relief and Rehabilitation Administration*. 3 vols. New York: Columbia University Press, 1950.

Zahra, Tara. *Lost Children: Reconstructing Europe's Families after World War II*. Cambridge, MA: Harvard University Press, 2011.

Zegenhagen, Evelyn. "Gross Rosen Subcamp System." In *The United States Holocaust Memorial Museum Encyclopedia of Camps and Ghettos, 1933–1945*, Vol. 1: *Early Camps, Youth Camps, and Concentration Camps and Subcamps under the SS-Business Administration Main Office (WVHA)*, edited by Geoffrey P. Megargee, 699. Bloomington: Indiana University Press in association with USHMM, 2009.

———. "Hinzert." In *The United States Holocaust Memorial Museum Encyclopedia of Camps and Ghettos, 1933–1945*, Vol. 1: *Early Camps, Youth Camps, and Concentration Camps and Subcamps under the SS-Business Administration Main Office (WVHA)*, edited by Geoffrey P. Megargee, 823–45. Bloomington: Indiana University Press in association with USHMM, 2009.

Ziemke, Earl F. *The U.S. Army in the Occupation of Germany, 1944–1946*. Washington, DC: US Army Center for Military History, 1990.

Zimmer, Bernd Joachim. "Arolsen." In *The United States Holocaust Memorial Museum Encyclopedia of Camps and Ghettos, 1933–1945*, Vol. 1: *Early Camps, Youth Camps, and Concentration Camps and Subcamps under the SS-Business Administration Main Office (WVHA)*, edited by Geoffrey P. Megargee, 307–8. Bloomington: Indiana University Press in association with USHMM, 2009.

———. *Deckname Arthur. Das KZ-Aussenkommando in der SS-Führerschule Arolsen*. Kassel: Verlag Gesamthochschule-Bibliothek Kassel, 1994.

———. *International Tracing Service Arolsen: Von der Vermisstensuche zur Haftbescheinigung. Die Organisationsgeschichte eines "ungewollten Kindes" während der Besatzungszeit*. Bad Arolsen: Waldeckischer Geschichtsverein, 2011.

INDEX

Page numbers in *italic* indicate illustrations and photographs.

111–113, *140*; diversity of, 193, *222*;
interviews with, 18, 220; in Lahnstein,
70–73; mapping, 192–193; misuse of
status, 32; Muslims as, 199–200, *225*;
nationalities of, 70–71; number of,
14–15; registration records of, 16;
research on, 191–193; second wave of,
15; securing status as, 17–18; unwanted,
208–211, 220; war criminals among,
72–75, *99,* 212–214, 216–218, *235*
Displaced Persons Act (1948), 216
displaced persons camps: conflict with
Germans in, 115; description of conditions, 69–70; at Lahnstein, 54, 69–71.
See also specific camps
Domagała, Jan, 171–172
DP-2 cards, 191–193; Golub (Greinom),
43; for infiltrees, 192; in ITS holdings,
16; prisoner numbers on, 123–124
DP identity card, Demjanjuk (Ivan), *51*
DPs. *See* displaced persons
Drahtwerke C.S. Schmidt, 66–67
Dünzl, Mac, 212–214, 220, *231, 232*
Dzierżązna subcamp, 151–152

Ebner, Gregor, 19–20
economy, forced labor in, 59, 75–76
Egenolf, Peter, 63
Eichberg, Emmy, 55–56, *79, 80, 81*
Eichberg, Ingeborg, 55–56
Eichberg, Josef, 55–56, *79,* 80, *81*
Einziger, M., 117
El-Mekki, Mohamed, 200–201
emigration: appearance and, 208–211; to
Brazil, 71; of ethnic Germans, 216–217;
to Greece, 116–118; to Israel, 122–123,
197–199; marriage and, 114–115; racism
and, 208–211; to the United States,
216–217
Emmel, Hilde (Levi), 57
employment organizations, ITS records of,
13
Eritrea, 206–207, *227,* 228
Estonia. *See also specific labor camps*: Jewish
population of, 102n2; labor camps of,
102–103
Ethiopians, 205–208, *227,* 228

ethnic Germans: displacement of, 15;
emigration of, 216–217
ethnic Italians, displacement of, 15
ethnicities, indexing CM/1 forms by,
193–194
ethnic minorities, studies of, 194
ethnic Poles, displacement of, 15
ethnic Ukrainians, displacement of, 15

Farbwerk Schroeder & Stadelmann AG, 63,
66
Feldmühle AG, 61–62
Finance Ministry of the Federal Republic of
Germany (FRG), ITS records of, 26
Flossenbürg concentration camp, ITS
records from, 5
Föhrenwald DP camp, 115–118
forced labor *(Zwangsarbeit):* at Auschwitz,
109; classifications of, 9; by companies,
61–62; extent of, 14; in Lahnstein, 54,
59–69, 75–76; Muslims in, 199–203,
225; POWs in, 68–69; prisoners in,
60–61, 66–68, *86–87,* 87–88, *94,* 95;
records of, 8–14. *See also* labor camps
forced laborers: death records of, 59–60, *85*;
in Lahnstein economy, 59–60, 61–63;
recapture of, 65; treatment of, 63–66,
76, *90–91, 92*–93
Foundation "Remembrance, Responsibility,
Future" (EVZ), ITS records of, 26,
27–28
France, authority over ITS, 4
Fuge, Hans Heinrich, 151–152, 175

gas chambers. *See* Auschwitz concentration
camp
Geisler, Lina, 17–18
geography, in Holocaust scholarship,
192–193
German Federal Archive (Bundesarchive), in
ITS administration, 6
Germany, authority over ITS, 4
Gessinger, E., 22, *48,* 49
Glauer, Charlotte, 160
Goldberg, Szulim, 5n15, *37*
Goldfields, 102
Goldsmith, Jean, 117n89

ABOUT THE AUTHOR

Suzanne Brown-Fleming, historian, is the director of the Visiting Scholars Programs at the Jack, Joseph and Morton Mandel Center for Advanced Holocaust Studies of the United States Holocaust Memorial Museum. She is also the author of *The Holocaust and Catholic Conscience: Cardinal Aloisius Muench and the Guilt Question in Germany.*